Wine and Architecture

Heinz-Gert Woschek Denis Duhme Katrin Friederichs

WINE AND ARCHITECTURE

Edition DETAIL

Authors:
Heinz-Gert Woschek (editor), Denis Duhme,
Katrin Friederichs

Editors:
Cosima Frohnmaier, Cornelia Hellstern (project manager)

Editorial services:
Niklas Fanelsa, Carola Jacob-Ritz, Florian Köhler, Sandra Leitte, Michaela Linder, Annette Müller (Rhineland-Palatinate Chamber of Architects), Jana Rackwitz, Eva Schönbrunner

Translations:
Kathrin Enke, Ludwigsburg; Christine Madden, Munich

Illustrations:
Nicola Kollmann, Martin Hemmel

Graphic design:
Heinz Hiltbrunner, Munich

Production and layout:
Roswitha Siegler

Reproduction:
ludwig:media, Zell am See

Printing and binding:
Kösel GmbH & Co. KG, Altusried-Krugzell

Bibliographical information published by the German National Library. The German National Library lists this publication in the Deutsche Nationalbibliografie; detailed bibliographical data are available on the Internet at http://dnb.d-nb.de.

A specialist publication from **DETAIL**
Institut für internationale Architektur-Dokumentation
GmbH & Co. KG, Munich
www.detail.de

ISBN: 978-3-920034-73-7

Contents

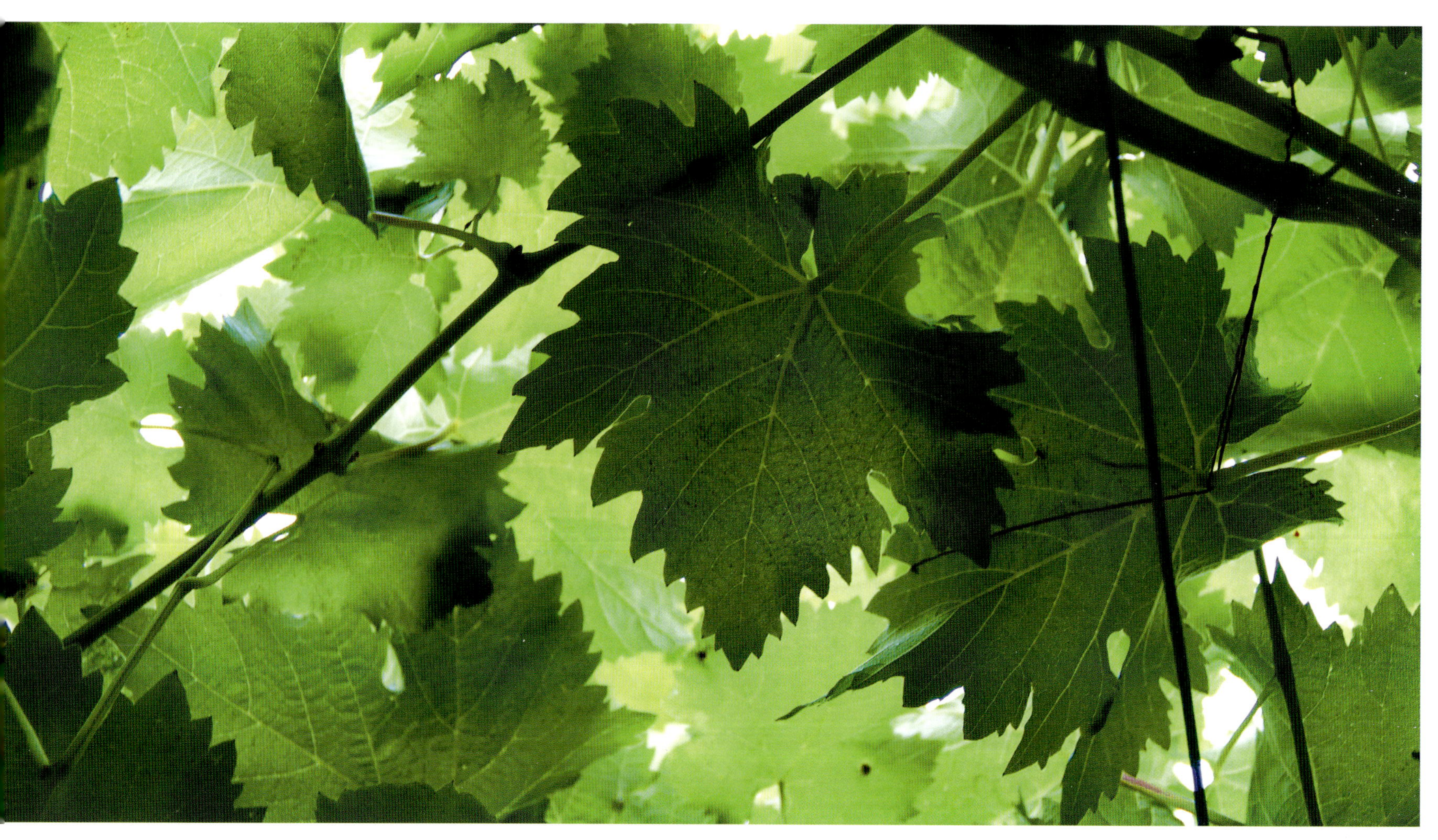

Foreword

The world of wine is currently undergoing a profound transformation. The spread of new oenological techniques, the globalization of viniculture and of the international wine market, and the division of this market into luxury and mass-market segments, are just some of the examples of the sea change in this sector. In addition, a number of newly built, architecturally innovative production facilities are garnering more and more attention, and not only in the world of wine. The mystique of that world is expanding into entirely new dimensions.

The design of new winery projects is, of course, influenced by the production techniques that will be applied there. At the same time, the conception and realization of new building projects in the wine trade is also now determined to a large extent by global changes in wine consumption and sales patterns, as well as by the increasing expectations of consumers when it comes to the image projected by wine producers and their marketing firms.
Previously of peripheral importance, architecture has become increasingly significant, even central, to winemaking. The heightened interest in what has come to be called "wine architecture" now extends far beyond the limits of the profession.
The need to optimize the production sequence is no longer the sole driving factor in the planning of the many new buildings, extensions and conversions of mid-sized wine estates, wine companies and cellars. Striking visual and tactile design elements, such as an aesthetic staging of the wines, or materials reminiscent of wine production and certain terroirs, are also paramount. In this way, wine estates and wineries have developed into marketing tools, with their impressively designed spaces often serving as venues for events. Their sometimes spectacular concepts and unusual solutions, their lavish structural language, and their use of unexpected materials set them apart from the old-fashioned romanticism of their predecessors and celebrate their liberation from the ballast of faux tradition. They interpret the wine experience in an accessible, inviting, authentic and creative manner, becoming a part of the new "wine philosophy" embraced by winemakers and wine lovers alike.

The examples in this book will give architects and their potential clients a wealth of inspiration. The project profiles do not solely depict architectural features and workmanship, but also look at the oenological side by including information about the estate's vineyards, winemaking techniques and marketing, describing its distinctive "wine atmosphere" as well as the particular collaboration between architect and client.
The choice of projects, which focuses on European wine-producing countries and their unique diversity and history, takes into account the major wine-producing countries, such as Spain and Italy, as well as smaller ones such as Austria. The examples include wine estates and cellars of all sizes and locations, with a focus on individual solutions for particular working areas, such as the fermenting cellar; tank, barrel and bottle storage; and tasting and sales areas.
The project descriptions are preceded by a short synopsis of the history of wine architecture and an introduction to oenology and wine production.
In this diverting way, the book hopes to achieve two goals: drawing architects into the fascinating world of viniculture, and giving vintners and wine-estate owners the opportunity to discover the exciting and rewarding possibilities of contemporary architecture in the world of wine.

Heinz-Gert Woschek
October 2011

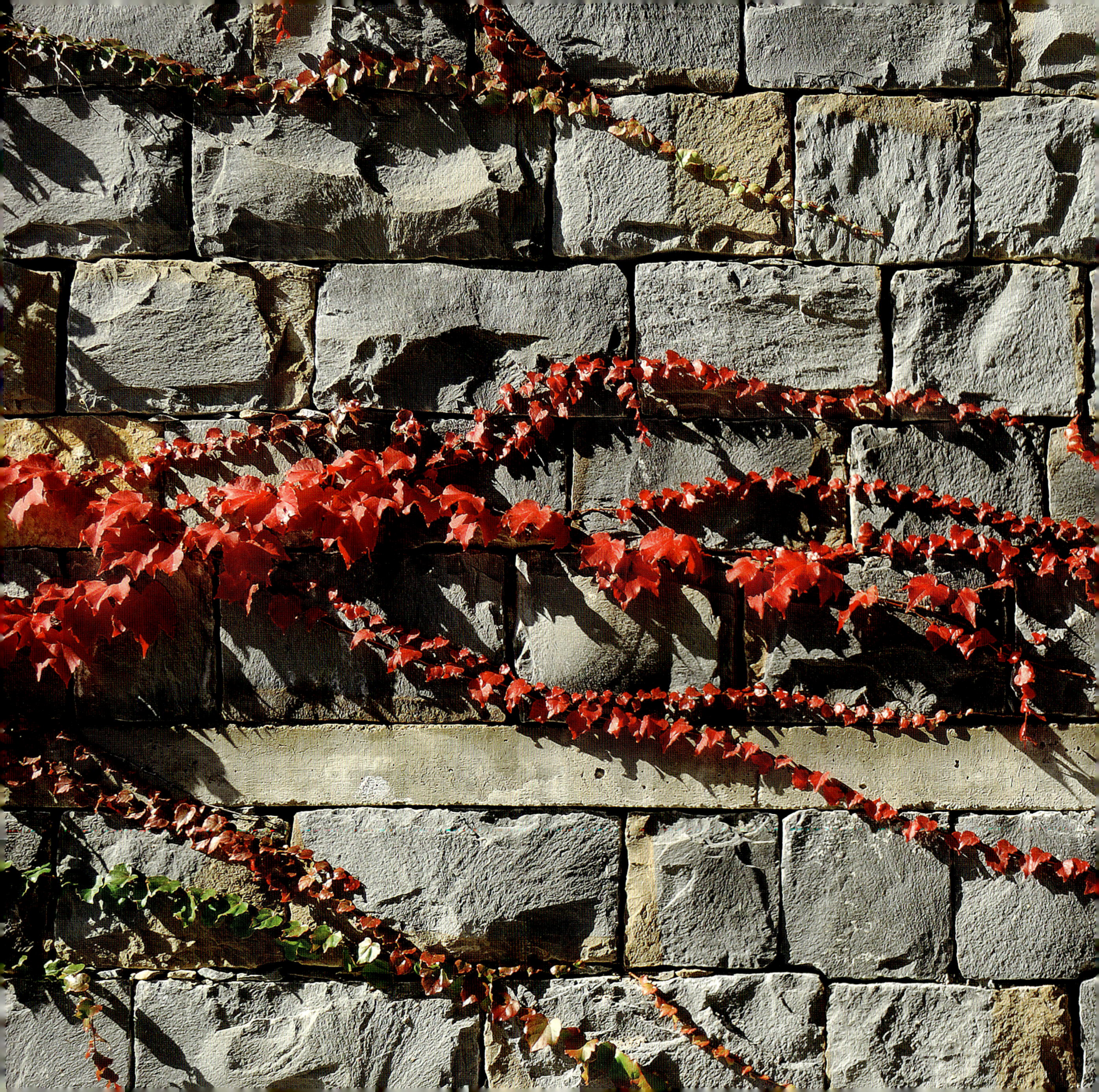

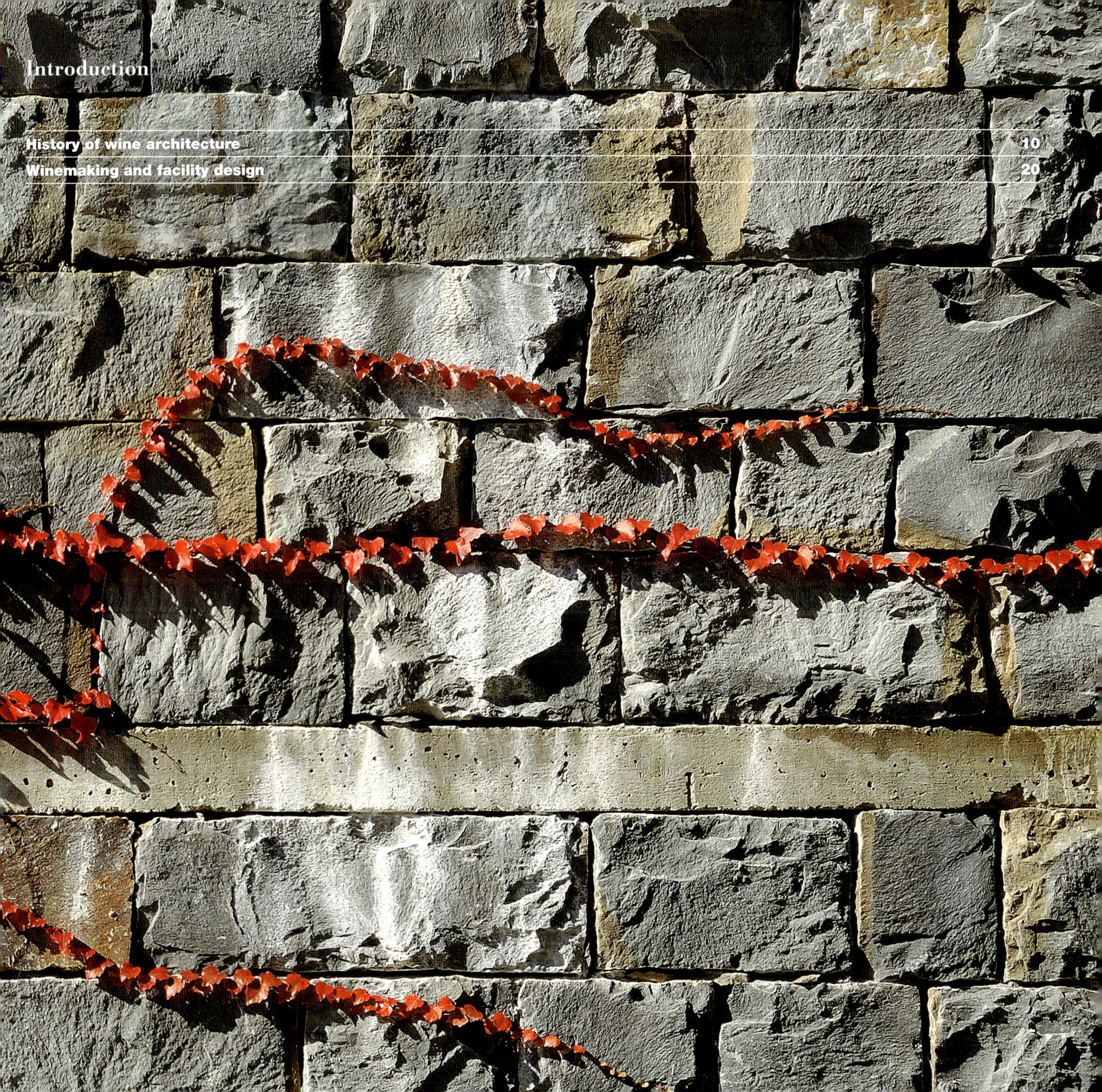

Introduction

History of wine architecture

Ever since humans first discovered how to turn grapes into a delicious, intoxicating beverage, there have been special buildings for wine production. Most likely even the peasants living in Asia Minor some 8,000 years ago, who grew grapes next to their huts, already had storage areas for wine. Although the ancient Greeks are considered to be the founders of viniculture in the Mediterranean, it was the Romans who, as well as fostering the extensive expansion of vineyards in their empire, erected purpose-built, free-standing buildings for viniculture from the first century AD onwards.
A typical Roman estate, called a *villa rustica*, usually consisted of a porticoed villa built on a slope, with a large courtyard around which the ancillary buildings were arranged. The main building was usually approached via an outside staircase leading to a colonnaded forecourt framed by two corner projections. The estate would usually include at least one heated room and a wine or provisions cellar that would, depending on the level of the water table, be either completely or partially underground. Cellars often featured exposed brickwork and a wooden-beamed ceiling. The estates would have pressing and fermentation rooms of up to 400 square metres in size. Because the fields and vineyards cultivated by any given farm could cover up to 30 hectares, a sizeable press or pressing basin for the crushing of the grapes would be in use. In the separate press house, there would be basins for the must (crushed grapes) and run-off juice as well as a beam or stone wine press. Since 1970, archaeological excavations – such as those carried out along the Mosel River and in the Palatinate region of Germany – have exposed the brick walls and stone basins of Roman press rooms in the first to fifth centuries AD. In the southern German state of Baden-Württemberg alone, 2,000 Roman farming estates have been identified.
In contrast to the *villa rustica*, the *villa urbana* was usually a single-storey Roman building. Its wine cellars featured ceiling beams or vaults supported by columns, a structural design element found in monastic wine cellars several hundred years later. Initially these buildings were made of wood or mixed materials, with a stone base and timber frame. From the second century onwards, stone structures predominated. In his *Ten Books on Architecture*, written about 27–22 BC, the Roman engineer Vitruvius gave precise recommendations for planning such landed estates. He advised that the wine storage room should be located close to the oil press and kitchen. The windows should face north to avoid an increase in room temperature through incoming sunlight.

Wine villas during the Roman Empire

In Pompeii, Villa di Diomede (second century BC), with its subterranean wine cellars arranged at right angles, indicates just how closely Vitruvius's recommendations were followed. When the villa was excavated in the late 18th century, numerous amphorae, vessels for the storage of wine, were discovered. The wine storage area at Villa Adriana, or Hadrian's Villa (AD 118–134), at Tivoli, east of Rome, was also underground, with a roof covering its southern side and cellar hatches facing north and east.
When the fermentation process was complete, further treatment of the must and wine in the press house included adding flavouring and neutralizing acidity, smoking to speed up the maturation process, and filtering and clarifying to improve taste. After that, the filled amphorae were brought into the wine cellar or a large storage room.
Nevertheless, the storage rooms and cellars in the estates were not always large enough for extensive wine storage, so the wine vessels, often together with other foodstuffs, were taken to multi-level storerooms, in which up to several thousand wine amphorae could be cellared. The remains of such storage depots from the second century have been found in Trier, for example. These consist of two parallel buildings, each of which is 70 metres long and 20 metres wide.
For the storage of wine, the Romans also made use of tunnels that had been dug into slopes either in prehistoric times or while they were quarrying for building material. Winegrowers in later centuries, too, benefited from the constant temperatures in caves, such as those hewn into the slate rock along the Mosel River or into the limestone quarries in Saint-Émilion, France. In the Tokaji region of present-day Hungary, wine caves kilometres long were carved into the tuff rock and clay soil.
Even 2,000 years after Roman times, winemakers, particularly producers of sparkling wine, utilized the catacombs as extensive ageing cellars. Underneath the Roman fortifications in the Kästrich quarter of Mainz, the sparkling-wine producer Kupferberg established 60 wine caves on seven subterranean levels in old Roman and mediaeval tunnels. Champagne houses built vaulted cellars in the many chalk tunnels dug 2,000 years ago, connecting them by means of kilometre-long passages. The Pommery & Greno cellars lie 30 metres underground and are connected by a system of passages 18 kilometres long. Veuve Clicquot Ponsardin, too, made use of old tunnels from Gallo-Roman times and extensively expanded them. Taittinger has a particularly impressive cave that connects its cellars to the 13th-century subterranean crypt of the Benedictine Abbey of St Nicasius in Rheims. Other historic cellars can be found in the chalkstone caves along the Loire River near Saumur. The deepest wine cave in France, Terra Vinea, belongs to Les Caves de Rocbère in Portel des Corbières near Narbonne. The 80-metre-deep cellar was established in a disused gypsum mine from the Middle Ages and houses about 800 wine barrels.

Rural vineyards

Around the time of the late Middle Ages, Roman wine villas in German-speaking regions gave way to Alemannic and Franconian building complexes, in which the main building and the ancillary buildings, some with barrel-vaulted cellars, were grouped around a central courtyard. Their broad entrance gates are a salient feature of the typical townscape of villages in many German wine-growing areas. A rectangular gate indicates a farm; an arched gateway characterizes a winery, as it allows a wagon piled high with barrels to pass through. The house's emblem, its year of construction or the name of its owner would be carved into the keystone of the arch.
Of the farms involved in both crop farming and winemaking, only few would feature dedicated buildings for wine production. Grape crushing would usually take place in the barns. In later centuries, wine press houses would be built on the slopes close to the vineyards in order to save time on grape processing. When these purpose-built structures nestled into the slope were built close enough to one another, they would often be linked by "cellar lanes" or "cellar alleys". This tradition was

primarily a feature of Lower Austrian wine-growing areas, but it was sometimes practised in Austria's Burgenland and in the Czech Republic as well. There is also a cellar lane in Guntersblum in the German wine region of Rheinhessen.
While the Mediterranean countries have always tended to situate their wine storage facilities at or near ground level, the underground cellar became a dominant fixture in the wine-producing countries north of the Alps from the 12th century onwards. Most of these underground storerooms were house cellars below private living areas. They served as storage areas for various goods – and, in times of emergency and war, offered protection from attack by way of a trap door or a chute known as the *Kellerhals*, or "cellar neck".

Wine cellars in castles and monasteries

Even today, fortresses and castles have storerooms and wine cellars that were hewn into the rock face, some of which were later lined with brickwork.
In German wine regions today, wine is often produced on castle estates, for example at Hornberg Castle near Neckarzimmern; Schaubeck Castle in the Bottwar Valley in Württemberg (documented as a wine producer since 1297); Staufenberg Castle near Durbach; and Ravensburg Castle near Sulzfeld in Baden. Vineyards surround Castel Noarna in Trentino, Italy, as well.
From the early Middle Ages, monasteries, church institutions and hospitals dedicated themselves to wine production on their considerable vineyard holdings. The work buildings were accordingly spacious and able to accommodate, among other things, the vineyard and harvesting equipment and wine presses as well as wine barrels and barrel-making supplies. Sometimes stills and beer-brewing equipment could also be found there.
Wine cellars, like other storage rooms, were a set feature of a monastery's infrastructure. The "ideal site plan" for the ninth-century Benedictine Abbey of St Gall in Switzerland shows a wine cellar 40 metres long and 10 metres wide in the middle of the complex, close to the cloister. In Burgundy, too, Benedictine monks were pivotal in expanding viniculture with their establishment of monasteries in Dijon and Cluny. The role of wine trailblazer was played even more intensely by the Order of Cistercians after the 11th century. Beginning with their mother house, Cîteaux Abbey, the Cistercians and

Medieval limestone cellar with riddling racks at Champagne Boizel, Epernay, Champagne

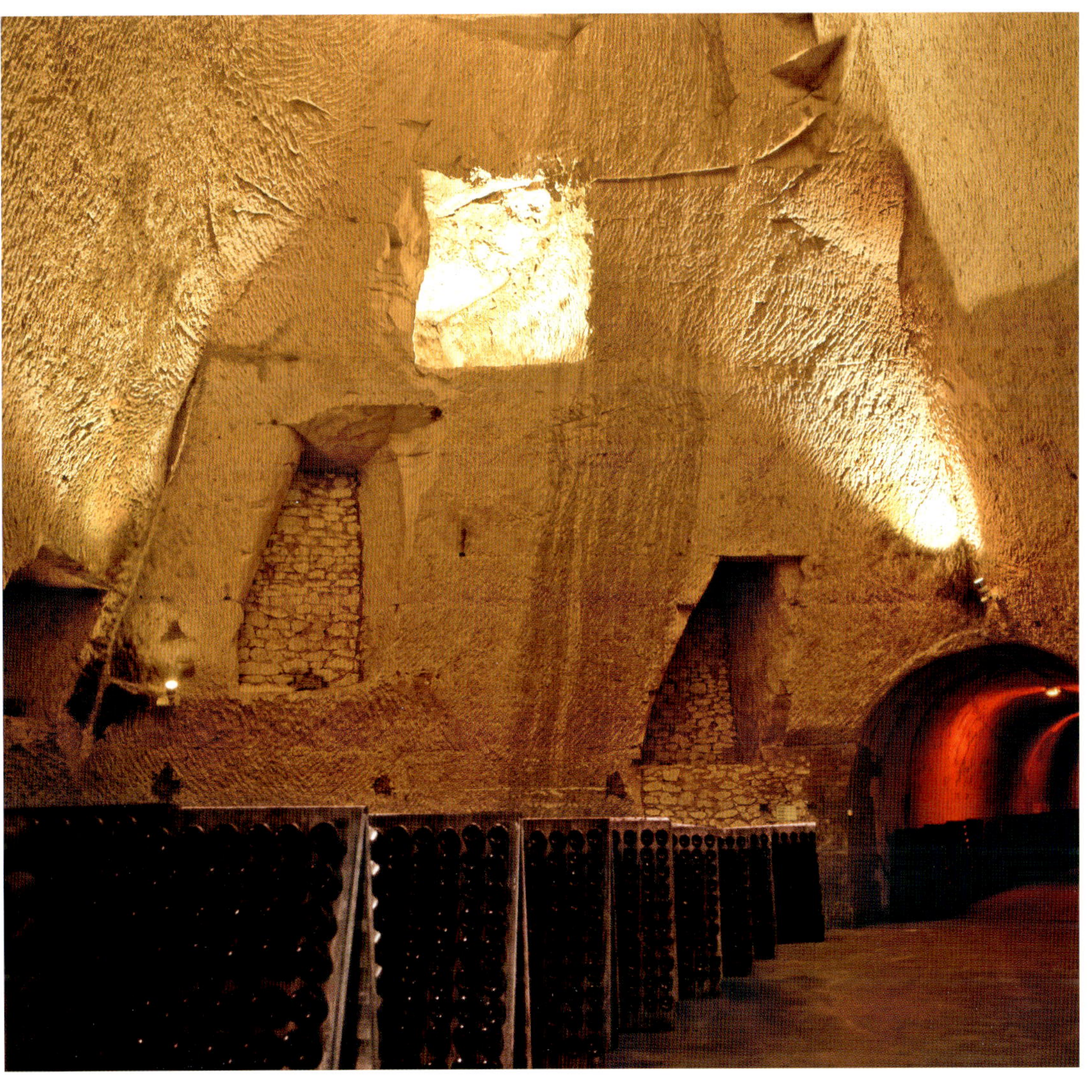

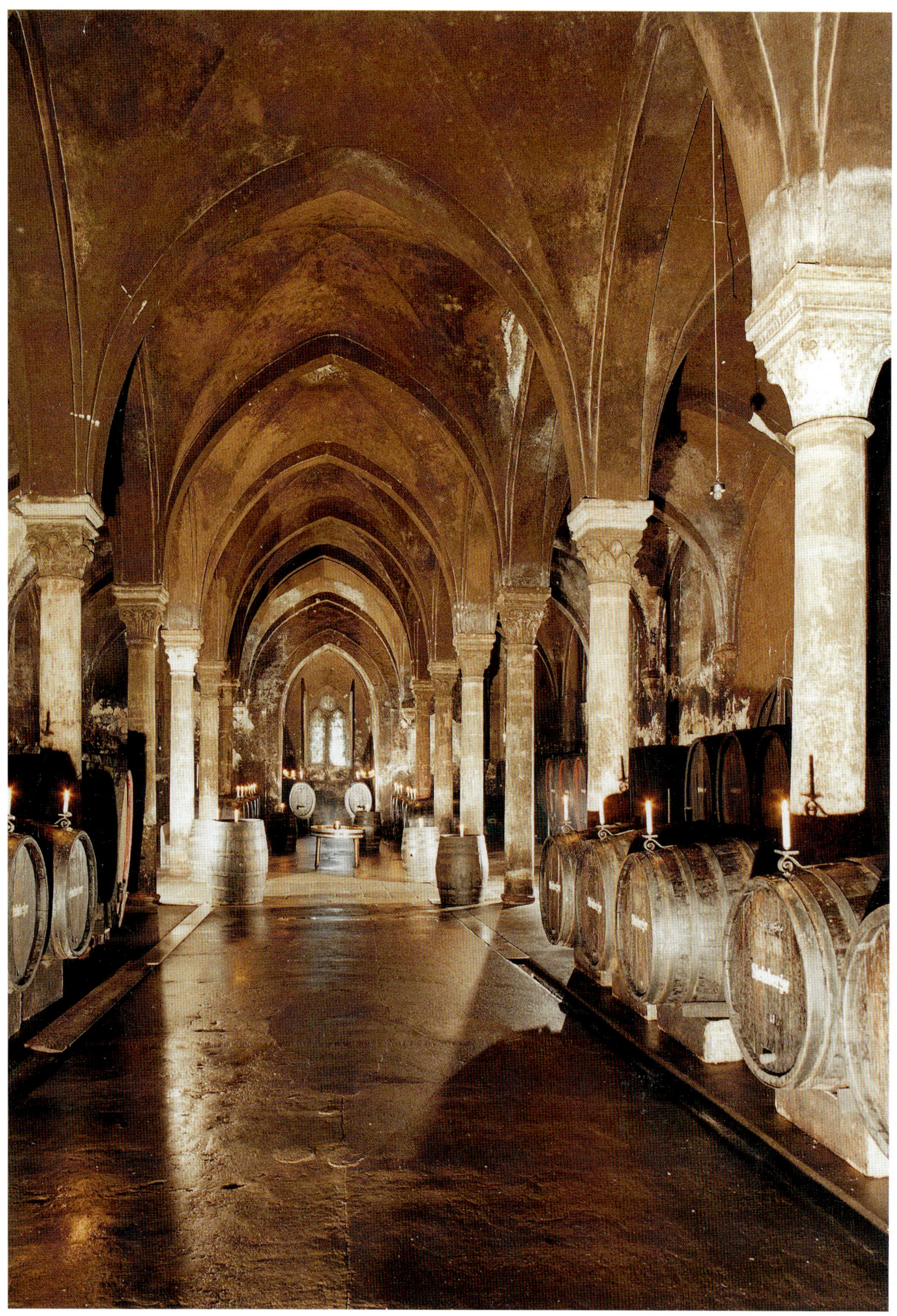

At left: 600-litre barrels in the three-nave, 13th-century *Hospitalkeller* at Eberbach Abbey near Eltville in the Rheingau
Opposite page:
Left: Lay brothers' refectory at Eberbach Abbey, featuring wine presses from the 17th century
Centre: Great Cellar at Schloss Johannisberg, Geisenheim-Johannisberg. The 600-litre barrels feature glass bungs. The vaulted ceiling is covered with the characteristic cellar mould (*Cladosporium cellare*).
Right: 1,200-litre barrels and an 18th-century wine press at Staatlicher Hofkeller Würzburg

their many affiliated abbeys and farming estates made a significant contribution to the expansion of vineyards and winemaking.

In 1136, the Cistercians founded Eberbach Abbey in the German Rheingau region. The building complex is considered one of the best-preserved Romanesque and early Gothic abbeys in Europe. It is also seen as a living reflection of the 800 years of continuous and successful wine production practised by the monks on numerous farming estates. In the 16th century, Eberbach Abbey was the largest wine-producing estate in the world, with recorded wine harvests yielding up to 250,000 litres a year. The "great barrel", built in 1485 with a 70,000-litre capacity, was a spectacular demonstration of the abbey's greatness. Modern-day visitors to Eberbach can marvel at three centuries' worth of massive historic wine presses, the oldest of them dating from 1668.

Eberbach Abbey combines an impressive presentation of wines with a magnificent sense of space. The early Gothic *Hospitalkeller* dating from around 1220, originally a hospital for the abbey's residents, was soon converted into a wine storeroom because of its very high humidity. A one-of-a-kind showpiece is the 47-metre-long *Cabinetkeller* in the double-naved, early Gothic former refectory, where the monks established a wine treasury in 1730.

The cultural wine legacy of the Eberbach monastery is now managed by the Hesse State Vineyards. The largely subterranean wine cellar complex built by architects Friess + Moster between 2006 and 2008 is one of the most modern in Germany. With

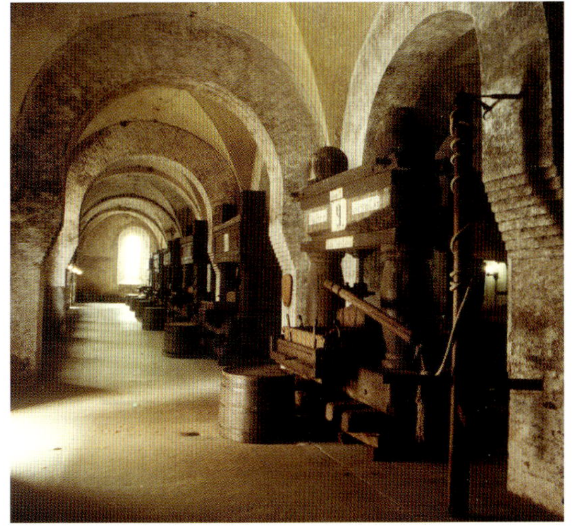

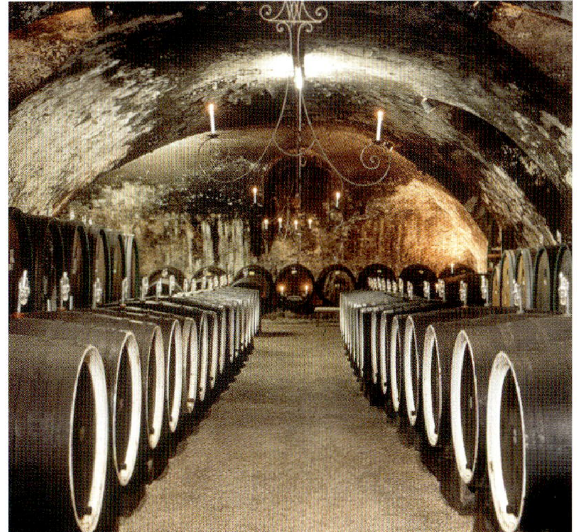

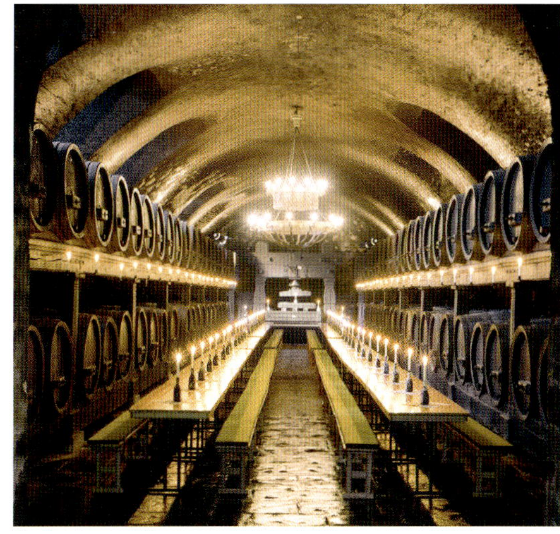

a storage capacity of 1.3 million bottles and a total tank volume of 1.8 million litres, it represents a fitting continuation of Eberbach's historic leadership in wine production in the Rhine region.

Ecclesiastical wineries with poetic names

In addition to Eberbach, there are currently about 20 wine-producing abbeys, cloisters and monasteries in the German-speaking countries. The leading facilities with significant vineyard acreage are Bürgerspital zum Heiligen Geist (ca. 1316) and Juliusspital (1579) in Würzburg; Spitalkellerei (1225) in Constance; and Vereinigte Hospitien (1464) in Trier. The wine cellars of Vereinigte Hospitien were established as part of a Roman storehouse around AD 300, which makes them the oldest in Germany. Abbazia di Novacella, near Brixen, is currently the largest monastic wine estate in Alto Adige, the German-speaking region of Italy otherwise known as South Tyrol. The Bavarian prelate monasteries in particular owned numerous vineyards in that region, and the yields were transported across the Alps and bottled in monasteries such as Andechs Abbey near Munich.

Other monasteries with a long tradition of wine production include abbeys in Austria such as Melk in Lower Austria, which has its wine cellar at Melkerhof in Vienna; the Benedictine Göttweig Abbey; the Augustinian Klosterneuburg Monastery (its wine estate, which features a four-level wine cellar built in 1114 that is 36 metres below ground, is considered the oldest and one of the largest in Austria); the Heiligenkreuz Abbey vineyards (1141) and its Thallern wine estate in Lower Austria; and the Schloss Gobelsburg winery (1171).

Most of the French monasteries still in existence can be found in Burgundy, such as the Hospices de Beaune (1443), whose wines have been sold in annual charity auctions since 1859. The Clos de Vougeot vineyard, with a château more reminiscent of a fort than of an early monastery winery, was founded by the Cistercians and now serves as a wine museum and a lodge for the Confrérie des Chevaliers du Tastevin in Burgundy. In this way, Clos de Vougeot shares the same fate as many formerly monastic wineries that were dissolved during secularization. The new owners of these estates – members of the nobility, wealthy citizens and the state – extended the grounds and rebuilt them according to their needs.

From the castle vineyard to the château

Schloss Johannisberg in the Rheingau, which goes back to a Benedictine monastery founded around 1100, provides an impressive example of structural changes made after secularization. When the castle changed hands in 1816 to become the property of Prince von Metternich, the estate was rebuilt in the Neoclassical style. The enormous, barrel-vaulted wine cellar, which was completed in 1721, was left untouched. It is 260 metres long and has a vault span of 11.5 metres. Another wine-related cultural attraction was created at Schloss Johannisberg with the establishment of an underground "wine bottle library", the *bibliotheca subterranea*. This became the prototype for countless wine treasuries for the storage of precious bottles of wine all over the world.

From about the 14th century, reigning princes began to prefer more lavish, impressive residential and administrative buildings to fortress-like enclosures and citadels. Accordingly, extended cellars were appended to their castles, some of them designed for the production and storage of wine. These cellars were sometimes so large that they would not have fitted into one of the earlier, more cramped fortress buildings.

Since then, the term "wine castle" has been used and interpreted in different ways. It may not necessarily refer to a majestic building with columns, turrets, battlements, pavilions, courtyards and landscaped grounds; rather, it may simply signify a country house or mansion whose owner is involved with winemaking and is content with the simplest architectural accoutrements.

The concept of "château", linguistically related to "castle", is equally ambiguous, especially with regard to wine production in the Bordeaux region. This term for a wine-producing estate emerged there around the mid-16th century. Most of the approximately 4,000 châteaux in existence today belong to non-aristocratic citizens or farmers. Particularly in the wine region of Bordeaux, the name "château" is associated with a particular *cru* (signifying a terroir or location), and is for this reason not an indication of a wine's renown or excellence.

Another term that is often confused is *domaine*. Particularly in Burgundy, the word is used to denote a wine estate with its own vineyards. In Germany,

Domäne indicates either a sizeable wine estate – in particular one belonging to the state – or an agricultural estate or its management.
The building complexes of the châteaux and castle estates are the products of centuries of change, featuring many diverse structures built at various times. In some cases, they began as residences, to which were later added facilities for the production and storage of wine. In the estates belonging to the aristocracy, in contrast, wine production was a feature from the start. Schloss Vollrads, one of the oldest German wine estates in the Rheingau, is a typical example of this long-term evolution. Its core is a 14th-century Gothic tower house, surrounded by a moat, to which the surrounding Baroque estate buildings were added in the 17th century.

Residences with majestic wine cellars

During the transition from the Renaissance to the Baroque era, while the castle estates were undergoing their architectural transformation, ancillary buildings and wine cellars were being expanded to be able to house ever larger barrels. The 17th century saw the emergence of vast facilities, some of which were able accommodate barrels with a capacity of up to 250,000 litres. These barrels included the now no longer extant *Riesenfass*, or giant barrel, in the Königstein Fortress in Saxony, and the Heidelberg Tun, the enormous wine barrel in the cellar of Heidelberg Castle, which is still on display there today.
Other German estates are perhaps less spectacular in this respect, but no less interesting to the architecture historian. These include Schloss Johannisburg in Aschaffenburg, the Altes Schloss (Old Castle) in Stuttgart, the Neues Schloss (New Castle) in Meersburg, the Fürst Hohenlohe Oehringen wine estate in Öhringen and Graf Neipperg in Schwaigern.

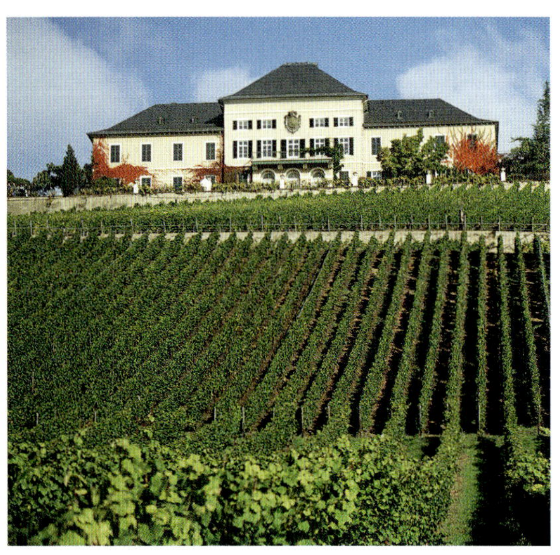

The Staatlicher Hofkeller (Bavarian State Wine Cellar, formerly the Fürstbischöflicher Hofkeller or Prince Bishop's Wine Cellar) is a special attraction in the Bishop's Residence in Würzburg. It was built by Balthasar Neumann and is the most notable Baroque palace in Europe. The cellar of this mighty building, on which construction began in 1720, covers 4,500 square metres and boasts walls four to five metres thick. Its passageways are nearly 900 metres long. The average temperature in the cellar is about 12.5 °C. The Hofkeller's great winemaking tradition, which spans more than three centuries, is illustrated not only by the imposing scale of the cellar, but also by its inventory. This includes a number of wooden barrels, many of them unique, dating mostly from the 18th century. The Hofkeller's famous "Swedish Barrel" was built in 1684 to house a precious vintage wine that had once been hidden by the people of Würzburg from the advancing Swedes during the Thirty Years' War. Other notable Hofkeller treasures include the *Beamtenfässer* or "civil servants' barrels", which can hold up to 50,000 litres each, and a Baroque wooden spindle press from 1784.
For centuries, walls two to three metres thick were not at all unusual in wine cellars. They served to maintain the cool and constant temperature required for wine storage. At the same time, their structural strength helped to absorb the significant lateral forces generated by the vault construction. Cellars were aligned on a north-south axis. Their entrances would be placed, if possible, on the north side, with sliding stone shutters to close cellar windows.
A similar development can be observed in the eastern European wine-producing countries. Here, too, we encounter the feudal architecture of various epochs as well as the construction of enormous cellars that were first in aristocratic, then in state hands. On the Crimean peninsula, Nicholas II, the last tsar of Russia, had a gigantic underground wine cellar built near Yalta starting in 1894, the entrance to which was "guarded" by a fortress-like building.

Palladianism, Classicism, Historicism

Various aristocratic dynasties – the Antinori, Frescobaldi and Ricasoli families among them – established themselves in traditional capitals of the wine trade, such as Bordeaux, Florence, Venice and Verona. Apart from erecting palatial city residences there, they also ran attractive agricultural estates still influenced by the style of the Italian and French Renaissance.
From the 16th century on, rural architecture began increasingly to come under the sway of Classicism, particularly Palladianism, the style pioneered by Andrea Palladio. With its clean lines and forms adopted from antiquity, the Palladian style came to define the patrician style of rural architecture. Villa Barbaro, built by Palladio in 1558 in Maser, near Treviso, stands as a prototype. The building is composed of five parts, with the reception rooms located in the upper storey of the central block. In the symmetrically arranged wings stretching out from the main portion of the building, the upper floor contains the private living quarters; the work areas are relegated to the lower floors. Pavilions round off the wings at either end, with the lower level housing wine cellars, stalls and other utility areas.
Designed by Palladio in 1564, Villa Emo in Vedelago, also in the Veneto, was the centre of an agricultural estate. The working areas were connected to the centre building by colonnaded wings.
Buoyed by their growing wealth and driven by a need to project a stately image, more and more proprietors of wine and agricultural estates embraced Classicism in the design of their manors. The concentration of this style of architecture is nowhere greater than in the Bordeaux region.
The historic trend begins with Château Haut-Brion. This wine estate was founded in 1525 in Pessac, now a suburb of Bordeaux. A characteristic feature of a château is that the majority of its built area is devoted not to living quarters but to wine storage buildings, or *chais*, which house the fermentation vats and ageing barrels. The typical structural elements of a château include a plinth that raises the structure and can incorporate about half of an underground *chai*; a terrace; and sometimes an outside staircase. A château's most salient features, however, are columns as well as decorative elements such as turrets and battlements. The predominance of Neoclassical buildings in the

Bordeaux region indicates the strong influence that Historicism wielded over wine architecture in the second half of the 19th century.
Its purest expression is found in several famous Neoclassical buildings, with pride of place going to Château Margaux. Dramatically situated at the end of a long drive lined with plane trees, the "Versailles of Médoc" boasts a grand Palladian facade with a broad outdoor staircase leading to a portico with four Ionic columns, and an interior design notable for its elegance and beauty. The château grounds also include buildings devoted to wine production. As well as accommodation for its more than 50 employees, the estate has its own cooperage (barrel-making facilities), as well as a 70-metre-long and 23-metre-wide barrel cellar whose oak ceiling is supported by 18 stone pillars at the centre of the space. This is where the wines are aged during the first year; the second-year cellar is in an underground *chai* built in 1982 with reinforced concrete, the first of its kind in Médoc. The Mazières architectural practice was commissioned with its planning and execution. In the 1980s, the architects undertook renovation and extension projects for about 20 châteaux in the area, as well as the renovation of underground cellars of iconic wine estates such as Château d'Yquem and Château Pichon Longueville Comtesse de Lalande.
With its subtle pageantry and clarity of forms, wine architecture in the Bordeaux region during the Belle Époque was undeniably shaped by a regional variant of Neoclassicism. Nevertheless, thanks to the influence of Historicism, other architectural styles played a role during this period as well, as is evidenced by a number of Neo-Gothic, Neo-Renaissance and Elizabethan-inspired buildings (Château Cantenac Brown, Château Lanessan). Still other châteaux display a surprising, even jarring mixture of styles. Some, like Château de la Rivière, are reminiscent of fairy-tale theatre architecture. Others, like the exotic-looking cellar building of Château Cos d'Estournel in St Estèphe, borrow from oriental models. The 1980 redesign of the *chais* with Far Eastern furnishings and barrels contrasts with the original Chinese pagoda style of the estate.
Baron Philippe de Rothschild was a pioneer of perfect cellar presentation. In 1924, he and Paris architect Charles Siclis started work on a new cellar with a 500-barrel capacity for his Château Mouton Rothschild. The ceiling of the 100-metre-long *chai*, part of which had to be blasted into the rocky ground, caved in during construction, but the cellar now stands without joists or supports.
The expanse of the cool, white walls is broken by columns of light. The only decorative element is the Mouton coat of arms on the front. Rothschild had the idea of showcasing wine as one would a work of art: through the effective use of light. The idea has since been copied all over the world.
The prevailing taste of the times left its traces not only in Bordeaux. Wine castles and cellars influenced by Historicism can be found along the Loire and in the Champagne region of France, in northern Spain and in Germany. The influence of Art Nouveau can also be seen.

Rustic and contemporary wine cellars

Meanwhile, in other wine-producing regions, most wine estates were constructed using local building materials. In Germany, these included quarried slate along the Mosel, central Rhine and Nahe rivers; and variegated sandstone and rubble limestone in Rheinhessen, the Palatinate and the Rheingau. Favourable economic and political conditions made it possible for a number of wine estate owners to construct grand mansions in a rustic version of the Baroque, Neoclassical or Empire styles – occasionally on properties that had been destroyed or seized from their former, aristocratic owners.
From 1830, vaulted cellars in Rheinhessen came to be built in a style typical of the region, with groin vaults resting on simple capitals supported by one or more rows of columns. This style was later to give way to repeating barrel-vaulted ceilings supported by steel girders and rebar. The first of the 300-odd work buildings that emerged in the groin vault style until about 1880 were converted cowsheds, so they came to be known as *Kuhkapellen*, or "cow chapels". These stone structures replaced earlier timber-framed buildings, as their greater fire resistance made them better suited to animal housing. From about 1950, an increasing number of farmers in Rheinhessen switched from dairy to grape and grain farming, so the stalls were put to other uses or torn down. In recent decades, the approximately 50 stalls still in existence have been restored and converted to wine bars and wine-tasting areas or turned into tourist venues.
On wine estates along the Rhine and Mosel rivers, a regional, relatively plain type of building emerged.

Opposite page: Southern facade of Schloss Johannisberg in Geisenheim-Johannisberg, built in the Baroque style. The Spätlese rating was created here in 1775.
This page, top: Château Margaux, Bordeaux, built in the Neoclassical style in 1816
This page, bottom: Château Pichon Longueville in Pauillac, Médoc, built in the Renaissance Revival style in 1851

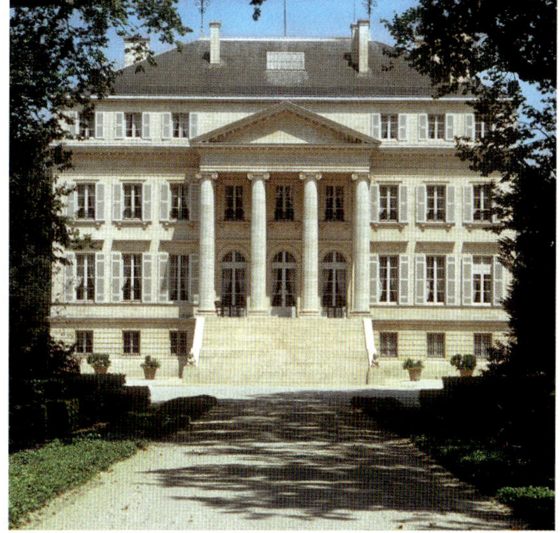

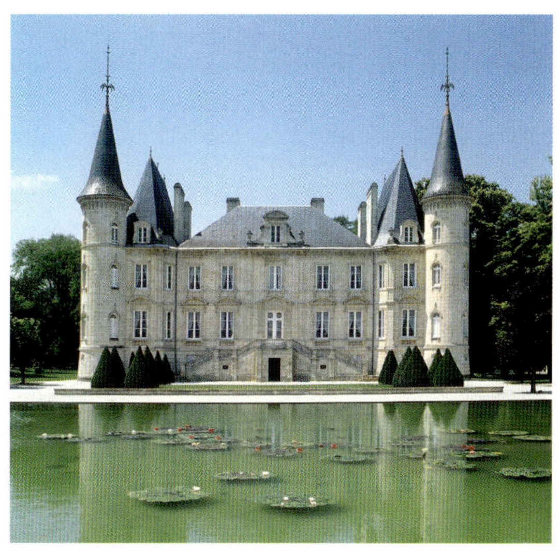

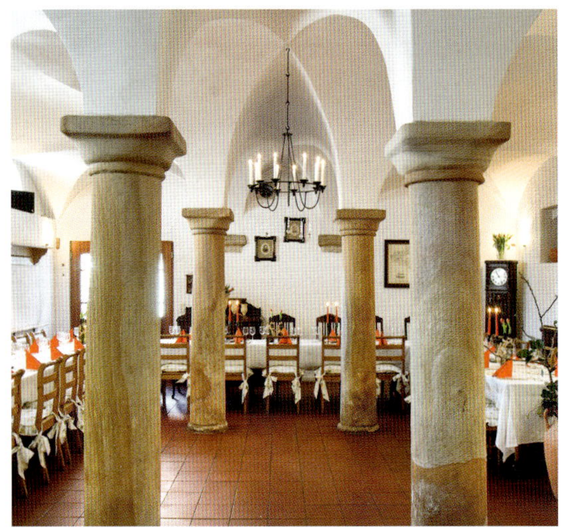

Lacking elaborate ornamentation, the style harked back to prototypes from the Renaissance, Baroque and Classical periods, sometimes incorporating elements of timber-frame construction.

From the end of the 19th century onwards, while wine estates and cellars were undergoing a structural redesign, step-by-step changes were taking place in winemaking. Novelties such as grape crushers with new extraction techniques; fermentation tanks; storage vessels of metal, plastic or steel; and bottling facilities all led to heated debates about ethics and benefits. Increasingly, steel tanks began to replace the traditional wooden fermentation casks used in red wine production. That development, in turn, had implications for the design of the press houses. Concurrently, large oak barrels came to be superseded by smaller ones, known as barriques. This allowed the transformation of barrel cellars into spaces marked by a new aesthetic: floors carefully tiled or dashed with white pebbles, stark walls featuring rubble stone or light-coloured render, contrasting wooden-beamed ceilings, and an almost clinical cleanliness.

New technologies transformed construction as well. Iron supports replaced stone pillars; brick and cement were increasingly used in cellars; and, for ground-level warehouses, cast iron (for wide spans) and reinforced concrete became the preferred alternatives to wood or brick construction.

Large-scale wine architecture

A new chapter in the architecture of wine began in the 19th century. In the wake of the Industrial Revolution, champagne and sparkling wine cellars, Sherry bodegas and port wine lodges, riding a wave of worldwide export success, stepped up their business activities. This increase in production created a need for new buildings of unprecedented dimensions. Just to remove the lees from the millions of champagne bottles produced (a process called disgorgement), for example, countless riddling racks were required – and an immense amount of space was necessary to accommodate them. Riddling halls and subterranean cellar passageways attained awe-inspiring dimensions. Cellars and tunnels at Moët & Chandon reached a vast length of 28 kilometres, but even this amazing figure was surpassed by the 30 kilometres boasted by Codorníu.

The underground labyrinthine cellars in the limestone quarries in and around Rheims, with their endless bottle galleries and riddling racks, are hardly distinguishable from one another except by their size. Because of this, champagne houses in search of publicity, and hoping to stand out from their competitors, gave their reception and administrative buildings exceptional, sometimes idiosyncratic designs.

During the founding years of cellars in the Champagne, the country-estate and Renaissance-inspired styles were in vogue, but also Gothic Revival. The most famous example of this is the curious architecture of the Pommery estate in Rheims, which was erected in the 1870s. Behind its imposing wrought-iron entrance gate stands an eclectic group of buildings constructed from a variety of materials. The ensemble is said to have been designed by Madame Pommery herself, although, officially, a number of master builders were also involved. The architecture is an obvious nod to the style of stately homes in England, whose owners at the time numbered among Pommery's best clients.

The ageing cellar built in Sant Sadurní d'Anoia, near Barcelona, for the Spanish Cava producer Codorníu, exemplifies the spirit of Catalonian Art Nouveau. It was designed by Josep Puig i Cadafalch, a contemporary of Antoni Gaudí, and constructed between 1895 and 1915. The *Celler Gran* ("Large Cellar") extends over an area of 2,000 square metres and is divided into three halls covered by a Catalonian vaulted roof.

Another example of the Catalonian Art Nouveau style, probably influenced by Gaudí and Cadafalch, is the majestic cellar built in 1920 by Cèsar Martinell for the wine cooperative Gandesa in the Spanish province of Tarragona. Here, for once, the lofty term "wine cathedral" applies. Most of the buildings from this period are, however, exclusively functional industrial structures – and regrettably forgettable.

The sparkling-wine house Kupferberg in the Kästrich quarter of Mainz is an illustration of the speed with which expanding wine producers abandoned their relatively modest pre-industrial look in favour of a more imposing style. The original Kupferberg building, built by Joseph Laské in 1856, was a stuccoed structure with a symmetrical facade and neo-Gothic motifs. In 1860, a three-storey building was added. Two years later, the Alexanderkaserne ("Alexander barracks") was erected next to them, a building made of variegated sandstone and ashlar masonry that has served the company as an office building since 1900. In 1866, Christian Adalbert Kupferberg commissioned Conrad Kraus to erect two neo-Renaissance buildings (with some Baroque and Neoclassical motifs), one of which features the magnificent Art Nouveau *Traubensaal* ("Grape Hall") and an impressive collection of champagne glasses. Kupferberg's brick cellar with sandstone details, dating from 1899, completes the diverse ensemble.

To avoid this kind of patchwork effect, Otto Henkell, founder of the Henkell sparkling-wine house, took a different architectural route. His growing company had become dispersed among 50 cellars throughout Mainz, and he wanted to bring it all together in a new build. Having bought an inexpensive plot of land in Wiesbaden-Biebrich, he invited architects to submit designs for the estate. It wasn't, however, the winner of the competition who ultimately got the contract, but architect Paul Bonatz, who was just 30 years old at the time. In accordance with his client's wishes, he erected a stately building in the Neoclassical style. The "Little Henkell Palace" boasts a central, five-bay projection crowned by a pediment. A steep hip roof of copper and glass rises above the travertine-clad facade. The colonnaded entrance walkway, with sweeping wings that end in pavilions, lends the building a particular charm. The sense of grandeur is amplified in the reception area, or Marble Hall, which was decorated in an elaborate Rococo style in 1928.

Moorish architecture served as the inspiration for several of the cathedral-like Sherry bodegas in

Andalusia. The first buildings of this kind emerged in the 19th century. They generally feature high, wide-span wooden roofs. Real Bodega de La Concha, however, is an exception. This impressive, shell-like steel structure was designed by Gustave Eiffel for the cellars of González Byass in Jerez de la Frontera in 1862. Nearby, the extensive La Mezquita bodega, designed by Javier Soto López-Dóriga for the Domecq Sherry house, features elements of Arabic architecture inspired by the mosque of the same name at Córdoba.
At the height of the international Sherry boom, Williams & Humbert built a 180,000-square-metre estate in Jerez de la Frontera, creating one of the largest bodegas in Europe. The ageing cellar measures 75,000 square metres and can accommodate 60,000 barrels. The cave's groin-vault-inspired ceiling is exquisite and, in combination with its supporting columns, recalls the shape of wine glasses. The ambition and commitment with which the large wine houses pursued their building projects 100 years ago declined in subsequent decades. Large and small companies alike suffered the impact of world wars and economic crises on their output and sales. Then, in the second half of the 20th century, building activity was largely restricted to renovation work – conversions and extensions for which mainly builders, not architects, were called upon.

Pioneers of the 20th century

Once again, it was from the Bordeaux region – more specifically, from Pauillac in the Médoc – that new ideas for a revolution in wine architecture came. In 1987, the new cave for Château Lafite Rothschild signalled a radical departure from the traditional rectangular floor plan. For owner Éric de Rothschild, the project was intended to bring considerable technical and economic advantages. The first priority was to streamline significantly the work processes in the *chai*, where barriques have to be shifted four times a year. Apart from saving time, the redesign was supposed to obviate the need for a cooling system as well as preserve valuable vineyard acreage, which necessarily meant choosing a subterranean solution. The result was an underground wine cave with a completely new spatial arrangement, designed by Catalonian architect Ricardo Bofill. His new solution was perhaps inspired by the circular arrangement of the barrels in some Sherry bodegas. The reinforced-concrete

Opposite page: Groin vault in a former cowshed from the 19th century. *Kuhkapellen* or "cow chapels" are found primarily in Rheinhessen.
Below: Vinothèque at Château Lafite Rothschild in Pauillac, Médoc. Established in the early 19th century, the cellar houses more than 20,000 bottles. The oldest wine dates from 1797.

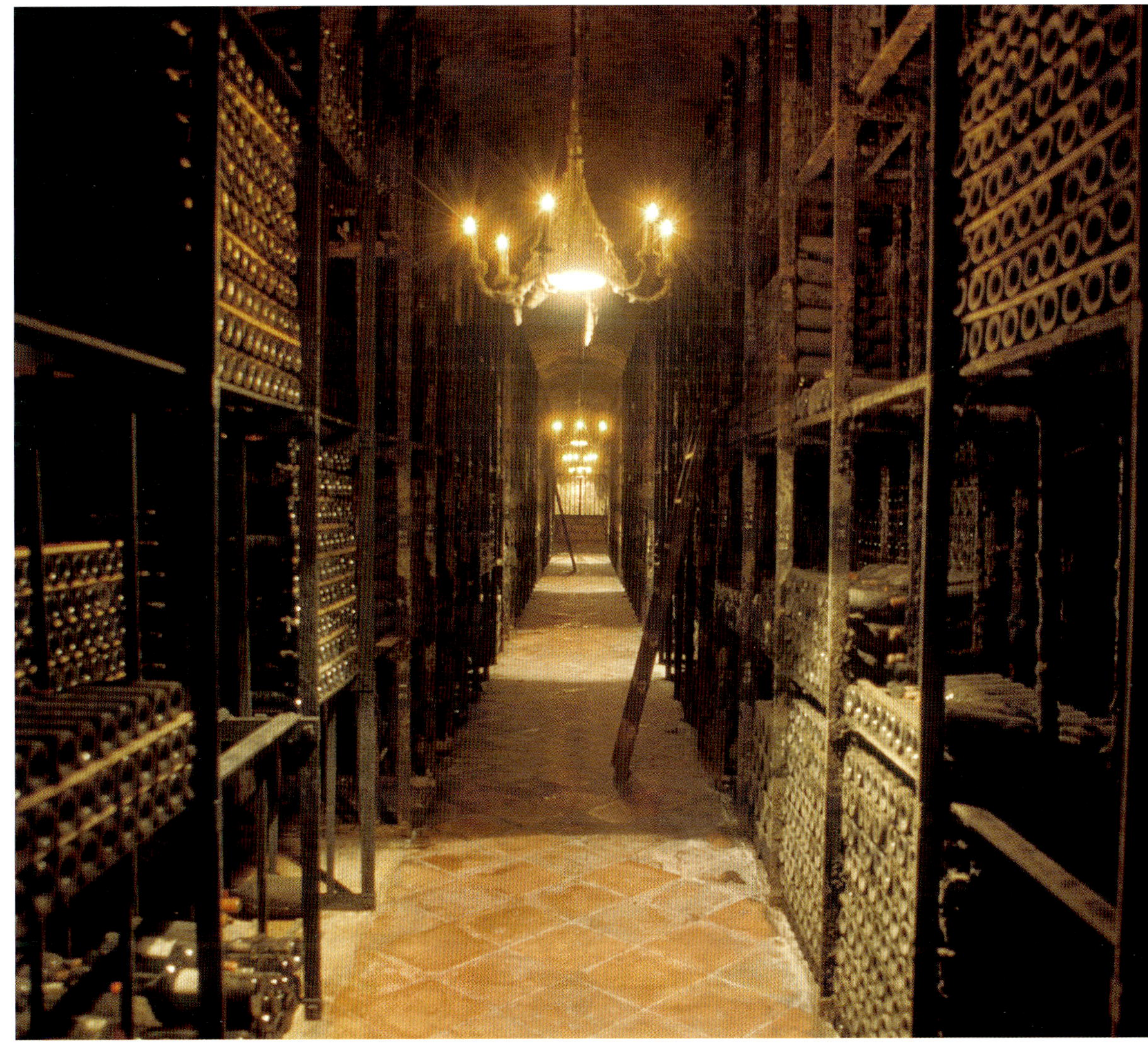

chai allows for the storage of about 2,000 barrels in concentric circles on an octagonal floor plan. At its centre, a well of light surrounded by 16 columns gives the cave the feel of a "wine crypt".
The sense of renewal that, from the mid-1980s, created an increasingly buoyant atmosphere in new wine architecture soon took hold even of winemakers who had previously been reluctant to try anything new. Fortuitous economic circumstances enabled the implementation of groundbreaking projects. The AXA insurance company, owner of the renowned Château Pichon Longueville in Pauillac, financed the construction of a new winery tract with *chais*, a circular press house for 30 fermentation tanks, and a bottle cellar. The 4,000 square metres of work area were expanded to include administrative spaces and a reception area with tourist facilities, making it possible to welcome up to 50,000 visitors a year. Architects Patrick Dillon and Jean de Gastines brought this project to fruition in the early 1990s. It was met, as is often the case, with enthusiasm and scepticism in equal measure. Out of deference to the neighbouring fairy-tale castle of Pichon Longueville, dating from 1851, the external appearance of the new structure is simple and minimalist. A large water basin mediates between the old and the new.
Projects such as this – including the new cellar also designed by Dillon and Gastines for Château de Bachen, located south of Bordeaux in the wine region of Tursan and belonging to celebrity chef Michel Gérard – helped inspire the Centre Pompidou in Paris to host an exhibition titled *Château Bordeaux* in 1989. The exhibition exhaustively documented the reciprocal, often symbiotic relationship between viniculture and architecture in the region.
The renewal process, however, was not restricted to France and its south-western wine regions. Similar developments followed, albeit with a slight delay, in the major wine-producing countries of Spain and Italy.
In the years directly after the Second World War, wine architecture in most European wine-growing countries saw little in the way of revival. This only emerged from 1980 onwards. Initially, new construction focused on a comprehensive modernization of production facilities and buildings, while reception buildings and living quarters were largely left as they were. In these interventions, functionality was the top priority, and results did not always blend harmoniously into their surroundings or the regional landscape. The variety of architectural styles was nevertheless broad, ranging from classical Modernism, such as the Bauhaus, to the futuristic architecture of Zaha Hadid.
Spanish wine producers were especially rigorous in pursuing new winery design. In Italy there was a similar development, although the affinity for new wine architecture was at first more pronounced in the country's northern wine-growing areas than in those in the south.
The close of the 20th century saw a veritable surge of activity in wine architecture in Austria. Almost 50 winemakers in the Burgenland completed new constructions, extensions and renovations of their work buildings in the years between 1999 and 2004. During the same period, the wine region of Styria recorded more than a dozen similar projects, and the situation was similar in Lower Austria. Though the new architecture allowed vintners to update and optimize their winemaking facilities and processes, the reasons for its rapid spread were not

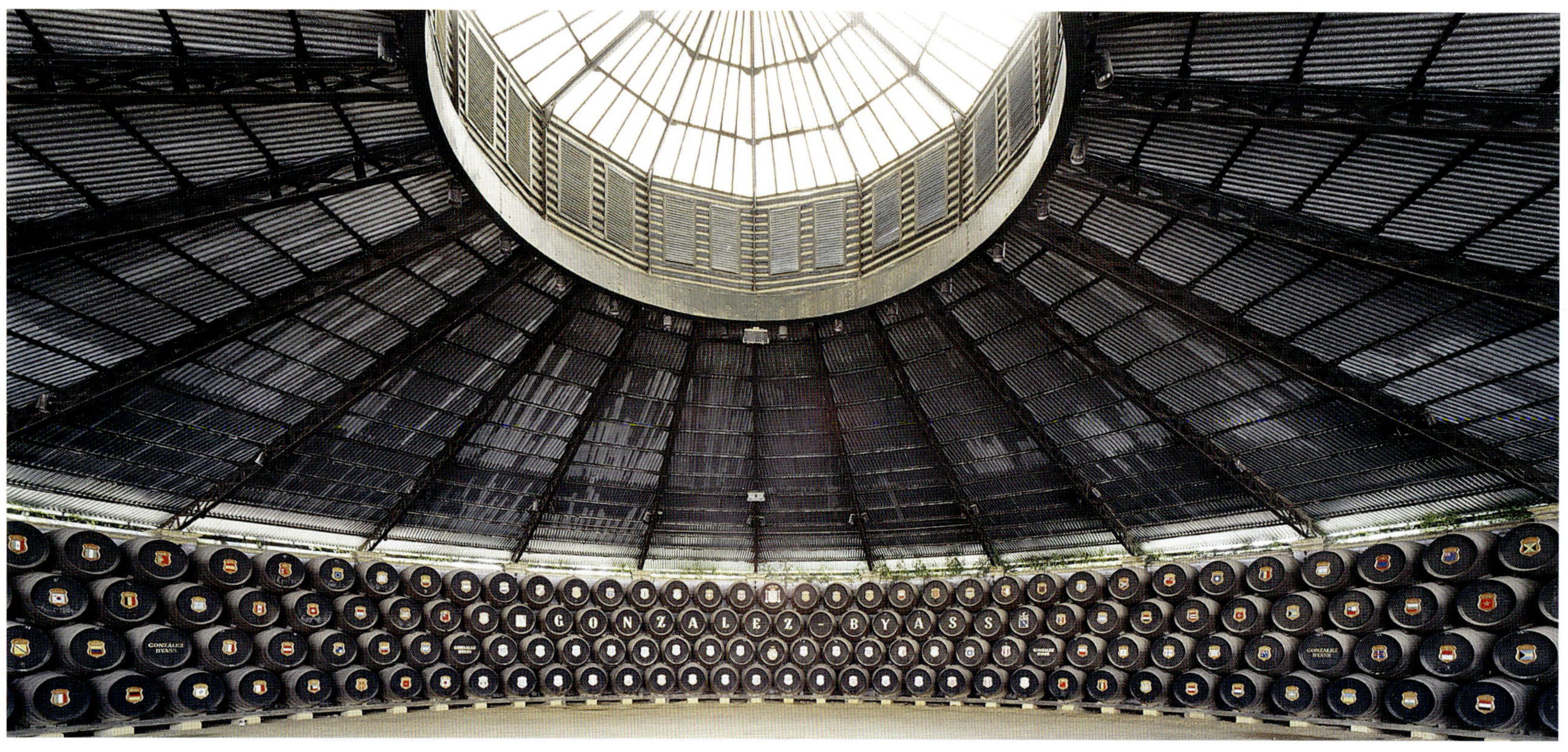

solely pragmatic. Owners and vintners also wanted to create high-quality wines, and to convey this aspiration through a distinctive, high-profile visual presentation. Such ambitious goals could, however, only be realized with the help of grants from EU structural funds, made available under the Maastricht Treaty, which declared Burgenland and other areas eligible for EU support.

Outlook and Vision

As this historical overview makes clear, the evolution of contemporary wine architecture has been subject to varying influences in each country and region. Economic conditions have certainly played a major role. Happily, experts predict positive sales trends for the wine industry to continue, particularly in light of the growing demand in the Far East. In Europe, too, particularly in the eastern part of the continent, wine is gaining new ground as a cult drink.

This situation is reflected in the growing acceptance and appreciation of new winery designs. As consumers become more and more interested in the fascinating world of winemaking, wineries that open their doors to the public are gaining a higher profile. The industry's embrace of direct marketing has led wineries to style themselves increasingly as tourist attractions, paving the way for new design possibilities within the constraints of agricultural, business and industrial architecture.

With their diverse, even exceptional, wine architecture creations, important names such as Frank O. Gehry, Renzo Piano, Zaha Hadid, Steven Holl and Mario Botta testify to the particular challenge and fascination inherent in what is, in fact, purely functional architecture. In this way, innovative architects and their clients have contributed definitively to the watershed in the development of wine architecture and its much-debated reinterpretation. Wherever contemporary architecture is practised, its unfamiliar design language can initially feel unsettling, even offensive, to fans of traditional wine cellar culture. Increasingly, however, the old, pseudo-romantic winery atmosphere is giving way to the pursuit of aesthetics, lucidity, clarity and functionality.

Visual considerations are becoming more and more vital to a winery's image and status. Here, architectural idiom knows no bounds. Whether simple and functional, spectacular or revolutionary, purpose-built architecture can help wine companies and winemakers to realize virtually all their aspirations. In doing so, wine architecture plays an important role in promoting and sustaining the public's fascination with all things connected with wine.

Opposite page: In addition to a wine cellar built for CVNE in 1879, Gustave Eiffel completed Real Bodega de la Concha in Jerez de la Frontera as a steel structure in 1862. Part of the Gonzáles Byass Sherry house, the cellar contains 214 Sherry casks.

At right: New underground *chai* for the second-year barriques at Château Lafite Rothschild in Pauillac, Médoc, from designs by Ricardo Bofill

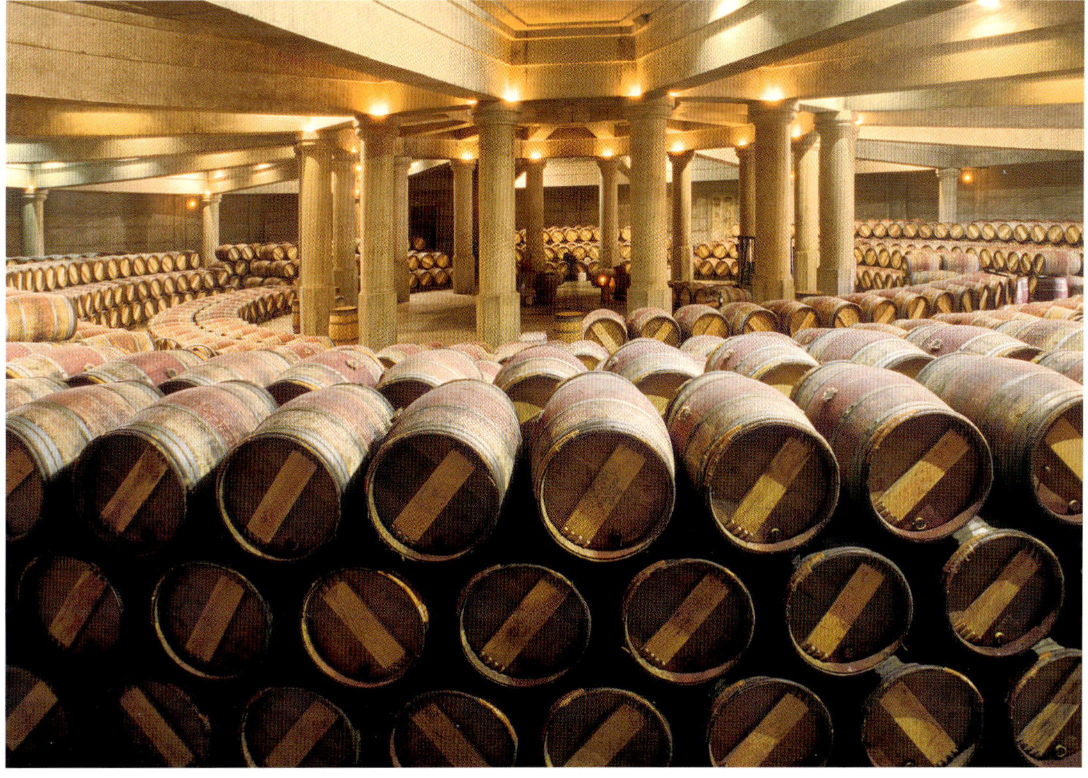

Winemaking and facility design

"Wine means the product obtained exclusively from total or partial alcoholic fermentation of fresh grapes, crushed or otherwise, or of grape must," according to EU wine regulations. The basic principle of winemaking has not changed substantially since ancient times, when people crushed grapes by stomping on them with their bare feet. In our high-tech era, however, the aid of physical, chemical and technological processes is enlisted to optimize and streamline wine production and to make the resulting drink an incomparably better product. Aspects such as sustainability and environmental considerations are playing an increasingly important role in this process.

The contrast between the ancient and the modern practice of wine production is therefore considerable. Must production and pressing used to be accomplished in one step, as the grapes were trampled in a basin with a drain to let the resulting juice run off. In ancient Egypt, grapes and skins would be pressed a second time in sacks. Filled into earthenware containers, the juice fermented spontaneously or was boiled. Certain herbs were added and the wine was often watered down before drinking.

While these rather primitive methods have long been consigned to history, a few processes, such as spontaneous fermentation, are being rediscovered by some winemakers. Other vintners eschew all chemical processing of their wines. Still others try combining old and new methods in various ways. In short, the process of wine production is a highly heterogeneous one.

The differences in approach already become apparent during grape receiving and processing. The first step to promoting quality is the grape selection, which is particularly important in the processing of red grapes. During selection, mouldy and unripe grapes, and particularly the remains of leaves and stems, are removed from the fruit either manually at the sorting table or sorting belt, or with the help of automated sorting facilities. This step in the process occurs together with destemming, a process by which the grapes are separated from the rachis. Today, the selection and destemming, like the crushing or maceration of grapes, no longer takes place at the vineyard but primarily inside the winery itself.

Maceration

To start the process of maceration, the crusher gently tears the grapes open and crushes them without breaking the seeds, which would add their tannins and bitters to the end product. The resulting thick mixture of fruit pulp, grape seeds, skins and juice is called the must. The less the must is exposed to oxygen, the smaller the danger of oxidation (browning). This is prevented by adding sulphur dioxide or carbon dioxide. The length of time the red wine is permitted to stay in contact with the skins and seeds depends on the characteristics and quality of the harvest. Extended maceration or extraction can result in a full-bodied wine, but it could also intensify unwanted tannins and pigments. As a general rule of thumb, maceration should be about as long as the fermentation process; depending on the desired style of wine, however, it could also last a bit longer.

Pressing

In the making of white wine, the pressing occurs right after crushing to separate the grape juice from the solids in the must. To this end, most wineries use pneumatic, hydraulic or mechanical presses. Modern presses can be set to regulate the pressing intensity and duration, which, depending on the type of wine, takes between one and a maximum of three hours. Varying according to the variety, ripeness and vintage of the grapes, between 65 and 80 litres of juice can be retrieved from 100 kilograms of grapes. Red wine grapes used to make rosé go straight into the press after crushing, without maceration and without a heating of the must. Immediate pressing gives the wine its characteristic light red colour, as only a little pigmentation from the grape skins leaches into the wine.

The solids remaining after the pressing, called pomace, can be used to make pomace wine or pomace brandy (such as marc or grappa), the quality of which improves with storage length. One hundred kilograms of pomace can yield about seven to nine litres of brandy. Often the must is clarified by various methods (sedimentation, flotation, filtration, fining) before pressing, in order to remove the insoluble matter.

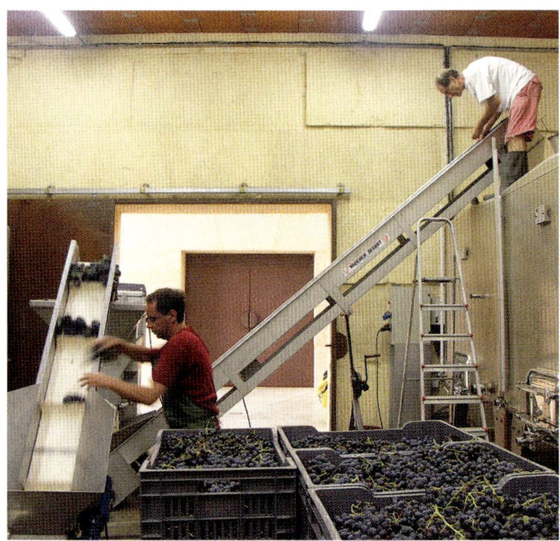

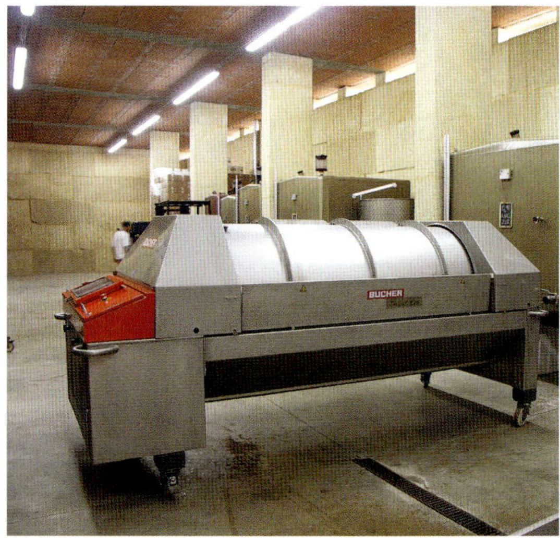

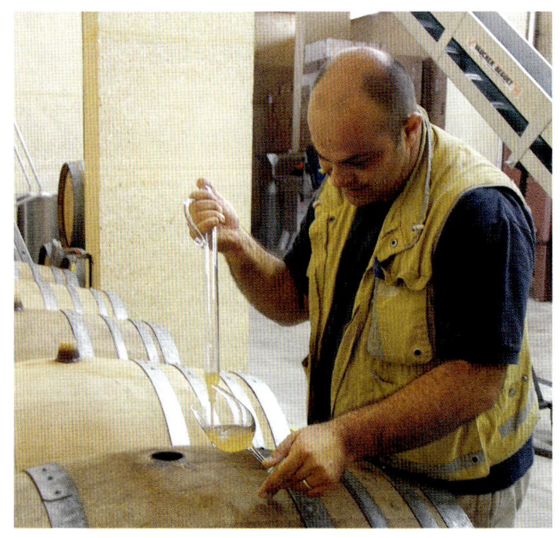

Fermentation

Fermentation is initiated by yeasts, which break down the sugars in the juice and convert them into alcohol and carbon dioxide. Nowadays, this process can be finely regulated in the temperature-controlled environment of metal fermentation tanks. Traditional fermentation, though, often still takes place in wooden barrels with fermenter lids (funnels or pots) to keep air out. Selected strains of cultured yeast influence the process of fermentation. To increase the alcohol content, some wines have sugar added to them before fermentation begins (chaptalization), although there are strict regulations governing the maximal amount of sugar allowed. The manner of fermentation, whether natural or controlled, as well as the fermentation method and length, have a direct bearing on the later character of a white wine. In keeping with customer tastes, most of the wines produced are dry or semi-sweet. The sugar left in the wine after fermentation only weighs a few grams per litre (according to wine regulations). By adding süssreserve (unfermented grape must) or potassium or sodium metabisulphite, the amount of residual sugar can be increased. The level of this is higher with wines that are classified as sweet or mild. Sweet wines (Auslese wines) retain their high content of unfermented sugar naturally, without additional sweetening. In many wine-producing countries, a secondary fermentation (malolactic fermentation) is done after the primary or alcoholic fermentation. In this process, lactic acid bacteria convert malic acid into lactic acid, giving the wines lower levels of acidity. In contrast to white wines, red-wine fermentation is carried out during the must stage. It takes place in traditional, usually rather small, closed or open vats, or in stirred tanks or pressure tanks. By keeping the must in motion and applying controlled amounts of heat, flavours and tannins are extracted from the grapes.
Ideally, the further transport of the must takes place by means of gravity. As fermentation vats are often situated at ground level, however, the must is usually transported with the help of pumps and pipes, and sometimes by conveyor belts.

Ageing

During the first racking, the young wines are siphoned off the lees (yeast that has settled to the bottom) and transferred to wooden barrels, tanks

Opposite page: Wine production at Domaine les Aurelles in Nizas, France
Top: After the grapes are received, they are sorted manually on a conveyor belt. Foreign material and imperfect grapes are removed. For a high-quality end product, only ripe and healthy grapes go on to the crusher.
Centre: Modern horizontal presses operate with hydraulic or pneumatic pressure to press the grapes in an almost entirely automated process.
Bottom: Taking a sample from the barrel to assist wine ageing and care.
This page, below: Red grapes often blush into different colours, according to grape variety.

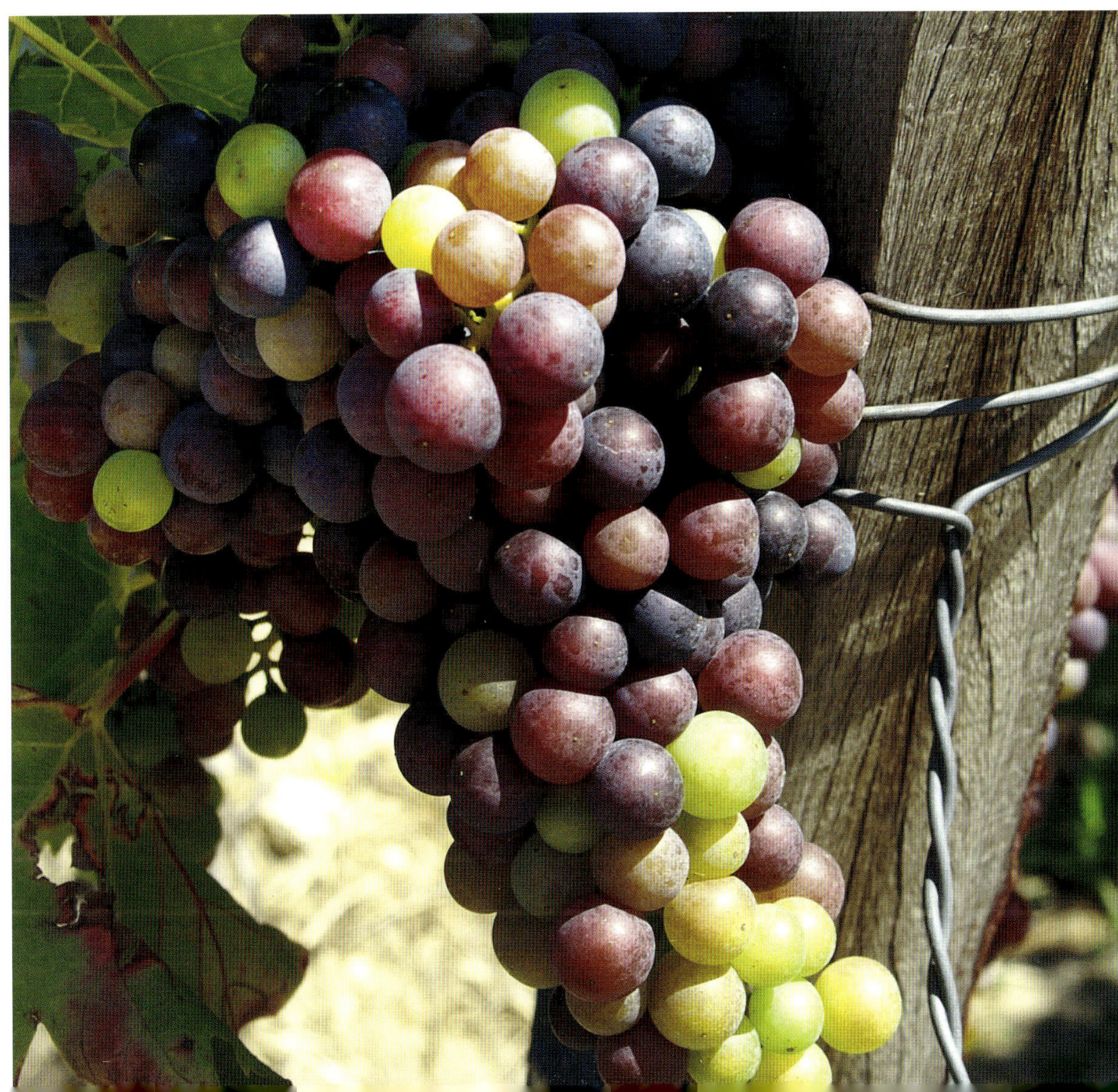

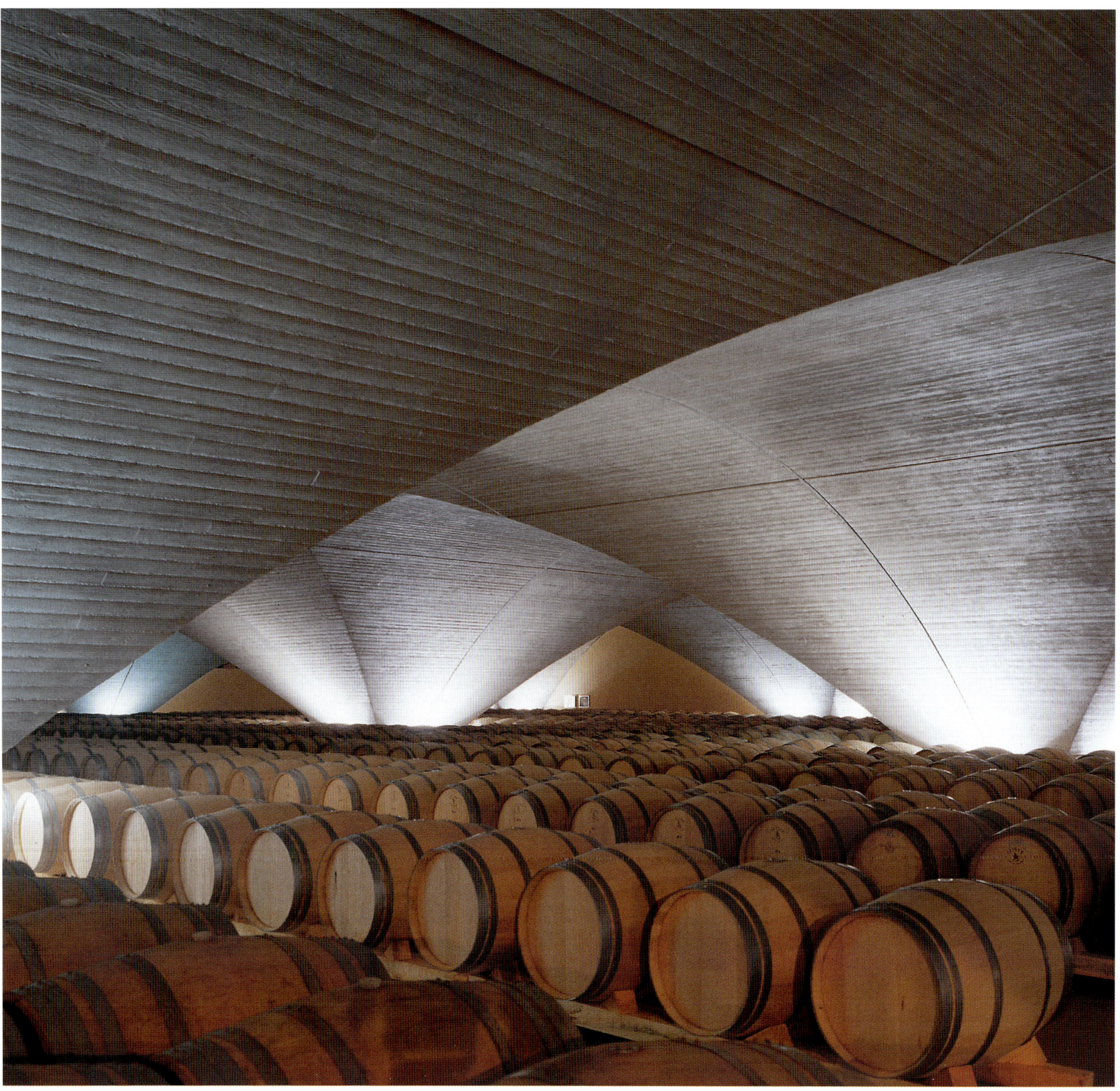

or other vats for ageing. The choice of container depends on the type of wine and the qualities desired for the end product. Crisp, uncomplicated white wines are usually aged in tanks for a short period of time. Wooden barrels are suitable for wines that require a long ageing process to develop their aromas and flavours fully. The traditional, large wooden barrels have a different impact on the wine than do the smaller, 225-litre oak casks called barriques. The effect a barrel has on the wine, and the intensity of this effect, is determined by the degree of contact the wine has with the wood of the barrel and by the wood's aromatic properties, which come from its kind, age and method of toasting.
Depending on the type of wine being made, further steps can be taken during barrel ageing. These include sulphurization, enrichment, deacidification, fining and possible blending. Clarification is done to prepare the wine for stabilization with additives (and in the case of white wines, filtration) before bottling. Red wine in particular continues to age in the bottle for some time – from one year to several years – before it is brought on the market.

Architectural solutions

In a wine-producing facility, the rooms in the work areas are arranged to accommodate the various phases of wine production. The fermenting cellar is actually a multi-purpose room, since the grape receiving, sorting, destemming, crushing, maceration, fermentation, pressing, and conveyance of the pomace takes place here. Moreover, since the space is used for these activities for only a few weeks a year, it can be utilized for other purposes as well, such as bottling, labelling, and storage of other equipment such as pumps, centrifuges and filters.
The tank storage area accommodates containers of many different sizes and materials (steel, stainless steel, plastic) as well as pressure vessels for various production processes (must preparation, fermentation, juice storage, etc.). Given the sophisticated technological equipment required for up-to-date production of quality wine, a customized, attractive design of production facilities makes sense not only in terms of streamlining the operational sequence but also because it permits the winery to project a positive, customer-oriented image.

Traditionally in European winemaking, barrels of wine are stored in a cellar – in other words, underground. Smaller wineries in particular often make use of subcellars and root cellars; in larger wine estates, vaulted cellars predominate. Newer buildings usually include concrete cellars. But no matter what cellar type is used, it must be able to offer an optimal climate for wine – in other words, be dry, cool (with average temperatures of 10–12 °C and free of frost in the winters) and odour-free – and hence fulfil certain structural engineering criteria. The humidity in barrel cellars has to be higher than in tank storage areas, but lower than in bottle cellars. Under no circumstances should the humidity in barrel cellars be so high that it leads to mould and mildew.
Tank and barrel storage areas usually make the strongest impression on visitors, which means that their fittings and interior design should be viewed with an eye to more than just practicality.
Together with the multifunctional production space, the wine storage area – whether at ground level or in a cellar – defines the architecture of a winery. Wine storage areas at ground level (often physically connected to the production space) are optimal from the viewpoint of transport logistics. In line with the development of the winery's output and sales figures, they can simply be extended or converted as needed.
The storage of wooden barrels requires the most amount of space, particularly when it comes to the increasingly popular barriques. This is the most work-intensive method of storage, but the most effective and impressive with regard to image and presentation. To reduce the amount of space needed, the barriques can be stacked one on top of the other. Wooden barrels require regular maintenance, so sufficient space has to be allowed between the rows. And they must be kept separate from the tanks, as barrels need a relative humidity of 85 per cent to prevent a large reduction in their contents.
The bottle warehouse – the storage area for full bottles – has to have enough volume to accommodate bottles from up to two harvests. It is usually on the same level as other work facilities such as packaging and shipping, as well as the customer reception and tasting areas.
In recognition of the fact that the in-house shop and wine bar has become an important part of a winery's image and its marketing, many winemakers have given their tasting areas pride of place. Offering an appealing product presentation and supplying their customers with background information, these shops are increasingly becoming wine discovery centres.
A winery's working areas include the machine halls for the equipment needed in the vineyards; offices; and, in larger facilities, the laboratory where the wine is chemically analysed.
The decision of whether and how working areas are to be united in one structure or divided among several buildings is dependent on a number of factors. Unquestionably, however, a well-thought-out arrangement of buildings and spaces, like a judicious use of mechanization in work processes, can achieve significant savings in work and time.
Many important aspects have to be considered and accommodated in the building, renovation and extension of wine production facilities. These include topographical factors (such as the location of the business on a sloping terrain): the environment of the site; the size, flexibility and functionality of the facility; the owner's aesthetic, financial and technological targets; and, last but not least, the creative imagination and stylistic language of the architect.

Opposite page: Señorío de Otazu in Echauri, Navarra

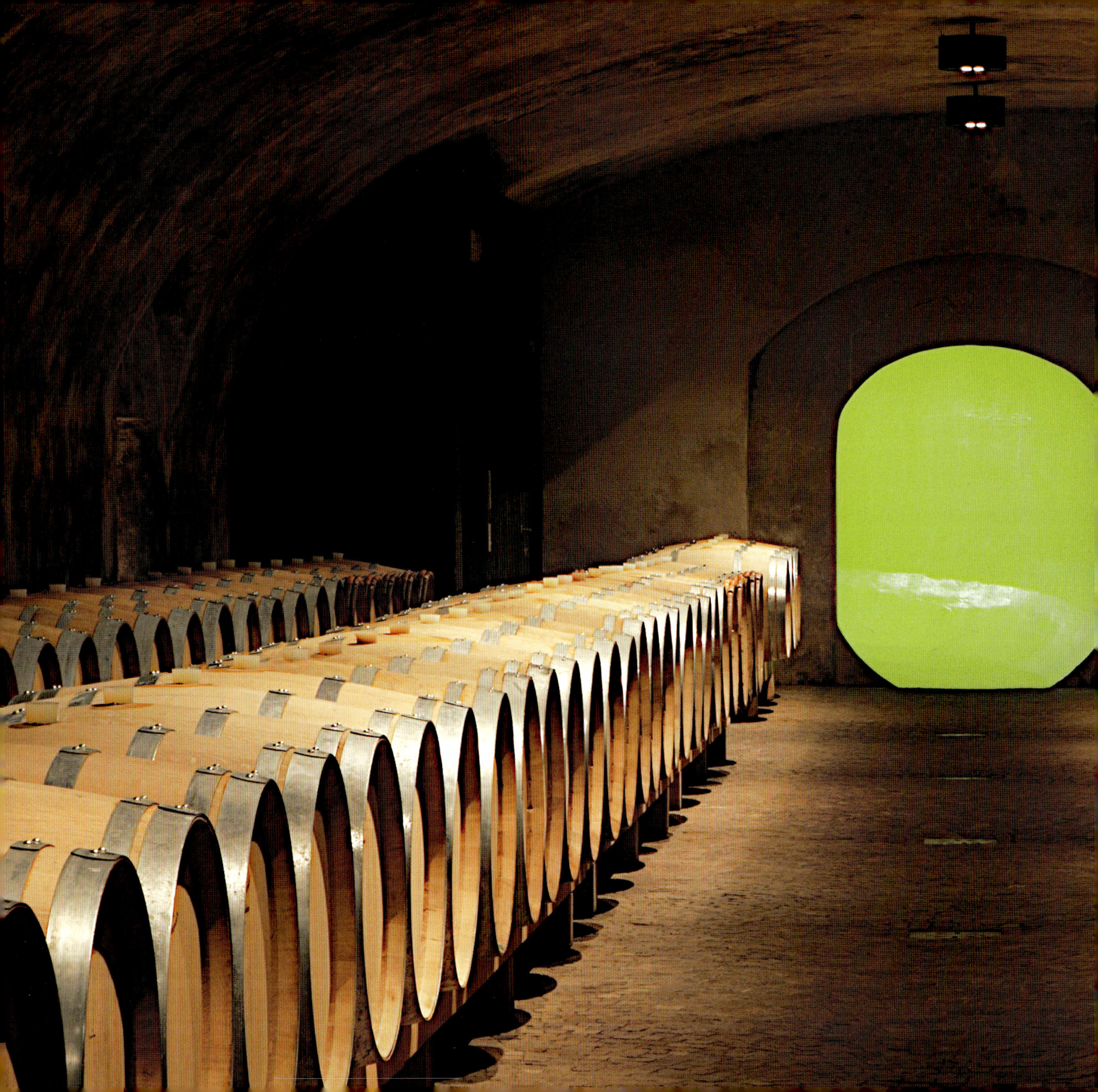

Projects

Adega Mayor in Campo Maior, Portugal

Architect: Álvaro Siza Vieira, Rua do Aeixo, 53, 2°
4150-043 Porto

Team: Avelino Silva (project head), Rita Amaral

Site area: 5,543 m^2

Gross floor area: 4,262 m^2

Start of design phase: 2003

Completion: 2006

Region: Alto Alentejo

Contact: Herdade das Argamassas, 7370-171 Campo Maior
www.adegamayor.pt

Oenologist: Rita Carvalho

Price range: €4.50–€30

●●○

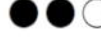

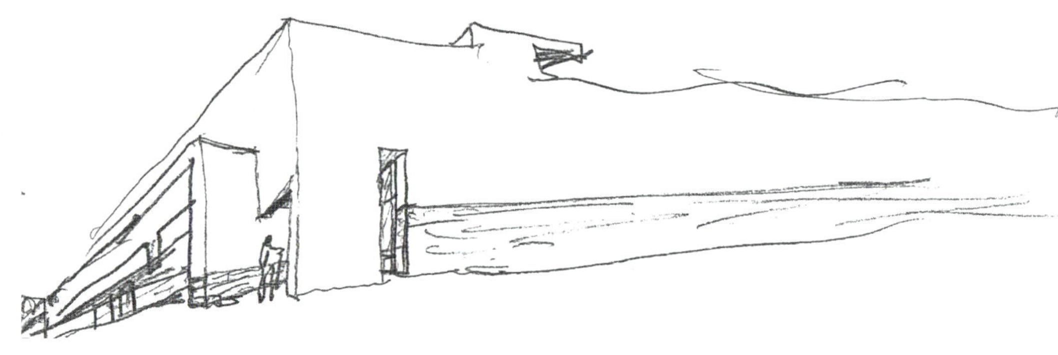

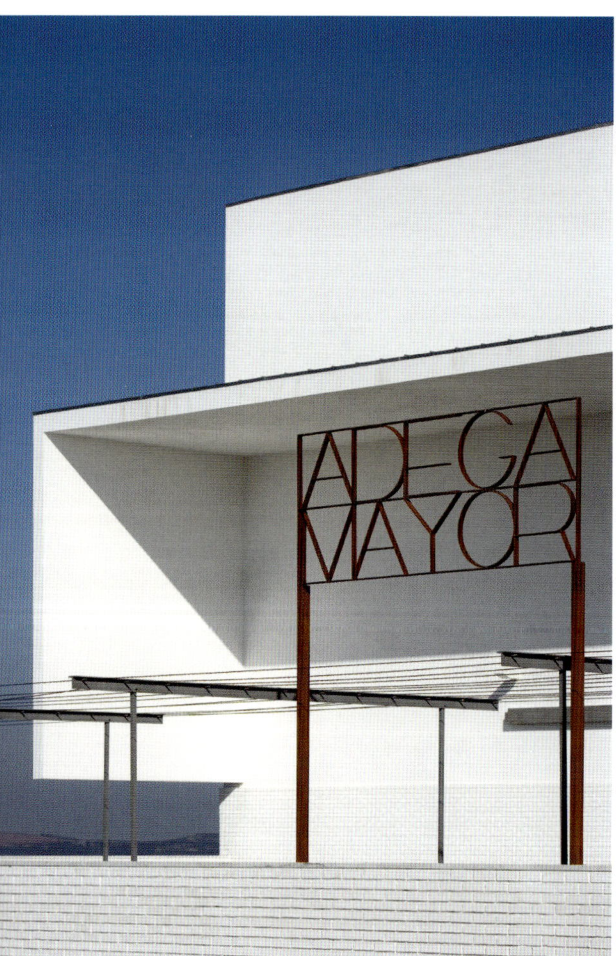

It all started with a coffee cup that the Portuguese architect Álvaro Siza designed for Portugal's largest coffee entrepreneur, Rui Nabeiro. When Nabeiro was considering building his own winery years later, it was again Siza he approached. Mutual understanding and respect bound the two grands seigneurs together.

The fruits of this friendship are impressive. At once purist and gleaming, Adega Mayor rises up from its throne on a hill in the wine-growing area of Alentejo, not far from the Spanish border. Without a doubt, the vineyard is architecturally among the most beautiful in Portugal. It embodies in every detail the Nabeiro family philosophy: "Passion is what drives us. It has always been that way. When we do something, many diverse emotions, desires and places play a vital role."

After more than two years of construction, the first harvest went to the press in the new, minimalist structure in 2006. The official inauguration followed in June 2007.

The foundation of the project was laid by Rui Nabeiro many years ago with coffee, when he launched Delta Café in the early 1960s. With more than 3,000 employees, it is today the market leader in Portugal. But for all his success, Nabeiro never forgot his origins. Campo Maior, originally a very poor agricultural town more than 200 kilometres away from Lisbon, is still the seat of his corporate headquarters. Showing great social commitment, Nabeiro champions the interests of the region and and its people, most of whom are directly or indirectly connected with his business.

In memory of the past and of his grandparents, whom he saw working in the local vineyards as a boy, Nabeiro fulfilled a personal dream in 1997 when he acquired his first vineyard in Godinha, about 10 kilometres from the current location of his winery. Bit by bit, he bought additional vineyards. From the very start, Paulo Loureano, one of the most respected oenologists in Portugal, contributed his expertise. Under his management, they developed their first red wine, Monte Mayor, in 2002, and followed it one year later with their first reserva, Comendador, both aged at neighbouring facilities. The quality of these wines was astonishing, leading to the conviction that top-notch wines could be produced in this northernmost part of the Alentejo region. Thanks to the climatic effects of the nearby foothills of the Serra de São Mamede, the air cools noticeably at night. This is beneficial for maintaining the acid content in white wines, which gives them a longer life and makes them an ideal accompaniment for food.

The search for an appropriate site for a wine estate was relatively simple. A small rise in the middle of the vineyards, just a stone's throw away from his company, appeared suitable. The search for an architect also met with quick success, as Siza immediately came on board. At the first meeting in

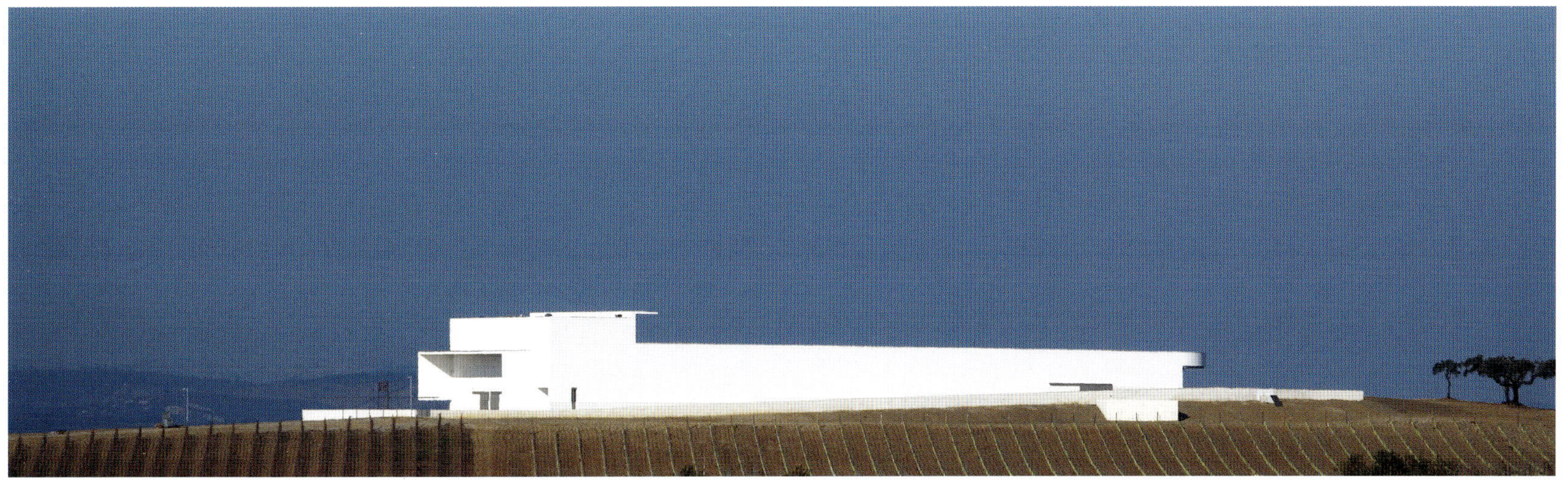

Floor plans
Scale 1:1000

1 Entrance
2 Reception
3 Shop
4 Bottle warehouse
5 Bottling plant
6 Fermenting (white)
7 Storeroom
8 Fermenting (red)
9 Barrique cellar
10 Vestibule
11 Laboratory
12 Administration
13 Void
14 Grape receiving
15 Technology

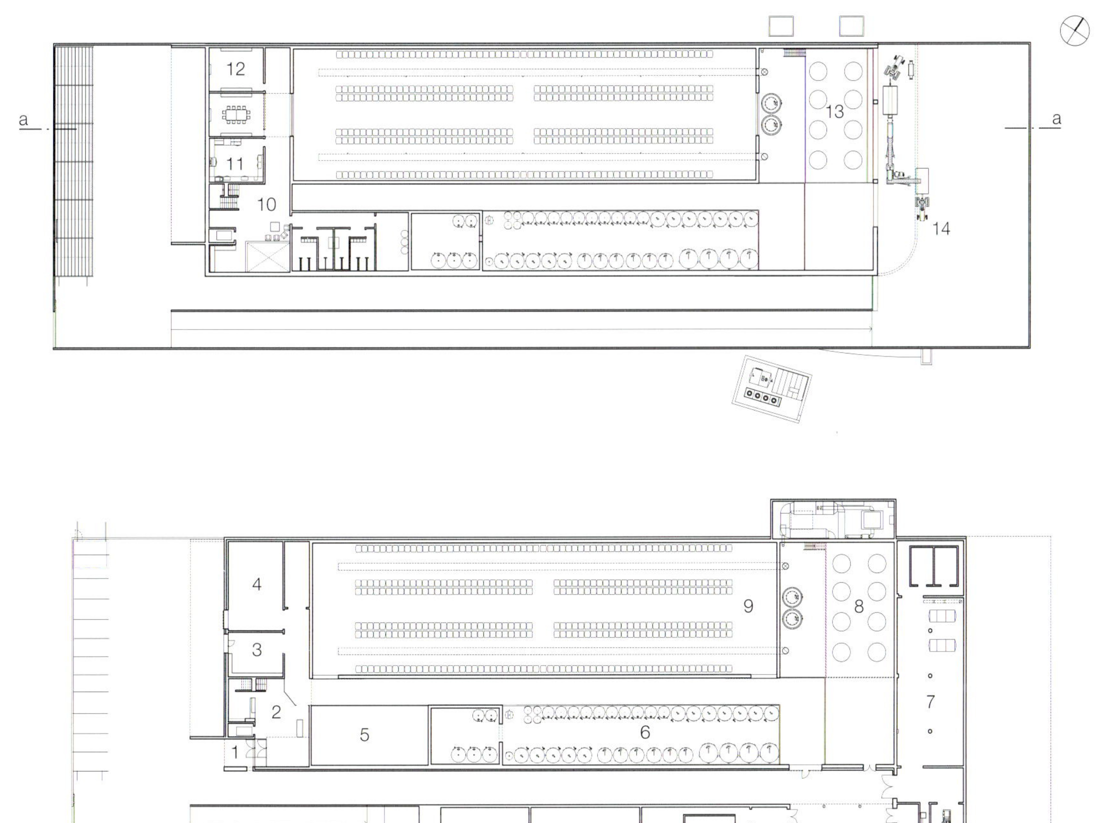

2003, he already started sketching the first draft of what was to become the Adega Mayor winery on a serviette. Siza suggested a functional, outwardly purist structure that could map the consecutive steps of wine production. During the entire planning phase of the facility, he was guided by the requirements put forth by Loureano; Nabeiro made no further stipulations.

When visitors first pass the Delta Café headquarters on their approach, they see Adega Mayor rising up amid the green of the vineyards. The building nestles against the slope of the hill. The entire outer facade is white, featuring the same whitewash traditionally used on the houses in Alentejo. The paint reflects the sunlight and protects the interior from too much heat.

The wine estate has its own access road, which ends at the car park at the front of the building. Upon entering, visitors immediately feel the pleasant coolness of the lofty, white reception area. The combination of the beige marble tiles on the floor and walls, light-coloured timber, and a cream-coloured leather seating arrangement – also designed by Siza – conveys an instant feeling of ease. In addition to the reception desk, this area contains a staircase leading up to the laboratory as well as the administrative and tasting areas. Two doors at the back of the reception area lead to an auditorium and a shop that sells not only the wine produced by the estate, but also olive oil, choco-

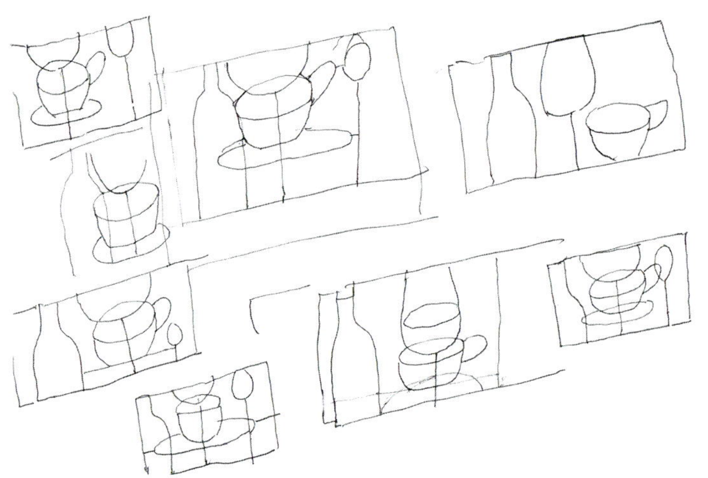

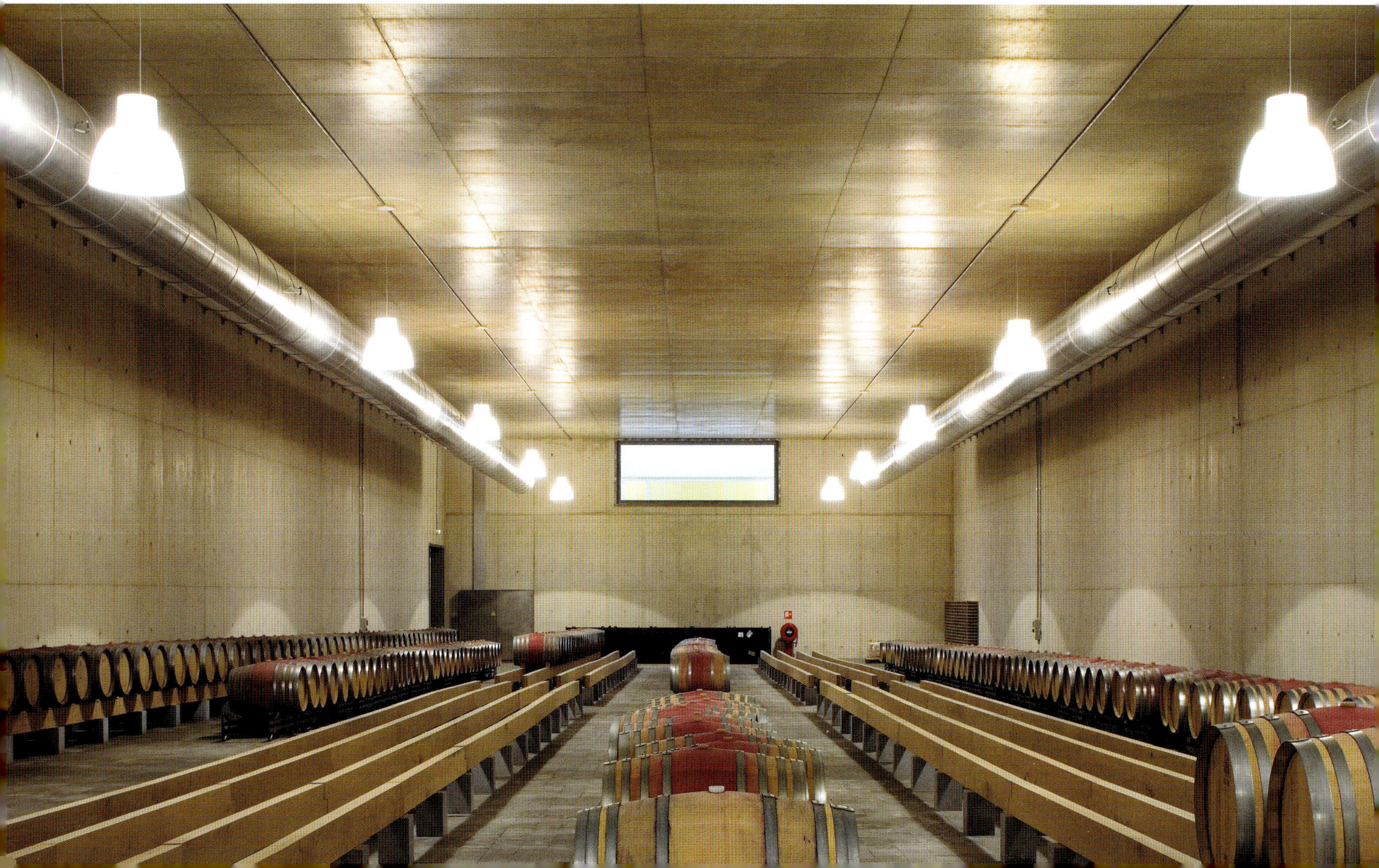

Section
Scale 1:1000

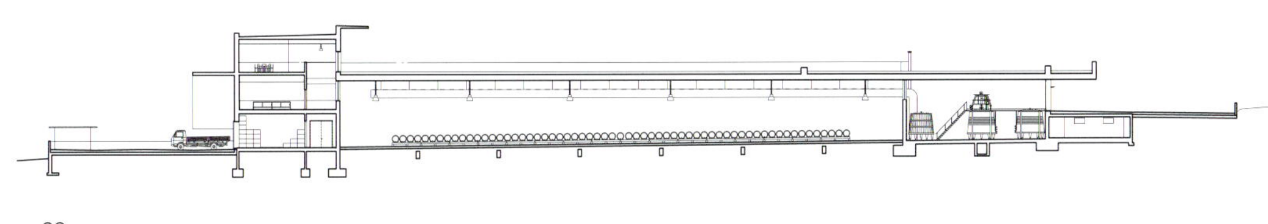
aa

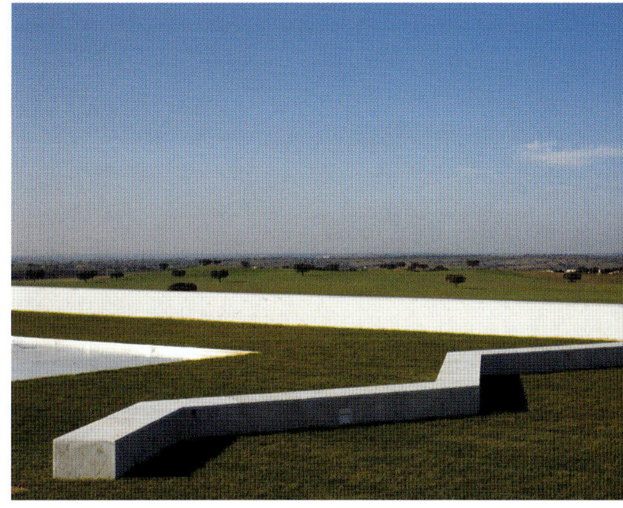

lates and gift items. A large glass door opens into a hallway that leads directly to the production area. Simple exposed concrete and a grey floor of poured epoxy resin dominate the tunnel-like corridor, production and storage areas. Here, Siza, in consultation with Loureano and Nabeiro, was successful in meeting the requirements of grape processing. A large, two-storey hall is situated at the end of the corridor. Grape receiving takes place by way of an access road behind the building, on which tractors bring in their valuable cargo. The red wine grapes arrive in 20-kilogram containers and, after sorting, are destemmed and crushed. Then, following the flow of gravity, they travel through a downpipe into individual large maceration tanks. The white wine grapes are similarly processed, except that they are pressed into juice immediately. The rectangular barrel cellar, which is located parallel to the corridor that leads to the production area, is stark and divided into clearly designated sections. The wine ages in numerous, seemingly endless rows of oak barrels. A window at the centre allows daylight in and gives the cool, concrete storage room a delightful sense of peace.
The same materials, themes and colour schemes found in the ground-floor reception area dominate the interior of the upper storey. A window affords another look from above at the impressive wine cellar. Upon arrival at the upper floor and its tasting area, visitors can experience the indescribably beautiful panoramic view over the Alentejo plain from the extensive roof terrace of Adega Mayor: a visual treat that requires more than a quick glance to be fully taken in. The rich green of the lawn (which also helps insulate the cellar) contrasts with an azure blue pool (also a cooling device) and the white marble walls. Here, too, Siza's characteristic style is unmistakable. From above, the roof styling recalls a face with eyes, nose and mouth – a personal touch of Siza's, who often includes these surprise elements in his work.
Today, the philosophy of this new wine estate is embodied and guarded by the founder's granddaughter, company director Rita Nabeiro. In close partnership with oenologist Rita Carvalho, she has produced wines solely from traditional Portuguese grape varieties since 2007. Rui Nabeiro's vision was to produce wine for everyone, from wine novices to wine experts. With its current range, which encompasses five different labels of wine, the company has succeeded. All its wines are blends made from regional grape varieties such as Trincadeira or Aragonez. Thanks to the area's special soil as well as Adega Mayor's stringent reduction in crop yield, the normally less significant Alicante Bouschet variety produces particularly good wines here, playing an important role in the red wine blends. The label on the introductory-level wine, the Caiado, which is sold in red and white versions, is reminiscent of the limestone wash on the houses in Campo Maior. The Monte Mayor collection offers the only rosé produced by Adega Mayor. Nabeiro's granddaughter's favourite is the Solista. As the name suggests, these wines derives from a single grape variety. The red wine is made from Touriga Nacional, the white from Antão-Vaz grapes. The red and white Reserva do Comendador wines age in oak barrels for 18 and six months, respectively. The Pai Chão, with a label decorated with a likeness of founder Rui Nabeiro, crowns their wine selection. All of the labels are also printed in Braille.
Today, Adega Mayor encompasses a vineyard area of 67 hectares; eventually it is to reach 100 hectares in size. The demand for Adega Mayor's wines is growing steadily; the total yearly capacity of 450,000 bottles is already sold out. A new warehouse – naturally, in collaboration with Siza – is already in planning. Rui Nabeiro has realized his dream.

Bodegas Portia in Gumiel de Izán, Spain

Architects: Foster + Partners, Riverside, 22 Hester Road, London SW11 4AN, www. fosterandpartners.com

Team: Norman Foster, David Nelson, Gerard Evenden, Pedro Haberbosch, Nadine Pieper Bosch, Ana Agag Longo, Juan Gabriel La Malfa, Luca Latini, Chris Lepine, Emanuele Mattutini, Josep Mercader, Jaime Valle

Gross floor area: 12,500 m²

Start of design phase: 2004

Completion: 2010

Region: Ribera del Duero

Contact: Carretera N1, km 170, 09370 Gumiel de Izán www.bodegasportia.com

Oenologist: Raúl Quemada

Price range: €5.50–€20.50

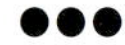

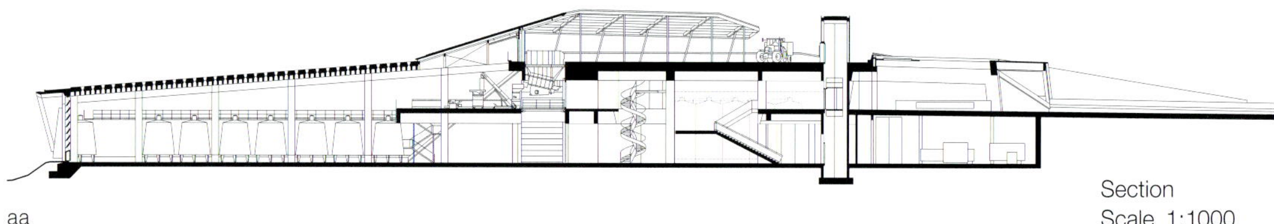

aa

Section
Scale 1:1000

A year's production of Trienna, a varietal pressed from Tinta Fina del País grapes, is limited to a maximum of 3,000 bottles. Its malolactic fermentation takes place in French oak barrels, where the wine ages for 18 months. Intense shades of red, a bouquet of dense, complex aromas in the nose, dark red berries on the palate with a long finish – this is the beauty of Bodegas Portia's flagship wine.

Trienna: a unity of three, as the label designed by Lord Norman Foster conveys. Foster took his inspiration from the shape of Bodegas Portia itself, one of his own architectural creations. Near Gumiel de Izán, about 150 kilometres north of Madrid and in the Ribera del Duero wine region, Bodegas Portia is surrounded by its vineyards. "The genesis of our wines lies in the vineyard. For us, the vineyard is a priority. We can only produce our wine thanks to it." That is the credo of the Faustino group, which was founded in 1861 by Eleuterio Martínez Arzok with the purchase of his first vineyard in Oyón Álava in La Rioja, which he named after his son. Since then, the company has been directed by four generations of the family and now encompasses seven bodegas in Spain's finest wine-growing regions.

Bodegas Portia was Foster's first wine project, "so we had no preconceptions about how it should work. It was an opportunity to start from first principles – to examine the different stages of wine production and try to create the ideal conditions for them to unfold. The wine was the starting point, as well as the beautiful setting in Ribera del Duero." His idea was to bring the area's topography and the necessary requirements of wine production together to create optimum working conditions. By embedding the building in the surrounding terrain, the amount of energy required for cooling could be reduced. At the same time, the building integrates itself visually into its environment in the best possible way.

To distinguish the three steps in production – fermentation, barrel ageing and bottle ageing – Foster chose the form of a three-pointed star with the reception and administration areas in the middle. The barriques and bottles are stored in two of the wings, which are partially underground to maintain an ideal temperature – a crucial factor in the quality of the wine. Currently the barrel cellar contains only 1,200 barriques, or 225-litre barrels of American and French oak. It can accommodate up to five times that number, or approximately 6,000. The bottle cellar, designed by Norman Foster, is particularly distinctive. Thousands of bottles age there in absolute darkness, inserted into vertical oak panels shaped like a honeycomb.

Throughout the cellar the light effects are fascinating. Futuristic red light lends the dark, cool spaces a warm yet intriguing atmosphere. The walls of the bodega are made of reinforced concrete, which keeps out the strong summer heat. The roof extends out over the walls to offer extra shade. On the outside, the concrete walls are covered with plates made of Corten steel, which blends in perfectly with the colour of the surrounding vineyards. Grape receiving during the harvest takes place from above using two gently inclined access roads that

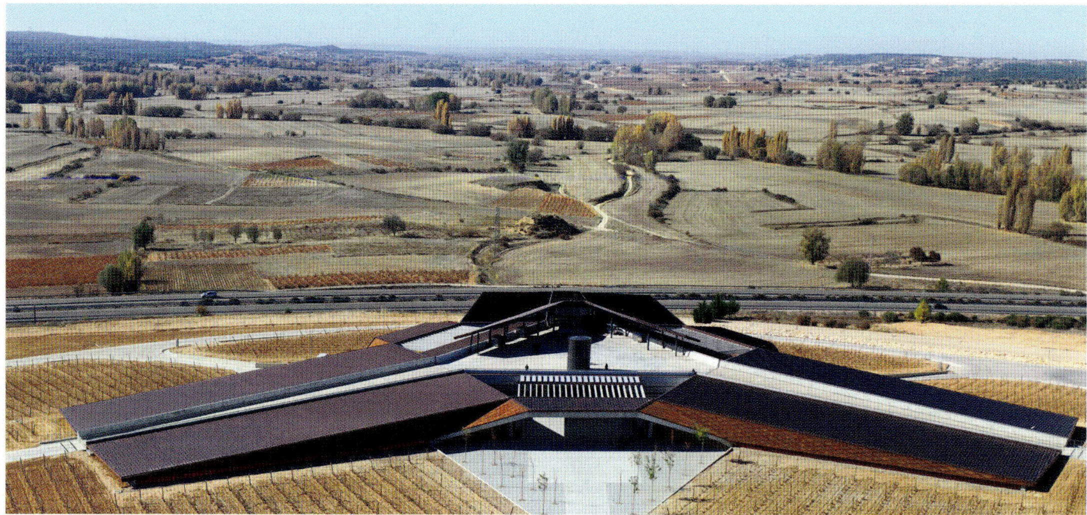

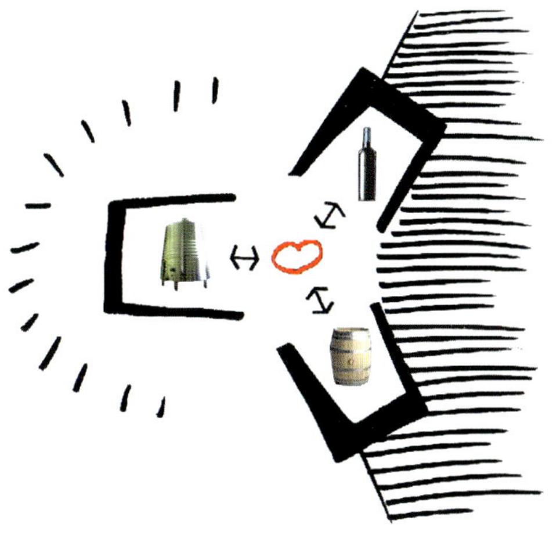

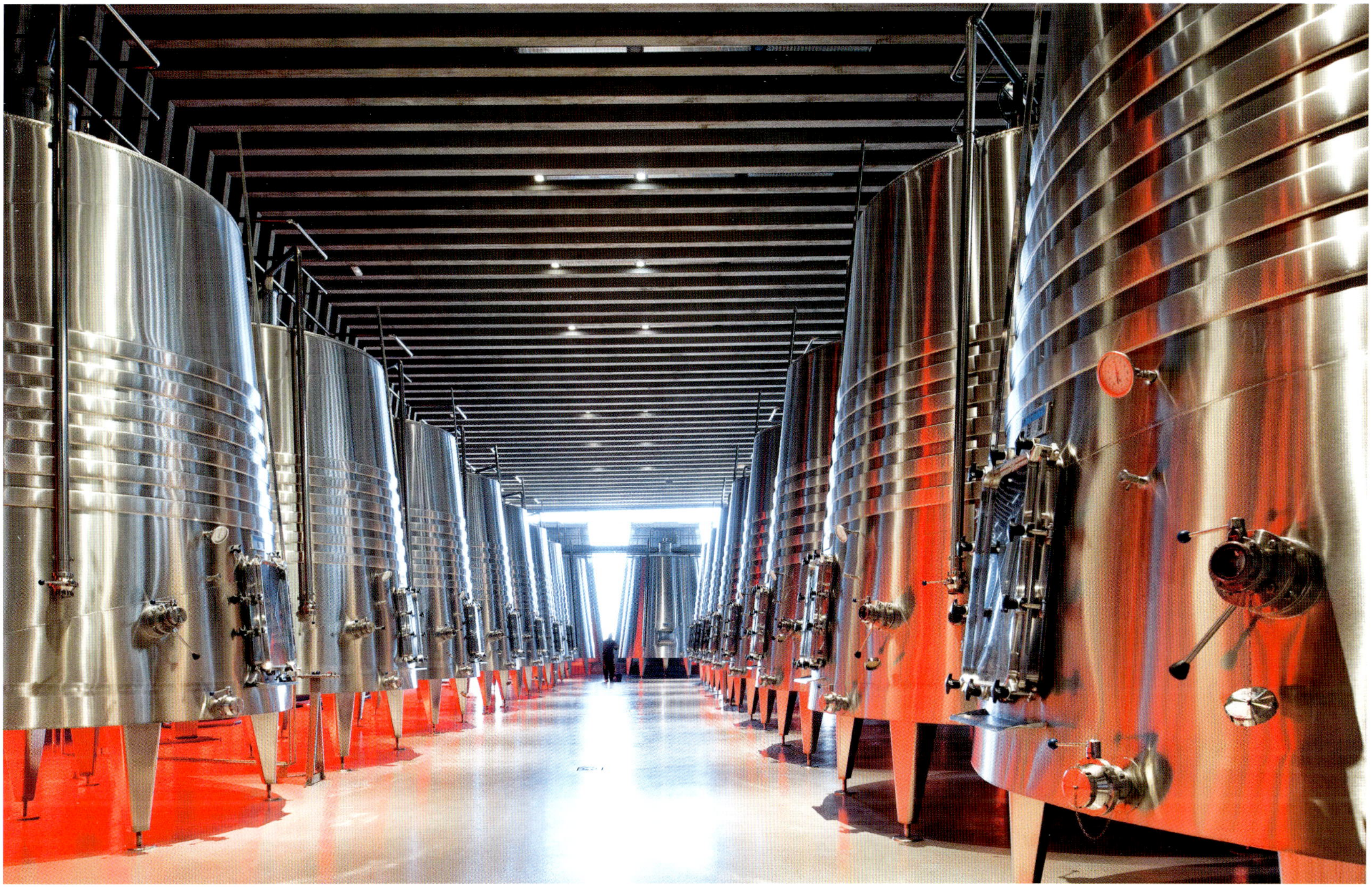

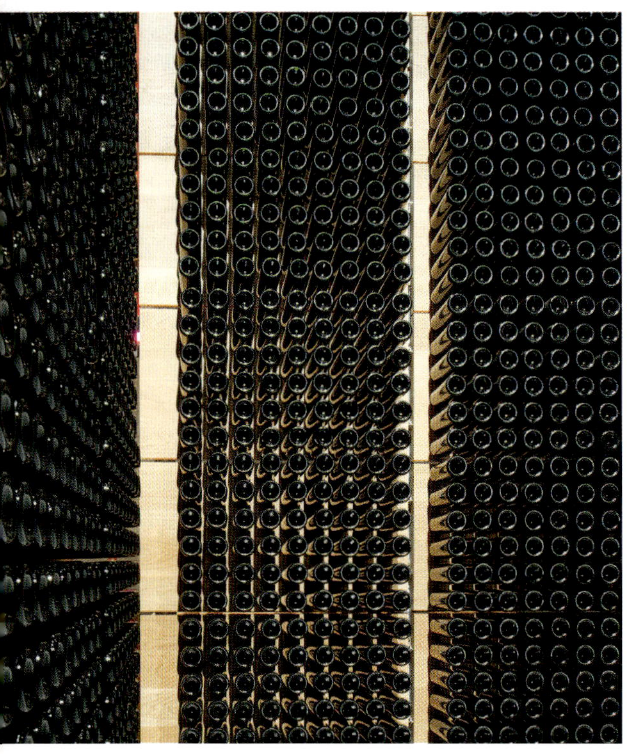

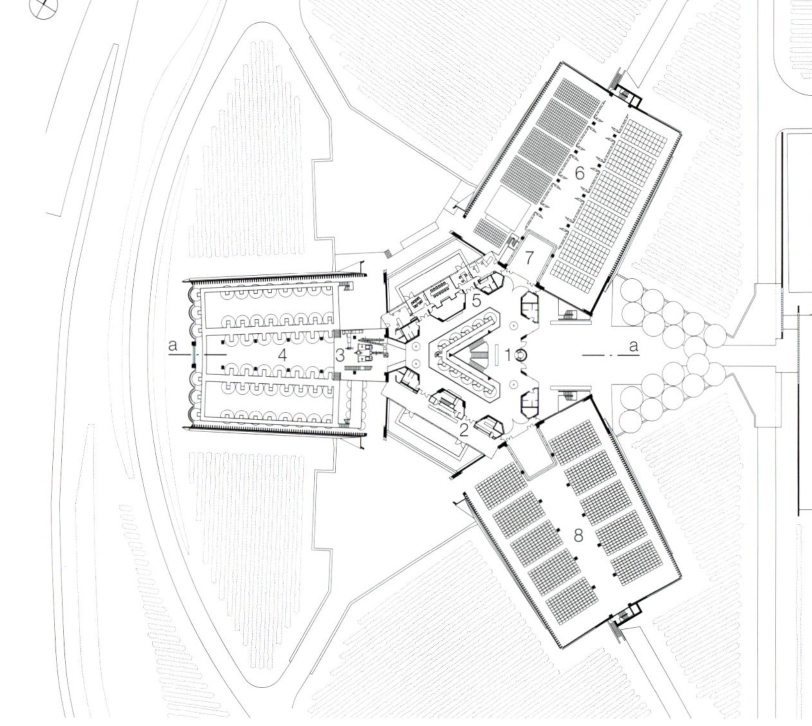

Floor plan
Scale 1:2000

1 Reception
2 Restaurant
3 Grape receiving
4 Fermenting cellar
5 Administration
6 Bottle storage
7 Seminar room
8 Barrique cellar

lead up on to the roof of the winery. That way, gravity is used to feed the grapes to the crusher, thereby guaranteeing gentle treatment of the fruit.
As well as the production of high-quality wines, it was a priority for the Faustino Group to have their new building become a tourist attraction in the region. This, it was hoped, would help to accommodate the increasing wine tourism trend and at the same time bring in new customers.
Visitors driving up to the building first circle it before reaching the car park in the back. That way, the building's exterior has a chance to intrigue visitors and make them curious about the interior. The car park is shielded from the entrance by a wall, so that the cars do not disturb the view of those looking out from the inside. The area in front of the entrance is extensive, designed with an attractive material combination of concrete, glass and wood. The stark exposed concrete contrasts sharply with the sheathing of vertical oak planks. The lattice fence on either side, made from the staves of old wooden barrels, draws a connection with the wine and recalls the long winemaking tradition of the Duero Valley.
Inside, visitors enter a generous reception area, where they can join a tour through the wine cellars every day of the week. Large windows in the entrance area offer an initial glimpse into the three wings of the lower cellar level, each supporting different winemaking processes. The house restaurant behind the reception area serves regional specialities, and its terrace affords a view of the surrounding vineyards. A pool on the terrace promises at least visual refreshment on hot days.
Bodegas Portia's 160 hectares of vineyards in the middle of the Ribera del Duero wine region, which extends across an area measuring 115 by 25 kilometres, grow only the Tempranillo grape, known regionally as Tinta Fina del País. The soils are diverse, the winter climate harsh for Spain; the summers, however, are still hot.
The total production capacity of the 12,500-square-metre winery amounts to one million bottles, divided among four different wines. In addition to the Trienna, the most recently created wine and the flagship of its product range, Bodegas Portia produces three other red wines. The Portia Prima ages for 15 months in French oak, and thereafter eight more months in the bottle. The Portia Crianza gets its intense berry aromas from its 12-month maturation in American oak, followed by six months in the bottle. Ebeia represents the base of the product range. After a minimum of four months in American oak, this appealing wine combines good acidity with pleasant tannin notes and a long finish on the palate.
The most remarkable thing about Bodegas Portia is its combination of perfect functionalism and impressive architectural style. The winery offers a captivating contrast between architecture and environment, between the surrounding gentle landscape and the cool sobriety of the building and its cellars.

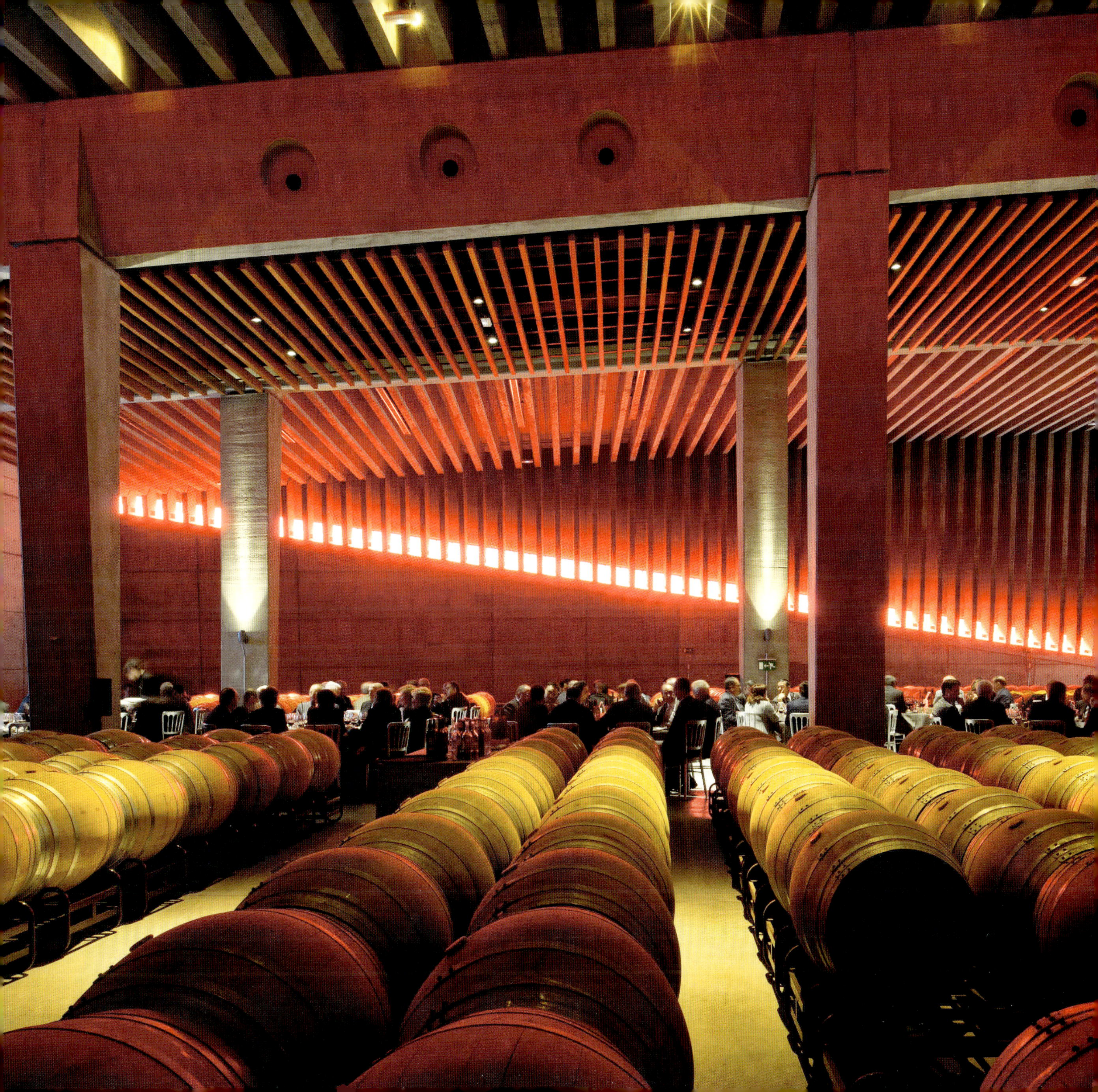

Weingut Claus Preisinger in Gols, Austria

Architects: propeller z, Mariahilferstr. 101/3/55, 1060 Vienna
www.propellerz.at

Site area: 17,961 m^2

Gross floor area: 1,779 m^2

Start of design phase: 2008

Completion: 2009

Region: Burgenland

Contact: Goldbergstr. 60, 7122 Gols
www.clauspreisinger.at

Oenologist: Claus Preisinger

Price range: €6.50–€50

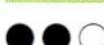

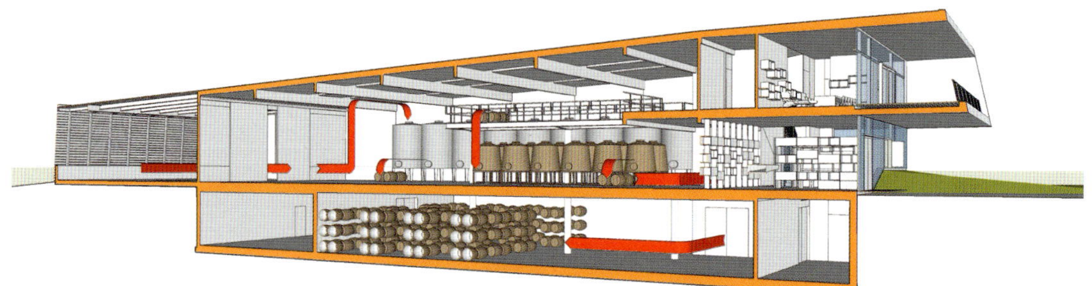

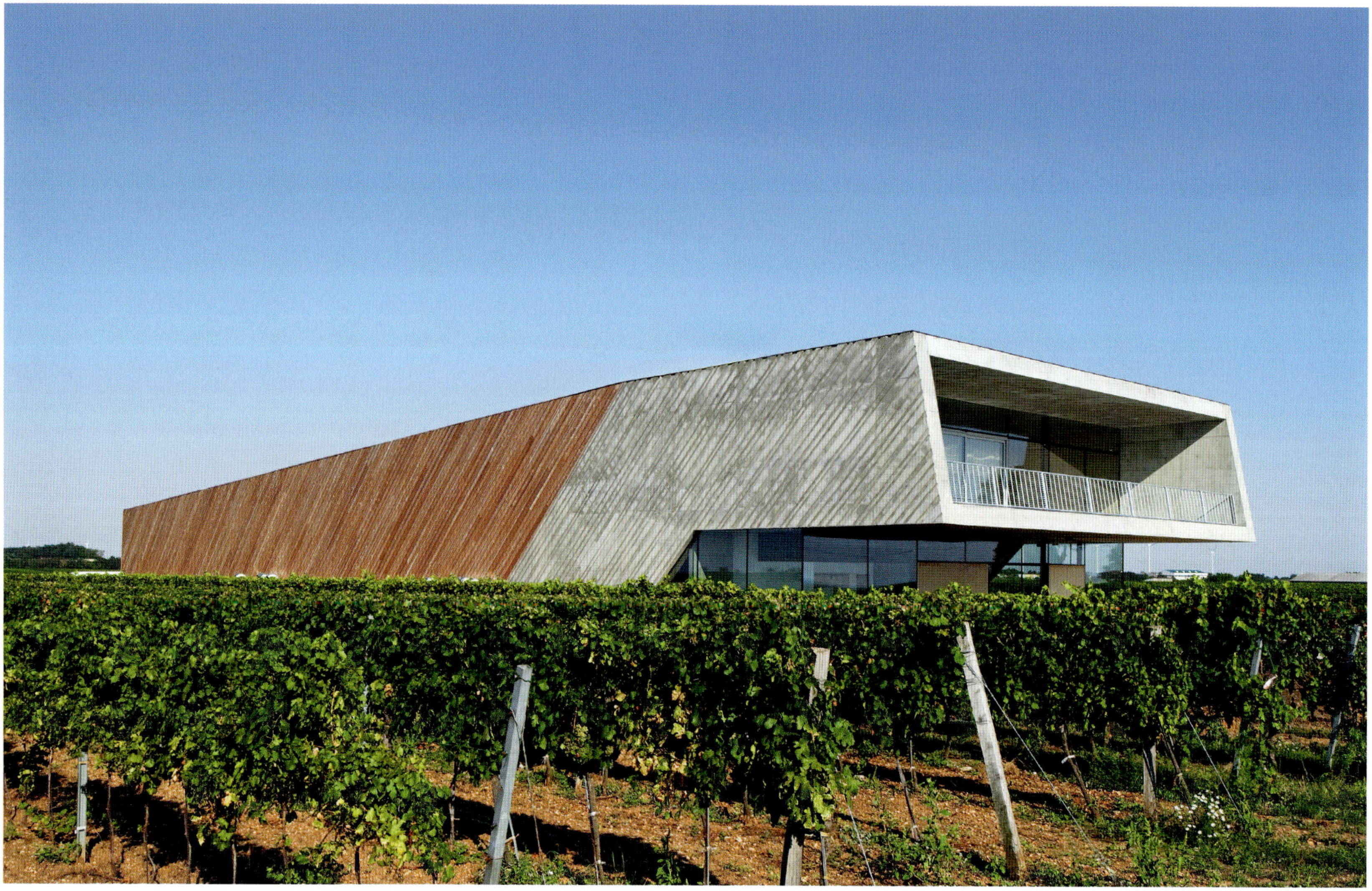

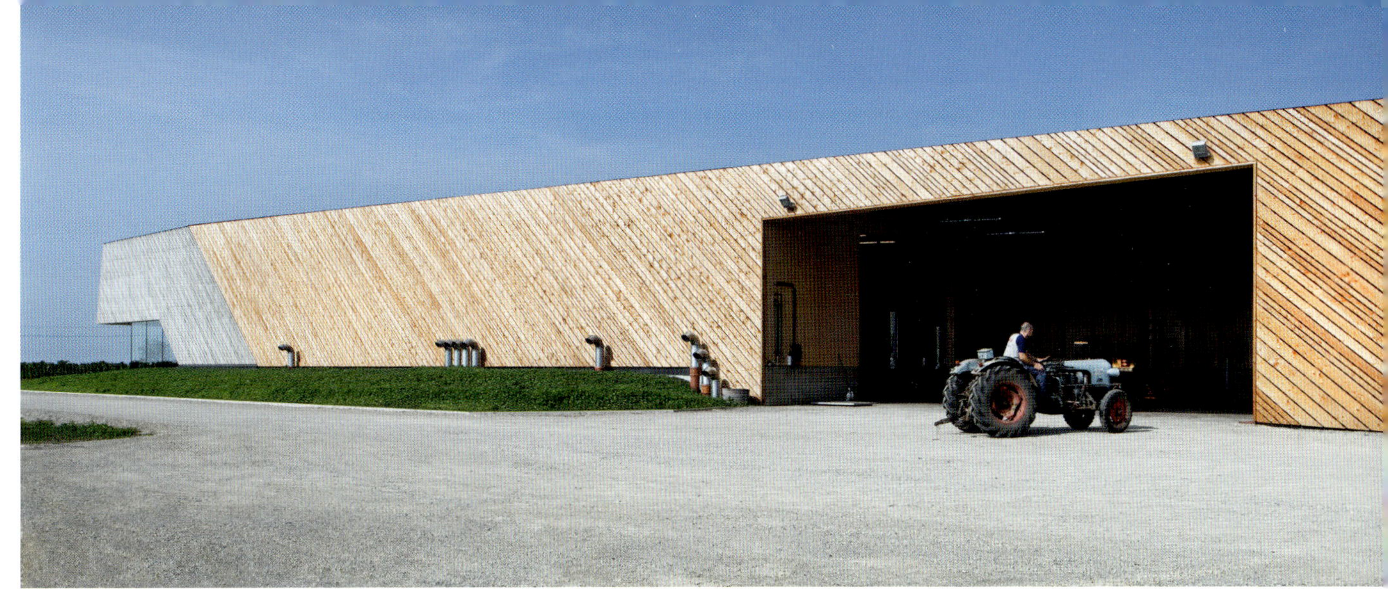

When Claus Preisinger looks westward from the terrace of his wine estate in Gols, in Austria's Burgenland region, he can take pleasure in the striking view across his vineyards to Lake Neusiedl, the second-largest endorheic lake in Europe, on the border with Hungary. "I wanted to create something grand, to make a statement," he declares. The young, committed winemaker has certainly succeeded. When he took over the family business in his early 20s, it was situated in the centre of Gols and only three hectares in size. Preisinger, who travelled the world after his completing his studies in oenology and viticulture to become a master vintner, extended the business to more than 20 hectares within a few years.

This expansion soon meant very little room for daily operations, and the cellaring of the wine was outsourced to a third-party logistics provider. Because of these adverse working conditions, it was no longer a question of "if" but where the facility would be relocated. Preisinger didn't want to leave the town of Gols, as his vineyards were situated in its immediate area and the short distances were an important factor in maintaining wine quality. His proposed solution was to locate the new production facility directly in the bordering vineyards – a task that proved difficult to accomplish. "It was primarily the acquisition of individual, adjoining lots which, because of the minutely allotted structure of the vineyard areas, became very drawn-out and involved," Preisinger explains. "Not everyone looked kindly upon my project and was willing to sell." In the end, however, he succeeded.

Inspired by his vintner friends Franz Weninger and Gernot Heinrich, Preisinger turned to the propeller z architectural practice, which had completed new cellars or cellar extensions for both winemakers (see pp. 110ff.). After his initial consultations with propeller z, Preisinger set aside his original plan to put the project out to tender. Both sides reached an immediate understanding. Preisinger gave the practice no architectural specifications, stipulating only that "it should be something special and blend in well with the natural landscape". As for the production areas, Preisinger's requirement for excellent quality lay at the heart of every consideration. To this end, he defined a series of elements that he considered necessary for the production of top-class wines, elements that needed to be taken into account in the plans. The building had to be large enough to accommodate everything under one roof, from winemaking to bottling, bottle storage and vehicle parking. Also, gravity was to play a vital role in the entire production process. Preisinger wished to forgo as far as possible the use of pumps in order to guarantee a gentle treatment of the wine. For financial reasons, it made sense to achieve temperature regulation chiefly by using the structure and materials of the building itself. All the various annual production steps in the cellar were to be made possible on the existing floor space, thereby allowing for a flexible use of the area.

The actual planning period took about a year, but as difficulties with official permits were a recurring impediment, the building project was delayed for six months.

Sectional view, wine production
Site plan Scale 1:5000

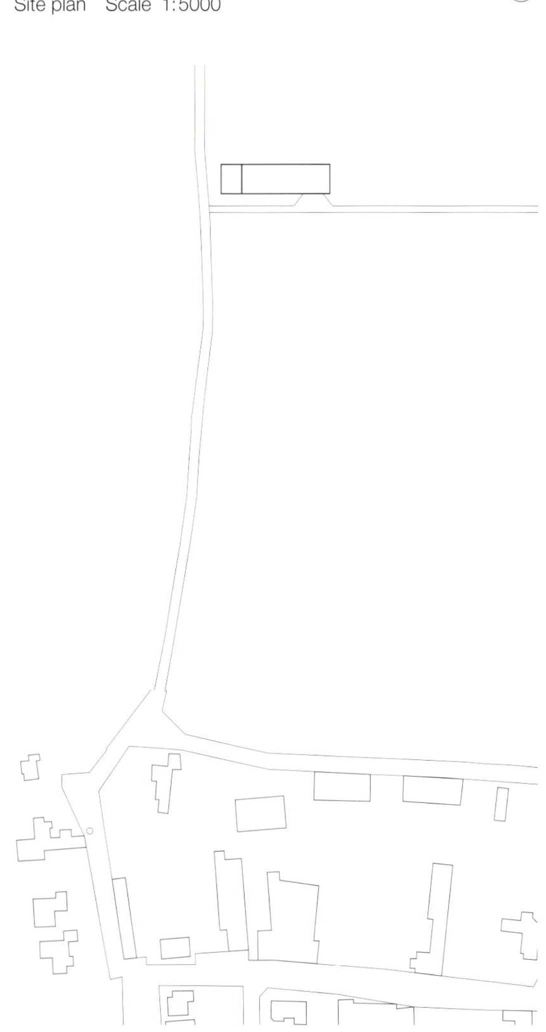

The initial design envisaged a much larger building. After the first cost projections, though, the original plans had to be retracted because of financial considerations. The erection of the building took place from November 2008 to August 2009, so that the harvest of the new vintage could already be processed in the new building without any delays in production.
The architects were able to implement all of Preisinger's wishes and stipulations in their plans and in the finished building. To make use of the temperature-regulating effect of the earth, one-third of the building was dug into the slope of the vineyard. To enhance this cooling effect, half of the ground floor, too, was set beneath ground level. This also helped integrate the entire building into its surroundings and prevent its full size from becoming apparent. The concrete foundation lacks insulation and is in direct contact with the earth, enabling temperature and humidity to regulate themselves naturally. Built of wood, the lofty main hall is two storeys high. The roof is made of fully prefabricated wooden modules interspersed with window elements that let in a generous amount of light. The hall was planned with an eye to functional considerations, featuring a bridge that creates a second work level. The levels are connected by a freight lift located to the side. The filling of the barrels takes place from the upper level solely with the aid of gravity.
The production area leads into a multifunctional space in the back, which is accessible even to large vehicles via a large side door. This space can be used in different ways, depending on what is needed at different times of the year. It can, for example, accommodate grape receiving and processing during the harvest, be a warehouse for empty bottles prior to the bottling process, and house the press after the harvest. Dozens of barriques are stored in the cellar, which maintains a year-round constant temperature of approximately 15 °C. Although an additional cooling system is installed, it needs to be used only during the hot summer months, thanks to the cellar's superior insulating qualities.
The building's distinctive slanting roof measures 7.40 metres at its highest point, the entrance area. Here the upper level cantilevers out over the reception area below. The south-west-facing facade is made mostly of glass, creating a sense of transparency. This allows Preisinger to look through the glass walls of his office at one side of the entrance and watch the arriving visitors as well as see past them into the large production hall. A striking table made of bare concrete welcomes visitors and invites them to pause and enjoy the view.
Above the entrance hovers the upper level with its tasting area, enclosed on two sides only by glass, which offers a look into the great hall on one side and a spectacular view of the lake on the other. The glass wall facing the lake can be opened out completely, allowing access to the terrace. For Preisinger, who is otherwise constantly busy, this is a place for introspection; for the interested vineyard visitor, it is simply impressive. The interior is minimalist: white walls and white tables, a large painting on the wall. The ceiling is of exposed concrete, bare of any adornment. This clearly expresses Preisinger's philosophy: "Less is more. Everything has to fit together and create a harmonious whole – from the wine to the vintner, from the architect to the bottle decor." The label design underlines this statement, featuring simple white paper, the name of the wine on the bottom right, and Preisinger's signature in the middle in an elegant grey.
The wines that Preisinger offers for tasting are also impressive. In his vineyards, which currently encompass 19 hectares, he grows mostly Zweigelt and Blaufränkisch grapes, which make up about 80 per cent of his vines and from which he produces rich red varietals and blends with a strong ageing potential. The rest is Pinot Noir, St. Laurent and Merlot – and some white wine from Chardonnay grapes. He

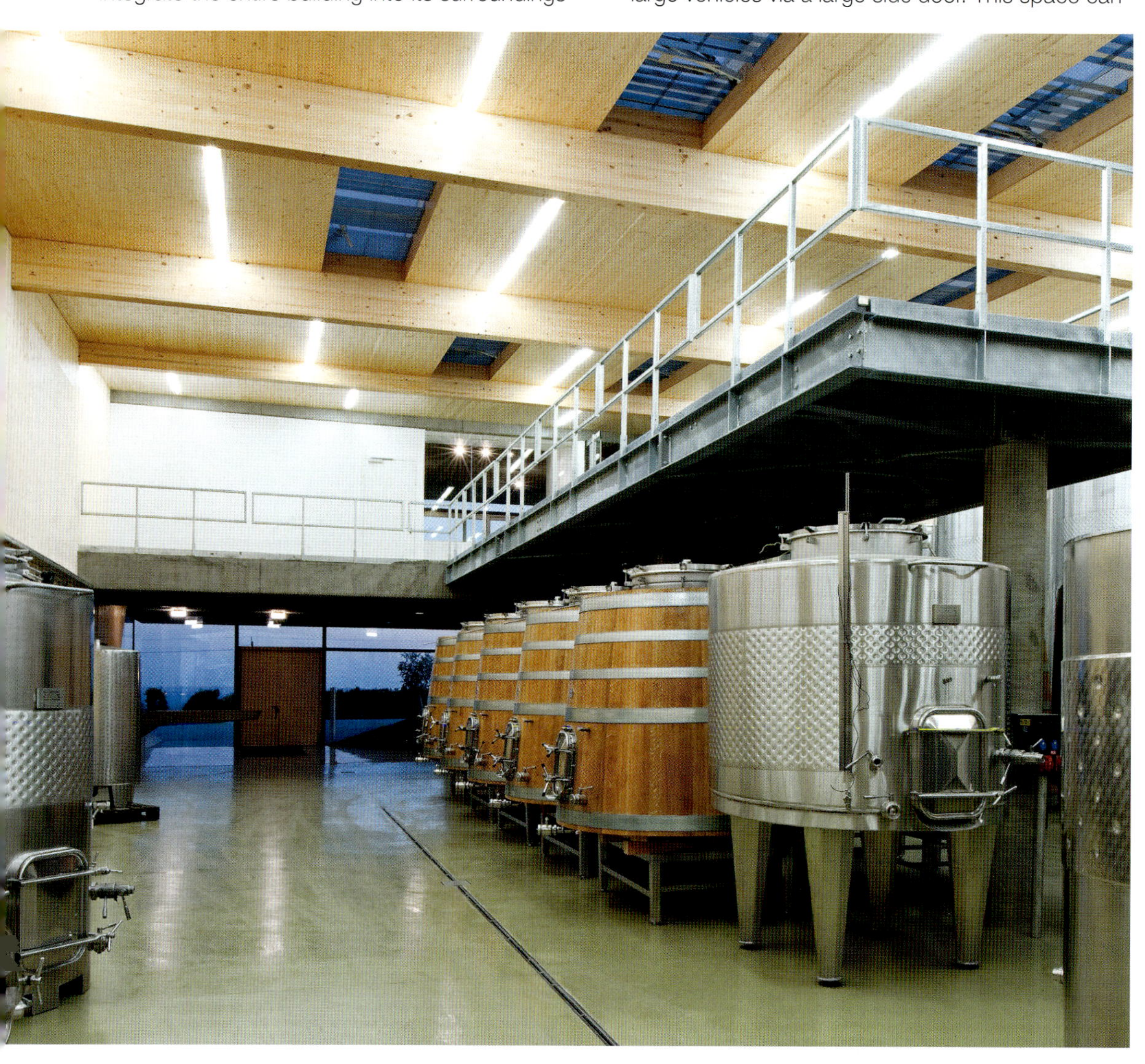

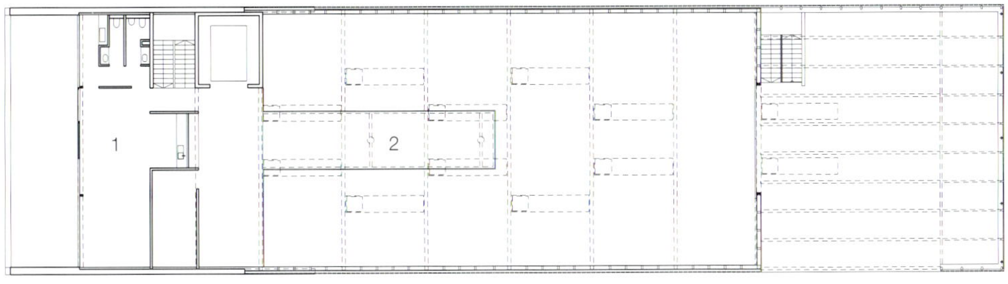

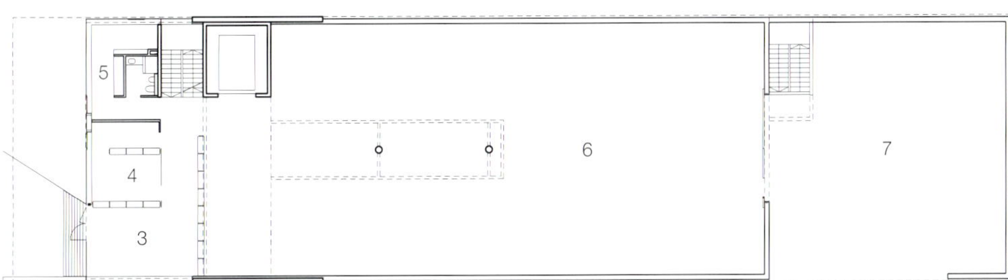

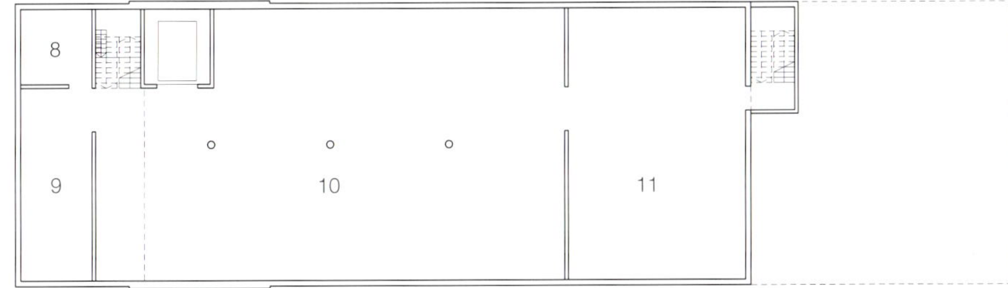

Floor plans
Scale 1:500

1 Tasting area
2 Catwalk
3 Reception
4 Office
5 Changing room
6 Production area
7 Multifunctional area
8 Technology
9 Storage area
10 Barrique cellar
11 Bottle cellar

also buys an additional 15 hectares' worth of grapes from contracted neighbouring vintners.
Preisinger runs the entire facility with only a small team. Apart from the workers in the vineyards, there are just three people who handle the sales and the wine production in the cellar. His father still lends a hand and gives him support with the work in the vineyards.
Preisinger has made his dream a reality. Looking back, would he do things differently today? "No," he answers, "at least not fundamentally. If possible, I would try to connect a kitchen to my tasting area, and set up a guest room to give customers the opportunity to stay overnight." But at age 31, Preisinger still has enough time for that.

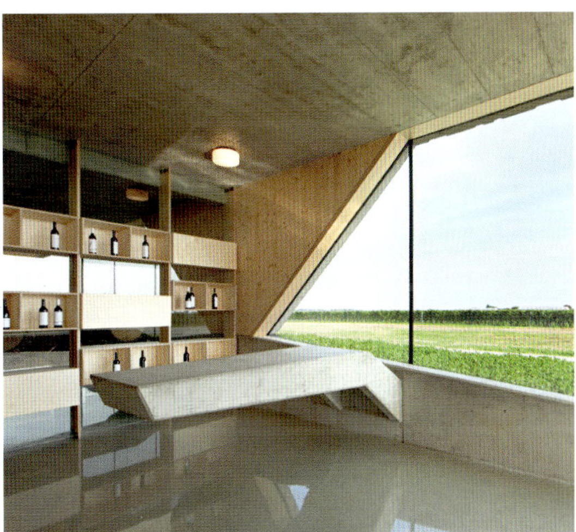

Tenuta Peter Zemmer in Cortina sulla Strada del Vino, Italy

Architects: bergmeisterwolf architekten, Via Bruno 3, 39042 Bressanone, www.bergmeisterwolf.it
Gross floor area: 249,60 m^2
Start of design phase: 2008
Completion: 2008
Region: Alto Adige
Contact: Strada del Vino. 24, 39040 Cortina sulla Strada del Vino, www.peterzemmer.com
Oenologist: Peter Zemmer
Price range: €6–€15
●○○

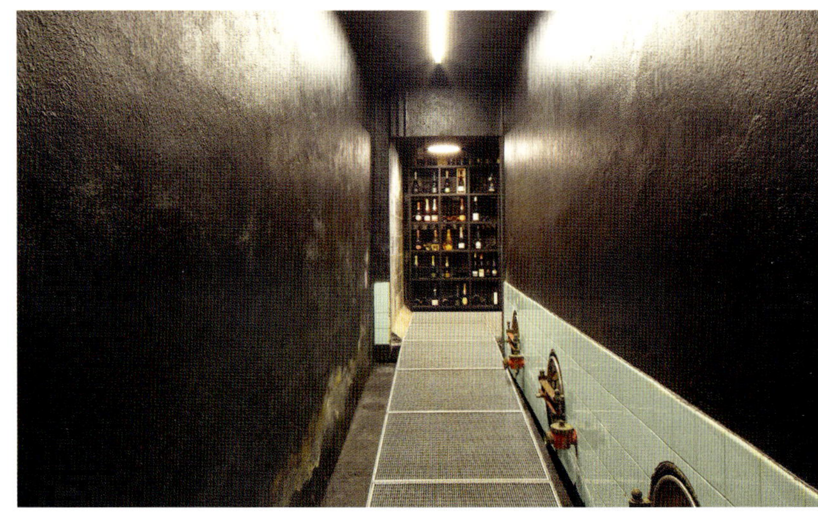

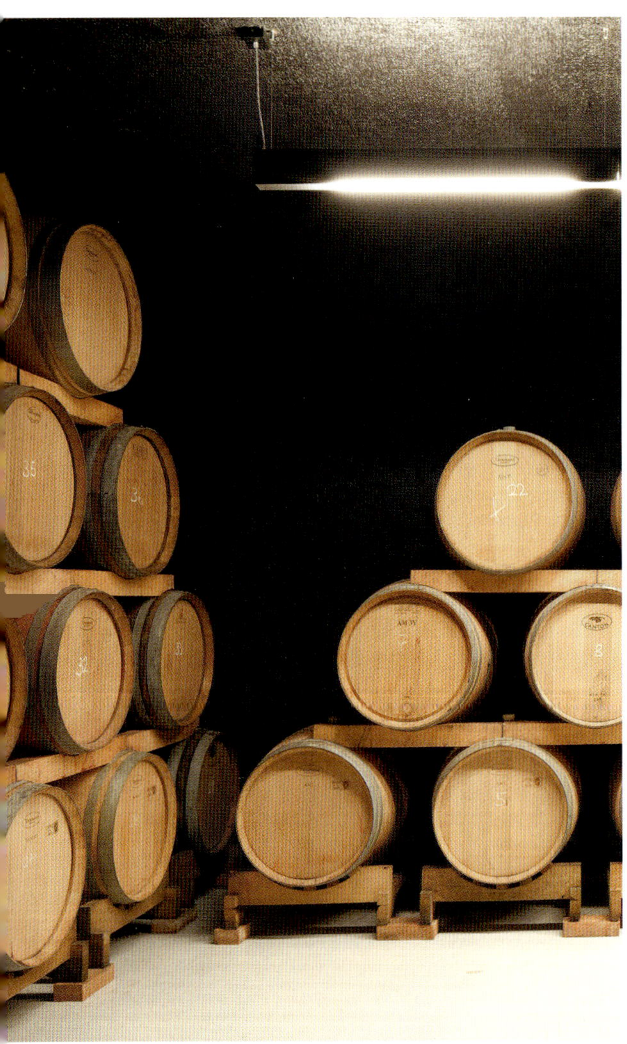

The village of Cortina, or Kurtinig, lies about 36 kilometres south of the Colterenzio winery in Cornaiano/Girlan (see pp. 52ff.). With its 600 residents, it is one of the smallest communities in Alto Adige (South Tyrol). It is also the location of Peter Zemmer's wine estate, which was established in 1928 and has been in the family for three generations. Under the management and direction of Zemmer, the wine estate makes wines using grapes from its own vineyards, and has become one of the most internationally successful in the Alto Adige region. Zemmer's philosophy is grounded in the idea that true rootedness in the soil – the notion of origin, of belonging – is the hallmark of authenticity, and that wines should reflect and typify the character of the terroir, which in this region is marked by various microclimates and diverse soils. His approach has been crowned with success; in 2002, it won him the distinction of being South Tyrol's "Vintner of the Year".
In the course of remodelling the winery, Zemmer got the idea of renovating the wine cellar as well. He wanted a dignified space in which to receive visitors and present his wines. On recommendation, he turned to bergmeisterwolf architects, who had already handled the renovation of the Colterenzio winery. They suggested cutting open a large concrete tank, which was lined with glass tiles, and converting it into the presentation area for Peter Zemmer's wines. Not only the special wines from his wine estate but also rarities from other winemakers were to be presented there.
The result is as simple as it is brilliant: over the years, the glass tiles in the cement tank, some of which were cracked, had been tinged by the red wine stored there. Their colour spectrum ranges from Bordeaux red and purple to dark blue. Wine diamonds glitter in the seams. The wines are presented on black shelves. With the iridescent tiles bestowing a sense of elegance to the space, the rooms are dark but not dreary.
A cleverly designed connecting path to the adjacent barrel cellar leads across galvanized grating. After entering the room by way of the courtyard entrance, the visitor proceeds three steps down to the bottle cellar and approaches the shelves where the rarities are displayed. Industrial grating is used for the floor here as well. Only after closer inspection does it become clear that the side shelving continues on beneath it, which creates the illusion of the grate hovering over the bottle inventory.
Around to the left, the metal bridge pathway slopes slightly as it passes the concrete back wall of the tank, which is painted black like the rest of the cellar. Only a one-metre-wide strip is tiled and still has the iron hatches, which once let the wine flow out, as a decorative feature. The original tiles of the light green hue popular in the 1950s and 1960s draw a connection to the past.
At the end of the path is an entrance/exit door that leads to the barrel cellar, which is, apart from the sand-coloured floor, also in black. Zemmer entrusted the cellar furnishings, including the lighting, to the architects.

Floor plan
Scale 1:300

1 Cellar entrance
2 Barrel cellar
3 Display area
4 Barrique cellar
5 Concrete tanks

Visitors to this small, mysterious microcosm in the shape of a mini-labyrinth can also sample Zemmer's wines there. Indigenous grape varieties form the basis of the varietal wines the estate produces. The signature products are the reserve-label wines made from Chardonnay, Gewürztraminer and Lagrein grapes from selected areas and vintages, the elegant sparkling wine Cuvée Z and, of course, the Cortinie collection (based on the ancient name "Cortinie" for Cortina): brilliant red and white blends, vinified from the best areas in the locality.
The blend made from Chardonnay, Pinot Grigio, Sauvignon and Gewürztraminer grapes is blond in colour, its aromas reminiscent of tropical fruits and spices. It has rich fruit on the palate with a salty minerality and refreshing acidity. A particularly complex wine with development potential.
The relationship between the client and the architects was consistently congenial. The original concepts were of course developed jointly; nevertheless, Zemmer laid the final decisions and execution of the project fully in the hands of the architects, and was very happy with the results.
The goal was to attract more public attention and create more space. The architectural aesthetic was meant to instil a lasting sense of well-being in visitors and employees alike. In this way, the project garnered a great deal of attention and accolades, even in a region like Alto Adige, which is used to innovative architecture.

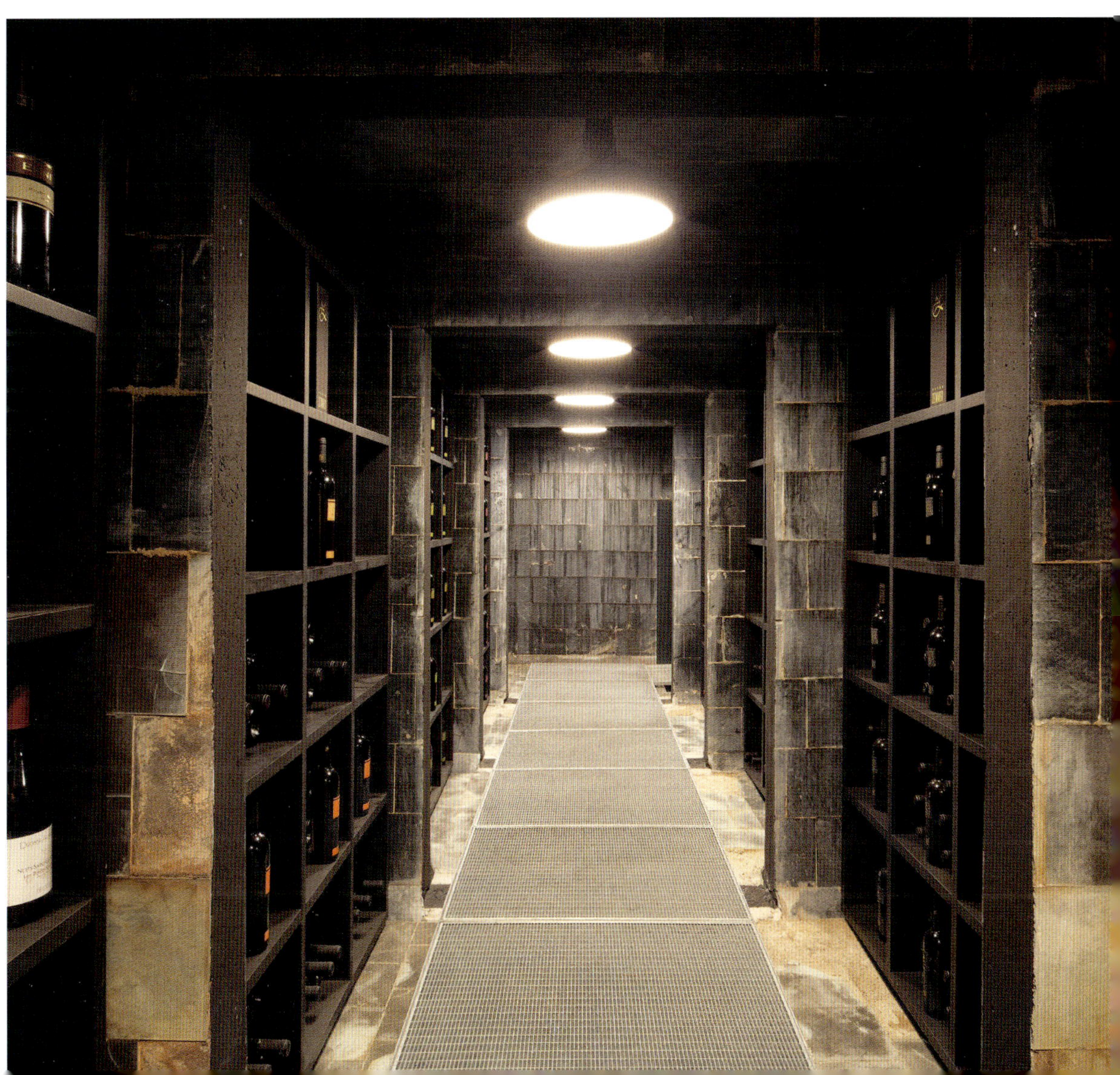

Château Thuerry in Villecroze, France

Architects: Leibar & Seigneurin, 9 Rue Emile Zola, 33000 Bordeaux, www.leibarseigneurin.com

Team: Nathalie Arriau

Gross floor area: 2,200 m²

Start of design phase: 1999

Completion: 2001

Region: Provence – Cote d'Azur

Contact: 83690 Villecroze
thuerry@chateauthuerry.com

Oenologists: Serge Gombert, Florat Lallemand

Price range: €9.90–€55

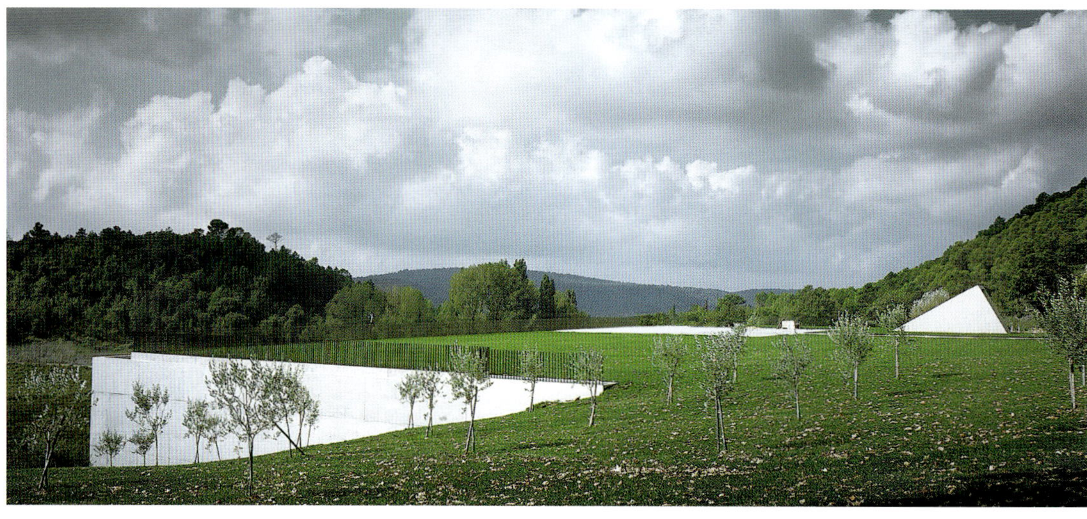

Floor plan
Scale 1:2000

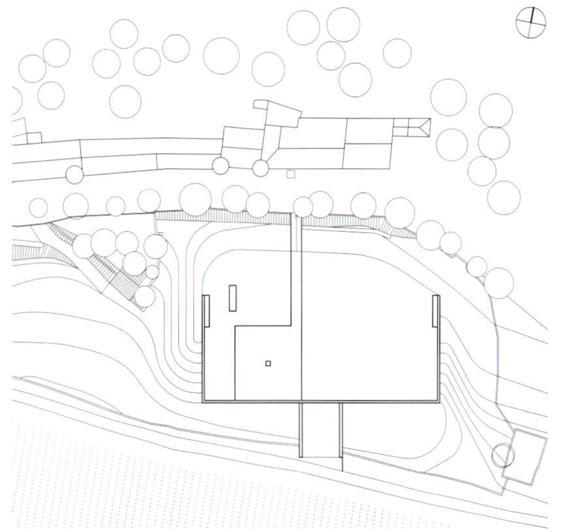

What began as a small vineyard in the wine region of Chablis became an estate of 380 hectares, of which 45 hectares lie near Tourtour-Villecroze, in the most beautiful part of Provence between Nice and Aix-en-Provence. For Jean-Louis Croquet, the work with the wine was, at first, simply a way to balance out the daily stresses of running a company. "It was a good introduction, having Chardonnay as the sole grape variety, with no marketing stress," he said.

But clearly the experience was enough to give him the bug. Soon he decided to spend the rest of his life as a vintner and devote himself to the task of producing superb wines. He enlisted the help of oenologist Stefan Paillard in seeking out suitable properties. The first trip took him and Paillard to Bordeaux, followed by a visit to the south of France. In all, they inspected 10 wine estates that were up for sale. With the winery in Provence, though, it was simply love at first sight. As soon as he arrived, Croquet felt that he had found the place for him.

It started with the first harvest in 1998, after Croquet took his leave of Chablis and sold his vineyard there. From the beginning, he focused on quality. For him, the three elements – terroir, grape variety and vintner – had to interact successfully and complement each other.

Only 4,000–5,000 vines per hectare of vineyard grow on the sparse, stony soil of clay and limestone. According to Croquet, the keys to exceptional quality lie in consistent yield reduction, a factor considered even during winter pruning; use of organic fertilizers to preserve micro-organisms in the soil; green harvesting to encourage the growth of the best fruit; manual grape harvesting; and careful processing in the cellar. About 30–35 hectolitres of red wine are produced per hectare. To retain their aromas, the wines are only minimally filtered before bottling. Croquet is convinced that the best wines come from a blend, or cuvée, of different grape varieties. "Depending on the vintage, there's always one grape variety in a cuvée that has had a superlative year," he explains. Like in the exemplary wine region Châteauneuf du Pape, almost every wine produced in the south of France combines the most diverse grape varieties of the region. Varietals are hardly available. Along with the classic southern French grape varieties Syrah, Grenache and Cinsault, Château Thuerry also cultivates the two famous Bordeaux varieties Merlot and Cabernet Sauvignon. As for white grapes, the estate grows Sémillon, Ugni Blanc and Rolle. The latter is a grape variety grown primarily in Languedoc, which can produce strong acidity and freshness in very warm and dry areas.

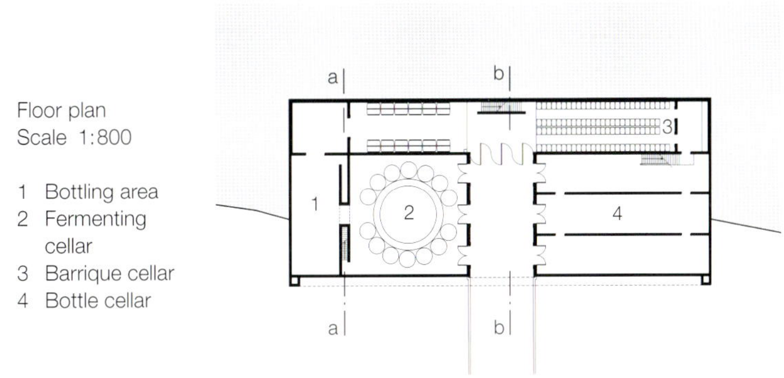

Floor plan
Scale 1:800

1 Bottling area
2 Fermenting cellar
3 Barrique cellar
4 Bottle cellar

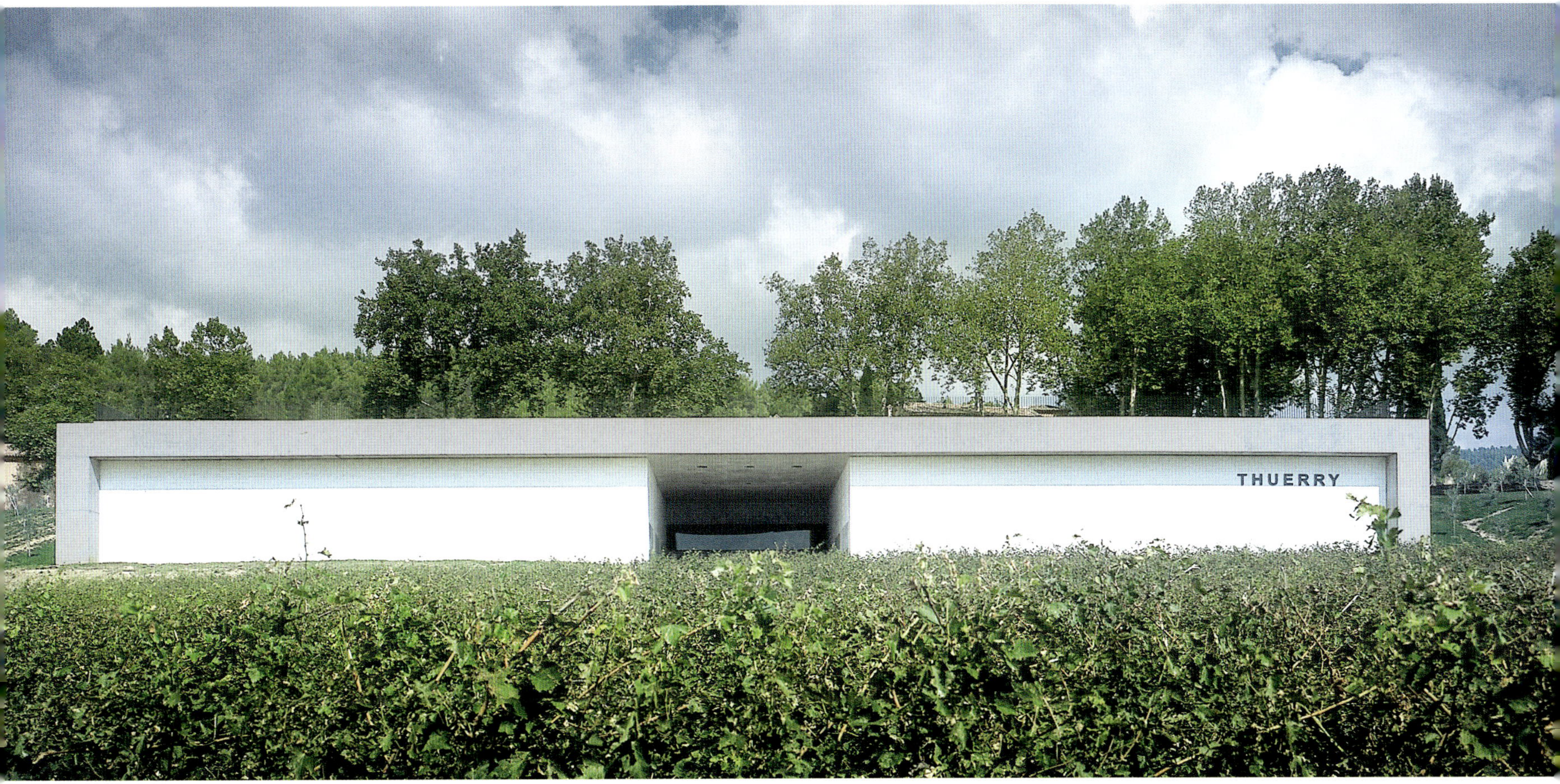

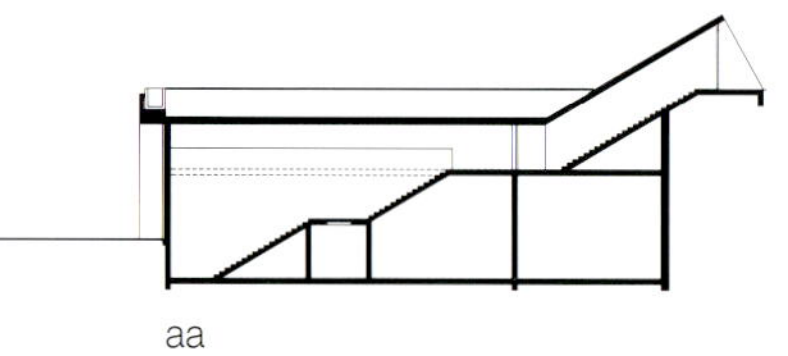

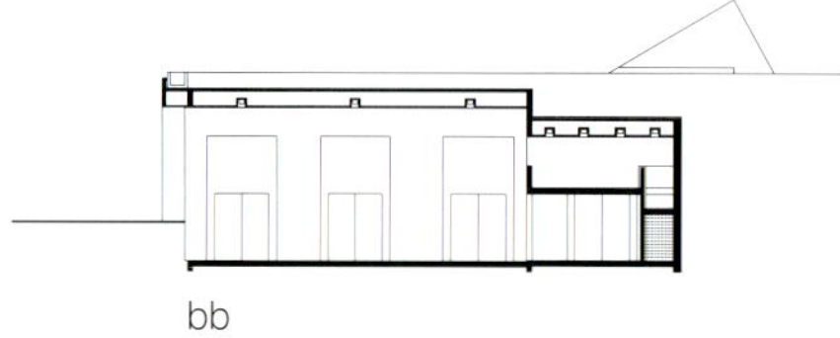

Sections
Scale 1:800

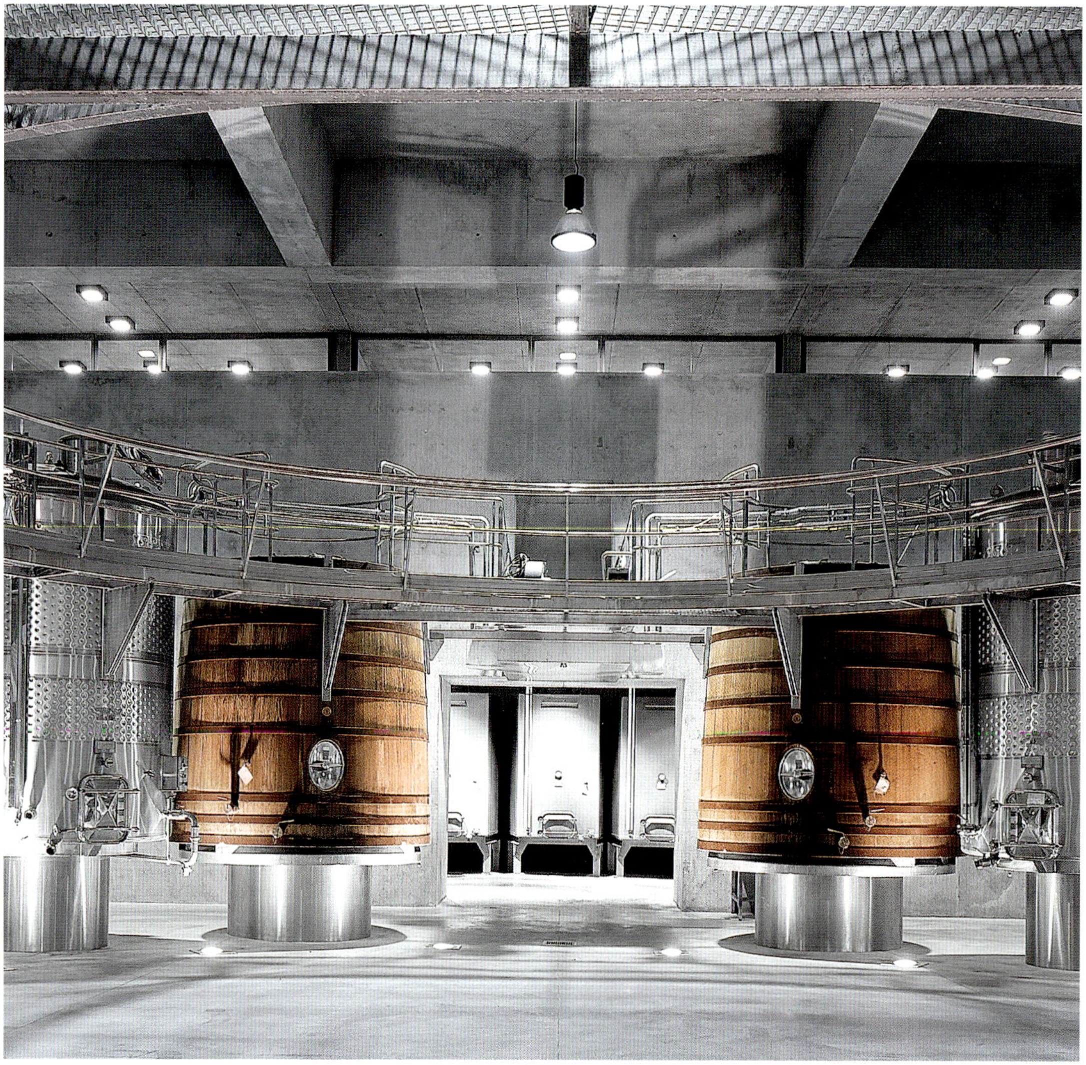

Rosés are characteristic of Château Thuerry, as they are for the rest of Provence. They amount to almost one half of the château's product range. Red wines, Croquet confides, will constitute a larger portion of his production in the coming years, increasing from 45 per cent to a target of 60 per cent. The white wines are only a small part of his range, but their share is also set to increase. Château Thuerry's market is primarily the Scandinavian countries, the United States, and, more recently, China.

In front of the old Thuerry manor house and the work buildings, a white, flat building lies embedded in the vineyards. A grey band encircles the sculpted white building, in the middle of which is the entrance. Only upon approach does one see that the white surface is made of white limestone masonry, which gives structure to the walls.

Soon after acquiring the wine estate, Croquet realized that the existing cellar was a limiting factor not only for the creation of top-quality wines, but also for further expansion. So he decided to build a new cellar to reflect the current state of the art. Two considerations were central to the planning process: firstly, that the grapes should be processed gently, which meant using gravity in all phases of

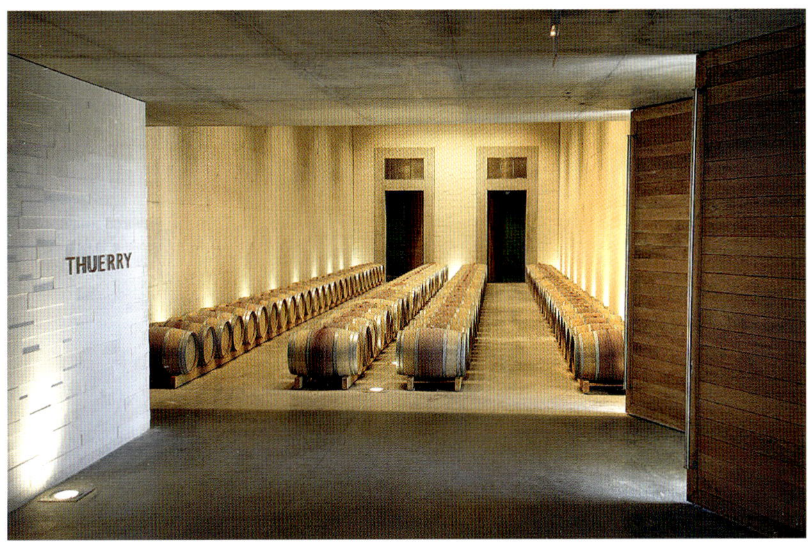

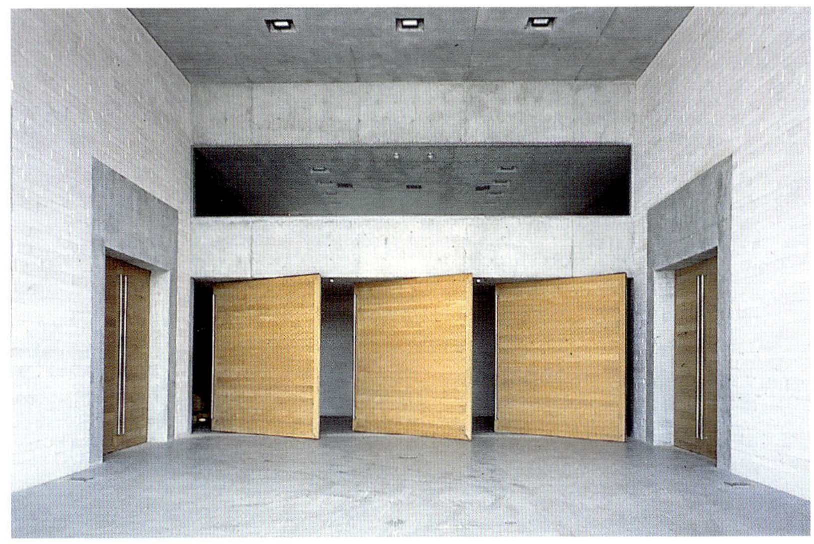

the production process; and secondly, that the fermentation process should be tightly monitored and controlled. Every individual phase of production was minutely analysed to see where work processes might be optimized, and then the technical specifications were laid down accordingly. Only then did the search for an architect begin.
Croquet only had one stipulation: that an architect should be chosen who had not previously completed any projects that had anything to do with wine. "I wanted it to be a joint process of discovery and development," he explains. After initial discussions and designs, it was architect Xavier Leibar, who comes from Biarritz and works in Bordeaux, who sufficiently impressed the client.
The building of the new cellar took exactly six months, from April to November 2000. During this period, 2,200 square metres of area were added and partially embedded into the slope in front of the historical buildings. The layer of earth over the cellar is two to three metres thick, allowing for an optimal temperature regulation. The entrance to the cellar looks like a pyramid jutting out of the ground, its stark exposed concrete creating tension between it and the surrounding green landscape. A plain oak door opens up to a staircase leading down into the interior, and the high temperatures felt just a moment ago yield immediately to a pleasant coolness.
The first stop is a cellar room with enormous steel tanks. Croquet's idea of using a circular system for arranging the tanks is ingenious in its simplicity. After the harvest, the grapes pass through an opening in the cellar roof to enter a downpipe that can be turned 360 degrees and connected to any of the tanks in the circle. That allows the filling of the tanks via only one access point.
Two thick walls border the steep stairs leading down to the lower floor. Here, too, nothing but exposed concrete was used. The cellars look clinical and pure. At the bottom of the stairs, large oak doors provide a strong contrast to the bare concrete. Long rows of small casks, mostly made of French oak, are stored in the narrow barrique cellar. The three wide oak doors next to each other in the middle of the cellar create a connection to the outside and allow for complete vehicle accessibility. Above them, a large pane of glass inserted into the exposed concrete allows daylight into the interior, opening up the space to create a pleasant sense of transparency. The bottling area and the bottle storage area flank the room on either side. These areas can also be accessed individually by way of the oak gates. The entire layout of the facility, as well as its sequence of production areas, indicate absolute professionalism. At the moment, 150,000 bottles are filled here annually, with an increase of 50,000 bottles possible.
At the end of a visit to Château Thuerry, a cool glass of rosé offers refreshment. This fresh, fruity beverage, made in equal measures of Merlot and Caladoc, a French hybrid of Grenache and Malbec, is an ideal summer wine. The idea for this cuvée came from Croquet's friend, the award-winning, Michelin-starred chef Alain Ducasse, who asked him to create a good rosé that "goes with many things". The name of the wine – L'exception, "exceptional" – also describes its creator, Jean-Louis Croquet.

Quinta do Vallado in Peso da Régua, Portugal

Architects: Guedes + de Campos, Rua S. Francisco 5, 3°, 4050-548 Porto, www.guedesdecampos.com

Team: Mariana Sendas, Cristina Maximino, Inês Mesquita, Luís Campos, Adalgisa Lopes, Francisco Lencastre, Joana Miguel, Tiago Souto e Castro, Ana Fernandes, João Pontes

Site area: 2,049 m²

Gross floor area: 4,142 m²

Start of design phase: 2007

Completion: 2010

Region: Douro

Contact: Vilarinho dos Freires, 5050-364 Peso da Régua, www.wonderfulland.com/vallado

Oenologist: Francisco Olazabal

Price range: €7.50 – €80

●●●

One of the first port houses in the Douro Valley, Quinta do Vallado was founded in 1716. It had long been the property of Dona Antónia Adelaide Ferreira. In honour of this very social-minded, highly respected lady, the Quinta's best wine carries her name to this day. In exceptional years, the best grapes from more than 100-year-old vines are meticulously selected and pressed. They yield about 1,500 to 3,000 bottles, depending on the vintage, with the name Adelaide emblazoned on the label. The first 150 bottles of a vintage are sold to well-known personalities in Portugal, with the earnings from the sale price of €80 euros a bottle going to charitable causes.

In 1987, the port wine brand name Vallado was sold and the estate's production converted to non-fortified wine. Today very little port wine comes from the estate. Almost 80 per cent of the 130-hectare vineyard area is planted with red wine grapes. These are without exception traditional Portuguese grape varieties such as Touriga Nacional, Touriga Franca and Tinta Roriz, which produce wines that are among the country's best. Although these wines originally had a high level of tannins and were therefore hard to sell even on the Portuguese market, they have now been brought in line with international styles featuring softer tannins. After the Quinta do Vallado Douro Reserva received its first prizes in 2003, the wine estate became one of the most highly regarded in Europe and can now look back on a number of international awards. This recognition, of course, also increased demand for the wines, so in 2006, the proprietors were already

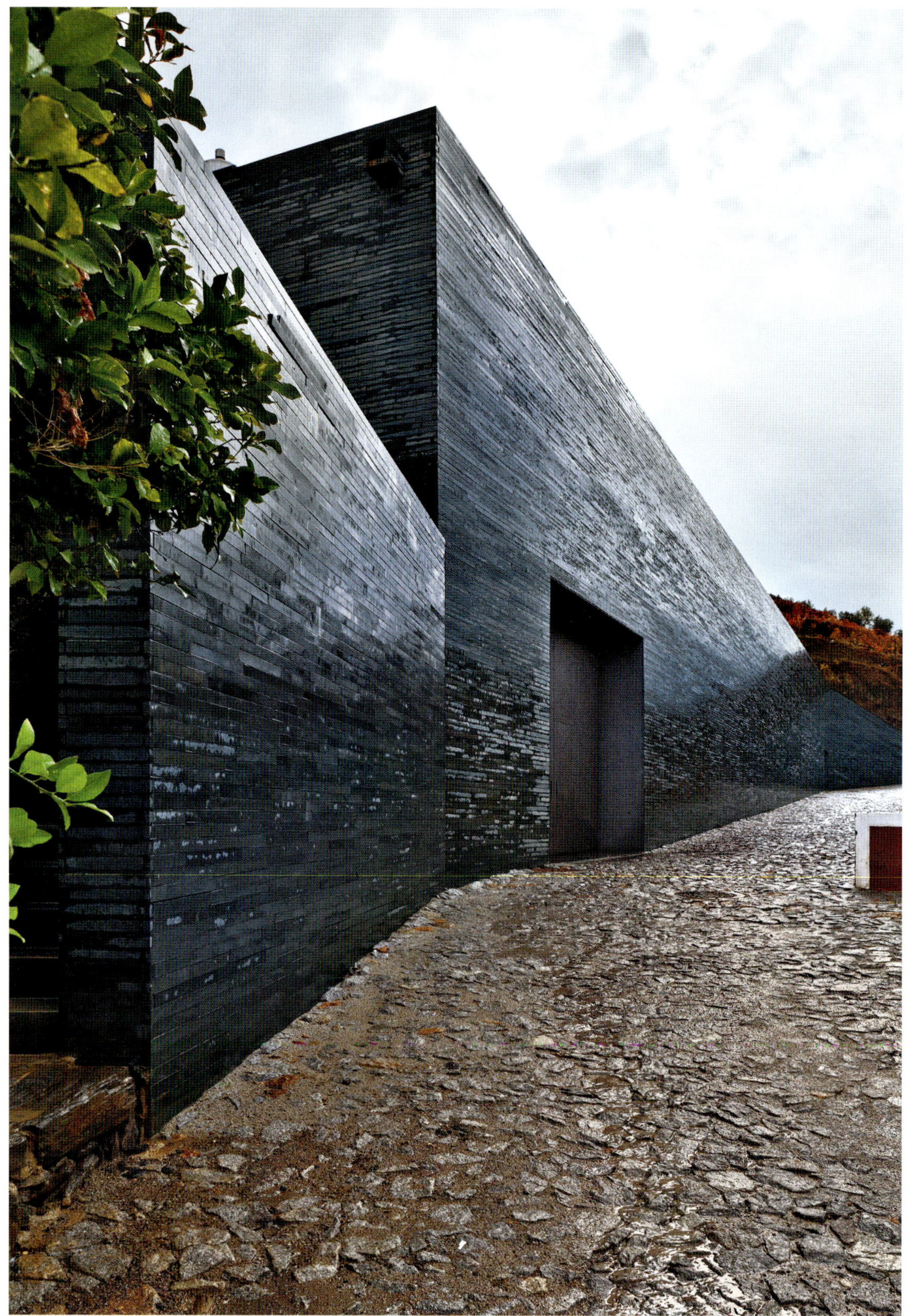

Floor plans
Scale 1:1000

1 Press area
2 White wine fermentation
3 Barrel cellar
4 Technology
5 Barrel-cleaning room
6 Grape receiving/ press area
7 Red wine fermentation
8 Laboratory
9 Multifunctional space

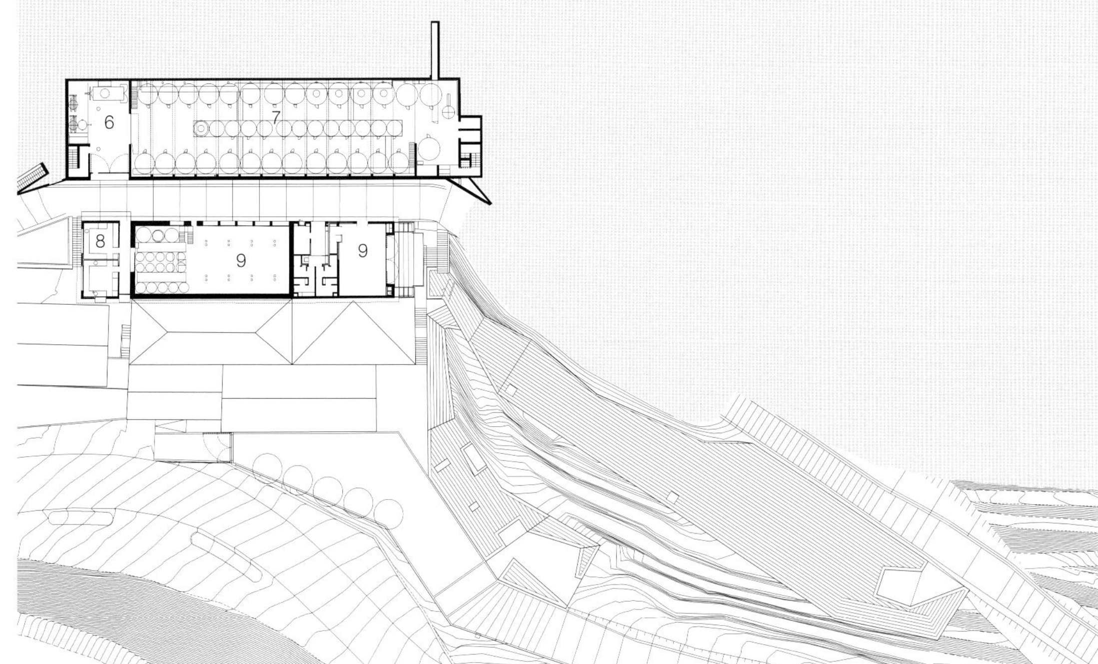

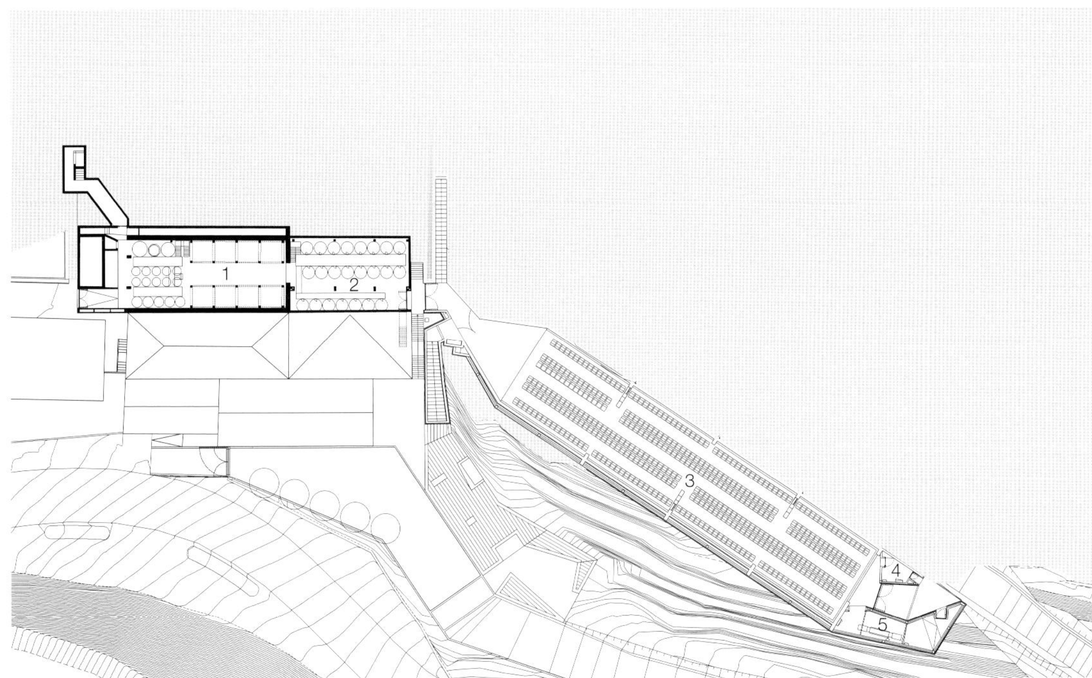

thinking about extending the estate. João Ribeiro, who together with Francisco Ferreira is responsible for Quinta do Vallado's management and finances, contacted the Porto-based architect Francisco Vieira de Campos. The recommendation had come from Portuguese architect Eduardo Souto de Moura, who had designed Ribeiro's private home; at the time, Vieira de Campos was working on that project with Souto de Moura's project team. Functional considerations of wine production were at the heart of the extension of the existing wine estate, so that the quality of its wines could be even further improved. Another important goal in adding the new build was to better tie the wine estate in with the company-owned hotel, thereby allowing the estate to accommodate and profit from the growth of wine tourism in the Douro Valley. For Vieira de Campos, there were two key aspects: making use of traditional regional building materials, and emphasizing the building's relationship to the surrounding landscape. He felt that the new structure should not compete with the estate's existing historical buildings, but rather present a natural contrast to them. The orange gleam of the quinta can be seen from far away. In contrast, the slate-covered exterior of the new building is very modestly designed. The extension imitates the natural form of the slope and is partially dug into the hill. That way, gravity can be harnessed to allow the most careful processing of the grapes.

The first meeting with Vieira de Campos took place in December 2006 at Quinta do Vallado. Apart from a minor alteration, the first sketch dating from this meeting was to become the basis of the plans and everything that followed. According to Vieira de Campos, the project was supposed to "ideally blend into the natural landscape and not look too bulky and heavy".

It was not clear at the time whether portions of the building would be able to be set so deeply into the slope; however, these reservations were dispelled during the implementation phase. The time scale of the project presented a further challenge. Normal business operations, the autumn harvest in particular, had to be guaranteed; the construction work had to run parallel to that.

Together with Francisco Ferreira, who manages the vineyards and wine production in Quinta do Vallado, Vieira de Campos – who had never before carried out a project involving wine – worked out a

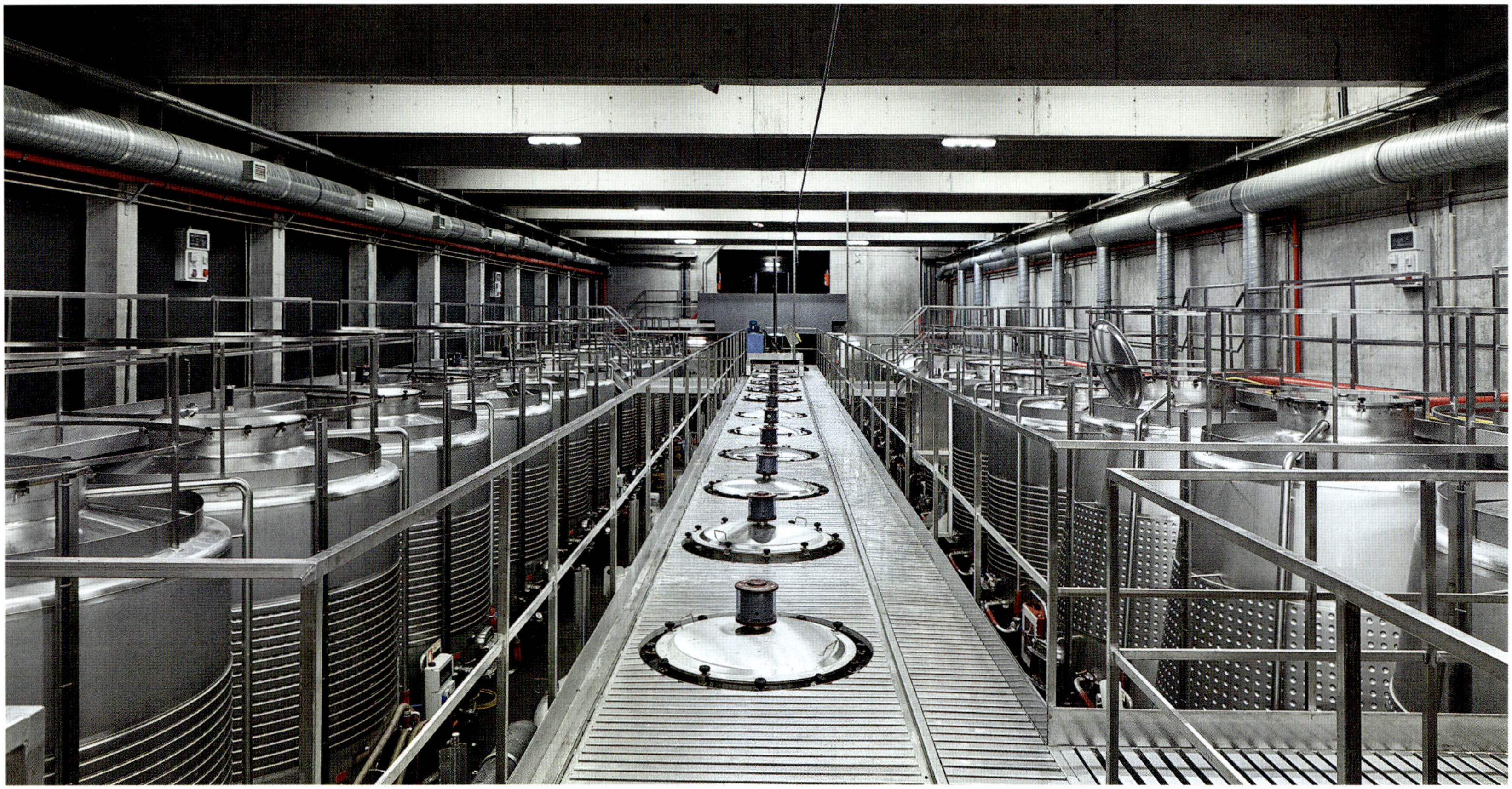

spatial layout in accordance with the technical requirements.
The first presentation of a model in September 2007 was already enough to convince the relevant authorities as well as the owners. Construction then officially began after the wine harvest in 2008. “The challenge lies in bringing architecture, building and landscape together into a unified whole,” says Vieira de Campos. He is convinced that “it’s the people working together on a project like this that make the difference”. From the beginning, therefore, he brought all those involved in the project together, from the labourers to the engineers. Midday meals were taken jointly, offering opportunities to discuss any current challenges. Vieira de Campos was constantly on the building site, as he found it important to be in direct contact with the workmen.
“It was the achievement of the entire team, in which everybody did his bit, that led to the goal,” says Vieira de Campos. The completed project certainly vouches for that.

Visitors coming from Peso da Régua first see the historical orange building of the quinta far above the road on the opposite slope. The name Quinta do Vallado is emblazoned in large letters on the roof. Then a futuristic-looking, lengthy building stretches out next to it. The flat, silver-grey exterior appears understated yet elegant. Only upon closer inspection can one see that the outer facade is made of thousands of elongated slate panels. One would never think that more than 3,000 square metres of floor space for the production and storage of wine are concealed beneath.
Visitors taking the winery tour follow the journey of the grapes after the harvest and so can more easily comprehend the production process. During the ascent up the stairs to the entrance of the fermenting cellar, the successful synthesis of the traditional and the new is already visible. The slate walls on either side of the stairs date from different periods, and so create a clear sense of dynamic tension in the design. Within, on either side, there are so-called *lagares*: flat granite troughs in which grapes

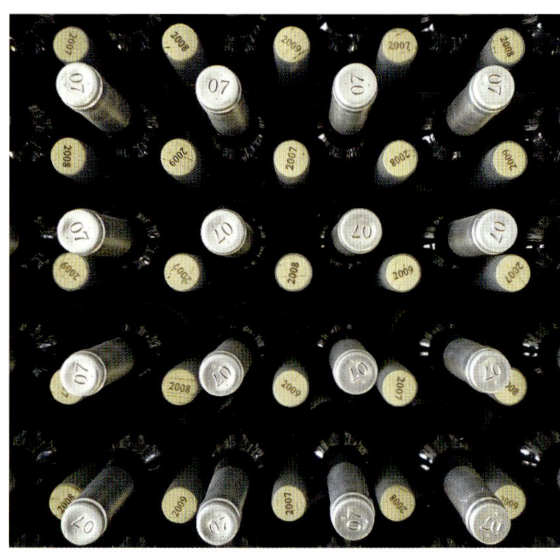

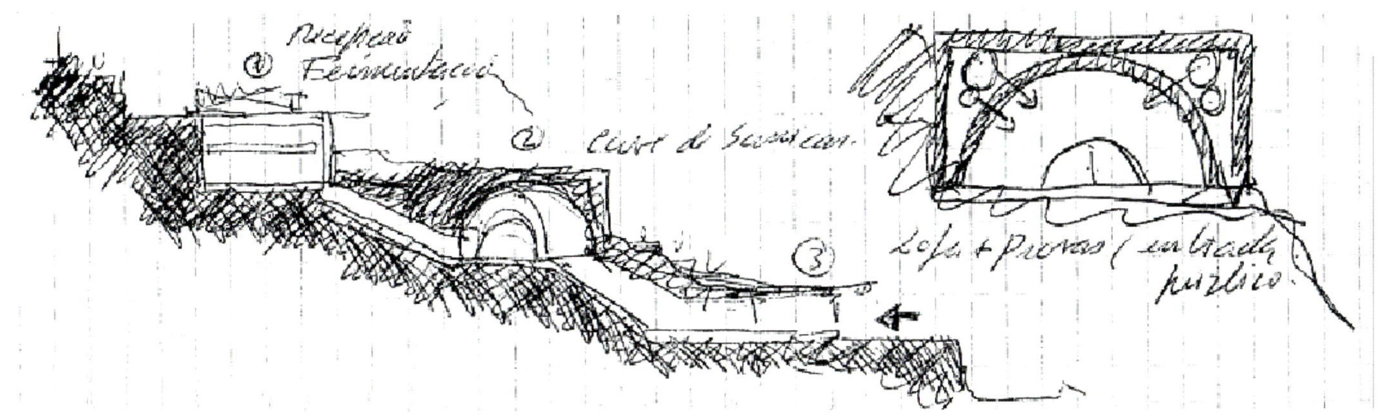

were trod upon by labourers as late as the 1970s. These, however, are facsimiles of the originals to show visitors the historic process of port wine production.

The pressure and the softness of the human foot combined to extract a maximum of fruit, colour and tannins from the grapes. Moreover, the seeds remained unharmed and were thus not able to release any unwanted bitters into the wine. This ancient system was replaced with modern crushers and maceration tanks less than 30 years ago. It soon became clear, however, that the new technology did not produce the same concentrated, balanced, richly fruity wines as before. About 10 years ago, a few top cellars therefore returned to the age-old technique of pressing by foot in the stone troughs.

After passing the *lagares*, the tour takes visitors to the actual fermenting cellar, the centre of red-wine production. Gravity ensures that the grapes received on the roof of the cellar reach the enormous steel fermentation tanks through a downpipe. Depending on the quality of the product, the tanks can hold five to six tons of grape must for the top-notch wines, and nine to 11 tons for the massmarket wines. In order to get the cap – the solid matter that rises to the top during fermentation – to sink back down, which achieves a more intense extraction of pigments from the grape skins, two techniques are employed. For the top-quality wines, the process takes place with the help of sieves that move slowly up and down; the rest are subject to a so-called remontage process. This involves pumping the new wine out from under the cap and back over the cap. The old fermentation tanks of cement, which are still in the main building, have been converted into storage tanks for white wine.

A long, plain staircase made of exposed concrete leads down into the impressive barrique cellar, where 600 casks are stored at cool temperatures. The space extends out in front of the entering visitors like a historic vaulted cellar. Long rows of the 225-litre French oak barrels are stored here for 16 to 20 months, depending on their contents. Three

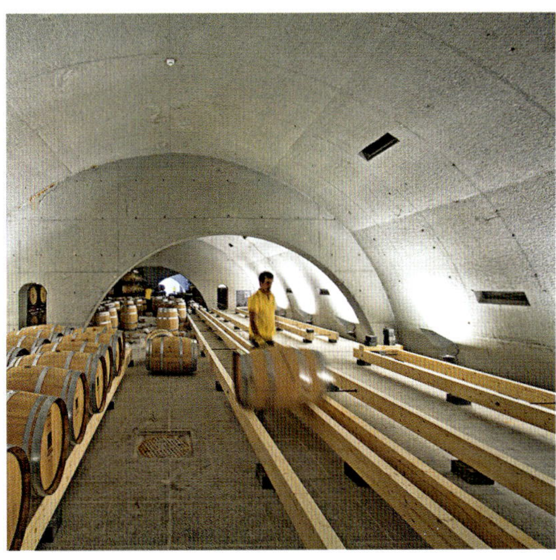

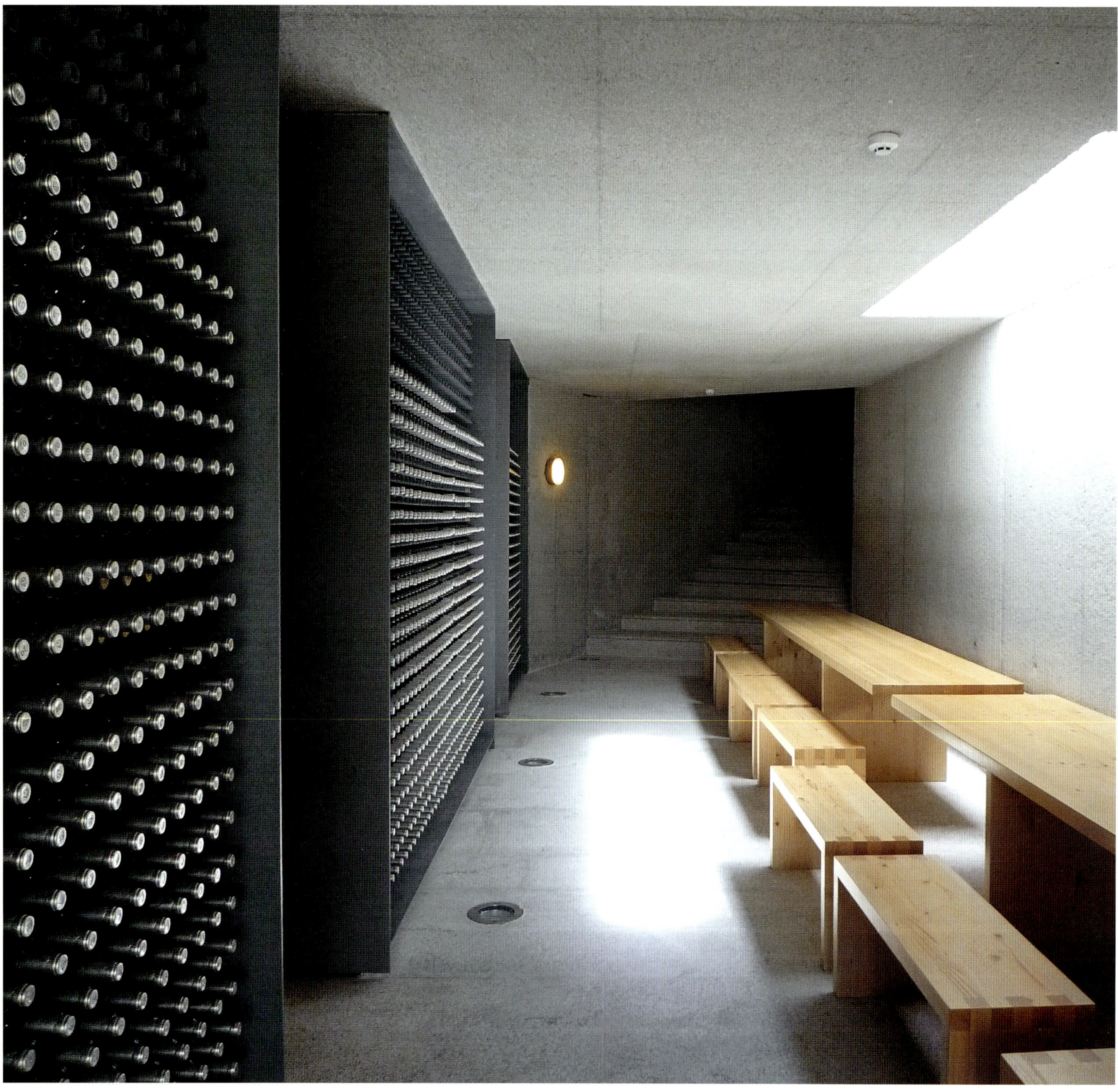

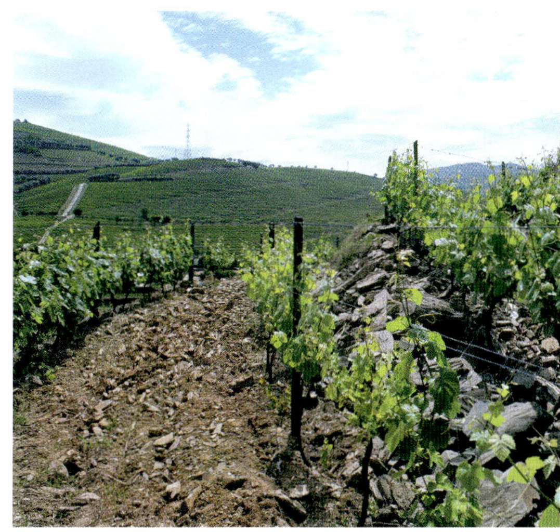

partition walls, which open out into large arcs, focus the eye and allow the depth of the room to be properly appreciated. This impression is strengthened by the indirect lighting beneath the casks, which bathes the space in an ethereal light. At the end of another staircase, visitors arrive at the tasting room, which is also dominated by exposed concrete. The only decorative features are wooden tables and benches as well as a large bottle rack doubling as a wall. An opening in the ceiling lets daylight filter in; spotlights installed in the floor along the racks provide illumination in the evening. Opposite the stairs, a sweeping glass facade offers an impressive view of the Douro Valley. Visitors who wish to try the Quinta do Vallado wines without taking a tour can access the tasting room here. By keeping the design minimal, Vieira de Campos was able to keep the focus fully on the wines. There is nothing to divert attention from the taste of the Touriga Nacional Douro Red 2007: very concentrated, with well-integrated oak notes and a rich nose of red fruit. Pressed entirely from Touriga Nacional grapes and aged for 16 months in oak barrels, this is an exciting red wine with unbelievably soft tannins, gently sweet and spicy notes and a long finish.

"Do what you feel is right and always be yourself," is Vieira de Campos's credo. He is already at work on his next project, the extension of the adjacent hotel, a commission he received from the owners. It seems that Vieira de Campos is not the only one with the credo; the wines at Quinta do Vallado are proof of that.

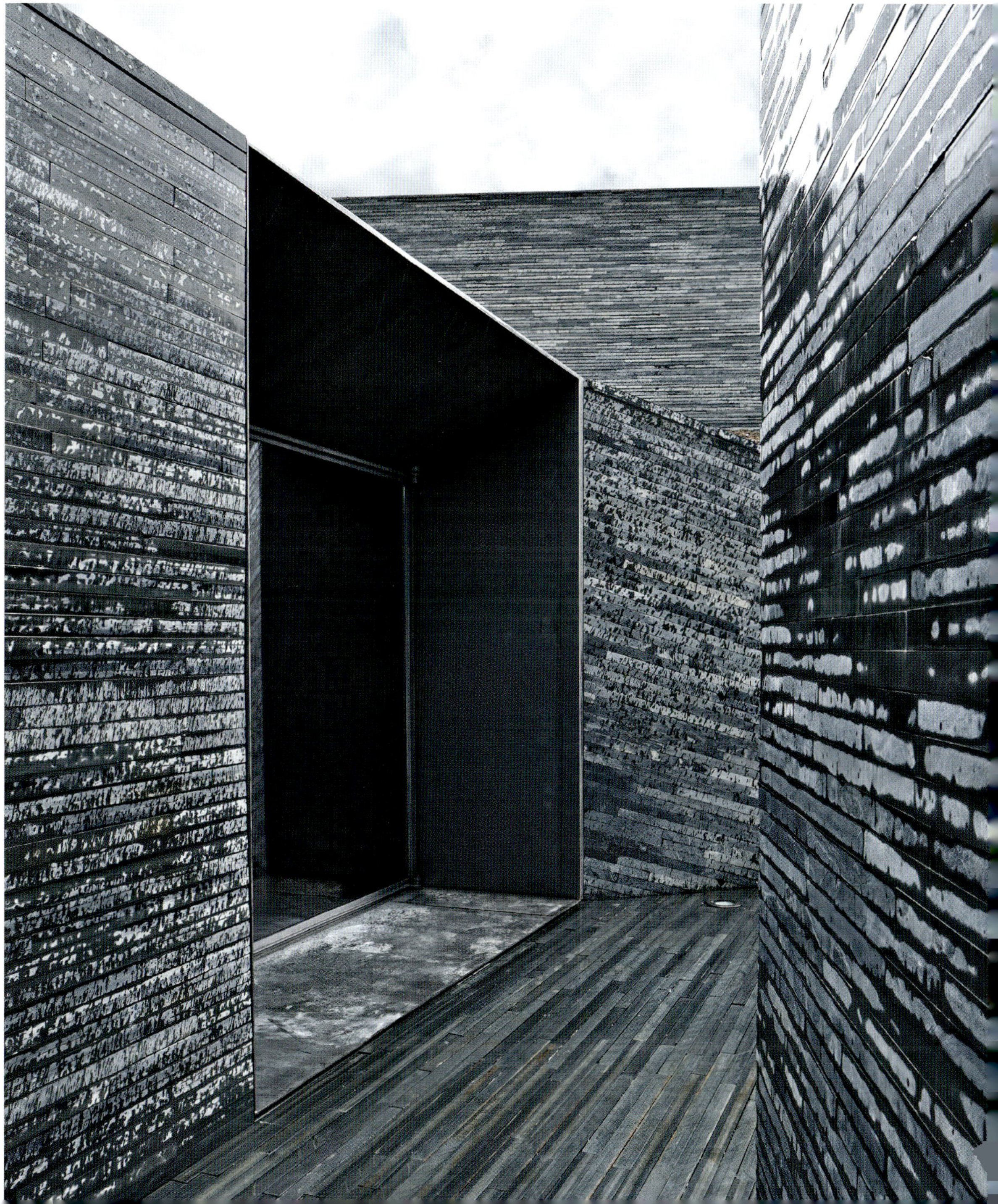

Domaine Perraudin in Vauvert, France

Architects: Perraudin Architectes, 16, Rue Jacques Imbert Colomès, 69001 Lyon, www.perraudinarchitectes.com
Team: Elisabeth Polzella
Site area: 3,000 m^2
Gross floor area: 900 m^2
Start of design phase: 1997
Completion: 1999
Region: Rhône Valley
Contact: Chemin des Salines, 30600 Vauvert www.domaineperraudin.com
Oenologist: Gilles Perraudin
Price range: €10–€16
●○○

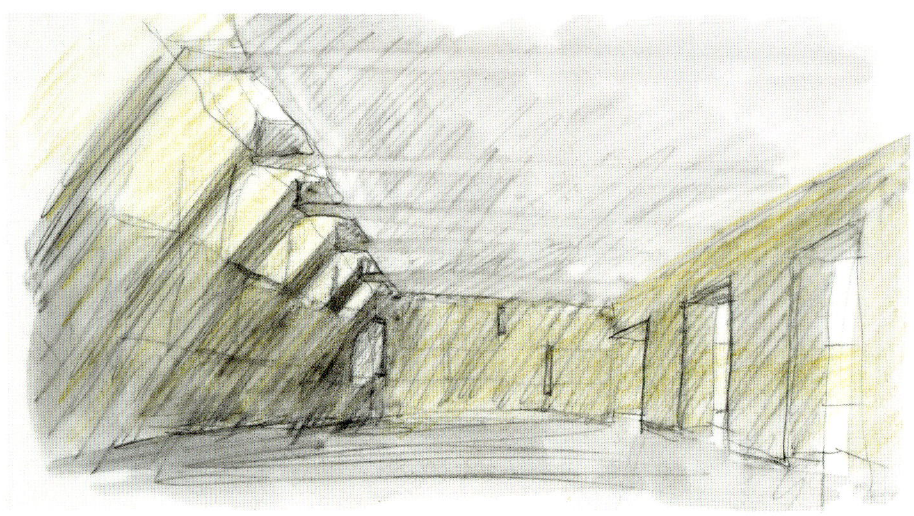

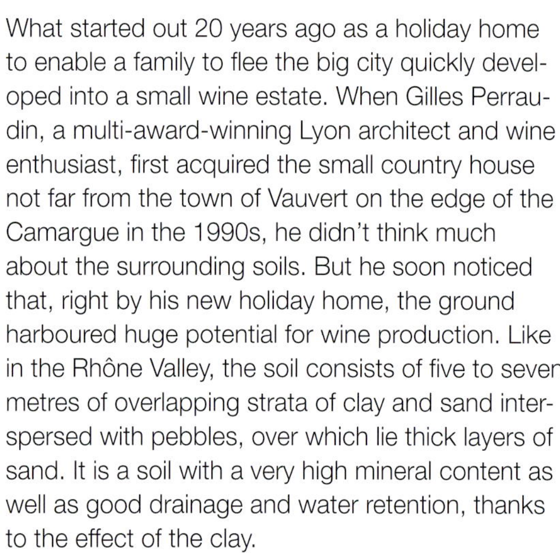

What started out 20 years ago as a holiday home to enable a family to flee the big city quickly developed into a small wine estate. When Gilles Perraudin, a multi-award-winning Lyon architect and wine enthusiast, first acquired the small country house not far from the town of Vauvert on the edge of the Camargue in the 1990s, he didn't think much about the surrounding soils. But he soon noticed that, right by his new holiday home, the ground harboured huge potential for wine production. Like in the Rhône Valley, the soil consists of five to seven metres of overlapping strata of clay and sand interspersed with pebbles, over which lie thick layers of sand. It is a soil with a very high mineral content as well as good drainage and water retention, thanks to the effect of the clay.

At first Perraudin was only interested in cultivating white grape varieties, thinking that he had a terroir before him that was most suited to producing white wine. He purchased surrounding vineyards from vintners, who had let their grapes be vinified by a so-called cave cooperative, and replanted them with Chardonnay, Sauvignon Blanc, Petit Marsanne and Chenin Blanc, the latter a grape variety that originally comes from the Loire. In choosing the Viognier variety, which he also planted, he went for a clone especially developed in Condrieu in the northern Rhône that was known to have a particularly low yield and was a good match for the mineral-rich soil in Vauvert.

The Mediterranean Sea, just 20 kilometres away, creates good climatic conditions for the grapes to thrive. The air cools considerably at night, thereby giving the grapes a refreshing acidity during ripening. The constant wind allows the grapes to dry soon after rainfall, thus preventing mould, mildew and other vine afflictions.

From the beginning, Perraudin focused on quality. "Très petits, mais très grands" – a small area producing a great wine, that was his goal. He consistently reduced yields; harvested minimal amounts, by hand – just eight hectolitres per hectare; and took care to let the wine develop in the cask and rest a long time on the lees. In 1995, a first blend was aged and bottled at a neighbouring vintner's. Just a year later, Perraudin got his first international award. The desire to age the wine himself and wield more influence on its quality led him to establish his own wine estate in 1999. Perraudin, who teaches architecture at the University of Montpellier, was driven by the challenge of adopting an architectural style that would blend harmoniously into the surrounding landscape and, at the same time, address the technical requirements as well as economic concerns of winemaking. He decided to use natural stone for the walls, and found these in the form of coarse yellow shell limestone in the region of Pont du Gard, a Roman aqueduct between Nîmes and Orange. Inspired by Roman ashlar building techniques, Perraudin used large, monolithic stone building blocks with identical dimensions (210 by 105 by 52.5 centimetres) and weighing 2.5 tons. The individual building blocks were simply laid down without mortar. The pressure of the stones against each other and the ensuing

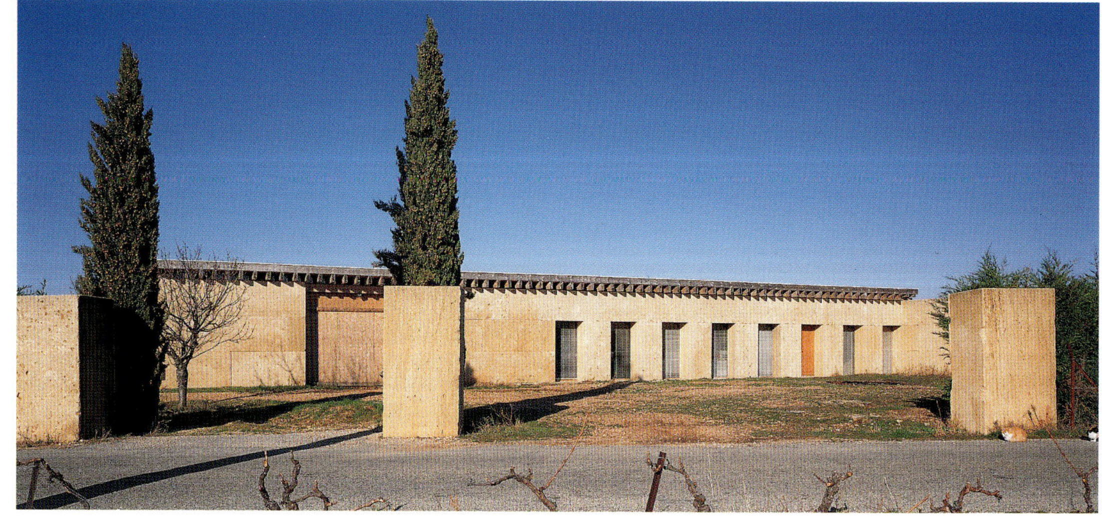

friction ensure the necessary stability. The thickness of the stone walls alone creates a cool temperature that remains more or less constant all through the year – a necessity for storing wine.
In building his wine estate, Perraudin created a prototype for the following projects: Domaine Les Aurelles (Nizas, 2001; see pp. 76ff.) La Bastide d'Engras (Gard, 2008) and the Musée du Vin in Corsica (Patrimonio, 2010). Two further buildings are currently under construction or in planning: Château Marsyas in the Bekaa Valley in Lebanon as well as a wine estate in Romania.
After taking a creative break as a vintner from 2003 to 2009, Perraudin returned to winemaking in 2010. On the six hectares of vineyards he has today, 2.5 hectares of which are planted with five-year-old Syrah and Grenache grapes, he has already produced 3,000 bottles.
The white wine Perraudin produced in 2010, a blend of 40 per cent Viognier with Petit Marsanne, Sauvignon Blanc and Chenin Blanc, has a powerful mineral elegance with a long, impressive finish. Its charm is to the palate what Vauvert is to the eye.

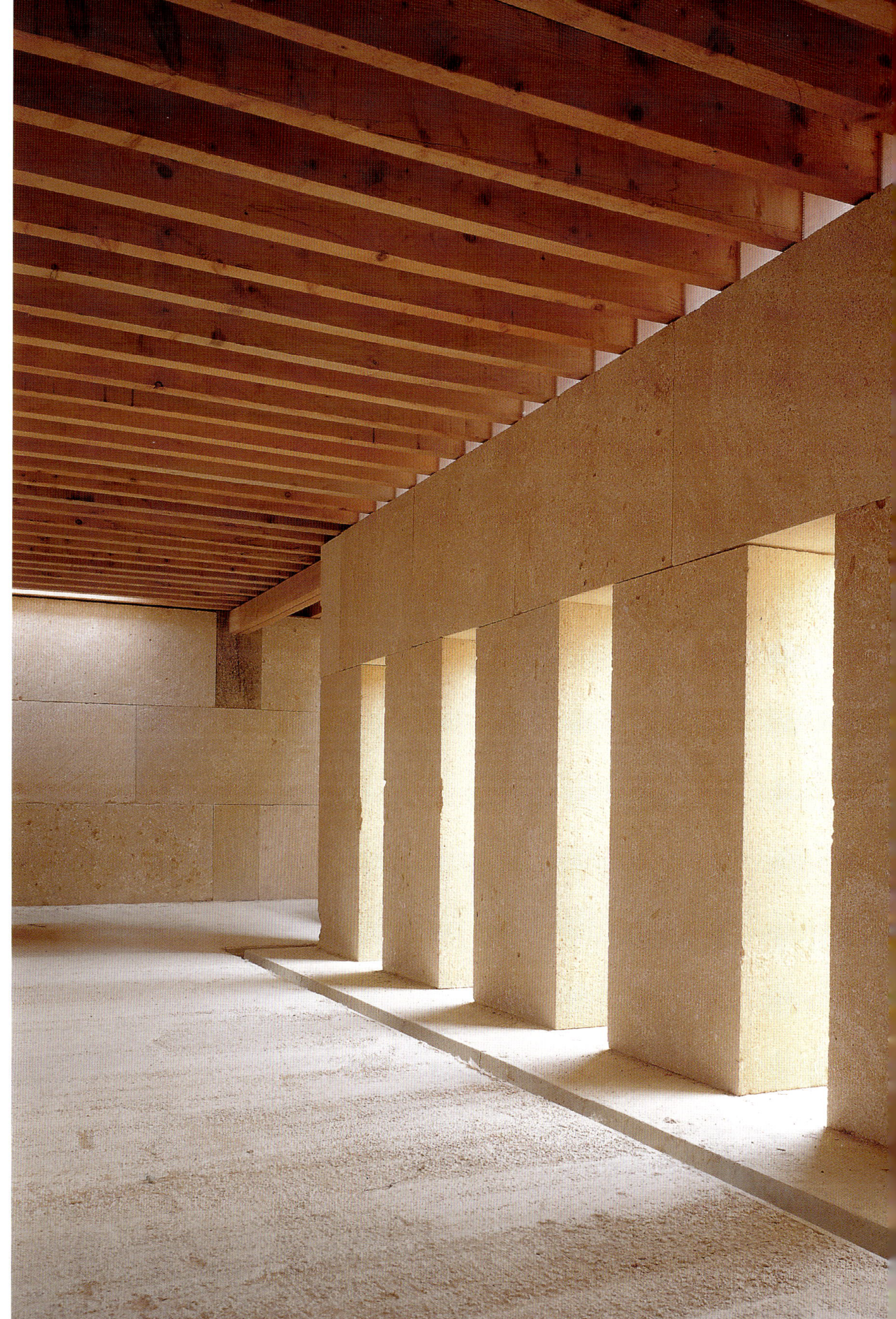

Cantina Colterenzio in Cornaiano, Italy

Architects: bergmeisterwolf architekten, Via Bruno 3, 39042 Bressanone, www.bergmeisterwolf.it
Team: Roland Decarli, Edoardo De Cicco, Jürgen Prosch
Site area: 11,140 m²
Gross floor area: 2,940 m²
Start of design phase: 2007
Completion: 2011
Region: Alto Adige
Contact: Strada del Vino 8, 39057 Cornaiano www.colterenzio.it
Oenologist: Martin Lemayr
Price range: €7–€40

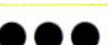

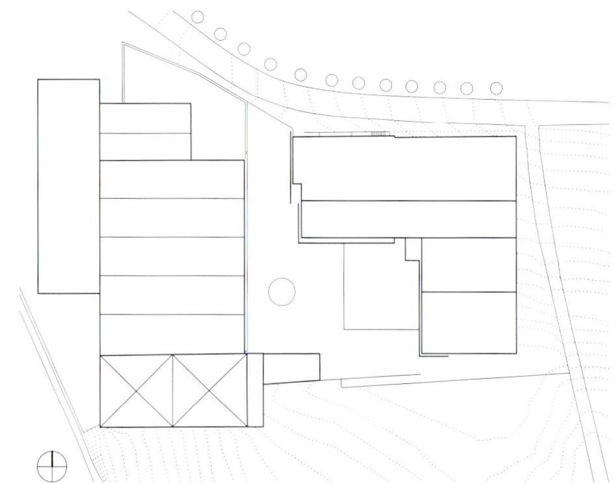

Site plan
Scale 1:2000
Axonometric projection, facade construction

On the plateau of Colterenzio, or Girlan, in the gentle Oltradige landscape formed by ice-age glaciers, lies the Colterenzio winemaking cooperative. Founded in 1960 by 28 vintners in Alto Adige (South Tyrol), it is one of the more recently established wineries in the region. Today it has 300 members tending 300 hectares of vineyards. Here, at the juncture of multicultural wine traditions, white and red wine grapes are cultivated in equal measures on superb plots at altitudes between 250 and 550 metres.

Thanks to its high technical standards, its capable management and its production of outstanding wines, the winery has enjoyed an excellent reputation for decades.

Luis Raifer, the grand seigneur of vintners in the region, had a large part to play in the renaissance of Alto Adige wines in general and the fortunes of the cooperative in particular. During his stewardship of the winery, he brought it back to its roots, focusing on the uniqueness and typicity of native wines, thus establishing them in the consciousness of local vintners and wine drinkers alike as a cultural treasure. Raifer was president of the cooperative from 1979 to early 2010; since February 2010, his son Wolfgang, head oenologist since 2005, has directed the fortunes of the wine estate, which markets its products under the names Colterenzio as well as Schreckbichl (its name in Tyrolean German). His successor as cellarmaster is oenologist Martin Lemayr.

Recently, this respected cooperative was seeking a new, contemporary image. In discussions with architects Gerd Bergmeister and Michaela Wolf of bergmeisterwolf architekten, the management decided to combine the old with the new, following basic principles of environmental friendliness and sustainability. The goal was to unify the winery, with its many buildings from the 1960s and 1980s, and give it a whole a new image. Existing entrances and connecting spaces were added to or covered with an oak or mesh metal facade. The new look is reminiscent of the oak barrels and steel tanks used in winemaking.

The purely functional building to the west of the complex, in which the stainless steel tanks, bottling facility, bottle storehouse and office are located, was fitted with a shell of oak panelling with a 50-centimetre gap between it and the building walls, a stylistic reference to wine barrels. The shell extends beyond the existing build and varies in width from 70 to 300 millimetres, and in seam spacing from five to 60 millimetres. Bevelled door and window reveals of galvanized and painted sheet steel emphasize the openings in the facade while maintaining its original form and structure.

The shell continues on to encompass the side yard, the so-called “flower trough”. This area was designed by landscape architect Roland Dellagiacoma. Myriad plants, from winter jasmine to woodbine, wind their way up a steel trellis. During the growing season, they transform themselves into a green patio, providing a dash of colour. On the facing side, the new mesh metal facade encases the older structure like a bracket, leaving a gap of 60 to 100 millimetres. Technical facilities have been

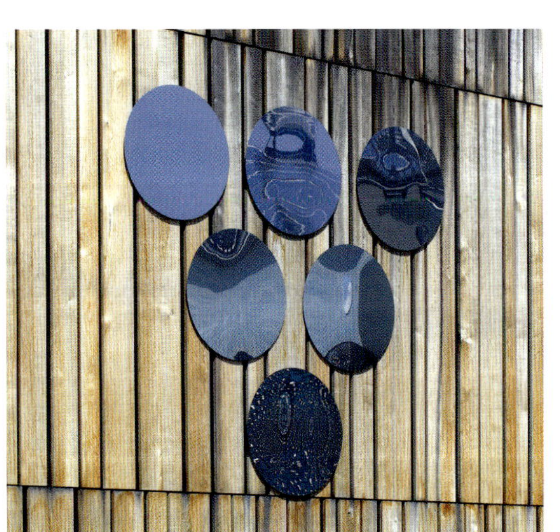

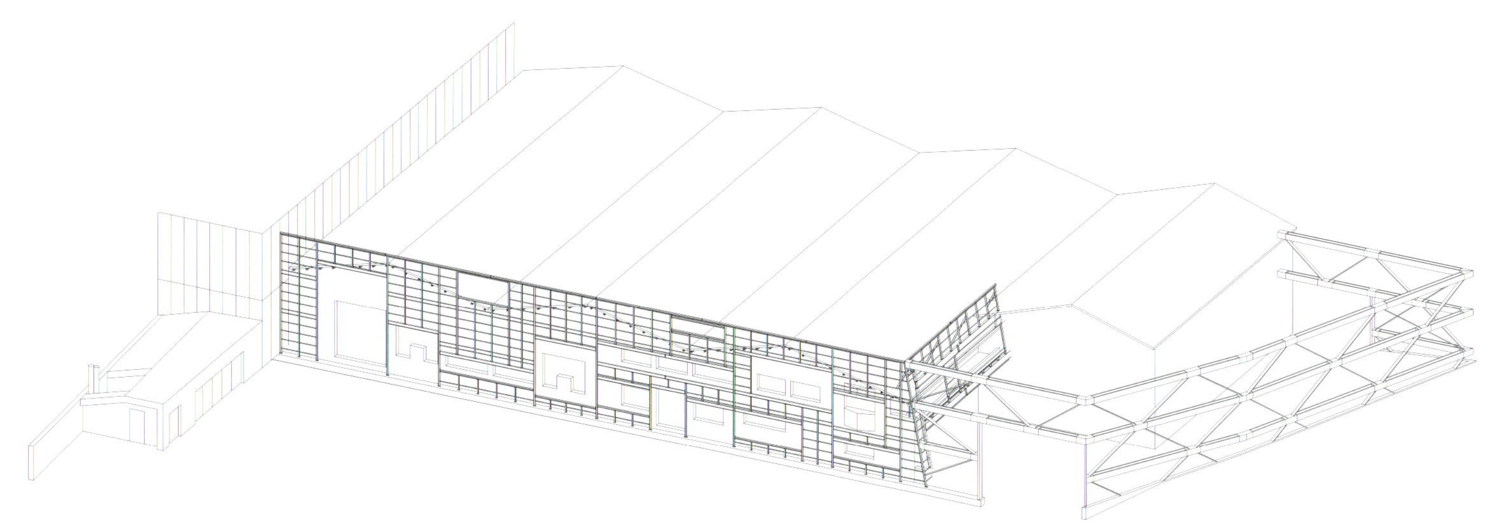

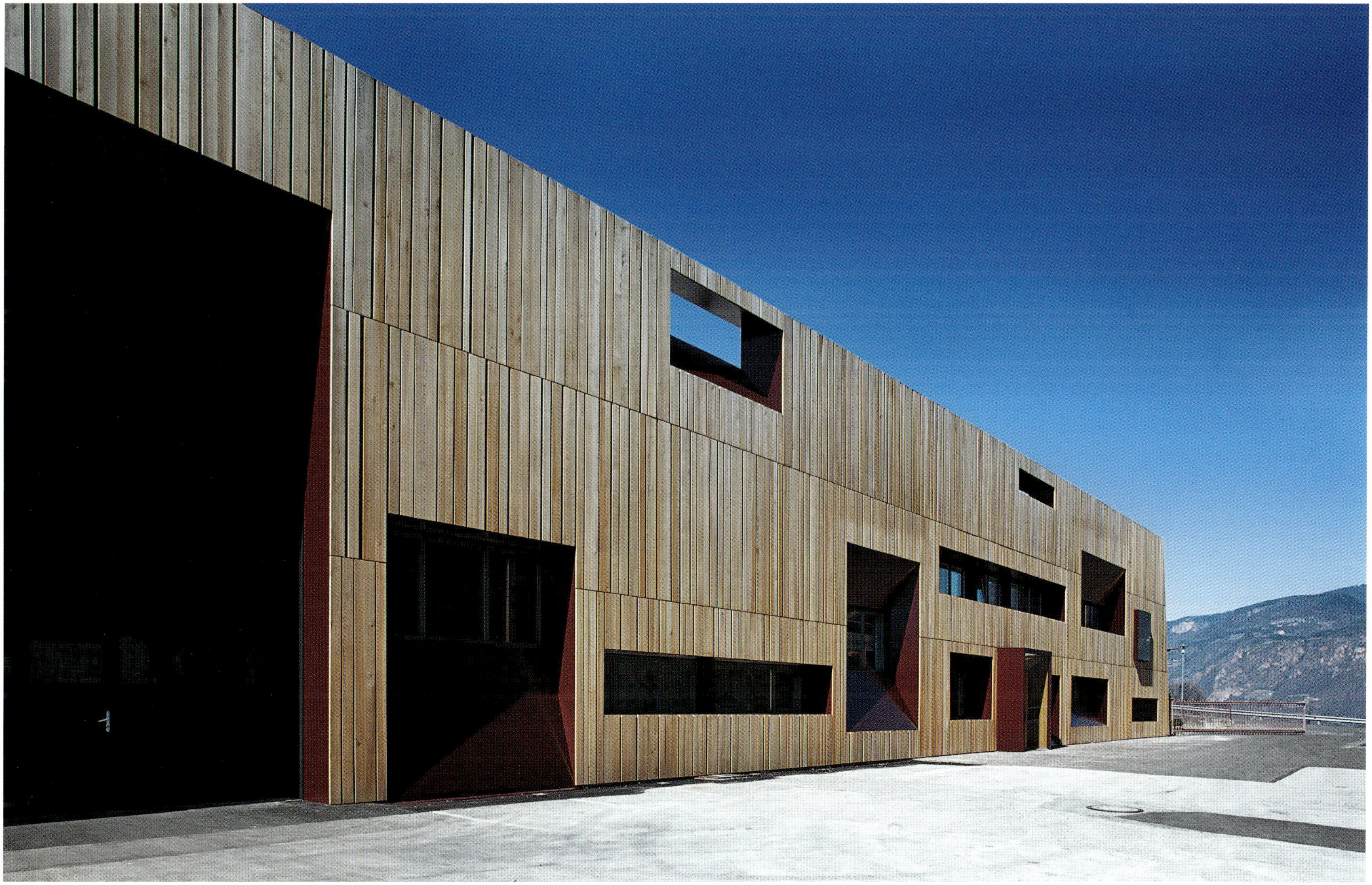

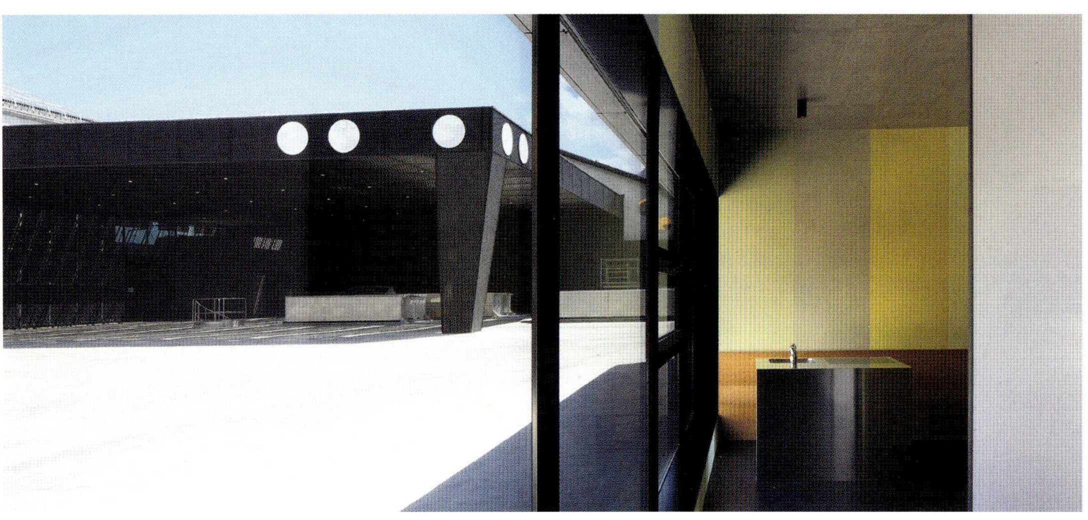

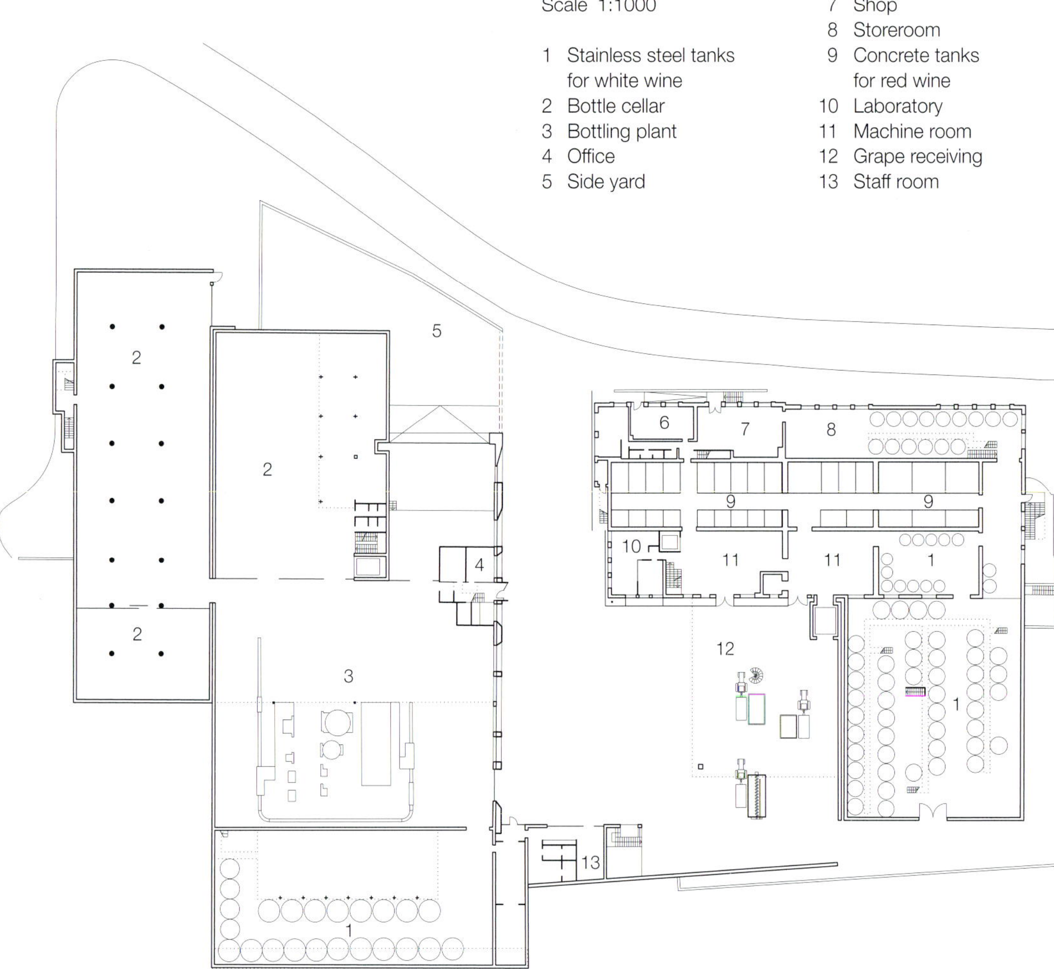

Floor plan
Scale 1:1000

1 Stainless steel tanks for white wine
2 Bottle cellar
3 Bottling plant
4 Office
5 Side yard
6 Tasting area
7 Shop
8 Storeroom
9 Concrete tanks for red wine
10 Laboratory
11 Machine room
12 Grape receiving
13 Staff room

installed in the newly created connecting space. The shell becomes a ribbon, jumping forward and back and ending over the delivery bay in a broadly cantilevered, protective roof. This offers constant shelter to all operations taking place below. The underside of the roof is covered with sheets of mesh metal. Photovoltaic elements, alternated with glazed skylights, form the upper roof covering. These various materials project interesting light effects on to the ground, allowing the building itself to become a significant light source at night. Stainless-steel discs, polished like a mirror, are set at intervals into the entire facade area. Designed by the Munich artist Philipp Messner, they provide an arresting contrast to the building envelope.

The photovoltaic cells on the roof of the receiving area produce 175,000 kWh of power a year to supply 30 per cent of the entire winery's requirements. Solar panels and a heat recovery system from solar energy provide 70 per cent of the hot water needed. The electricity generated by photovoltaic technology can, for example, be used to regulate the temperature in the tanks and storage areas. At the same time, the hot water produced by solar energy and heat recovery systems is needed to sterilize the rinsers and fillers in the bottling line and to clean the cellar's tanks.

The staff room lies in the southern part of the building, next to the receiving area. This is the heart of the estate. The reinforced concrete ceiling was left exposed, while the floor was painted black. The walls are painted in broad, vertical blocks of pastel colours. Simple oak benches line the walls, situated behind sturdy tables with crossed steel legs. A cooker and sink are integrated into a free-standing stainless steel island. Warm and peaceful, this room with its floor-to-ceiling windows directs attention to the courtyard beyond. After work or during their breaks, employees can cook here or just get together.

The theme of sustainability, central to the entire concept, carries through to the integrated vineyards. The average age of the vines is 30 years. The grapes form the basis of four wine collections. Classic is the name of the upmarket standard range. Praedium (Latin for "estate") is a collection of wines grown on single vineyard sites near historic wineries and wine farms. The premium range, featuring wines from Colterenzio's best vineyards, is called Cornell. Luis Raifer's favourite wine, Char-

donnay Formigar, is one of them – a strong but elegant, Burgundy-style wine with well-integrated woody notes. Moscato Rosa Rosatum is also noteworthy – like Amarone, it is made from 50 per cent dried grapes. Its name hints at its intense aroma. The private estate Lafóa produces a Sauvignon Blanc and a Cabernet Sauvignon. They represent Colterenzio's highest-quality wines and are produced entirely from grapes grown in vineyards on a mountain slope between Cornaiano and Colterenzio. The Sauvignon Blanc Lafóa, half of it aged in oak, has a gooseberry nose and, when young, is still somewhat frisky. Its racy acidity mellows after just a few years of bottle ageing to harmonize with the fruit and woody notes – a complex wine with ageing potential, which, despite its individuality, is reminiscent of high-quality white Bordeaux wines. The two top ranges, Cornell and Lafóa, represent about 10 per cent of the winery's production. The other 90 per cent receives just as much attention, however, as a constant high quality is the declared aim of the cooperative.
The international wine media have honoured Colterenzio's work with diverse awards and excellent reviews, for example for the Lagrein Riserva Mantsch 2007 and the Sauvignon Blanc Lafóa 2009.
Also newly redesigned by bergmeisterwolf architects, the tasting room in the old building over the wine shop features a stunning view of the vineyards. The people who tend the vines form the cornerstone of the winery. Social responsibility was a vital part of the plan from the beginning, and it has paid off in the winery's good staff retention and long-term supplier relationships. These factors, ultimately, are factors contributing to the continued high quality of the grapes.

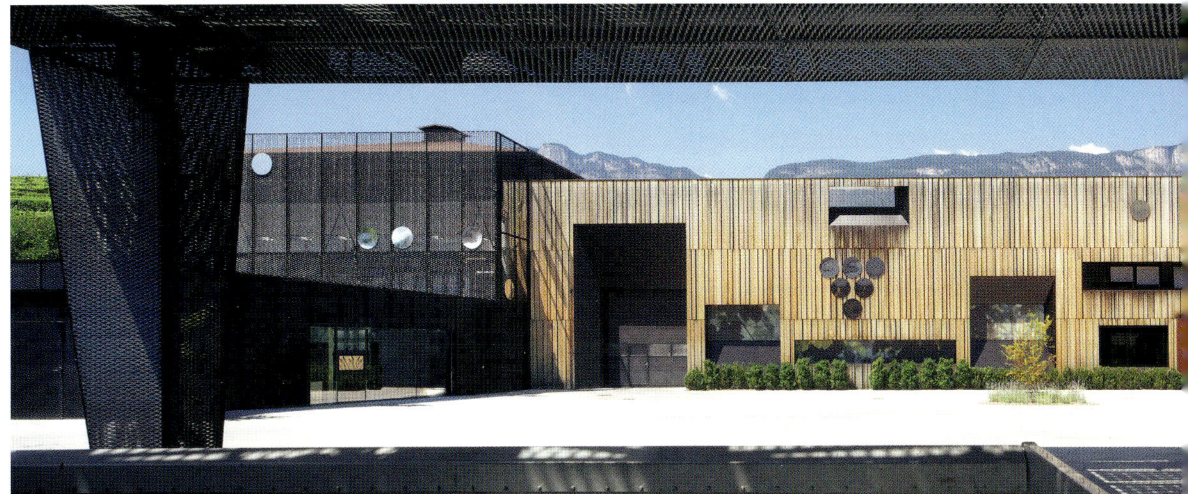

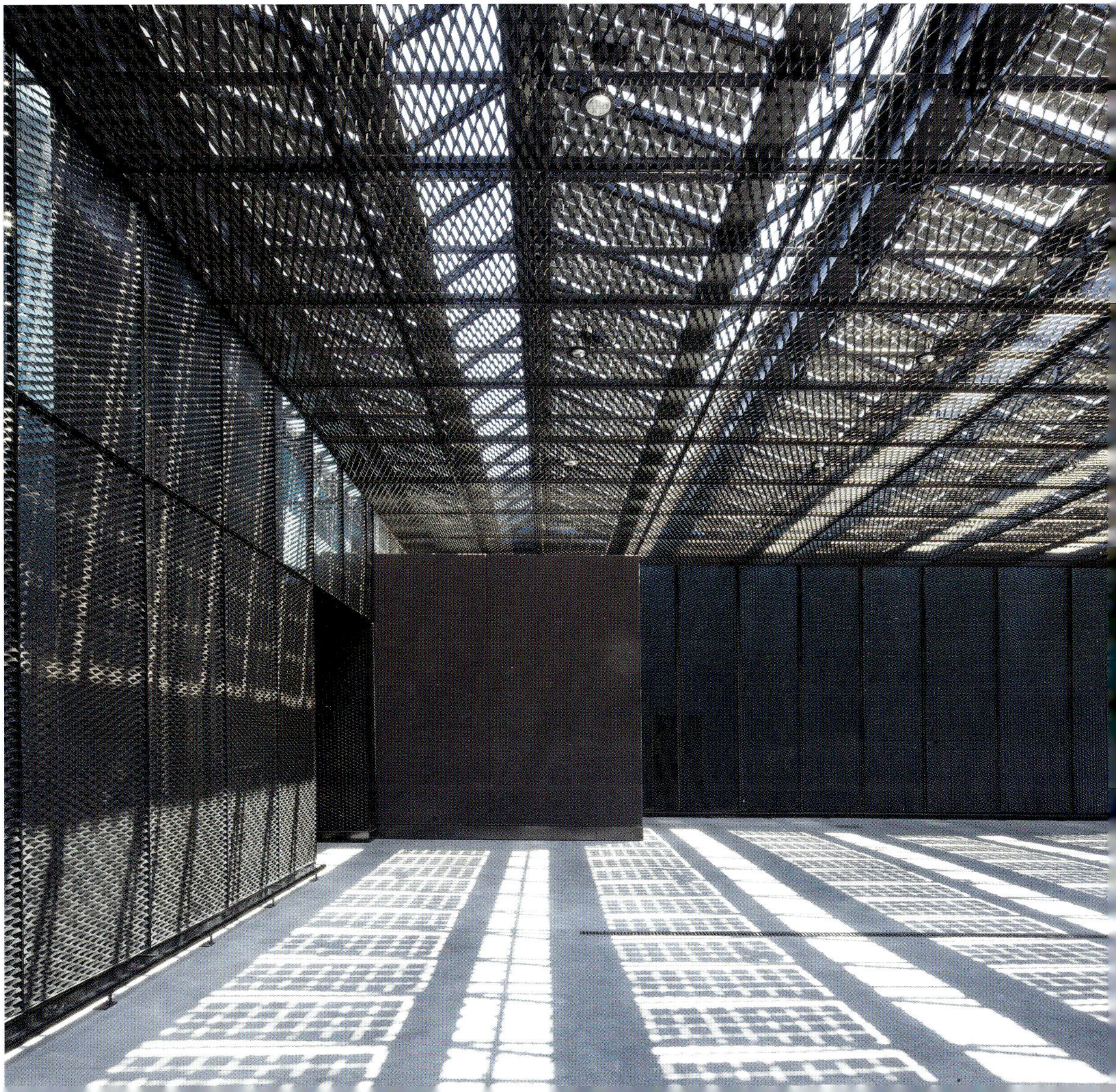

Weingut Leo Hillinger in Jois, Austria

Architects: gerner°gerner plus, Mariahilfer Str. 101/3/49, 1060 Vienna, www.gernergernerplus.com

Team: Klaus Rösel, Matthias Raiger, San Hwan Lu, Eduard Begusch

Site area: 4,700 m^2

Gross floor area: 2,000 m^2

Start of design phase: 2001

Completion: 2004

Region: Burgenland

Contact: Hill 1, 7093 Jois
www.leo-hillinger.com

Oenologist: Edgar Brutler

Price range: €6–€35

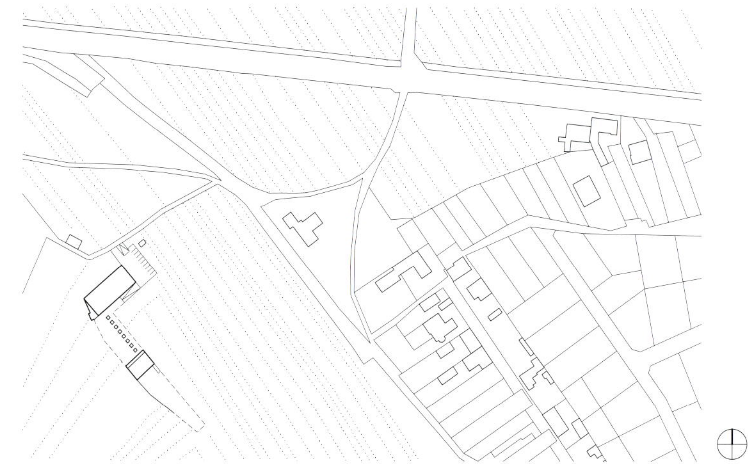

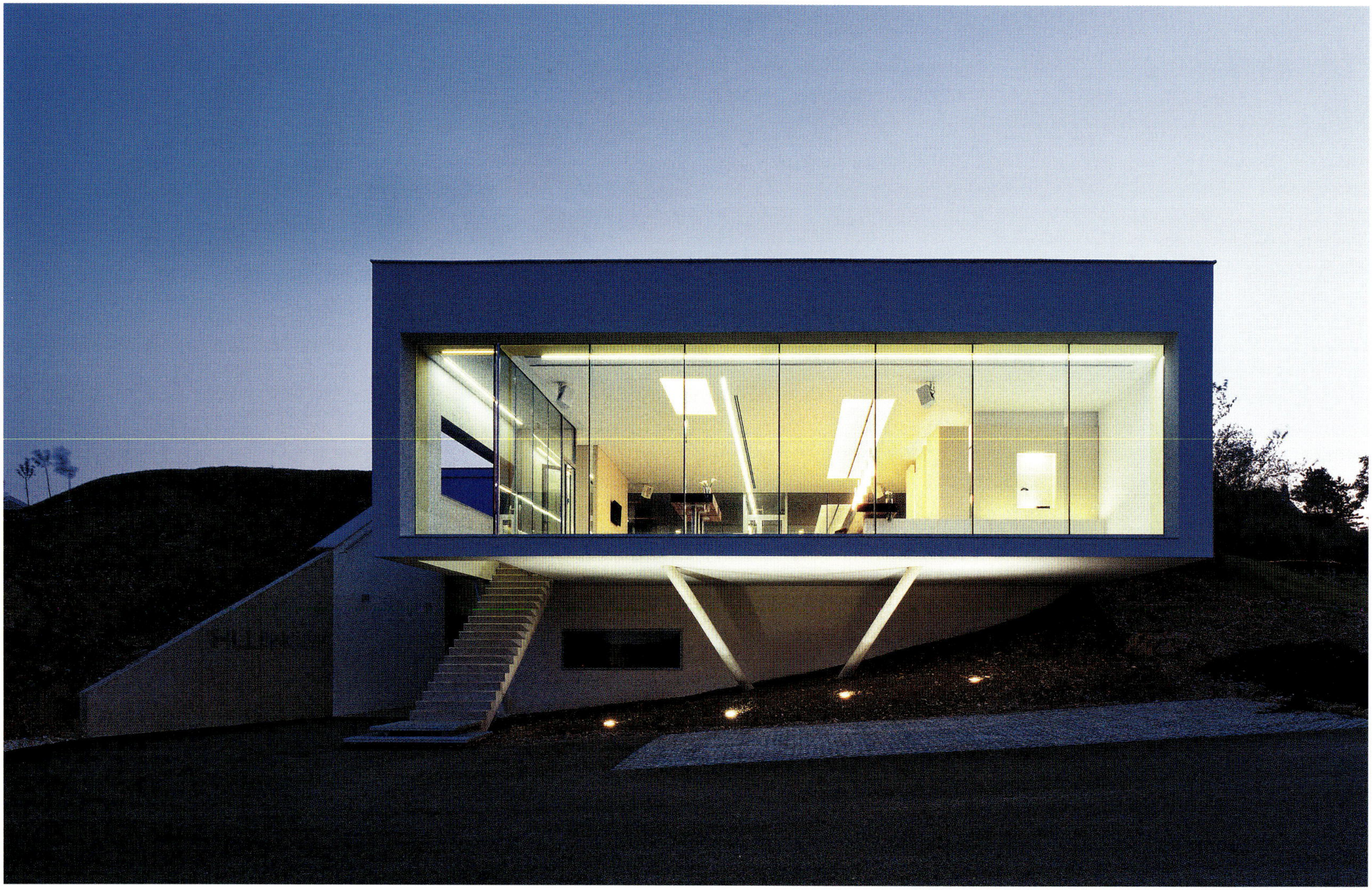

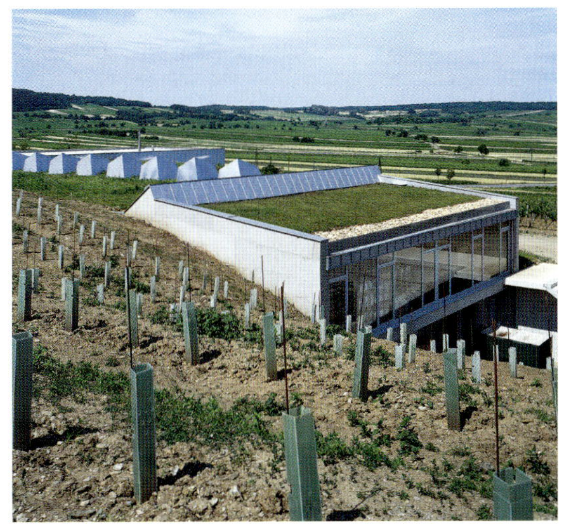

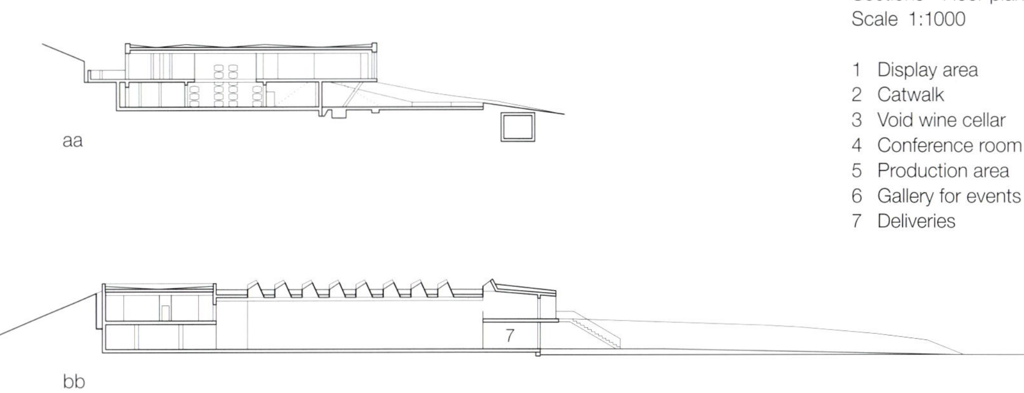

Site plan
Scale 1:5000
Sections • Floor plan
Scale 1:1000

1 Display area
2 Catwalk
3 Void wine cellar
4 Conference room
5 Production area
6 Gallery for events
7 Deliveries

On the outskirts of Jois, a vineyard town on Austria's Lake Neusiedl, a futuristic building captures the attention of passing motorists. Nobody would guess it was a wine estate. The name Hillinger blazes out from a large sign. The small "Leo", placed vertically in front of it, is only noticeable upon closer inspection. As if both were created together, the building and the writing are a perfect fit: sober, modern, straightforward, and yet just a bit extroverted – come to think of it, a little like owner and vintner Hillinger himself. Growing up in his home town of Jois, Hillinger took over the small family business in 1990 when he was just 23.
At that time, the vineyard area was only one hectare, which his father, a wine dealer, cultivated alongside his day job. Hillinger had already completed a viticulture and oenology course as well as several internships abroad, and had gained practical experience in California, South Africa, Australia and New Zealand. Back in Jois, he focused consistently on quality, acquired surrounding vineyards, and rapidly expanded his wine estate. When the village became too small for the growing winery in its midst, a new start "out in the green fields" was unavoidable. The question of where was never an issue for Hillinger, who is far too attached to his Burgenland home and Lake Neusiedl to leave them.
A family home built by the architectural practice gerner°gerner plus caught Hillinger's eye. After an initial meeting, it was clear that something had clicked between the architects and the vintner.
The first step was the drawing-up of a study that Hillinger then presented to the local authorities.
After that, the project was put on ice for six months while they waited for the results of the local elections. Planning permission was finally granted, with the proviso that the project had to blend into its natural surroundings as much as possible.
Building started in early May 2003. The extremely hot summer without a single drop of rain made the completion of the cellar possible in less than four months – just in time for the harvest in September. Temperatures of up to 50 °C heated up the building site; a thick layer of dust settled on the surrounding vines. A total of 24,000 cubic metres of earth were moved. The project was completed in its entirety in May 2004.
The site, located in a nature reserve between the northern shore of Lake Neusiedl and the south-eastern edge of the Leitha Mountains, and featuring a Mediterranean microclimate as well as strong westerly winds, inspired the two architects to design an L-shaped structure, two-thirds of which is sunk into the ground, that blends respectfully into the protected lakeshore area. All that is visible above ground is eight north-facing skylight domes rising out of the fields. From far away, they look like tents in the grass. These obliquely cut structures, resembling sectioned pyramids, provide an optimal source of light for the production and storage areas below, which benefit from the cooler climate underground. Thanks to the direct contact of the building with the earth, the temperature and humidity regulate themselves naturally. The built-in climate control systems need not be switched on, even on hot

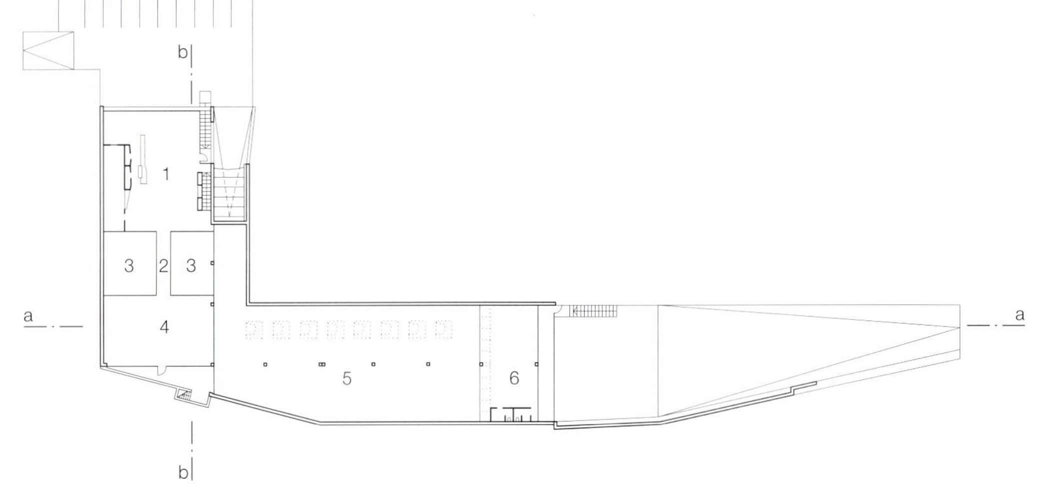

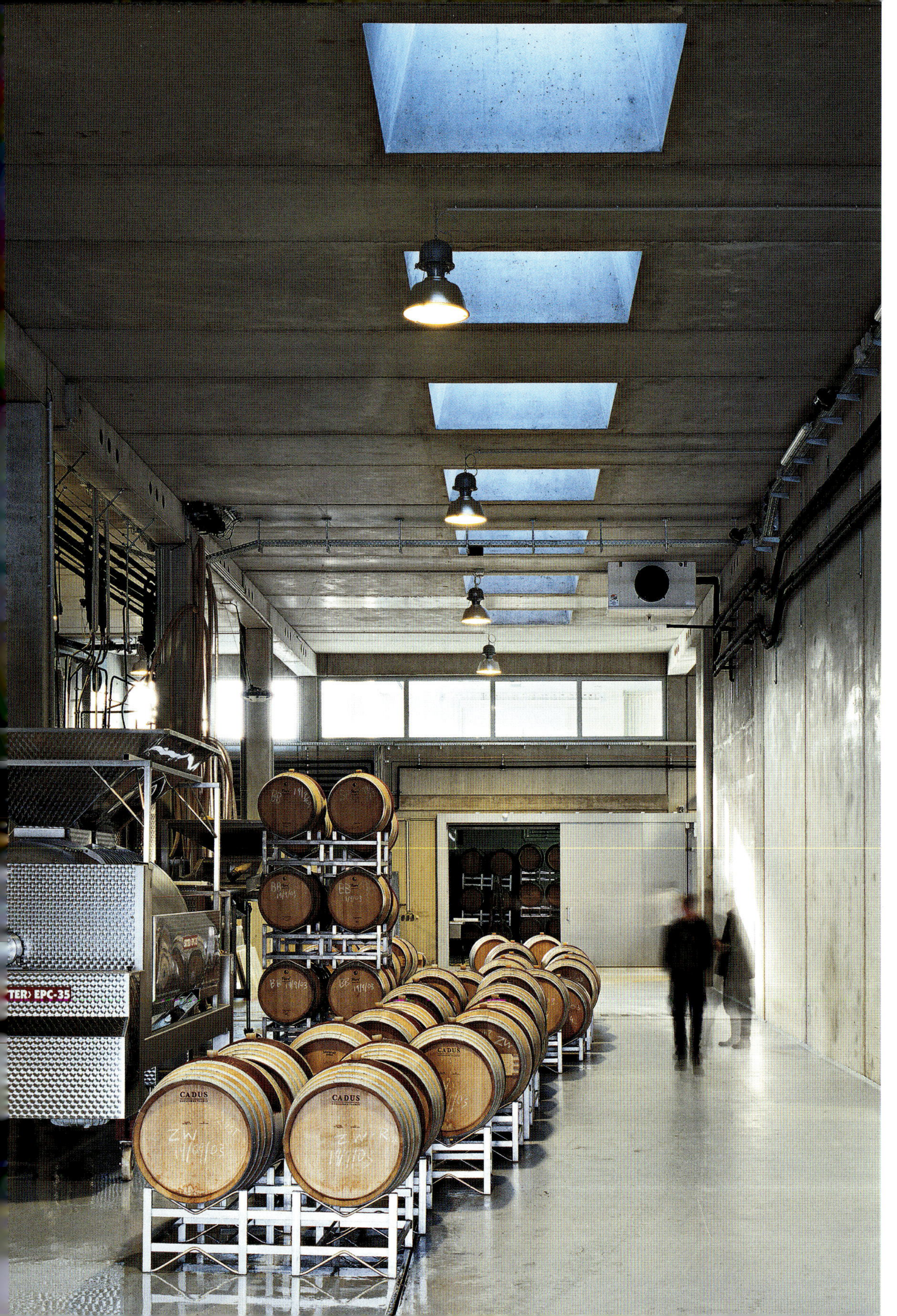

summer days. There is a constant temperature of about 15 °C. The illumination provided by the prefabricated, reinforced concrete skylights gives the interior a hallowed feel.
In contrast to the largely underground wine cellar, the sales, tasting and seminar room juts out of the slope as a box perched on V-shaped spun concrete supports. The entire upper storey can be used and hired for all kinds of events.
The architects themselves designed the dark walnut furniture that brings a sense of nature into the interior; the bar lit from below seems to float over the gleaming epoxy resin floor.
A picture window affords a magnificent view of the surrounding landscape. Illuminated at night, the cube is a distinctive feature of the wine village. There is also a wonderful view of the surrounding vineyards and the lake from the accessible roof. It was just these visual relationships that were particularly important to Hillinger.
Within the building, continuous sightlines create a sense of openness: the vintner can oversee production while his customers can get a glimpse into the art of winemaking. The barrique storage area on the lower floor can be viewed from a concrete catwalk glazed with insulated glass. Nevertheless, Hillinger had to outsource most of the bottle and barrel storage to an external service provider in a neighbouring town; a total of 900 barriques are cellared there. The bottling also takes place externally, in a facility in nearby Mönchhof.
A solid stone table with a monolithic tabletop measuring seven metres in length stands outside the winery building. For Hillinger, the table has become something of a trademark. Two smaller versions of this table stand in shops in nearby Parndorf and in Salzburg, opened in 2005 and 2008, respectively. The tables let the customers know they are visiting a "real" Hillinger shop.
"That was a project where everything worked," says architect Andreas Gerner. "And a team that worked together perfectly." This is thanks partly to the exceptional site management provided by an external office, but also to Hillinger, who, after handing the architects the commission, remained in the background, giving them only one stipulation: "It's got to be fabulous!"
All in all, €6 million were invested, made possible by a 30 per cent EU development grant. The building that emerged created media excitement well

beyond its launch in May 2004, to which 500 guests were invited.

Today Hillinger, together with 40 employees, cultivates 50 hectares of vineyards, of which 30 hectares are located near the town of Rust and 20 near Jois. Depending on the vintage, additional grapes from a further 40 to 50 hectares are purchased from cooperating vintners. And although this makes Hillinger one of the biggest private wine companies in Austria, he still succeeds in producing excellent wines. For him, quality starts in the vineyard: "When the grapes are good, you don't have to do so much in the cellar. After years of experience and lots of experiments, I know that the fruit has to be perfect, and should go into the bottle unchanged." That is his credo.

Hillinger has focused on organic grape cultivation since 2010. Thanks to his untiring work in the vineyards and strict yield reduction, he produces rich, intense wines.

Hillinger's range features a broad palette of wines to suit every taste: the "small HILL" series, young wines for every occasion; the reds and whites carrying the full name HILLINGER to indicate varietal wines; and the multi-award-winning HILL series, which consists of cuvées: HILL 1 for red wine and HILL 2 for white.

Hillinger is not considering further expansion. He would rather concentrate on developing the Leo Hillinger brand. A glimpse into the products being sold alongside the wine in his tasting and shopping lounge indicates how far he has already come in this endeavour. The selection includes chocolates and various jams, fruit brandies and coffee, and even merchandising products. How much longer until he has his own perfume?

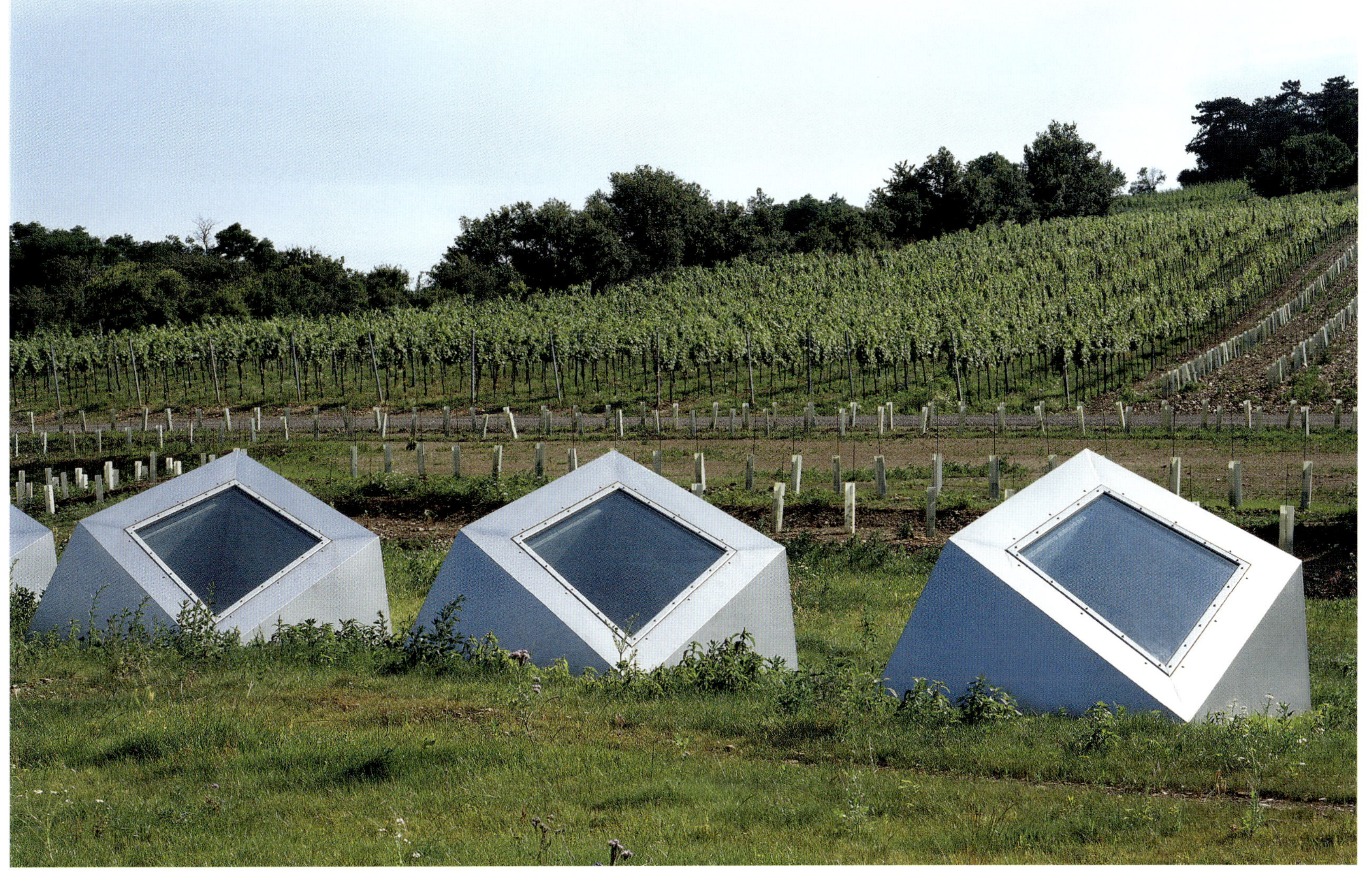

Cantina Tramin in Termeno, Italy

Architect: Werner Tscholl, Mühlweg 11/a, 39021 Morter
www.werner-tscholl.com
Team: Andreas Sagmeister
Site area: 10,468 m²
Gross floor area: 5,514 m² (existing build), 4,300 m² (new build)
Start of design phase: 2007
Completion: 2010
Region: Alto Adige
Contact: Strada del Vino 144, 39040 Termeno
www.cantinatramin.it
Oenologist: Willi Stürz
Price range: €6–€25
●●●

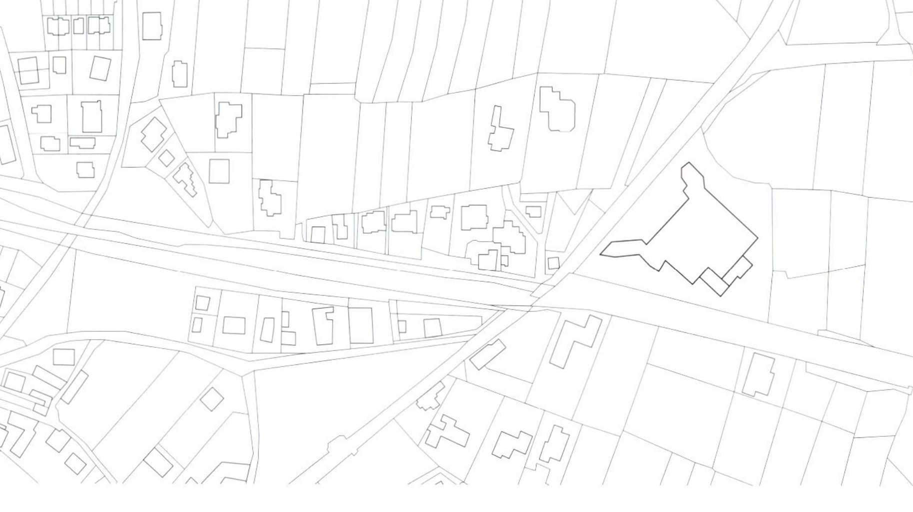

Site plan
Scale 1:5000

Futuristic and yet organic: these are the visitor's first impressions on seeing the two new wings of the Cantina Tramin winery. With a form that recalls the surrounding steep vineyard slopes and mountain crags, the building blends harmoniously into the landscape.

Founded in 1898, Cantina Tramin is one of the oldest winemaking cooperatives in Alto Adige (South Tyrol). The wine farmers in the area often do a combination of fruit and wine farming, which has resulted in small vineyards, some of them under one hectare in size. The 230 hectares belonging to the winery are cultivated by 270 "co-owners". They are the foundation of this strong community, delivering grapes with peak biological maturity for the production of wines of consistently high quality.

It is sometimes difficult to describe the benefits of a cooperative, says cellarmaster Willi Stürz, who was born in Termeno and has been head oenologist at Cantina Tramin for 20 years. But it is just this structure, he explains, that provides the right conditions for the careful development of the wines on these small plots, and for the individual work of their members. Cantina Tramin's philosophy is one of quality and sustainability. It is an aspiration that has paid off, winning the winery's wines regular accolades in respected wine guides.

Alto Adige is white wine country, and the king of its white wines is the Gewürztraminer, which owes its name to Tramin, as the town of Termeno is called in this German-speaking region. The star product of the Cantina Tramin winery is the Gewürztraminer Terminum 2007, the only wine in Italy to receive the highest overall rating in all of the country's wine guides.

Until the early 1970s, Cantina Tramin was located in the picturesque town centre. When the space became too small for the growing facility, the cooperative moved to the equally charming outskirts with an unencumbered view of the Adige Valley and its vineyards.

The main building is still at the heart of the structure. In 2006, the management decided to expand the existing ensemble, consisting of production halls, wine storage areas and a visitor centre. So they tendered a competition for a new concept, and were ultimately won over by the submission by Werner Tscholl.

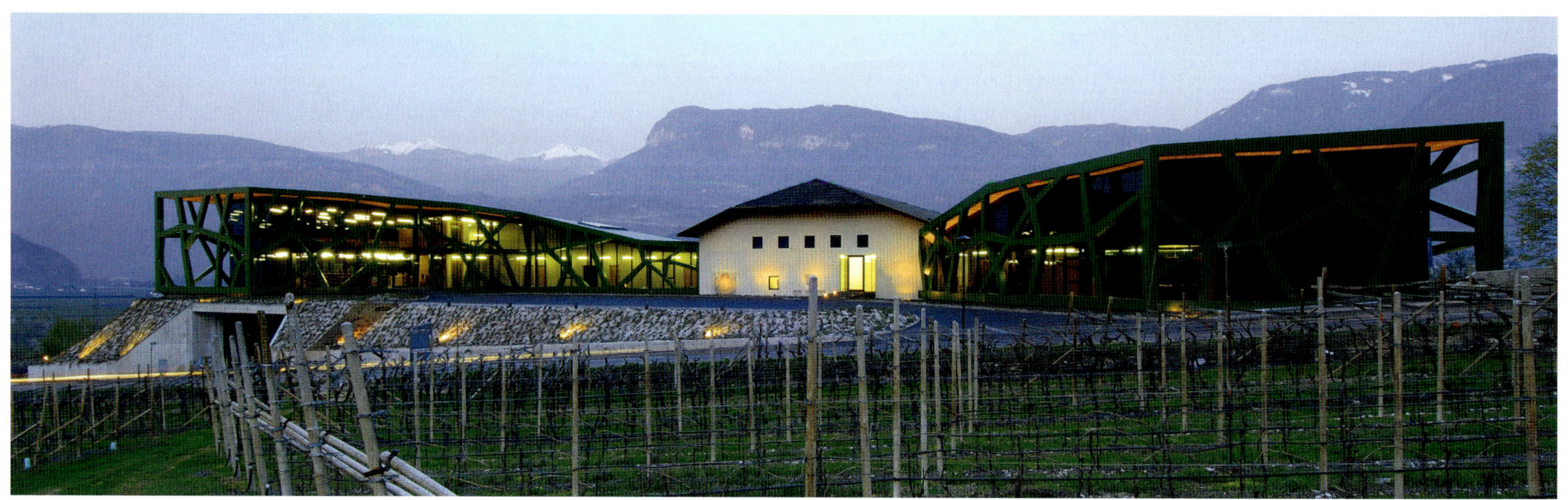

Tscholl found himself inspired by the landscape and the vines. "A purely emotional split-second decision," he says. His plan did not require the uprooting of a single vine. During the year-long planning phase and the construction of the building, Tscholl was in constant communication with Cantina Tramin president Leo Tiefenthaler, executive director Stephan Dezini, sales director Wolfgang Klotz and cellarmaster Stürz.

First, the men drew up a list of the winery's required specifications, a process in which every last detail was discussed. Even selecting which shade of green to use for the steel structure surrounding the new buildings took an entire year. From 50 colours, they chose the one that blends perfectly into the landscape.

Keeping the winery operations and the streams of visitors separate was the primary consideration. For each of these functions, a separate level was created. The existing level continues to provide delivery access to the vintners, the entrance and exit for goods, and anything else to do with the vital workings of the winery's operations, as well as the employee car park.

Guest access is located on the newly created level above, so that visitors can be welcomed separately from the facility's operations. The existing winery building serves as the reception area; the two new wings, which house the wine shop and the tasting room, are situated to the left and right of the old main building. They greet visitors like two open arms.

It was important to the project participants to retain the sweeping, unspoiled view of the valley. The green steel web-like structure surrounds the new spaces like a climbing vine, just the association that was intended. The basic idea for the project was a vine that grows out of the ground of the delivery area and then climbs up to envelop the building, giving rise to a sculptural structure that opens itself out to visitors and gives the whole ensemble a new face. The complex thus functions as a landmark for visitors and passers-by, and could become a welcoming feature of Termeno itself. The visitor reception is located in the newly configured winery building, which serves as a symbol of the winemaking tradition and thus constitutes the heart of the complex.

The vine-inspired, stylized steel framework is not only a decorative element. The placement of the

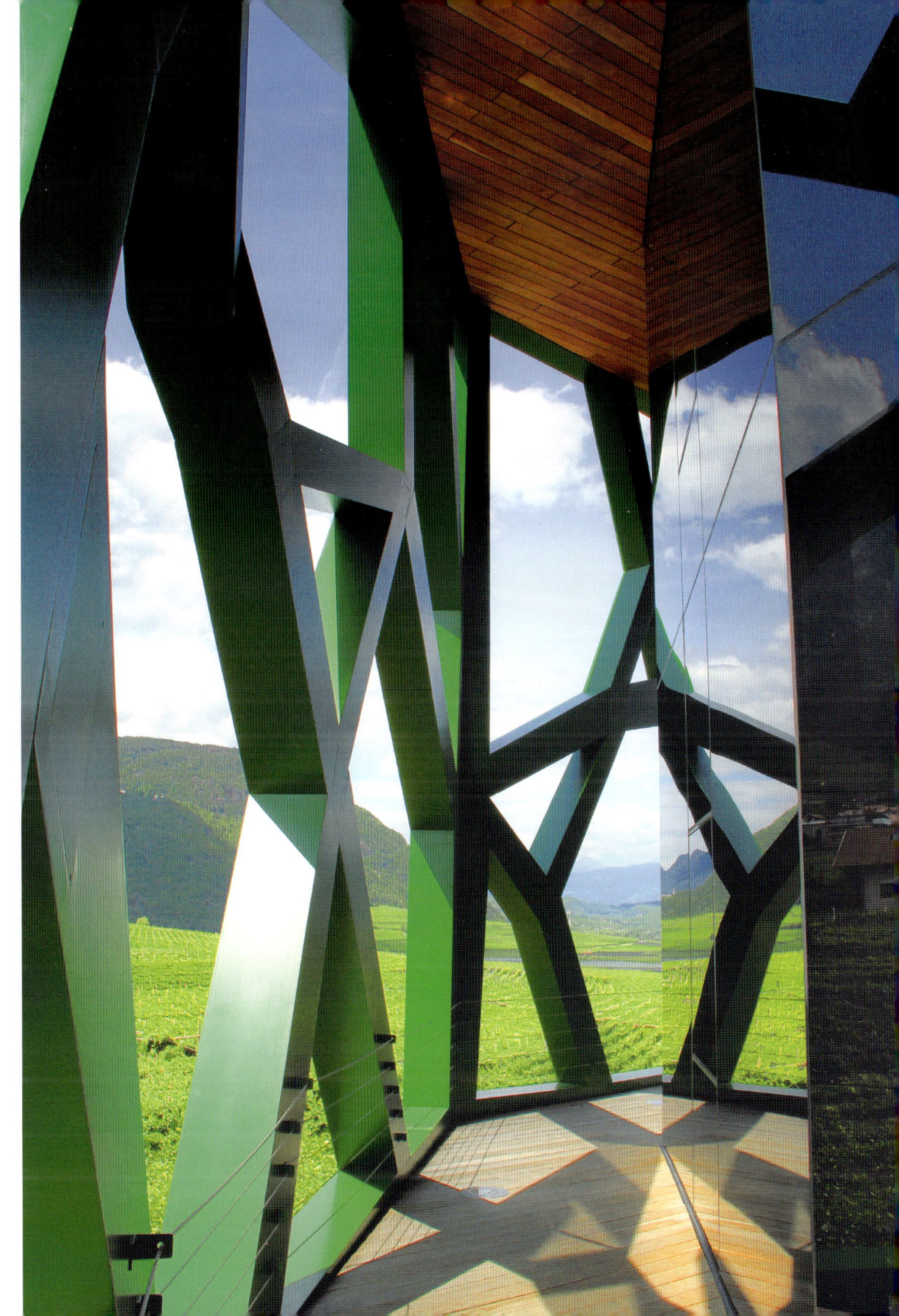

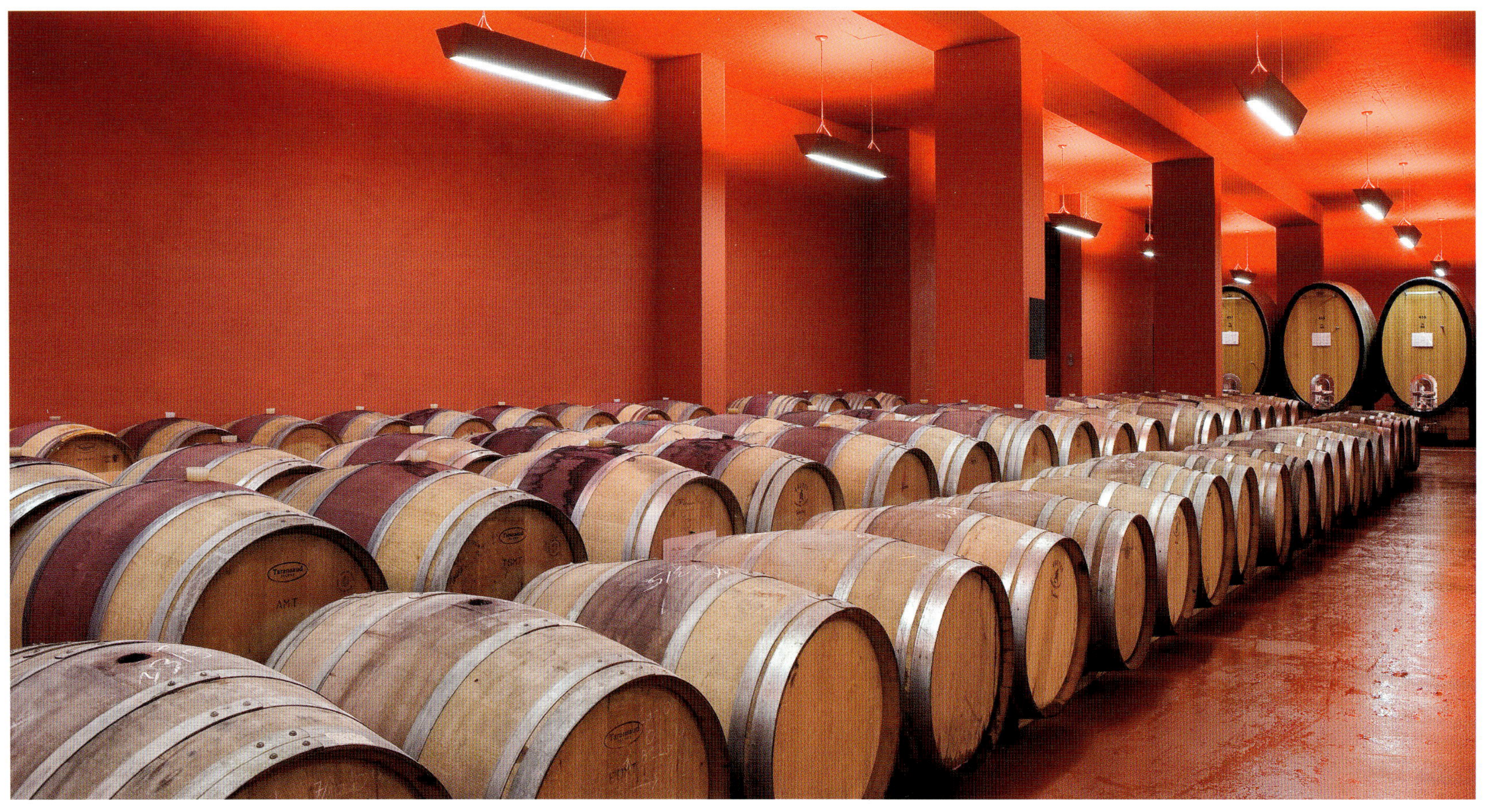

struts was precisely engineered to provide optimal shading to the glass facade behind. The composition and tint of the glass further reduces the amount of heat entering the building. A clever circulation system, fed with 12 °C water from the building's own well, ensures sufficient cooling of production areas.

The primary building materials used in the interior are concrete and wood. The purist elements of polished concrete create an interesting contrast to the oak furnishings, which allude to winemaking and oak barrels.

Along with the red and white varietals – the classic range named after the respective grape variety, and the special range after the location – Cantina Tramin also offers "special signature cuvées". These wines, bearing names taken from the local dialect – Stoan (stone) and Loam (clay or loam) – are particularly noteworthy, as they create a strong link to the soil and to tradition. The winery's best-known wine is of course the Gewürztraminer. This grape variety constitutes 21 per cent of its production and takes up almost half of its vineyard area. Conditions in Alto Adige are ideal for the variety. The plots lie at an altitude of between 250 and 850 metres. The difference between daytime and nighttime temperatures is considerable, a vitally important factor for the development of aroma in the grapes. The mountain range to the north protects the area from frost, the intense sunlight during the day ensures ripeness, and the warm, dry Ora wind coming up from Lake Garda prevents mould and mildew.

The captivating nose of the delicate Nussbaumer Gewürztraminer, with notes of rose and smoked ham, is the star wine of the Cantina. The wines from vintage 2000 prove its ageing potential, featuring a buttery palate with ripe yellow plum and straw aromas, yet fresh taste. The Urban Lagrein 2009, soon to come on the market, also deserves further attention. The wine from this red, indigenous grape grown on old vines is still a bit frisky, with gutsy tannins. Its rich bouquet of dark berries, plums, rummy fruit and kirsch schnapps hints at a promising development.

The "organic architecture" theme continues beneath the main building, where we find the dark-red barrel cellar with its walls lined with unfired clay. The connection to the red wine slumbering in the wooden barrels is evident. The clay keeps the humidity at the right level.

The wines of Cantina Tramin are aged in steel, concrete and wood. There is also a section in which wine is aged in small barrels according to area, so that the specific virtues of individual locations can be drawn out.

A large skylight illuminates part of the cellar. A special lighting system collects daylight and delivers it by way of mirrors into the room to create pleasant working conditions by almost natural light. Along with the new building, the winery's entire corporate identity got a makeover. The Milanese agency Robilant Associati redesigned Cantina

Tramin's homepage, labels and logo. The five lines that seem to emerge from the mist on the distinctive logo are meant to spark the imagination: Is this a play on the five senses? Do the lines symbolize vines? The idea was to focus on the creativity and integrity that underpin the philosophy of the cooperative.

Upon completion of the project in June 2010, the Cantina's co-owners, 300 of their customers, and of course fellow vintners from the region were invited to celebrate. During the building phase in particular, some critics viewed the building unfavourably. The reaction at the launch ranged from absolute enthusiasm to complete rejection. In the meantime, though, even dyed-in-the-wool critics have come round somewhat and now show grudging respect and admiration for the project.

From the beginning, Tscholl had had such a clear idea of the design that one could place his first sketch over a picture of the finished building without seeing any great difference.

In retrospect, the clients and the architect would do everything the same way again. And no wonder: the building is the product of a constant, intense exchange of ideas marked by a mutual striving for perfection.

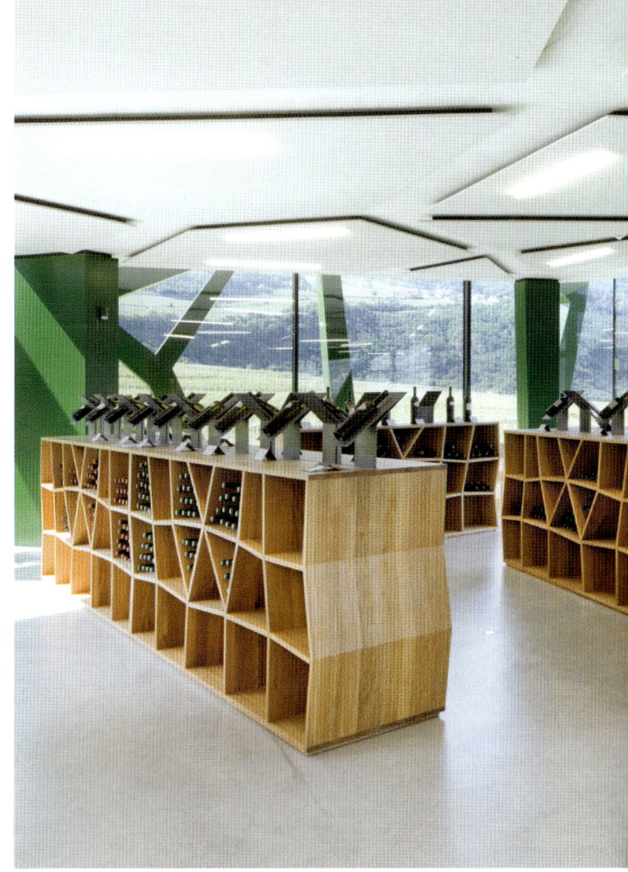

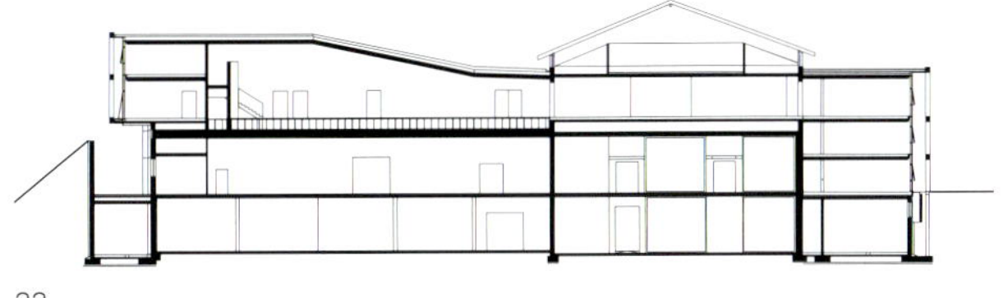

Section • Floor plans
Scale 1:1000

1 Grape weighing area
2 Staff car park
3 White wine fermentation
4 Staff room
5 Visitor car park
6 Sales and tasting area
7 Storeroom
8 Conference room
9 Staff entrance
10 Void
11 Administration

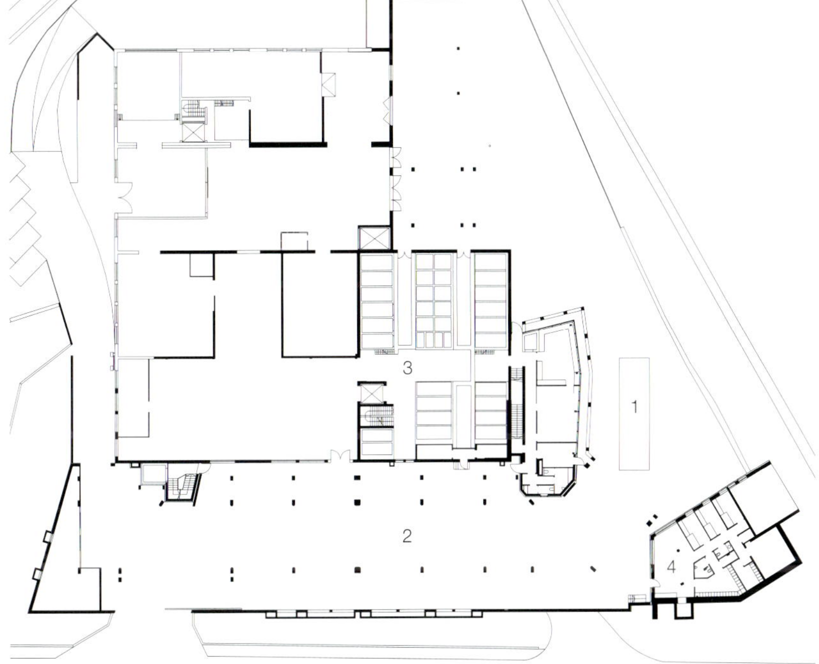

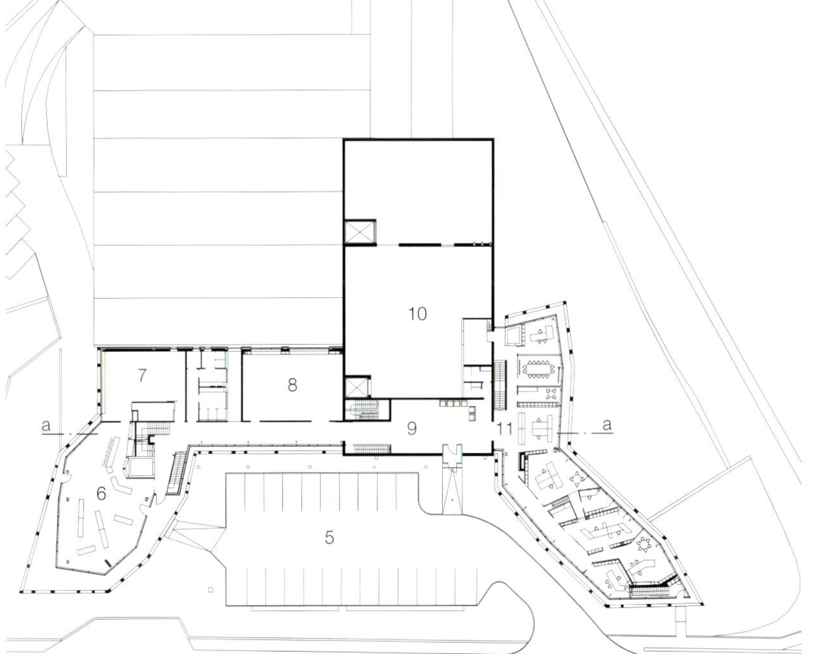

Weingut Heid in Fellbach, Germany

Architect: Christine Remensperger, Pfizerstr. 8, 70184 Stuttgart, www.christineremensperger.de

Team: Torsten Belli, Johannes Michel

Site area: 1,060 m^2

Gross floor area: 800 m^2

Start of design phase: 2000 (wine shop), 2007 (wine estate)

Completion: 2001 (wine shop), 2009 (wine estate)

Region: Württemberg

Contact: Cannstatter Str. 13/2, 70734 Fellbach www.weingut-heid.de

Oenologist: Markus Heid

Price range: €5.50–€23

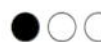

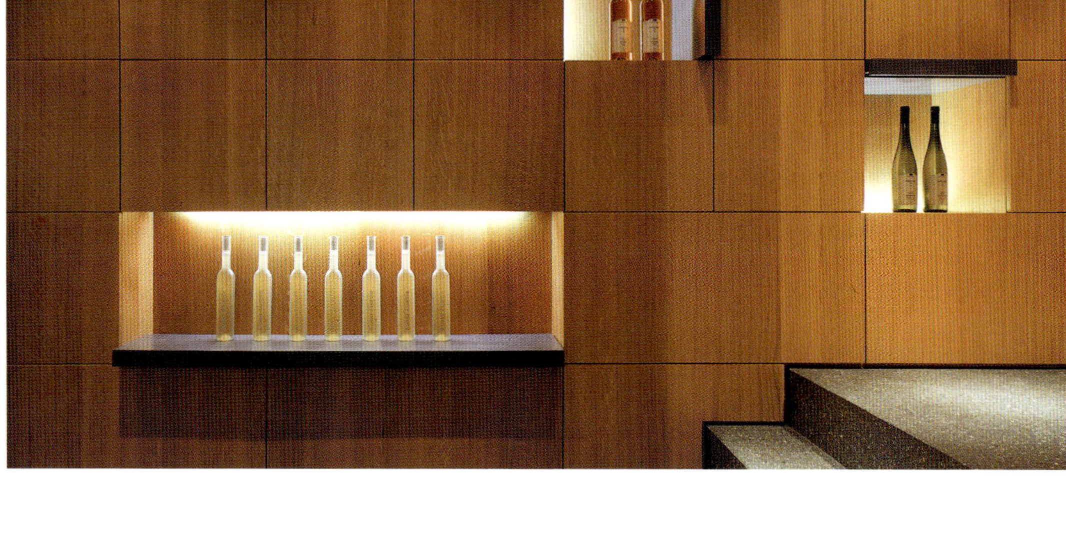

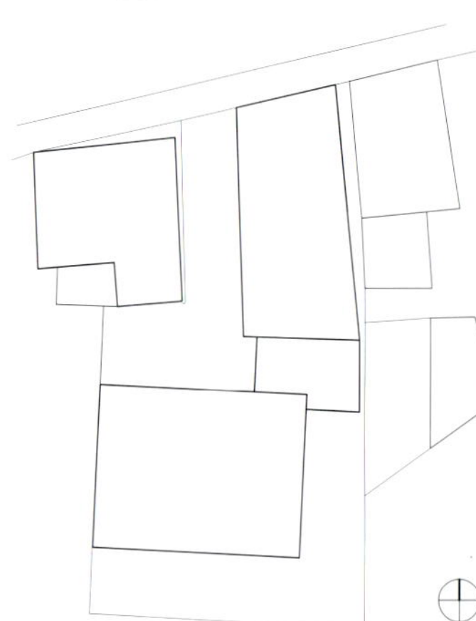

Markus Heid's tradition-rich family business lies right at the heart of Fellbach, next to the town hall. To accommodate changing production conditions and processes, Heid decided to increase his vineyard area from its previous size of four hectares and expand the wine estate. Initially, however, the town-centre location offered no possibilities for expansion. Heid's first thought was to move the entire estate to the outskirts of Fellbach; the town's administration, however, was quite interested in keeping the winery in the town centre, and so was very cooperative in consultations. During talks, it became apparent that the wine estate was in the middle of an area slated for redevelopment in 2007, and the rehabilitation, if not demolition, of the old neighbouring buildings was already planned. On the garden side of the building, a new housing estate was going to be built, which would provide access to the wine estate and consequently make construction a logistical possibility. This made it feasible to realize the building project without interrupting production. Given these developments, Heid decided to remain in town and extend the existing facility.

Another reason to remain in Fellbach was the fact that the ground floor and vaulted cellar in the old timber-framed house had just been converted to a tasting room and shop in 2001. The interior walls had all been lined with cupboard and shelf elements to display the small but exquisite selection of house wines. Evoking the old oak barrels in which wine is aged, oiled oak was used for the cupboards and other furniture. In designing this wine shop, Christine Remensperger had transformed the Heid philosophy into architecture – and did it once more when she was commissioned with the renovation of the entire wine estate. Since their first project together, she and Heid had enjoyed a friendly relationship, a factor that made their second project go all the more smoothly.

The task was to renovate or expand all the company spaces on the ground and lower floors of the family home, which dates from the 1980s, as well as its various extensions and its courtyard area. Improving the handling of the production processes, installing a freight lift, extending the bottle and tank areas, and creating a new design for the courtyard were all identified as important goals. A further challenge lay in connecting the new structure to the existing building within the limited space available, and within the time constraints determined by the surrounding redevelopment of the area. During close consultations from November 2007 to April 2008, the vintner and the architect came up with detailed plans for the renovation.

Heid, who has always been more interested in creating something timeless than in following trends, took over the family business in the mid-1990s. He is absolutely convinced that the quality of wine is determined in the vineyard, and that the cellar plays a subordinate role. In his view, the new cellar needed to combine aesthetics with practicality. To link the new building to the old one, Heid and Remensperger adopted and extended design elements previously used in the shop. These included a

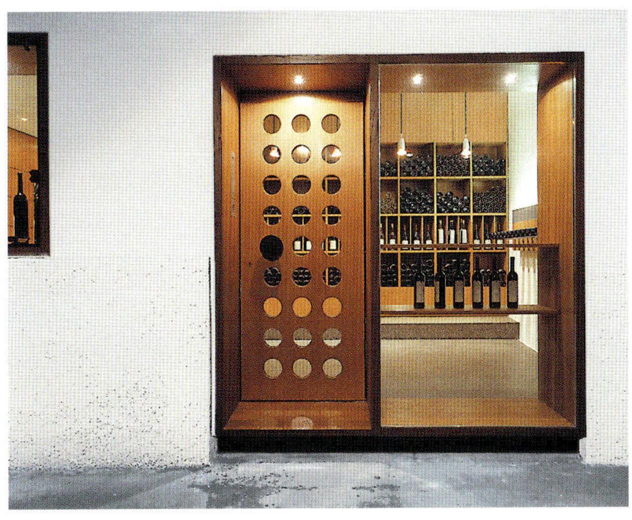

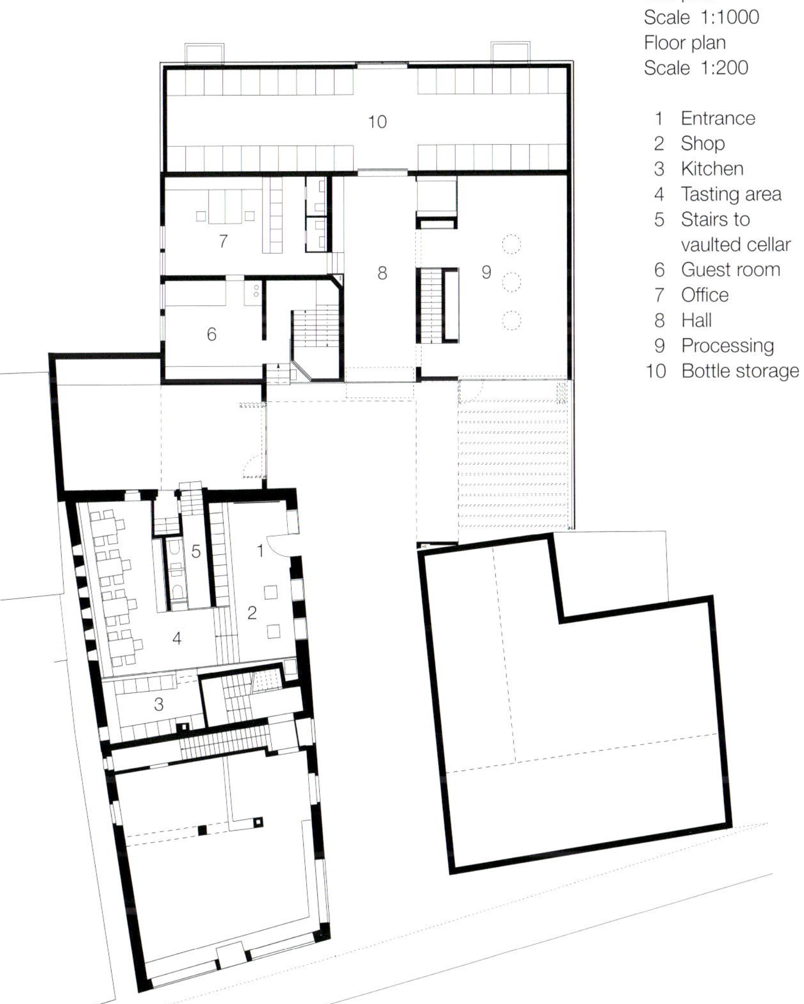

Site plan
Scale 1:1000
Floor plan
Scale 1:200

1 Entrance
2 Shop
3 Kitchen
4 Tasting area
5 Stairs to vaulted cellar
6 Guest room
7 Office
8 Hall
9 Processing
10 Bottle storage

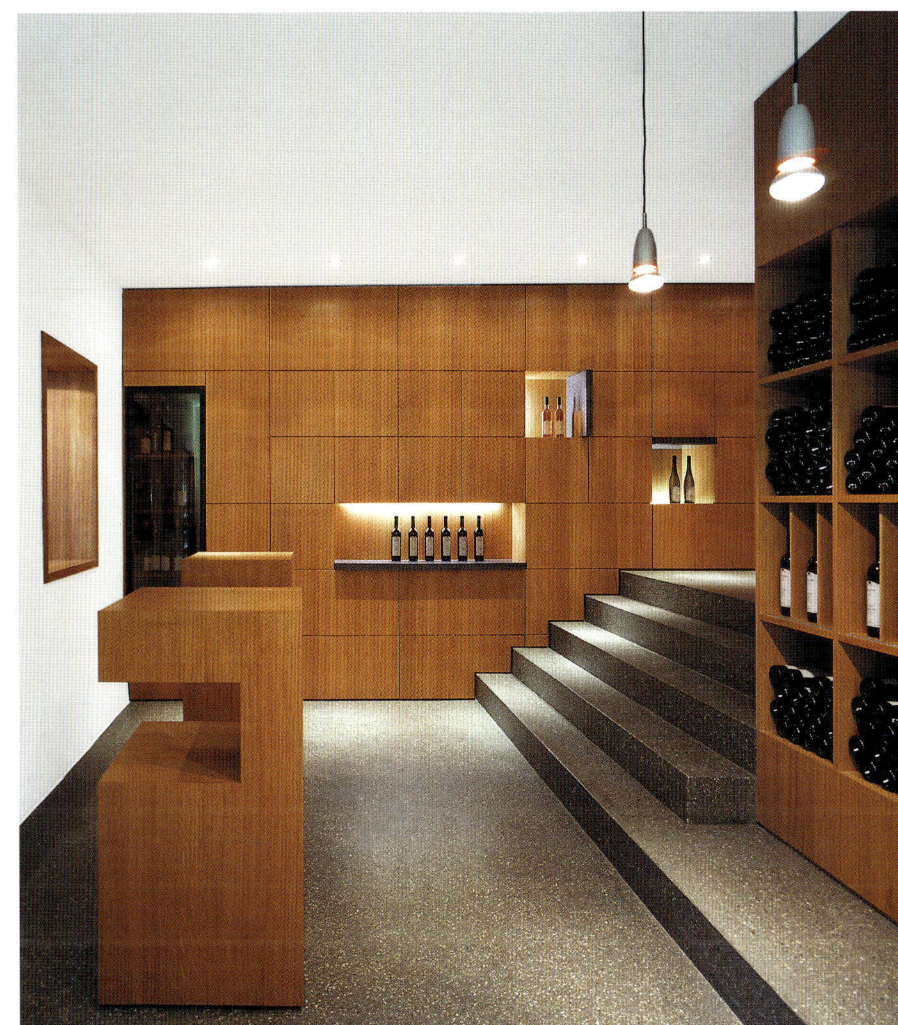

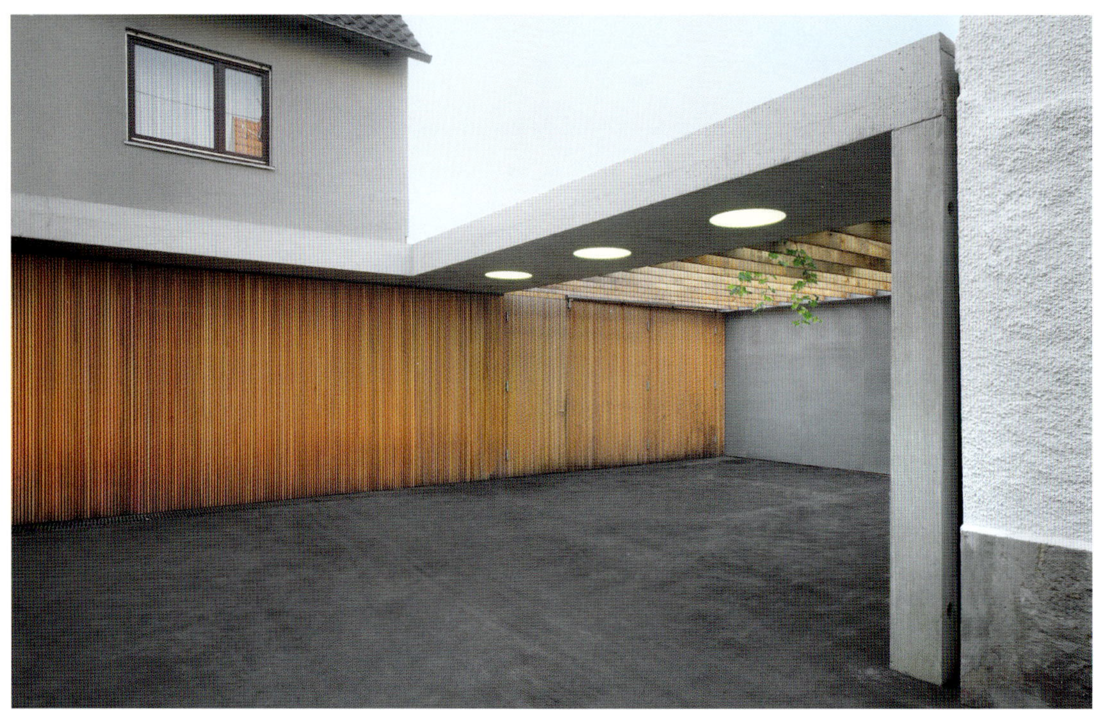

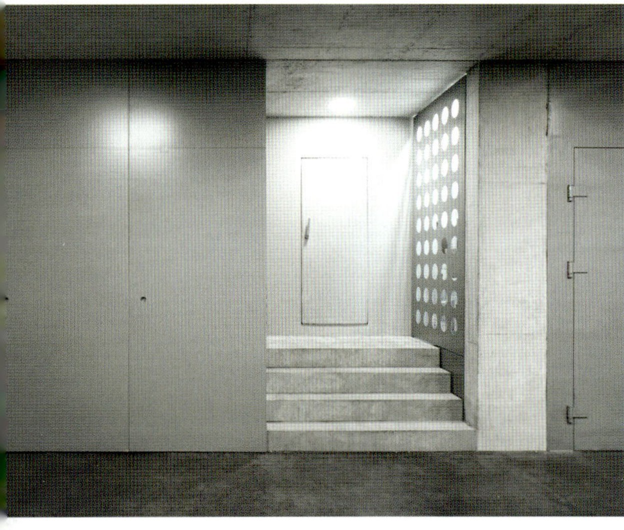

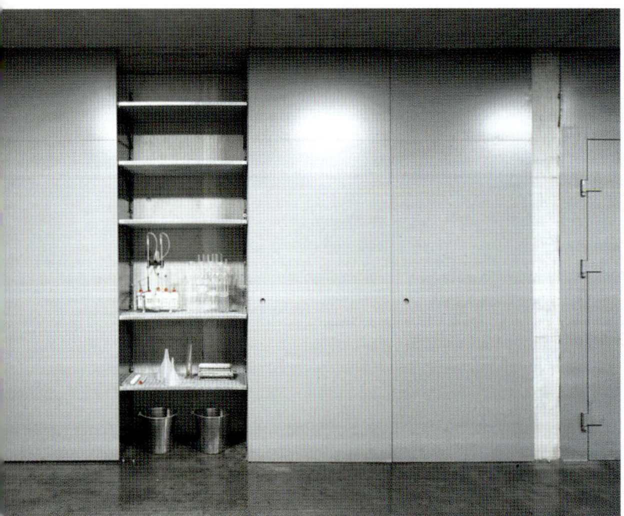

sparing use of materials. In the new build, too, the design concept was built on a few select, well-placed measures.

Remensperger connected the new building to the existing structure by adding a sizeable awning of reinforced concrete, which also provided the framework for a wooden pergola. The roofing created a new space for winemaking and for the traditional wine festivals. Sanding down the existing concrete surfaces made them look identical to the new ones. Additionally, all the walls and gate and door areas that had been created with various designs over the years, received the same cladding of narrow squared-timber strips. For these, the designer chose the same material that gives red wine its finishing touches during barrique ageing, and which had already been used in the shop for the wall cupboards and furniture: oak.

In keeping with practical considerations, the two floors of workrooms are laid out at angles around the existing house. An impressive reception area on the ground floor welcomes visitors. Space considerations necessitated a multifunctional design of the reception area and parts of the cellar. The crushers stand here during the harvest, followed shortly thereafter by the fermentation tanks. In early summer, during the bottling phase, the palettes of empty bottles and the bottling line are kept here. A conscious decision was made not to build a shutter gate leading to the courtyard, but instead to install a seven-pane folding door. A door integrated into a shutter gate would have meant a cumbersome obstacle for hand trucks. The folding door offers plane access as well as a variable opening.

The freight lift was placed centrally to allow for rapid loading and unloading. The high-tech areas on the lower floor were combined into "laboratories", each centrally located for the production sequence. A flexible, multi-sectioned sliding wall made of floor-to-ceiling steel plates closes off the laboratories or the access to the stairs and unites the space into a creative whole. All of the wiring leading in and out of the facility is integrated into one channel running underneath the cellar ceiling. "Every centimetre was taken into consideration to make the best use of the limited space available," says Remensperger.

The sphere, a motif inspired by the bottom of a wine bottle, represents a key design element in Remensperger's concept. The circular form is first featured at the entrance to the shop, and returns again by the staircase to the cellar. Circular holes in the wall give visitors a glimpse into the glass presentation cases, where numerous medals and certificates for Heid's award-winning wines are on view.

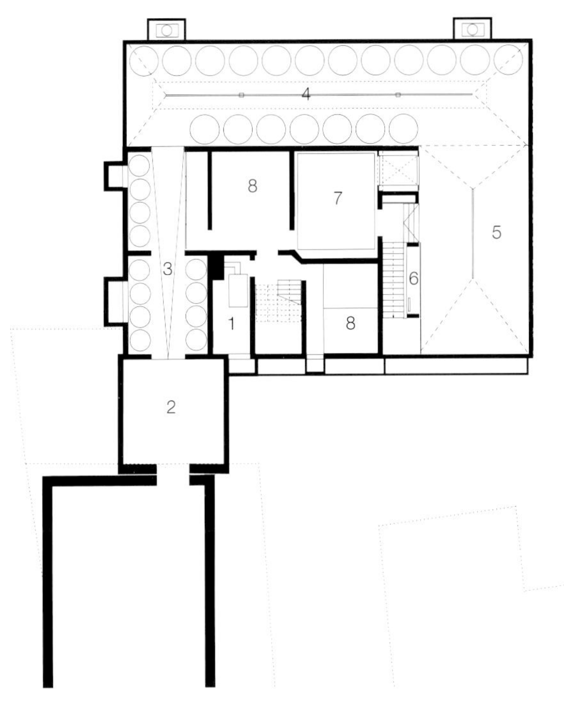

Floor plan
Scale 1:200

1 Technology
2 Linking space
3 Workroom
4 Tank storage
5 Processing
6 Laboratory
7 Cold storage
8 Storeroom

The skylights in the courtyard awning as well as in the production area have the same round form. A unique feature of the skylights is that they not only let light in during the day, but also function as light sources at night. This is made possible by lamps fitted at the sides of the skylights. This idea, as well as the entire lighting design, came from Remensperger. With his newly designed building, Heid has created a working environment that brightens every day for him. The purist, unfussy furnishings are not distracting and so focus attention on his wine and its creation. "I wanted a timeless atmosphere, because the wine always has to come first," he says. In this, the vintner has clearly succeeded. His red wines, made from Lemberger, Spätburgunder (Pinot Noir) and – unusually for Württemberg – St. Laurent grapes, have a lovely richness and elegance. Heid is constantly mindful of the quality of his wines. He got rid of the old, large, red-wine fermentation barrels and replaced them with traditional open fermentation vats. That makes it possible for him to observe and control the fermentation process more closely.
He is particularly fond of Syrah, which, here in the Rems Valley, takes on a certain coolness. Since taking over the family wine estate, Heid has reduced the share of the traditionally cultivated Trollinger (Schiava) grape variety in his wines from 70 per cent to a marginal amount. With regard to the white wines, his particular favourite is Sauvignon Blanc. He uses this grape variety, which comes from the Loire Valley in France, to produce fresh and expressive varietals. Currently he cultivates 10 hectares, three of which are subcontracted. He hopes to increase the size of his vineyards to 12 hectares, after which he plans to stop. Or does he? There is the possibility of taking over the neighbouring estate, a listed building...

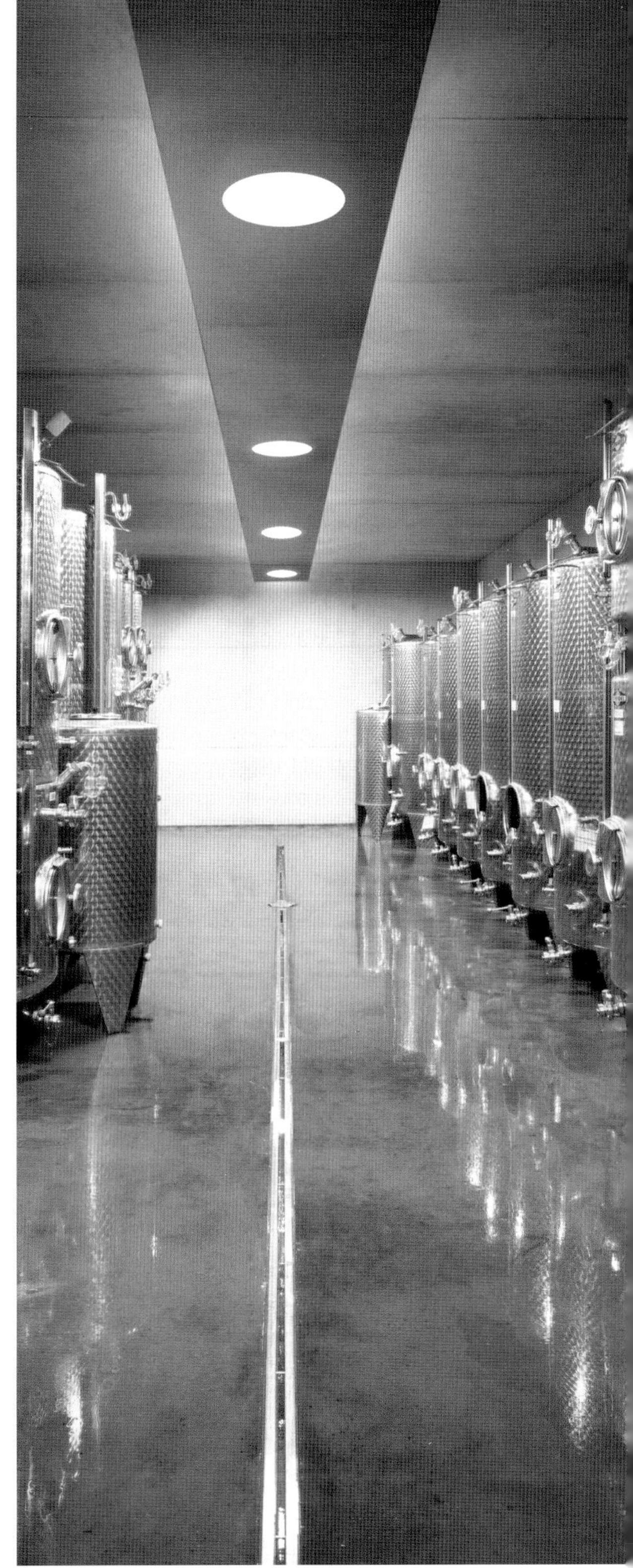

Quinta do Napoles in Santo Adrião, Portugal

Architect: Andreas Burghardt, Mariahilfer Str. 105, 1060 Vienna, www.burghardt.co.at
Gross floor area: 5,000 m^2
Start of design phase: 1999
Completion: 2007
Region: Douro
Contact: Têdo, 5110–543 Santo Adrião www.niepoort-vinhos.com
Oenologist: Luis Seabra
Price range: €9–€60
●●●

Port wines made the name Niepoort famous and put the Douro Valley, in the north of Portugal, on the map. Today, like no other, Niepoort stands not only for port – a highly ageable wine created by adding grape spirit to halt the fermentation process – but also for exceptional red wines from one of the oldest and most impressive wine regions in the world. Dirk Niepoort, of the fifth generation of the family, sees himself as an ambassador of port and of Douro wine, as the non-fortified wine pressed from traditional red and white Portuguese grape varieties is known.
Without directions, Quinta do Napoles, Niepoort's wine estate, is difficult to find. There are no signs to point it out along the narrow, serpentine road that winds up the slope next to the vineyards.

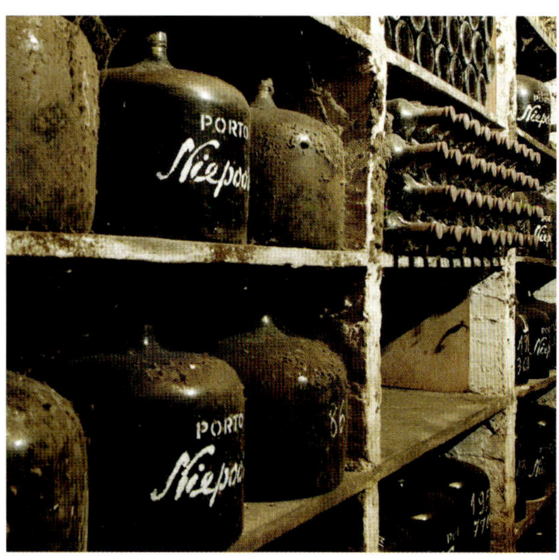

Majestic views illustrate what makes the Douro Valley so exceptional: the terraced vineyards carved out of the slate hills. Their creation hundreds of years ago under gruelling conditions made it possible to cultivate wine in this area, which is known for its steep slopes.
The wine estate blends effortlessly into its surroundings. "Essentially, we had an idea to erect an invisible winery – a building that disappears completely into the terraced landscape," explains Andreas Burghardt, the head architect. "Natural stone terraces, a completely invisible building, a hatch through which one descends." In the end, however, that was not entirely feasible. "We would have had to blast away too much rock to do it, and that would have swallowed huge sums of money," the Vienna-based architect says.
Niepoort and Burghardt met in 1999 at the launch of Fred Loimer's wine estate in Langenlois, in the Kamptal region of Austria (see p. 122). That was one of the first wine estates in Europe to have special architectural demands, along with the Neumeister wine estate in Straden, in south-eastern Styria – and both were designed by Burghardt. At the time, Niepoort had already been looking to expand the winery he had acquired in 1987. The planning phase for Quinta do Napoles took a full eight years.
Right at the beginning of their collaboration, Niepoort and Burghardt committed a design to paper. Afterwards, though, they visited a succession of wine estates together, and in the end it was their third design that was implemented.

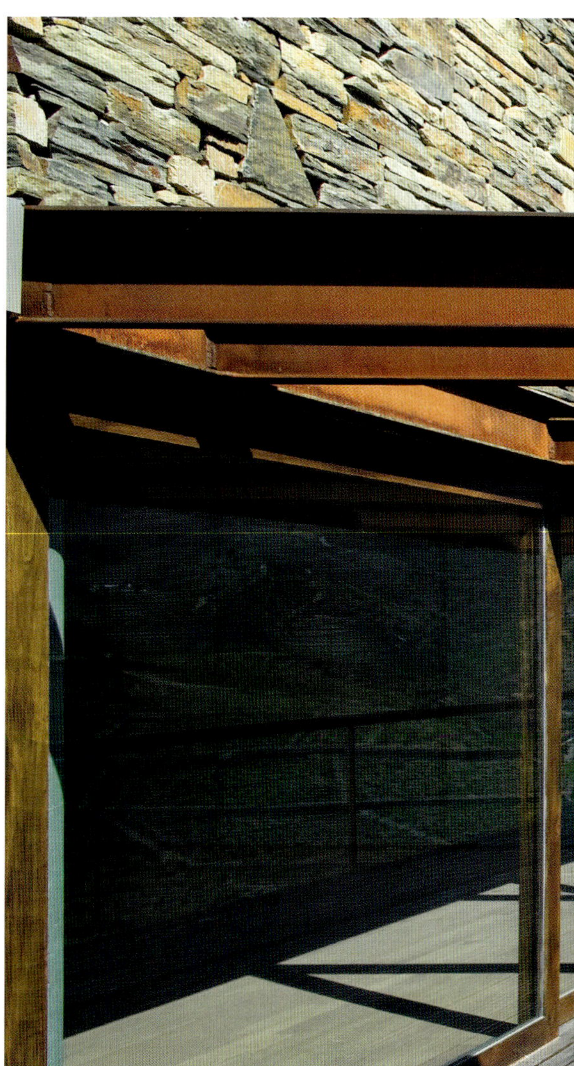

Floor plan
Scale 1:800

1 Veranda
2 Garden
3 Entrance
4 Tasting room
5 Catwalk access
6 Fermenting cellar
7 Laboratory
8 Access to house
9 Picture window

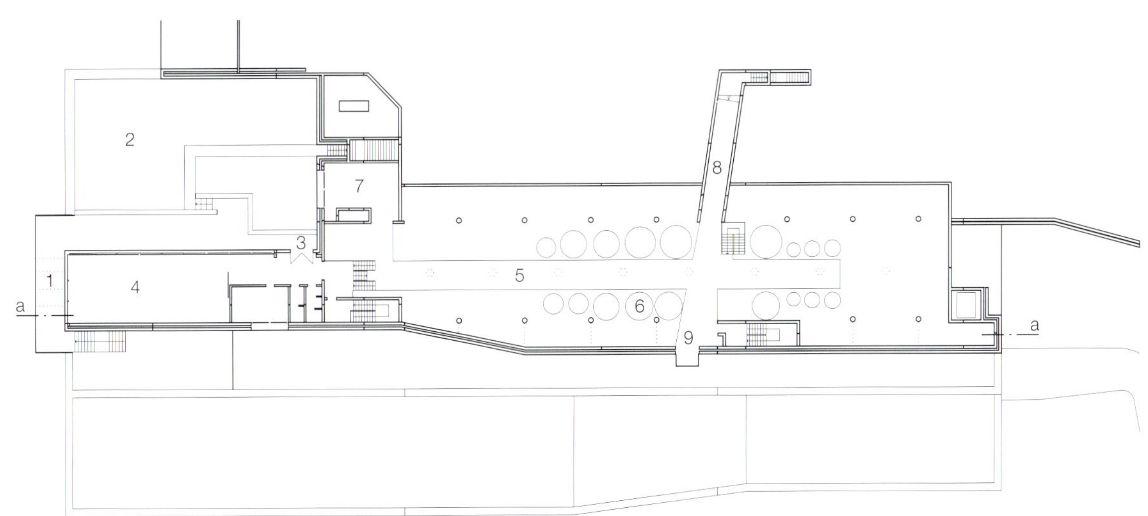

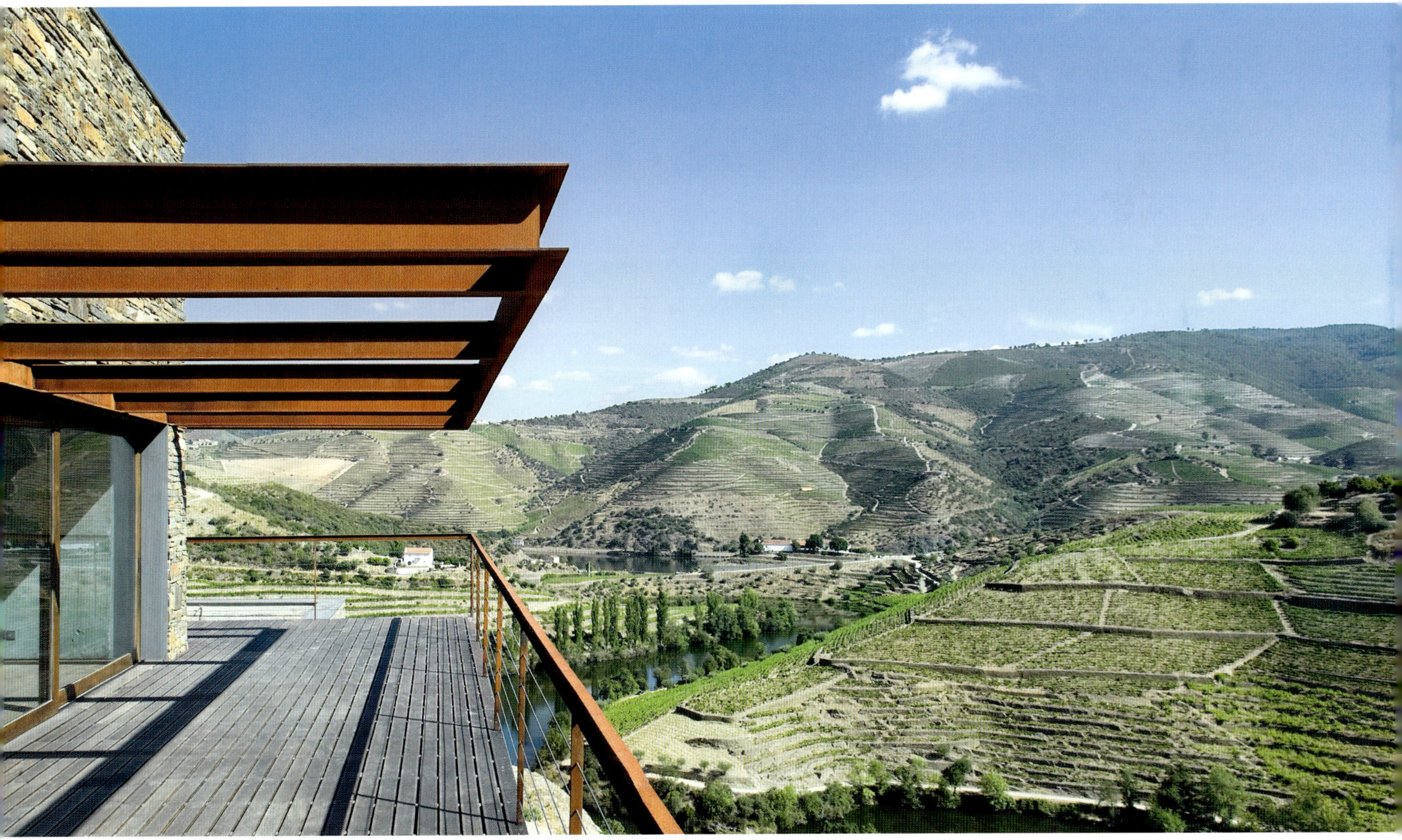

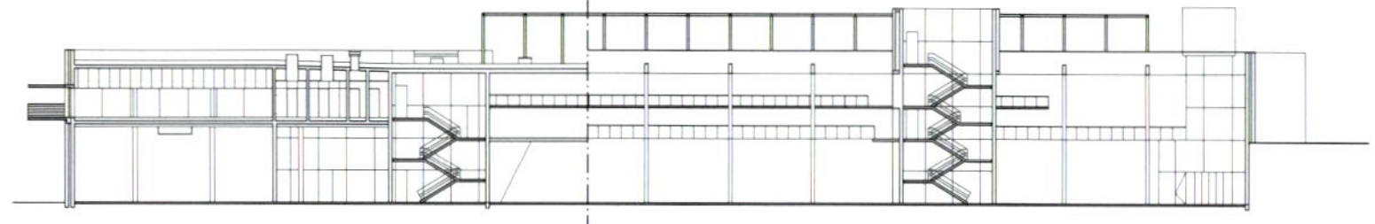

Section
Scale 1:800

aa

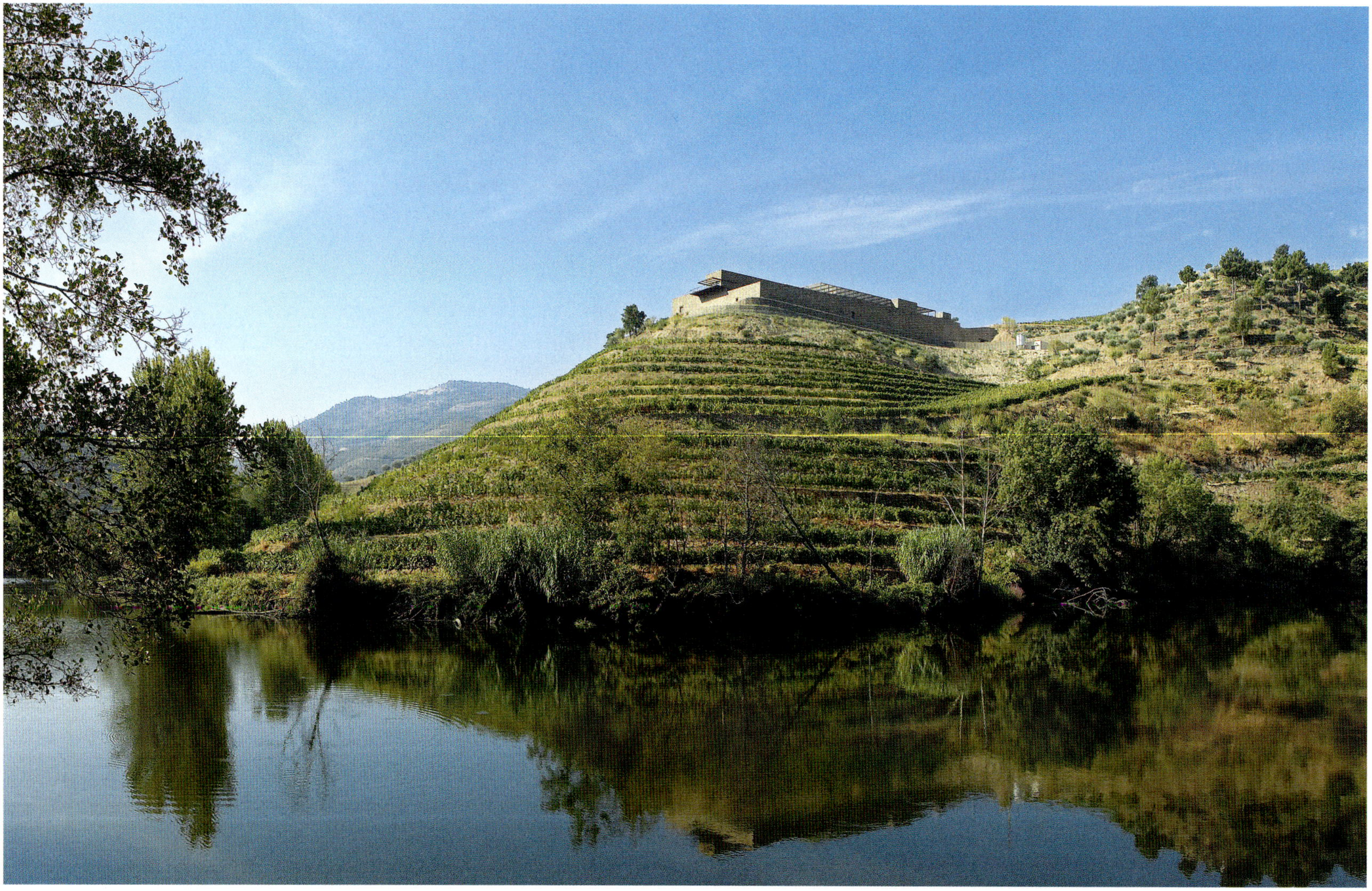

Even today, what they accomplished fills Niepoort with great satisfaction. "It's what I wanted, something to last generations." With conviction, he adds: "It will look even better in 50 years' time and be just as functional."
The building is an almost seamless continuation of the existing natural stone terracing, thereby blending perfectly into the landscape. Following the terracing concept, thousands of cubic metres of the slope were removed to set the wine estate up to 30 metres deep into the hill, so that only a small portion of it is visible.
The entire design was oriented towards the requirements for producing exceptional wine. Making use of gravity flow as well as ensuring passive cooling were part of the fundamental stipulations in planning. From the beginning, the winemakers, production engineers and architect were all involved in creating the concept. The organization of the rooms and the logistics were a collaborative effort. The technical equipment – apart from the tanks and the presses – was custom-made. "It was a mutually inspiring process," says Burghardt. For the most part, Niepoort kept out of the proceedings.
The building phase took only nine months. The production areas of the wine estate were finished in time for the 2007 harvest, and the rest followed suit. A number of technical challenges presented themselves. To build the cellar beneath, it seemed at first that the old quinta manor house had to be torn down due to its enormous weight. Instead, the suspended ceiling was removed and the building virtually hollowed out in order to make it lighter. Today the warmly lit, lofty interior functions as a tasting and presentation area as well as one of the entrances to the cellar. The walls of the enormous underground spaces are made of slate. The water that seeps through cracks in various places helps keep the temperature cool, maintaining a constant 15 °C throughout the year. The slate, whose layers run towards the interior of the building, is fixed in place by wall anchors set deep into the rock.
Ventilation openings bring hot air from the outside, where temperatures can climb up to 45 °C, into a lofty space – a kind of "lung" – at the side of the actual cellar, where it is cooled. In contact with the native slate on the walls, the air temperature sinks immediately to about 22 °C. On particularly hot days, dousing the rocks with water creates additional cooling through evaporation.

Large entrances into the cellar make it accessible for goods vehicles. "An important feature, should the fermentation tanks have to be replaced at some point," confides Niepoort.
Vans drive along the access road to the estate to deliver the harvested grapes in 20-kilogramme crates. Sorting, destemming and crushing take place on a large, roofed open space before the processed grapes travel down a flexible, adjustable pipe to the fermentation tanks below. The white grapes are immediately pressed and sent to ferment at low temperatures in French oak barriques with an open bunghole.
The two barrel cellars differ in more than just size. The walls of the larger, red-wine cellar are painted all in black, which makes the room look smaller. This is an intentional effect, as the area was originally planned to be smaller but, because of technical constraints, could only be realized in its current form. The much smaller white-wine cellar is painted in bright, light green, which emphasizes the freshness and acidity of the wines. In general, the entire facility is impressively laid out. Visitors never really get a sense of its immense 5,000-square-metre footprint, much of which is underground, or of the fact that enough grapes are processed and aged here every year to make more than one million bottles of wine.
The wines carrying the memorable name Fabelhaft (Fabulous), originally created for the German market and now sold to other countries under various names, are also a success story. Small cartoons on the labels tell stories in the respective languages of the countries to which the wine is sold. The stories come from well-known artists in these countries. For example, the work of Phil Mulloy, a British animator, is featured on the label of the UK version of the wine, called Drink Me. Niepoort markets 800,000 bottles of his red cuvée wine – 95 per cent of which is aged in stainless steel, the rest in oak – all over the world. "Without Fabulous, I wouldn't have been able to expand Quinta do Napoles into what it is today," he states.
Currently Niepoort cultivates 62 hectares of vineyards, 25 hectares of which are in the direct vicinity of the quinta, and purchases additional grapes from vintners who work according to Niepoort's quality directives. "As much involvement as possible in the vineyard, as little as possible in the cellar" – that is his philosophy, and he follows it with great determination. All of his wines are allowed to ferment spontaneously. By harvesting as early as possible, Niepoort endeavours to keep their alcohol content at a maximum of 13.5 per cent, which only first-rate work in the vineyard can assure. The slate soil gives rise to wines with minerality, elegance and great potential.
For what Niepoort has achieved in the Douro Valley, and for his efforts to market Portugal's wines worldwide, there is only one word: Fabulous.

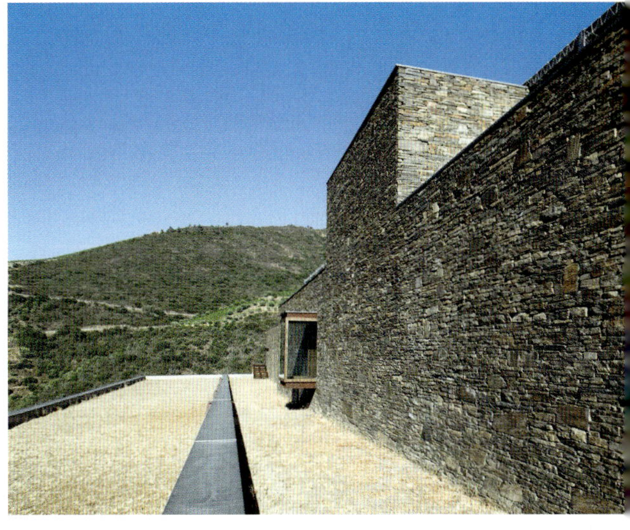

Winzer Sommerach in Sommerach, Germany

Architects: hofmann keicher ring architekten, Veitshöchheimerstr. 1, 97080 Würzburg, www.hofmann-keicher-ring.de with Reinhard May, Mergentheimer Str. 10, 97082 Würzburg, www.raymay.de

Team: André Stemann

Site area: 3,704 m²

Gross floor area: 1,424 m²

Start of design phase: 2005

Completion: 2006

Region: Franken / Franconia

Contact: Zum Katzenkopf 1, 97334 Sommerach www.winzer-sommerach.de

Oenologist: Anton Glaser

Price range: €5–€30

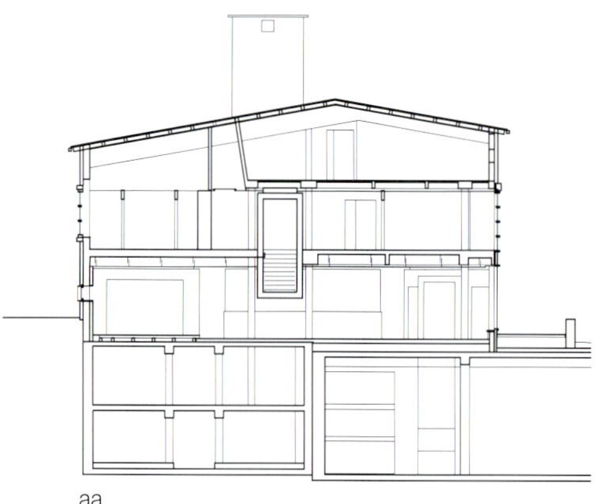

aa

Sommerach and its wine cellars are, in many ways, the very essence of Germany's wine region of Franken (Franconia). The name of this idyllic winemaking cooperative located on the so-called Wine Island in the bend of the Main River is, loosely translated, "Place on the sunny side of the river" — a name that vouches for the excellent grape-growing climate on the south-eastern bank of the Main. Fortuitous growing conditions particularly favour Sommerach's most famous vineyard site, the "Katzenkopf" (Cat's Head). Indeed, the perimeter of the area does recall the shape of a cat's head a bit, if one applies a bit of imagination to the task. What's more interesting, however, is that the soils here consist mostly of Muschelkalk, interspersed with clayey sand. This particular soil, common throughout Franconia, is predestined for the cultivation of the region's classic grape varieties, Müller-Thurgau and Silvaner.

To get the maximum benefit from these excellent natural conditions for wine cultivation, the vintners of Sommerach got together to form a cooperative 110 years ago, in 1901. After winemaking cooperatives had been founded in other German wine regions for decades, this was the first association of Franconian vintners. Now, the Sommerach winemakers call themselves simply "Winzer Sommerach" (Vintners of Sommerach), adding "Der Winzerkeller" (The Vintners' Cellar).

The name change was, of course, not the only improvement; indeed, it was just the beginning of a whole range of notable changes with which this establishment has been garnering attention for more than a decade. The centenary in 2001 was a watershed moment, the beginning of a new era. The earlier "Winzerverein Sommerach" (Vintners' Association of Sommerach), with its 250 members, was known as a solid, dependable winemaking cooperative. But the chairman of the winery was not content with being "respectably average". In 2004, Frank Dietrich, a certified agricultural engineer, took over the position of managing director and brought a new wine philosophy and market strategy into the company. Authenticity, sustainability and value now play an important role. The wine cellar sees itself as a safeguard of tradition, yet an open and innovative one.

This way of thinking is evident in the relaunch of the Sommerach wine range. It consists of six product

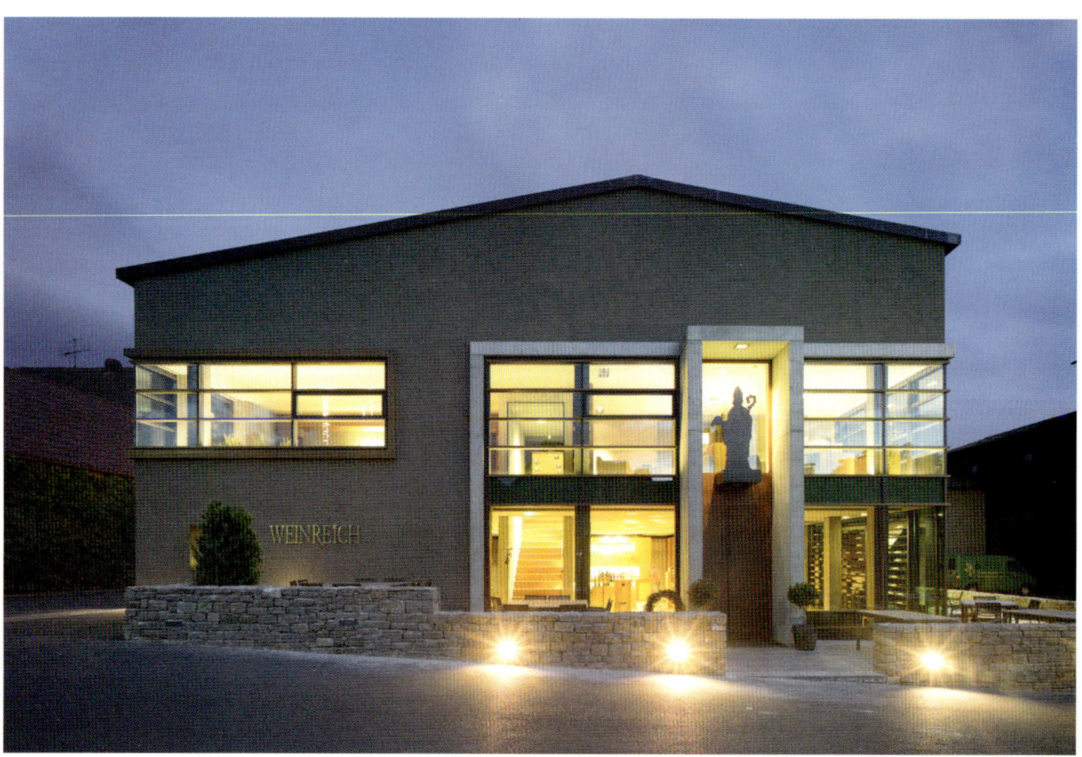

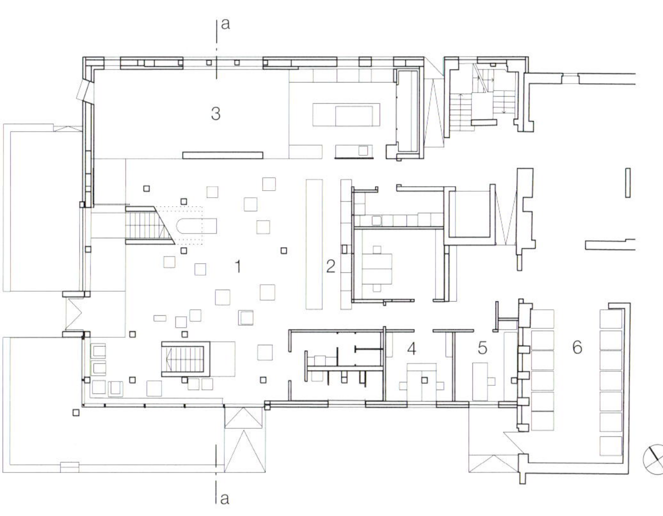

Section • Floor plans
Scale 1:800

1 Sales and presentation area
2 Tasting bar
3 Tasting area
4 Office
5 Laboratory
6 Storeroom
7 Steel barrel cellar (existing)
8 Barrique cellar
9 Historical barrel cellar

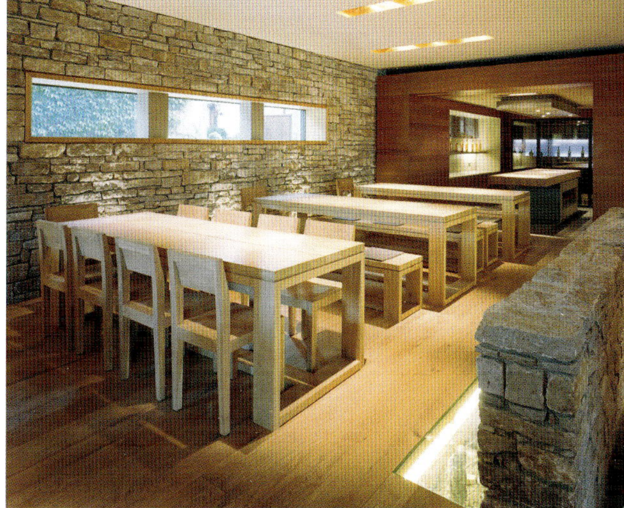

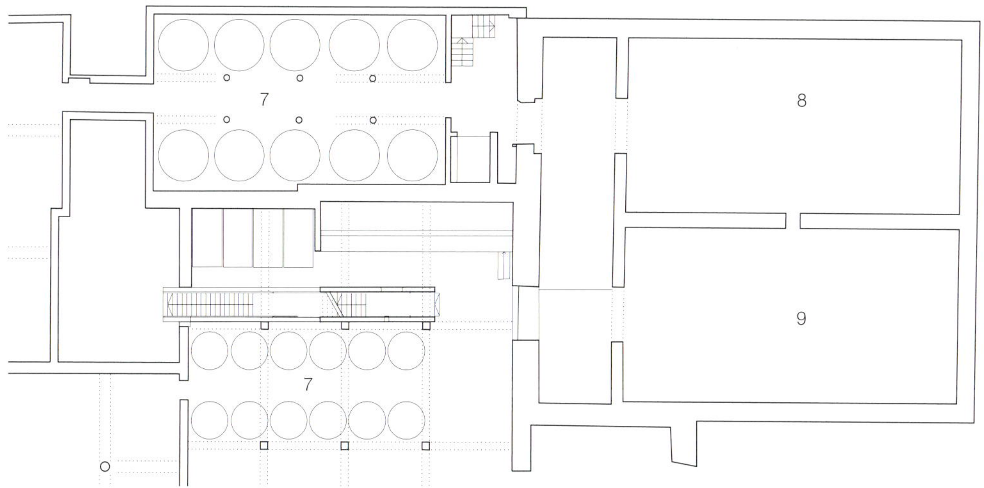

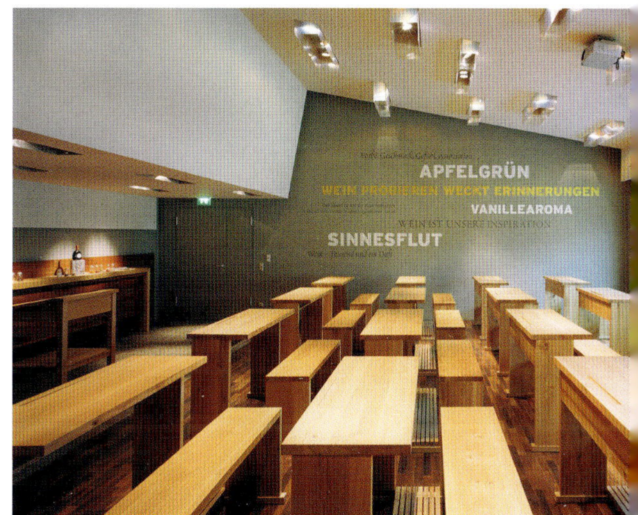

lines, only two of which are still bottled in the traditional Franconian Bocksbeutel flasks. Whether Edition St. Valentin, Frizzante Valentin, Fränkische Klassik, Weinreich Eins, Supremus or Wunderbar, the fresh, modern and attractive wines are heralded in an unconventional way by their contemporary styling. The countless accolades, competition awards, and top ratings from trade journalists that the Sommerach winery has received since then, prove that the new branding isn't just smoke and mirrors. Dietrich and his cellarmaster, Helmut Glaser, see all the recent recognition (include being named as best German cooperative) as a confirmation of their quality policy, in which great skill and exceptional ambition pervade all work done in the vineyards and cellar, and play a pivotal role in their success. Indeed, with its many-tiered selection process in the vineyard, its careful grape processing, and its tailoring of the ageing process according to grape variety, vineyard location and maturity, the winery has set the bar very high. So it was only a matter of time – and financial capability – before it took the next step in its pursuit of renewal and perfection: commissioning the renovation and redesign of its marketing, management and sales areas.

The first step involved organizing a competition for the project. Seven regional architecture practices took part. The jury awarded first prize to the design by Würzburg-based architects Hofmann Keicher Ring.

For the architects, who started work on their winning design in summer 2005, there were interesting parallels to a commission they had secured two years previously, also by winning a competition: the redesign of the Würzburg wine estate Weingut am Stein, which they completed in 2005 (see p. 119). Although certain basic elements were identical in both projects, the details and tasks involved in the brief as well as the ultimate implementation were completely different.

The main building features at its centre an ample ground-floor presentation space with a tasting and shop area, which includes an information counter, tasting islands, a service bar and a demonstration kitchen – all under the appealing name "Kostbar"

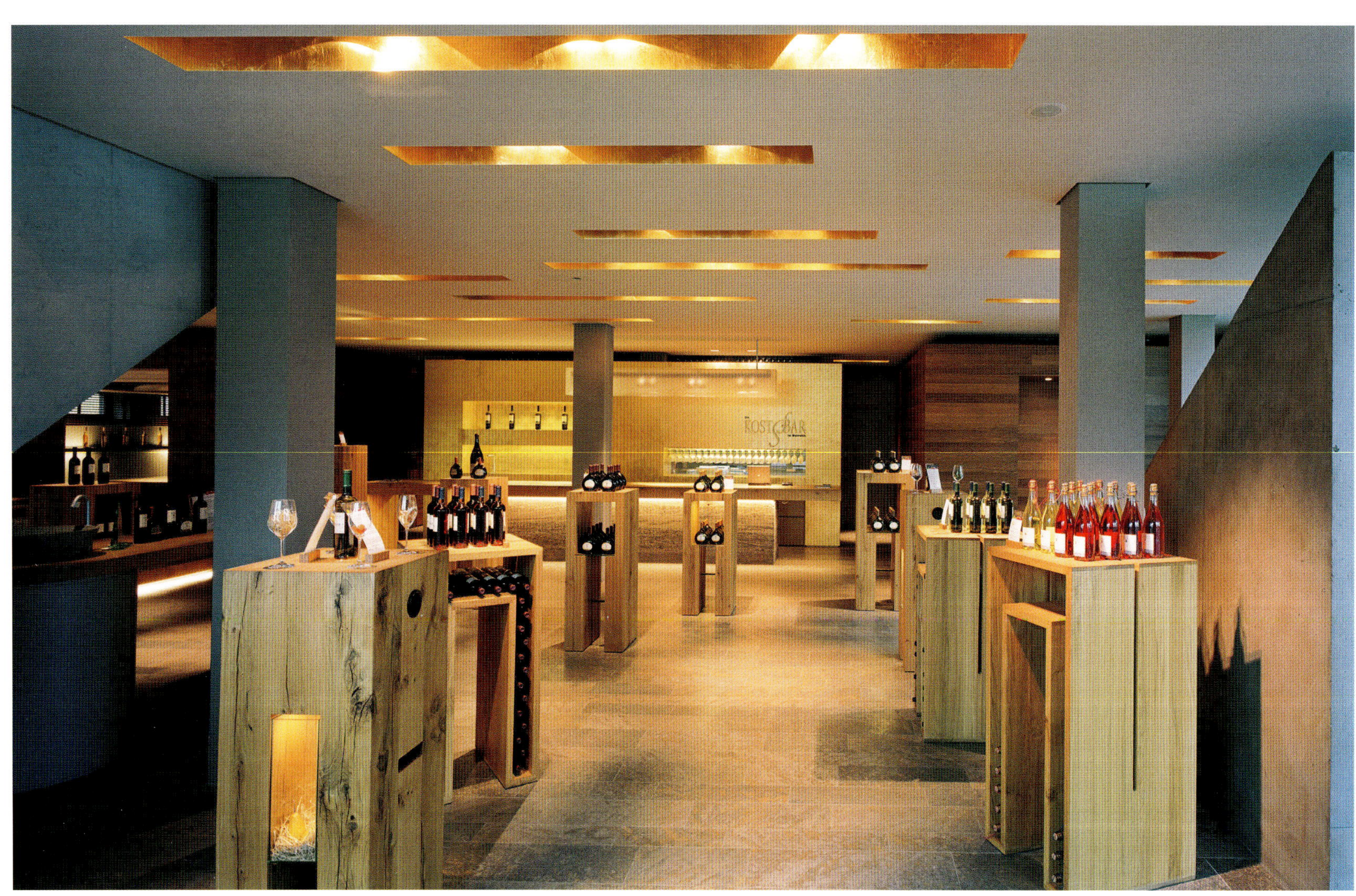

(meaning "precious", but also a play on the German word *kosten* – to taste – and bar). A counter situated in the middle and two staircases are the main elements of the room. A striking staircase leads from here directly into the underground complex.
In one area of the vaulted cellar, the architects tastefully restyled the existing wooden barrel cellar. In another part, they removed the 1970s' concrete tanks to lay bare the historical vaults of quarried stone. This created an atmospheric barrique cellar, where the designers also left enough room for wine tasting and events such as a sensory introduction to wine.
The wine school is located on the upper level of the "Empire of Wine" – the evocative title of the entire institution. Along with wine seminars and wine film showings, the vintners' meetings also take place here. The tasting room next door offers a lovely view of the vines on the Katzenkopf in Sommerach. The building technology and further storage areas are located at attic level. Outside, open terraces face toward the sun. The existing storehouses on the opposite side are all painted the same way to harmonize with the complex.
The main building was emphasized with a high-quality facade design. Green solar protection glass framed by wood and concrete beams, and a dark terrazzo render define the character of the exterior. The entrance portico on the gable side of the courtyard, featuring a statue of St Urban, is a modern interpretation of traditional Franconian building.
The same materials, forms and colours are echoed in the interior. The sustained colour and form motif, together with the Sommerach winery's existing corporate identity, create a unified image. The use of traditional materials such as stone, oak, glass and concrete underscores the winery's strong connection to the locality. Thus, the synthesis of the traditional and the modern is a goal not only in Sommerach's winemaking but also in its architectural expression.
The entire winery project, which had a budget of €2.4 million, was completed on time in the spring of 2006, after only 11 months of planning and construction.
The management of the cooperative had prepared itself for the project by means of comprehensive information-gathering visits to new wine architecture projects within and outside Germany. Investigating best practice, they researched which solutions would best suit their expectations and the conditions in Sommerach, and how they could be implemented.
In the end, the management and the architects took all the facts and requirements and turned them into a persuasive new concept. They transformed the sombre interior and the old jumble of elements from the post-war period into an open, inviting building that offers the quality wines of Sommerach an attractive and compelling setting. Ultimately, the renovation was resoundingly successful, enabling the Vintners of Sommerach to reach new target groups as well as significantly increase the number of visitors and sales.

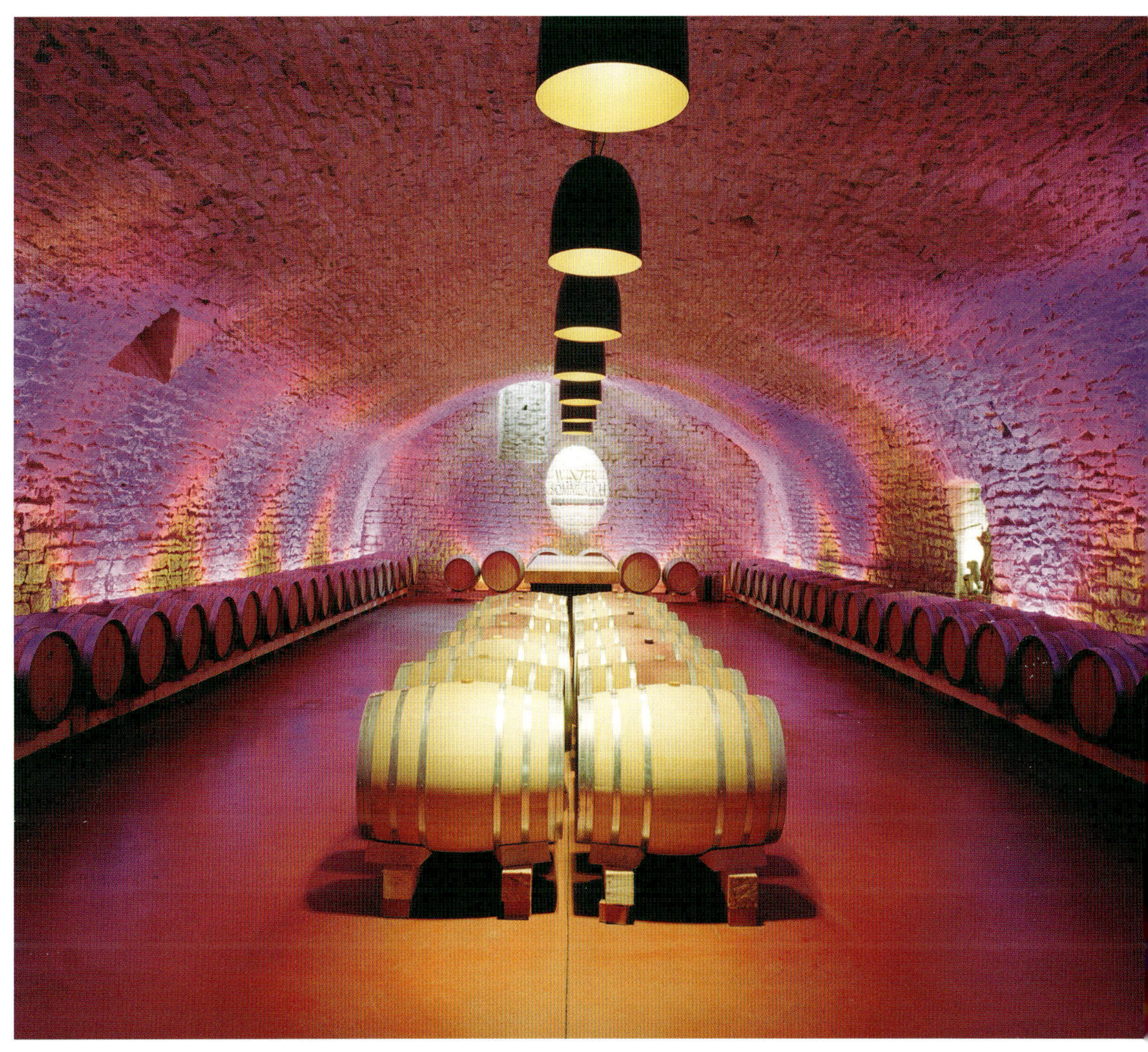

Domaine Les Aurelles in Nizas, France

Architects: Perraudin Architectes,
16, Rue Jacques Imbert Colomès, 69001 Lyon
www.perraudinarchitectes.com
based on a concept by Eric Castaldi

Team: Elisabeth Polzella, Olivier Schertenleib

Gross floor area: 665 m²

Start of design phase: 1999

Completion: 2001

Region: Languedoc-Roussillion

Contact: 8, Chemin des Champs Blancs, 34320 Nizas
www.les-aurelles.com

Oenologist: Basile Saint Germain

Price range: €12–€45

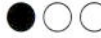

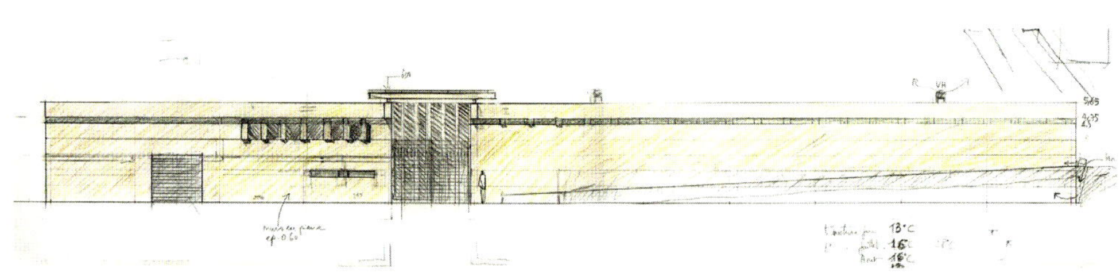

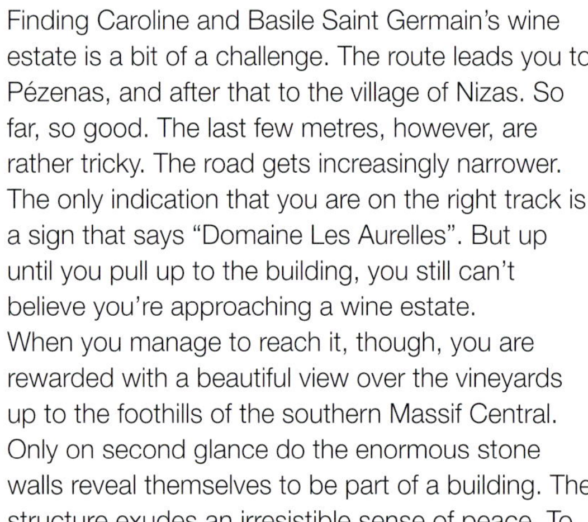

Finding Caroline and Basile Saint Germain's wine estate is a bit of a challenge. The route leads you to Pézenas, and after that to the village of Nizas. So far, so good. The last few metres, however, are rather tricky. The road gets increasingly narrower. The only indication that you are on the right track is a sign that says "Domaine Les Aurelles". But up until you pull up to the building, you still can't believe you're approaching a wine estate.

When you manage to reach it, though, you are rewarded with a beautiful view over the vineyards up to the foothills of the southern Massif Central. Only on second glance do the enormous stone walls reveal themselves to be part of a building. The structure exudes an irresistible sense of peace. To the eye of the visitor, it looks uniform, minimalist, a bit monumental yet discreetly reserved. Stacked, monolithic stone blocks form its outer perimeter, measuring 61 by 11 metres. In the middle of the long front facade is an imposing steel gate, which has purposely been allowed to develop a rusty patina. Here, steel and stone complement each other, both imparting their own timeless quality to the building.

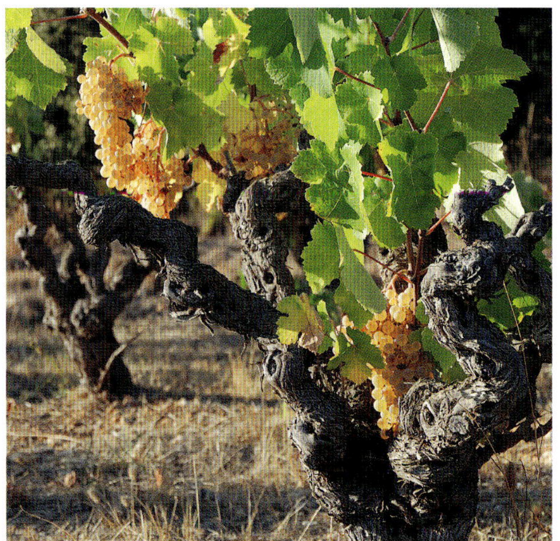

The gate conceals the entrance. When it is open, one can see that there are two buildings, one to either side of the entrance. A large shutter gate opens to one side for access to the northern part of the building, where large enamelled tanks are located in the ground-level cellar. The height of the single-storey space is about eight metres. At either side there are six stone columns supporting the roof.

The entire structure is reminiscent of a Greek temple. Daylight can enter only through the long, slit-like openings directly under the roof edge on both sides of the space. This is a place that offers no distractions – a place where Basile Saint Germain can devote his full attention to his passion of creating exceptional, exquisite wines.

The two-storey southern building houses a storage area on the ground floor. Above that there are offices illuminated by a row of vertical windows on the eastern side of the building. There is no separate tasting area. Instead, tasting takes place either directly in the cellar or under the olive tree in front of the winery.

Saint Germain's passion for wine began when he was a student of landscape architecture in Nice. Born in Forbach, in the Lorraine region of France, he also worked there as a wine seller on the side. He became obsessed with the south of France as well as with wine.

To improve his knowledge, he travelled to Bordeaux and began a two-year apprenticeship at the famous Château Latour. There he worked not only in the vineyards and the cellar, but also – as a landscape architect – in the park of the château. During his subsequent studies of viniculture in Bordeaux, he met his future wife, Caroline. Her roots led the couple to Cognac, where Caroline's family business was located.

After seven years, both of them felt drawn back to the south of France, determined to start up their own wine estate from scratch. Saint Germain went about the search for his future estate methodically and painstakingly. He was only interested in a superior terroir, with exceptional soil and climate conditions. Only there, he knew, would be able to achieve his goal of producing really tremendous wines. "In the end, it could just as well have happened in another wine region in France," says Saint Germain, "but I was convinced that, particularly here, in the neglected wine region of Languedoc with its exceptional conditions, greatness would be possible."

It was chiefly the southern French grape varieties – such as Carignan, Grenache and Mourvèdre for red wine and Roussanne for white – that fascinated him. He searched for the perfect site for two years, from 1992 to 1994. There were enough vineyards on offer, but he wanted very particular soil conditions. He finally found what he was looking for close to his current site, near Nizas.

The area boasts a white, clayey soil above 10 to 15 metres of low-lying, substantial seams of pebbles, which developed as fluvial deposits from the Hérault River. Similar to the renowned soils of Châteauneuf du Pape, the ground here is full of these round pebbles, which are about as big as the palm of one's hand. Saint Germain left the existing, up to 100-year-old vines standing. "On the slopes with southern exposure and lots of heat, and in the clayey soil with its good water-holding capacity and, thanks to the pebbles, excellent drainage, the Mourvèdre grape in particular has superb potential," explains Saint Germain.

After the harvest in 1995, he and his wife began to produce wine in their own vineyards, working according to organic precepts from the very start. As they did not yet have their own cellar to age the wine in, they looked for someone who could help them. This proved to be extremely difficult, however, because at that time almost all the vintners were working in cooperatives, which wielded enormous power in the wine sector and had little interest in a vintner who wanted to develop his own wines. Additionally, most of the *maisons des vignerons*, as the vintners' homes are called in France, had only a small cellar under the living area that was very difficult to access externally. "These two

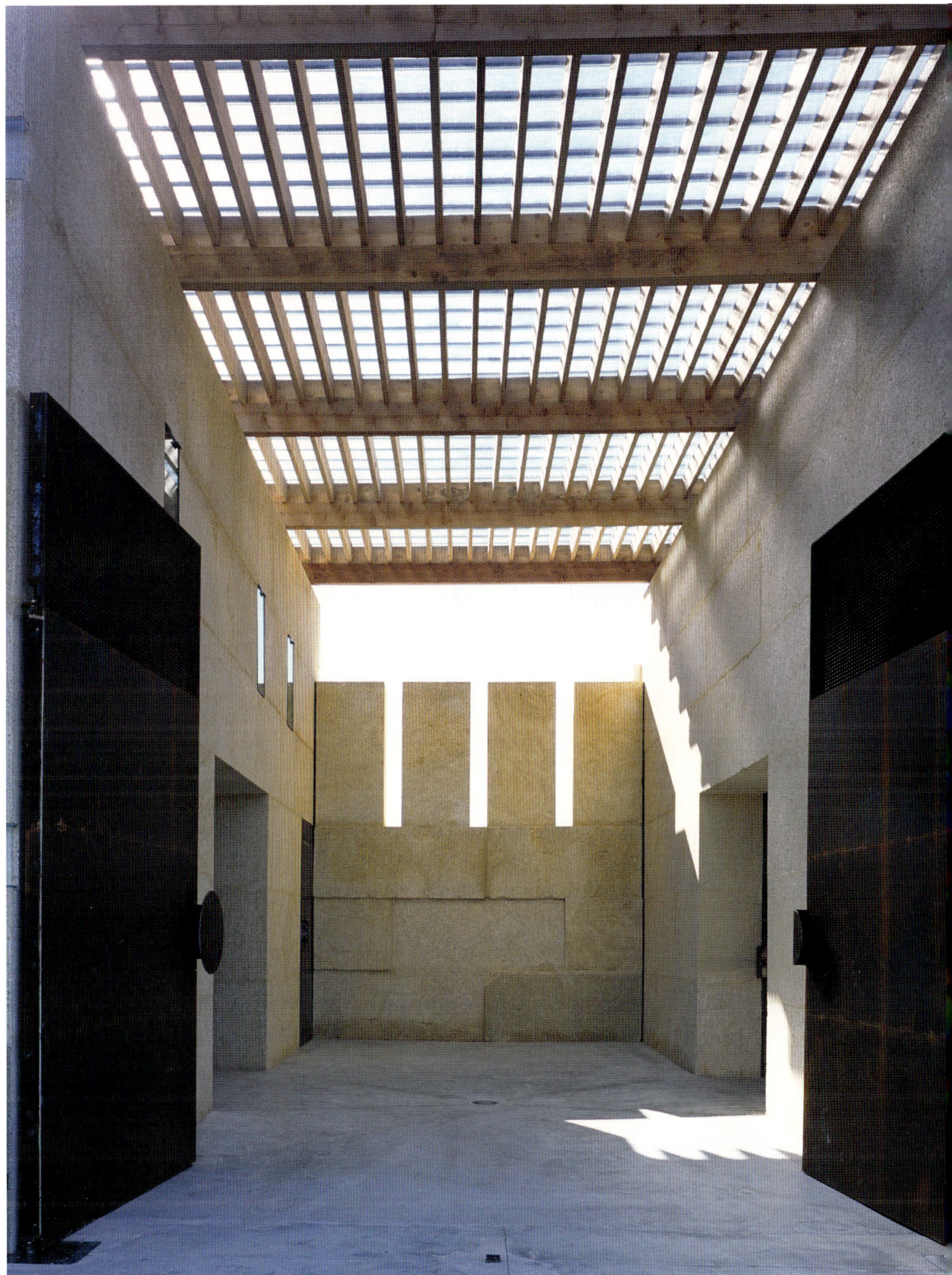

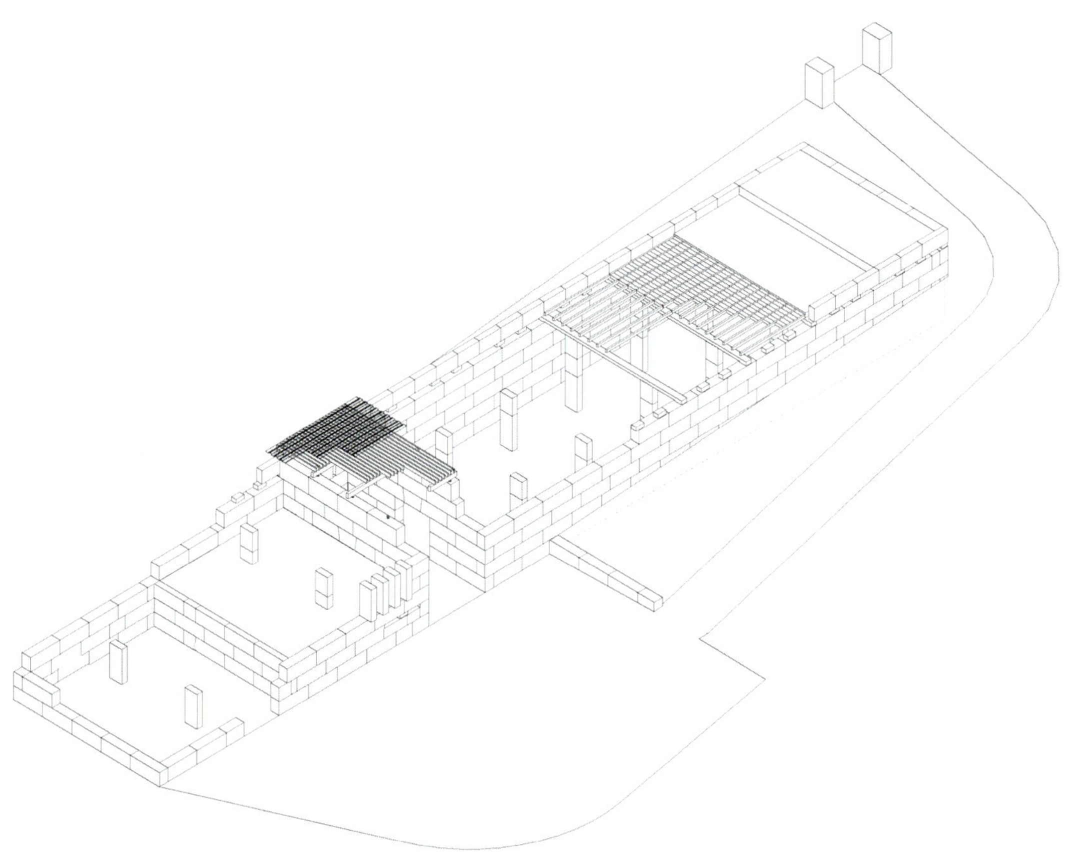

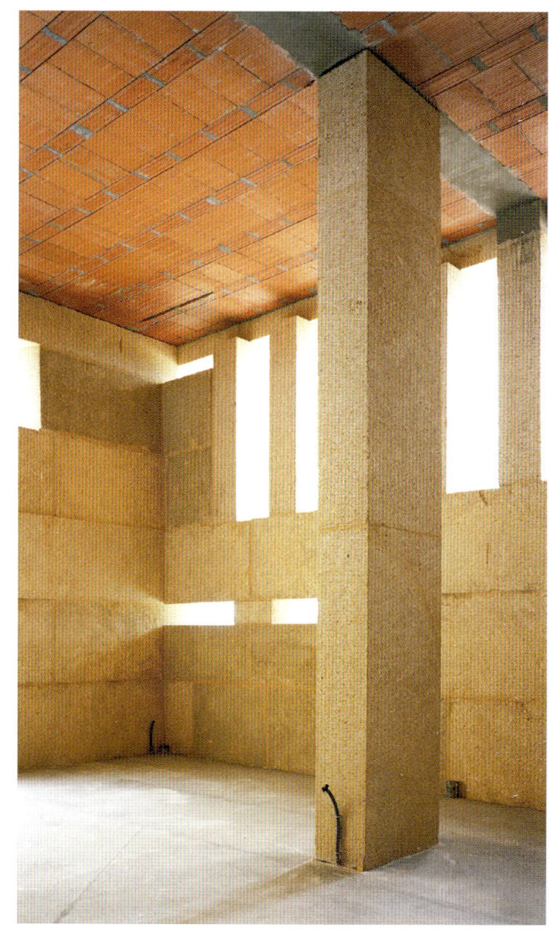

problems were very nearly the undoing of the whole project," says Saint Germain.

But then he found a solution. After four successful harvests, it became clear that he needed his own facility. His friend, architect Eric Castaldi, agreed to do the planning. They started work in September 1999. "We wanted a simple, functional structure on new terrain that would integrate itself perfectly into the landscape," says Saint Germain.

During planning, they got the idea of making the building out of solid rock using native stone from the area. The Lyon-based architect Gilles Perraudin, whose favourite materials have been wood, earth and stone ever since he completed his own wine estate in Vauvert in the Camargue (see pages 50ff.), took over the project from Castaldi, who did not have the time to continue with it. In the end, they chose the same stone that was used for the Pont du Gard, a Roman viaduct near Nîmes. Enormous blocks of solid limestone were cut to a depth of 65 centimetres and transported by lorry to Nizas – not an easy feat, considering that the average stone weighed three tons.

The original idea – to cement the monolithic stone blocks together – was discarded, as it was not known what effect the adhesive would have on the interior room climate. Instead, they decided to employ a tried and tested construction method from ancient Roman times: the blocks were simply laid down, layer for layer, to be kept in place by their own weight, and the seams were faced with lime mortar.

The stones act as a cooling unit, absorbing heat during the day and emanating it back into the environment at night. The green roof was also designed to be a climate buffer. This heavy construction with a thick substrate layer absorbs rainwater, which cools the building as it evaporates.

This impressive building was finished in 2001 in just four months, in time for the harvest in September. The wines of the Domaine Les Aurelles are just as impressive. From a total vineyard area of nine hec-

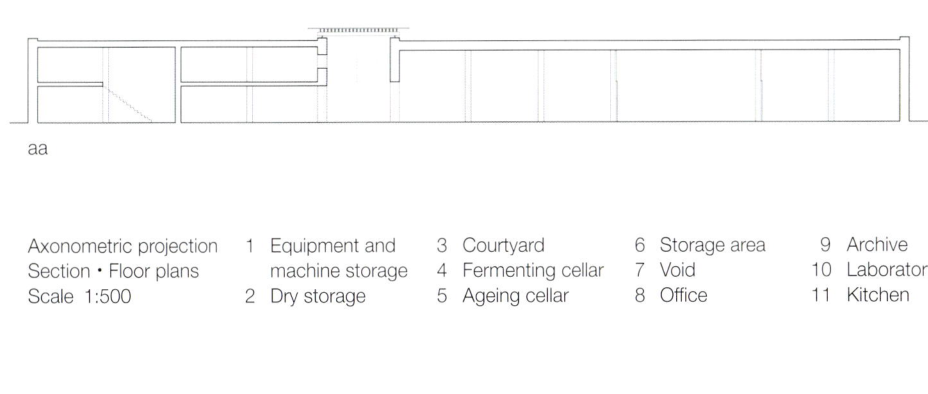

Axonometric projection
Section • Floor plans
Scale 1:500

1 Equipment and machine storage
2 Dry storage
3 Courtyard
4 Fermenting cellar
5 Ageing cellar
6 Storage area
7 Void
8 Office
9 Archive
10 Laboratory
11 Kitchen

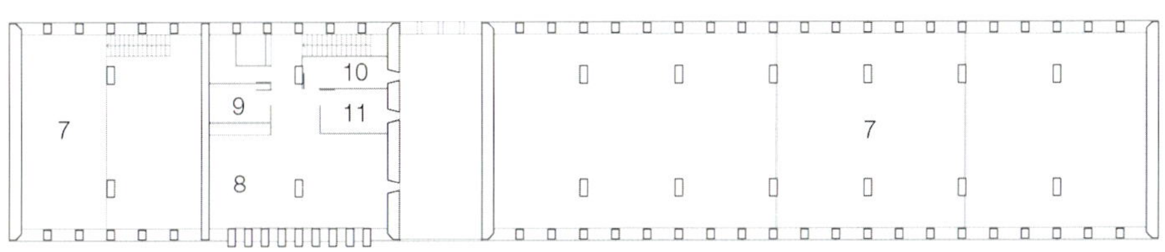

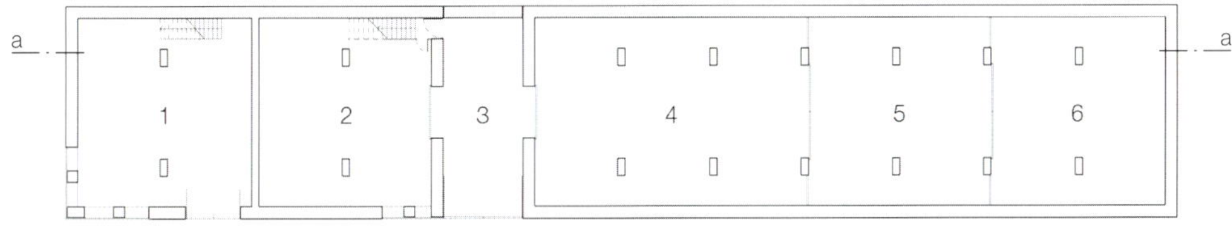

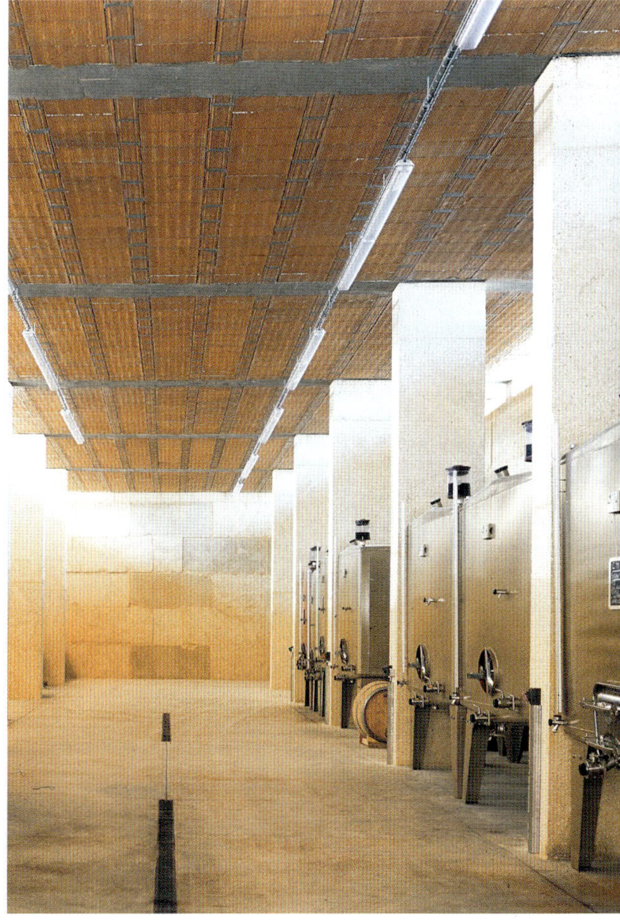

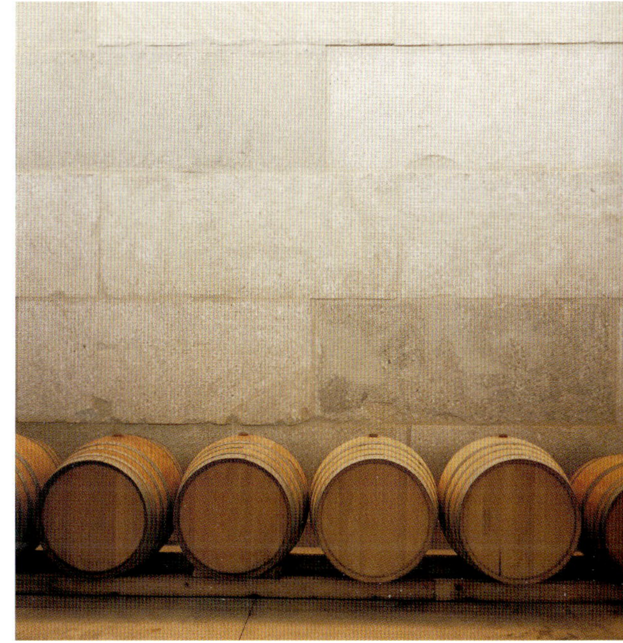

tares, only 200 hectolitres of wine are produced. With a yield of 18 hectolitres of white wine and 20–22 hectolitres of red wine per hectare, Saint Germain is operating at homeopathic levels – but at the very highest levels of quality. His vinification of the difficult and often underestimated white grape variety Roussanne produces one single wine: Aurel. Its name inspired by the name of the estate, the varietal is aged in barriques made of oak from the Vosges Mountains. Per vintage, there are only five casks of this wine, which has a fascinating nose and a complex aromatic structure, and is very rich with an almost endless finish on the palate.
There are just three red wines: Solen, a cuvée made of 60 per cent Carignan and 40 per cent Grenache; a red Aurel with 65 per cent Mourvèdre, 20 per cent Syrah and 15 per cent Grenache; and, last but not least, Déella, a wine that Saint Germain calls "the leftovers", as it only gets bottled when there is wine left over – meaning its composition is variable. All the red wines are aged in stainless steel, so that the fruit notes enter the bottle as unadulterated as possible. They are unbelievably rich wines with an intoxicating depth, fruitiness and great potential.
Saint Germain's wines have joined the top ranks of the world's wines, and are most often found on the tables of Michelin-starred restaurants.

Quinta do Portal in Celeirós do Douro, Portugal

Architect: Álvaro Siza Vieira, Rua do Aeixo, 53, 2º
4150-043 Porto

Team: Gabriel Flórez, Pedro Polónia, Ola Boman, Miguel Nery, Atsushi Ueno, Gonçalo Campello

Gross floor area: 4,700 m²

Start of design phase: 2001

Completion: 2010

Region: Douro

Contact: E.N. 323 Celeirós do Douro, 5060 Sabrosa
www.quintadoportal.com

Oenologist: Paul Coutinho

Price range: €4.50–€75

●●●

Site plan
Scale 1:2000

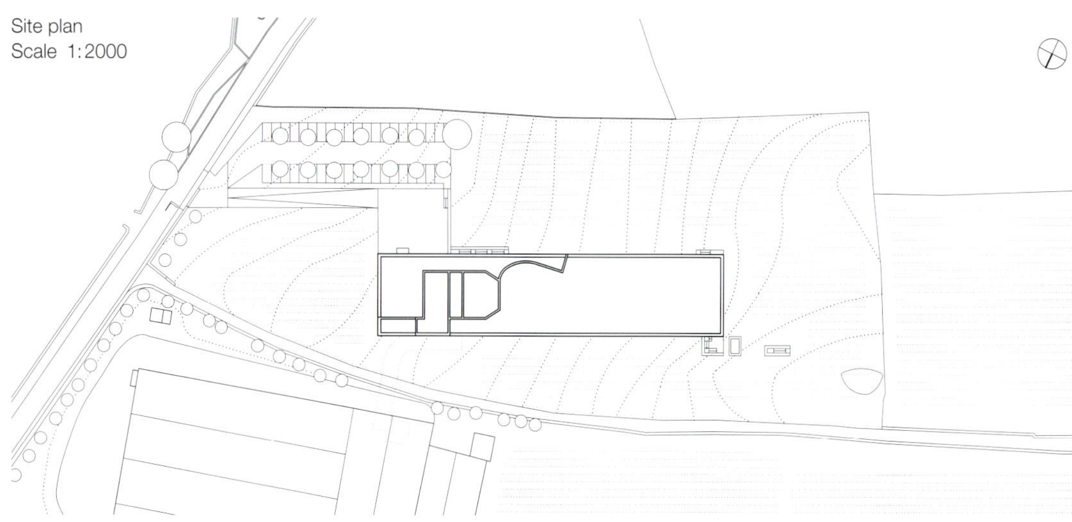

Portugal's Douro Valley is characterized by cork and slate – cork as a stopper for wine bottles, slate as the ground on which the vines grow. Both materials also envelop the new storehouse at Quinta do Portal, helping it to blend into the surrounding vineyards of the central Douro Valley. Completed in 2008, the 4,700-square-metre building in Celeirós do Douro, near Sabrosa, represents the fulfilment of a dear wish of Quinta do Portal's owner, Eugénio Branco.

The Branco family has been in the Douro Valley since the 15th century, and has been producing port wine for more than 100 years. The original estate was Quinta dos Muro; after 1974, they bought more vineyards, then four more quintas. The year 1991 saw the purchase of Quinta do Portal and the merging of all five wine estates under its name. The property now covers 100 hectares. Quinta do Portal started producing red Douro wine in 1994, which became a great success. Then, 10 years later, the wine Quinta do Portal Auru 2001 won its first awards. When the winery became increasingly short on space, Branco decided to build a new storehouse for wine ageing and storage. It was to be a functional building that blended into the landscape as well as possible. At the same time, together with the already existing hotel and neighbouring restaurant, it was to bring wine tourists to the estate.

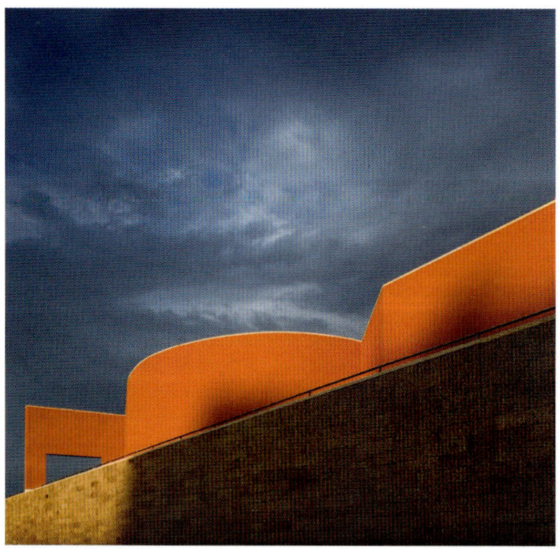

Branco managed to bring one of the most important contemporary European architects, Álvaro Siza, on board for the project. Siza's objective was to create a building that was in harmony with the landscape and that could be integrated into it as fully as possible. The planning of a building that was to function as a storage space for port wine as well as for red wine was challenging, as the two require different storage temperatures. Branco and Siza settled on a three-storey solution.

The bottom floor is set nine metres into the ground to provide the cool temperatures of about 12 °C required for cellaring red wine. If the mercury rises, a vaporizer installed in the ceiling distributes a fine mist into the air, ensuring further cooling and a humidity level of 80 per cent. One storey up, the port and muscatel wines are stored at about 17 °C, a significantly higher temperature. On the top floor, Siza created the Portal, a space that combines a panoramic terrace and presentation rooms. Here visitors can admire the view over the Douro vineyards. Right next door, an older hall still serves as a production facility, with large fermentation tanks, presses and bottling lines. A subterranean tunnel connects the two buildings.

The entire structure is made of steel and concrete, visible on interior cellar walls, which are left bare. The stairs that connect the two lower floors are constructed symmetrically and, seen from a distance, resemble a large W. Large ceiling lamps of white glass illuminate the area. On the side of the lampshade, in small letters, one can read the name of the designer: Álvaro Siza.

Both storage areas are designed to offer enough capacity for the coming years. At present, there are only about 600 barriques in the red wine cellar, which can accommodate up to 3,040 of them. In the port wine cellar, the enormous barrels can hold up to 800,000 litres. The barrels are made predominantly of French and American oak. On the bottom, all of them carry the characteristic icons for Quinta do Portal. The first, a P, stands for Portal. The second, a stylized gateway, is the sign for all port wines and is found on their labels as well as their crates. The third icon, a door knocker, represents all Douro wines; and a fourth, a wine glass, symbolizes the tasting of the wine.

A notable feature at Quinta do Portal is its use of oak from Russia; its special wood qualities are suited particularly well to very dry port wines. The 50-year-old barrels of Portuguese oak, in which port wine ages for several decades, are also noteworthy.

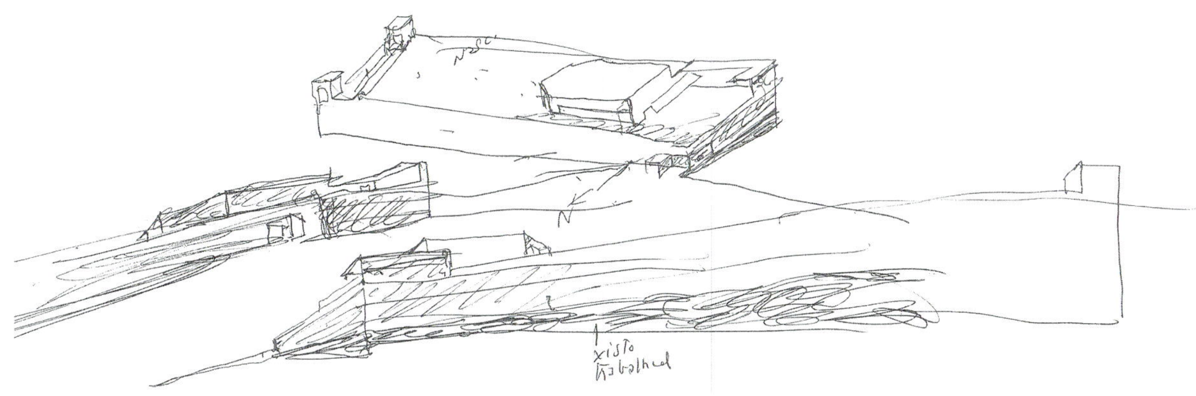
xisto

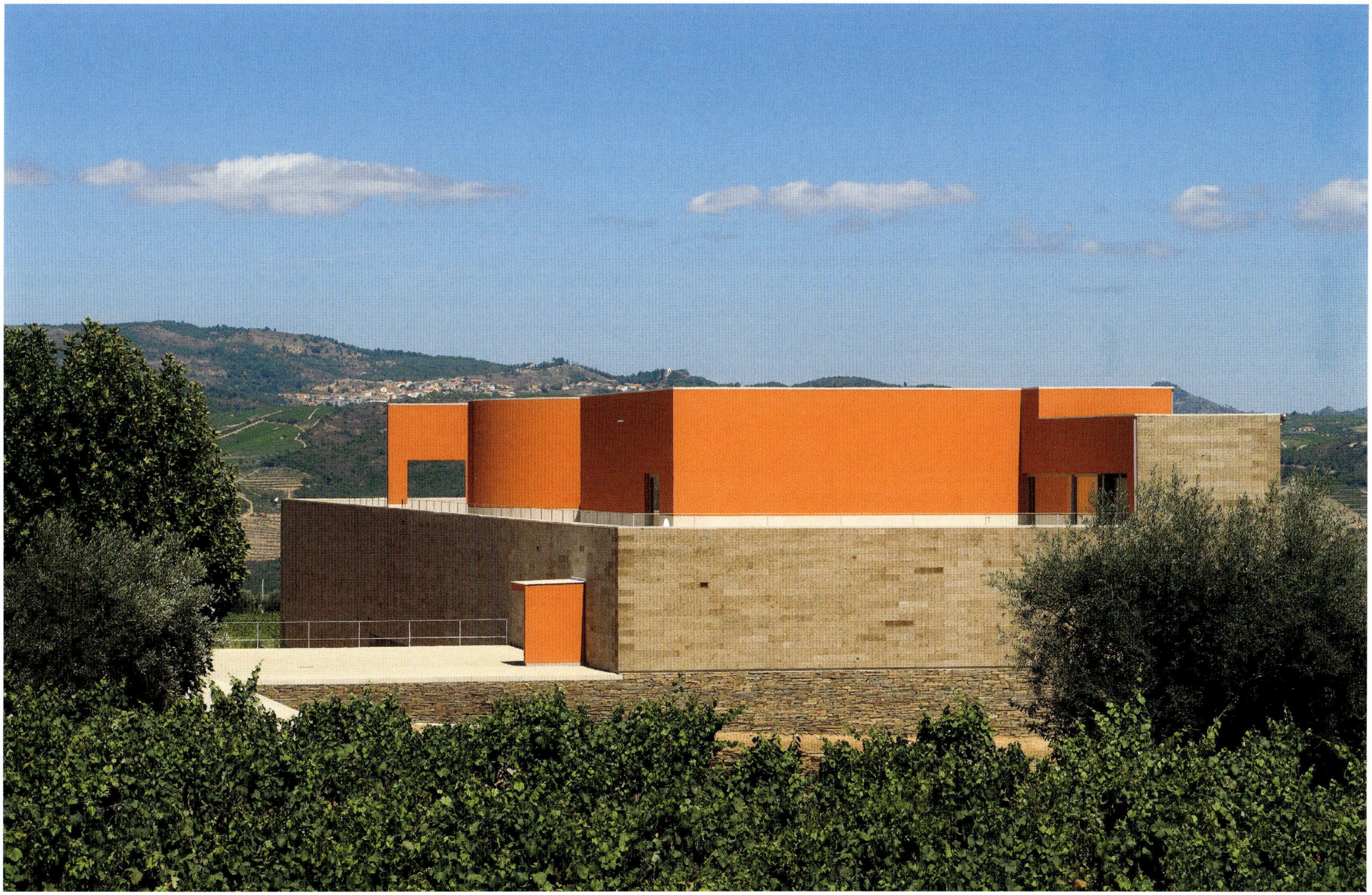

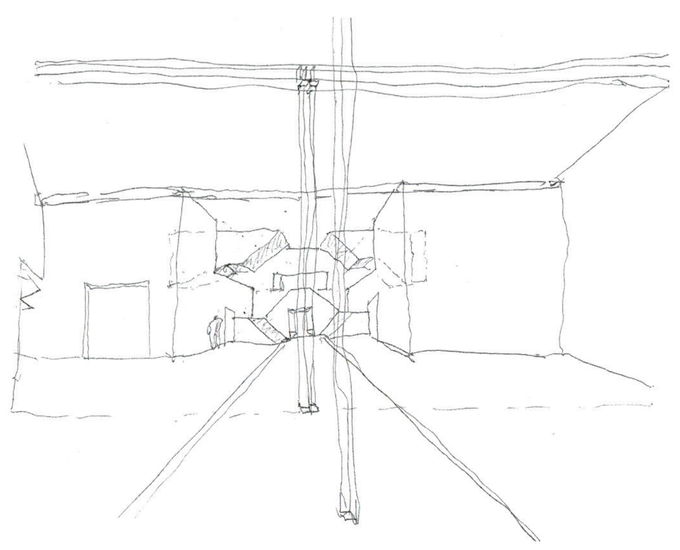

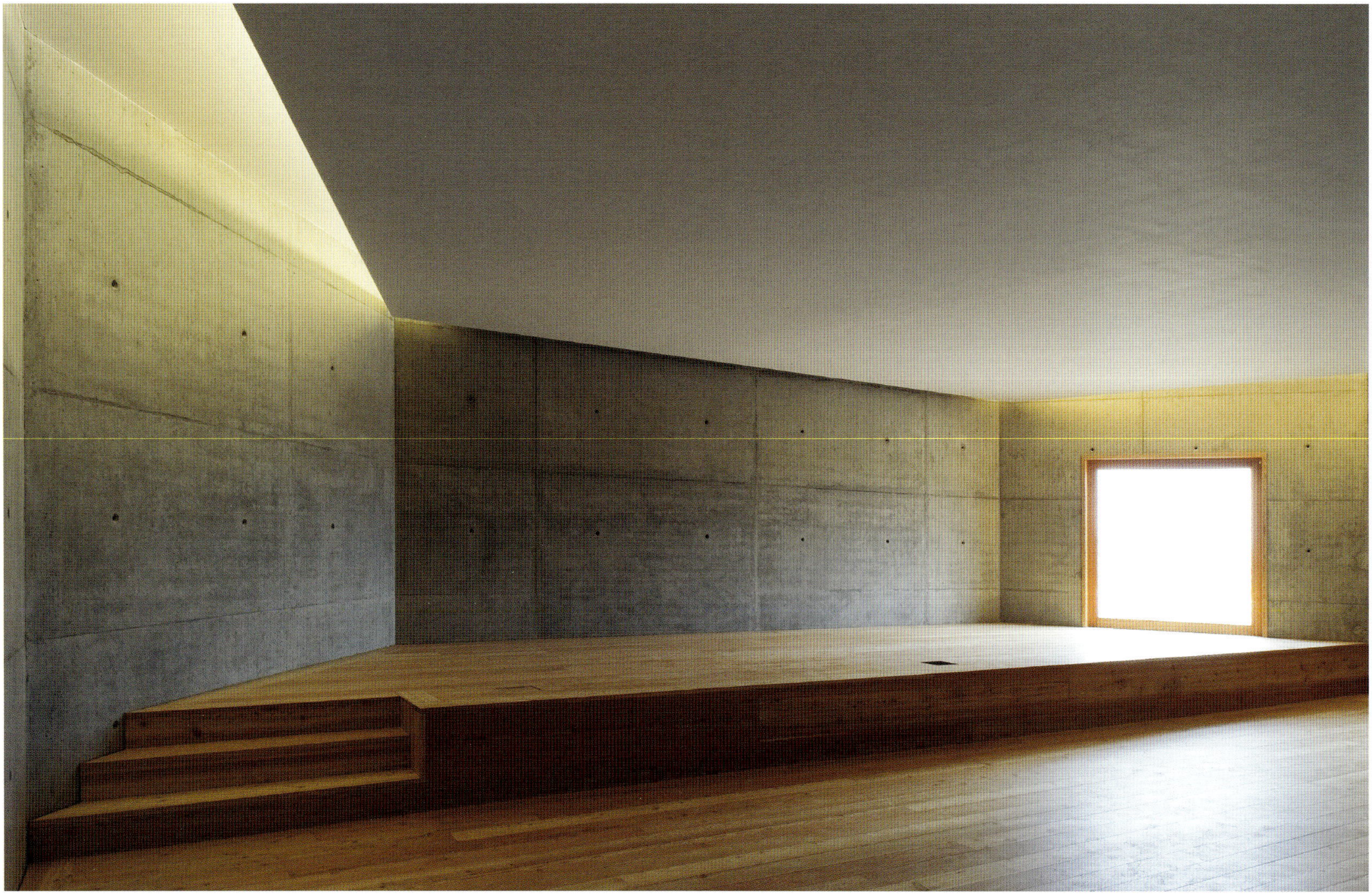

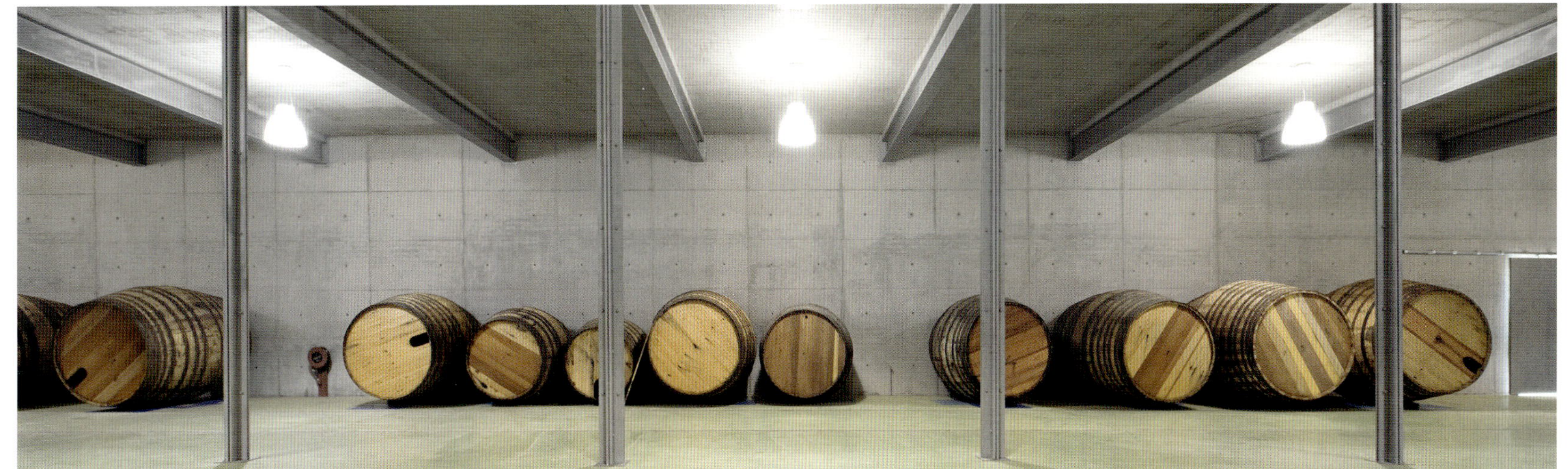

The idea of using cork, Portugal's characteristic material, on exterior facades, first came to Siza while he was designing the Portuguese pavilion for Expo 2000 in Hanover. Conceived initially as a temporary exhibition space, the pavilion was later reassembled in Coimbra, a town in central Portugal, for use as a concert hall. It became clear that cork is a first-rate, weather-resistant material that also provides very good insulation. For Siza, this was reason enough to use a layer of cork 10 centimetres thick to insulate the exterior of Quinta do Portal. The cork cladding covers a surface area of 1,506 square metres. The combination of this with the Douro slate, which covers the lower portion of the building over 1,140 square metres, creates a fascinating contrast.
Visitors arriving at the Quinta entrance from the enormous car park immediately enter the shop and tasting area. Here, the rustic pine parquet floor contrasts with the walls and ceiling of exposed concrete. A long wooden counter on the right displays the red, rosé and white wines, and further down the port and muscatel. The furnishings, also designed by Siza, are made of Riga fir, which comes from Latvia and was used in the 19th century to build houses in Porto. Siza made use of it for the first time in one of his earliest projects, the Leça Swimming Pools in Leça de Palmeira, completed in 1966. The material proved itself to be strong and stable, even after decades, without any treatment.
On the top level of the building, the roof area, Siza set a large structure in the shape of a keyhole. This

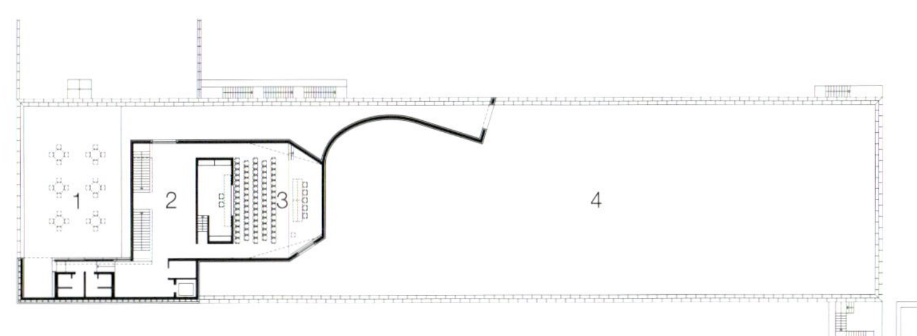

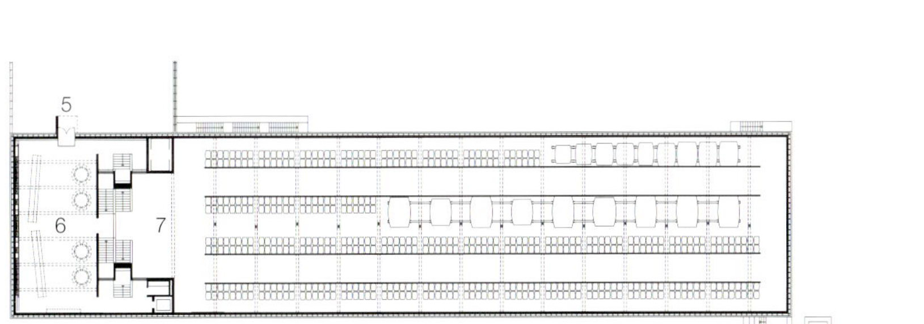

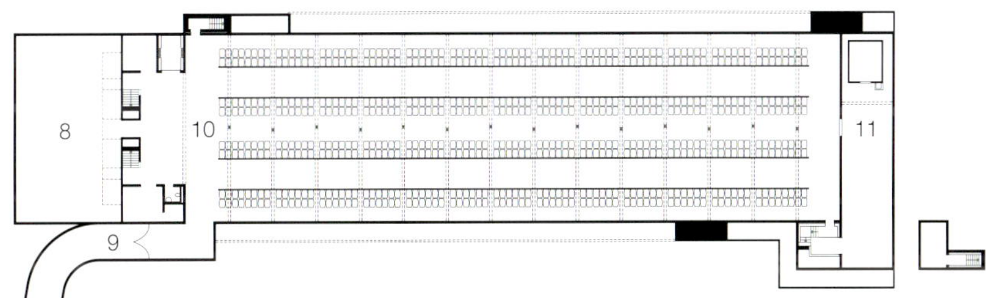

Floor plans
Scale 1:1000

1 Terrace
2 Vestibule
3 Auditorium
4 Roof terrace
5 Main entrance
6 Tasting area
7 Port wine cellar
8 Bottle storage
9 Linking tunnel
10 Barrique cellar
11 Technology

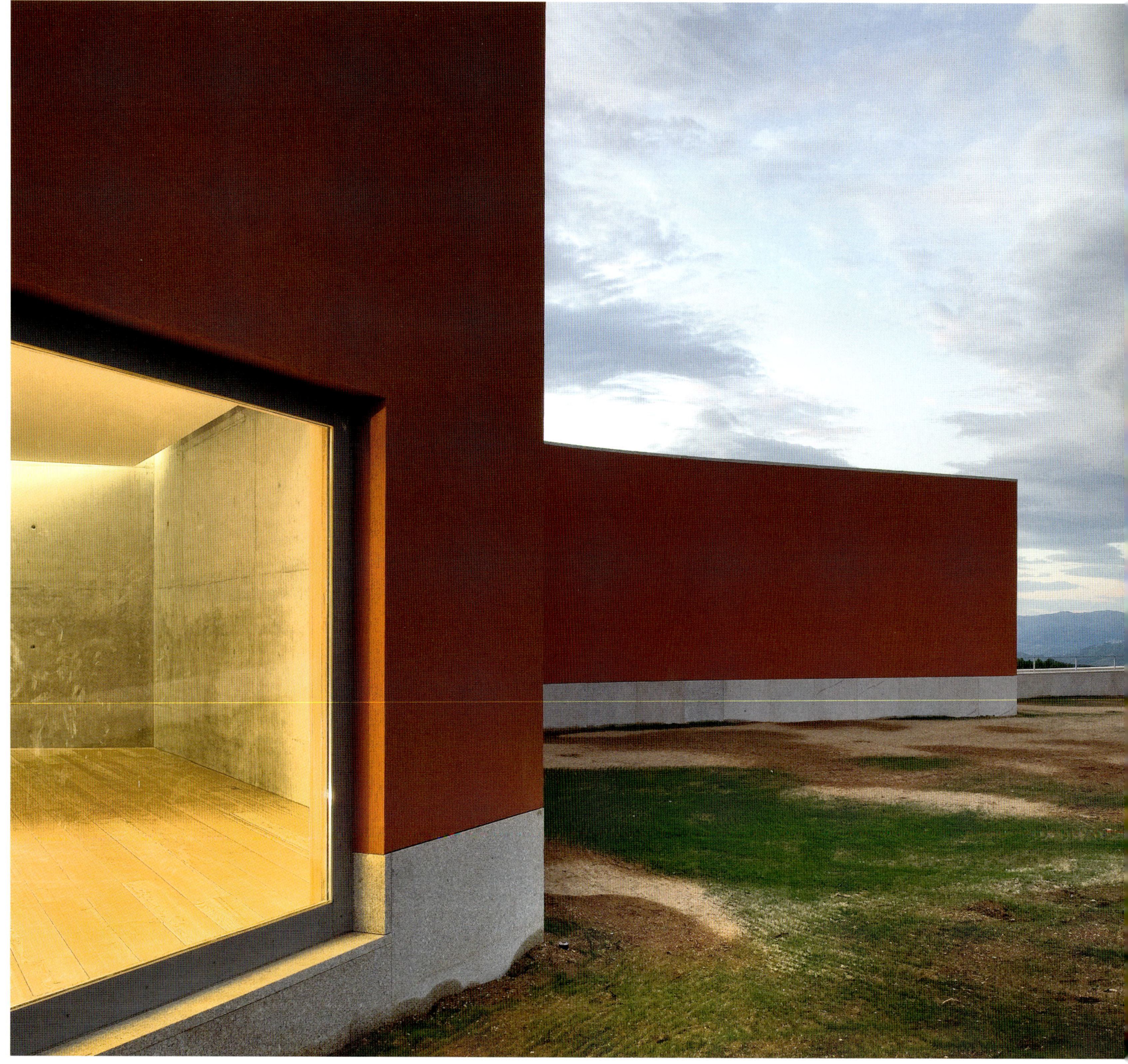

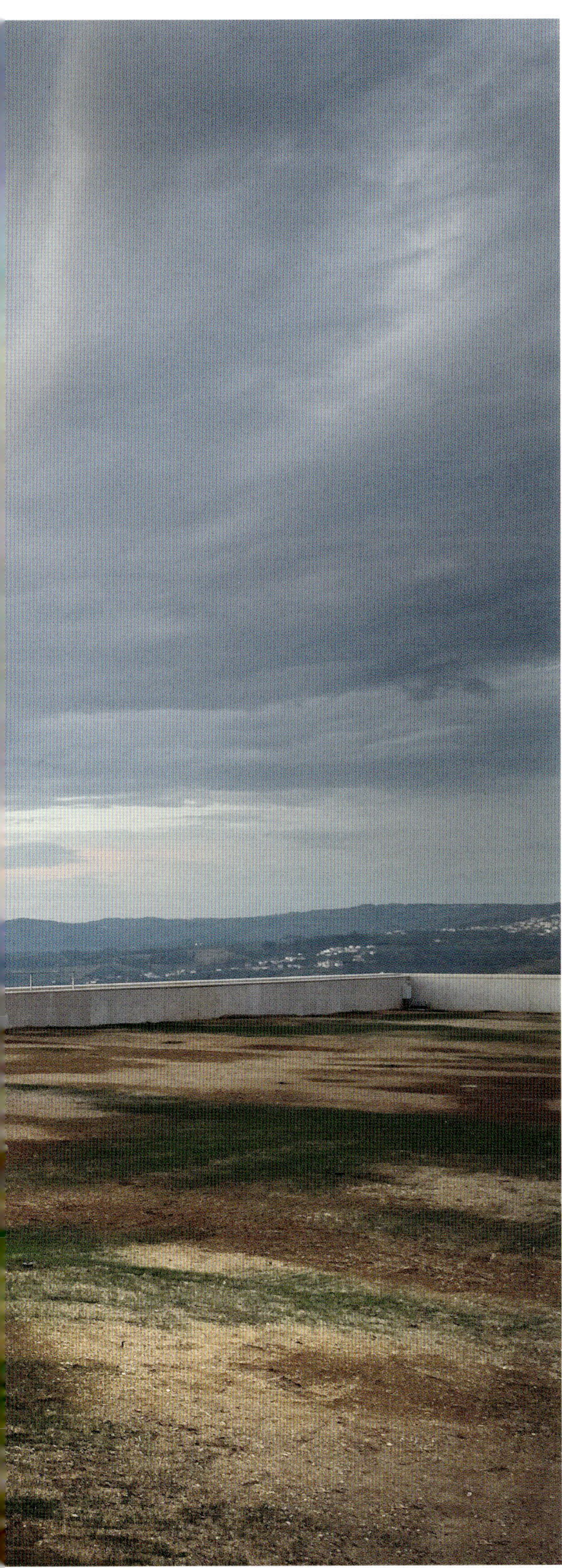

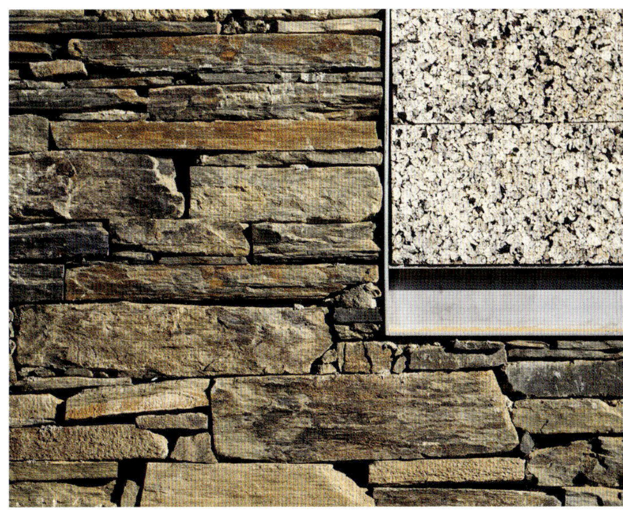

terracotta-coloured volume accommodates a presentation area that holds up to 60 people. A large window affords a view out over the surrounding landscape. The roof terrace, which can be hired for various events when not used by the quinta for its own, is covered with vegetation, which also benefits the climate in the storage areas below. This was Siza's second wine commission after the Adega Mayor wine estate (see pp. 26ff.). On this project, too, he worked according to the requirements of the vintner – in this case cellarmaster Paulo Coutinho, who has been responsible for wine production at Quinta do Portal since 1994.

Numerous accolades attest to Quinta do Portal's quality standards. Its wine range encompasses the entire spectrum, from the introductory white Relato wine, a blend of Gouveio, Malvasia Fina and Viosinho grapes, to the top wine of the house, the Quinta do Portal Auru, a red wine made from selected Touriga Nacional and Tina Roriz grapes. Today, the estate exports more than 1.4 million bottles of wine and port wine to more than 50 countries of the world, and the numbers are steadily climbing.

Winning the 2011 Prémio de Arquitectura do Douro, the Douro Valley's architectural award, Quinta do Portal opened another chapter in a success story that began more than 100 years ago with the production of port wine.

Rocca di Frassinello in Gavorrano, Italy

Architects: Renzo Piano Building Workshop, Via Rubens 29, 16158 Genoa, www.rpbw.com

Team: L. Couton (associate), B. Plattner (partner) with L. Dal Cerro, G. Ducci G. Pasquini, P. Hendier and K. Demirkan; Y. Kyrkos, C. Colson, O. Aubert (models)

Start of design phase: 2001

Completion: 2007

Region: Maremma

Contact: Podere Poggio Alla Guardia, 58023 Gavorrano www.castellare.it

Oenologist: Alessandro Cellai

Price range: €15–€100

Rocca di Frassinello in Gavorrano, in the Grosseto province of Italy, is a collaborative project by Paolo Panerai, owner of the famous Tuscan wine estate Castellare, and Baron Éric de Rothschild, managing director of the renowned Bordelais family business Domaines Barons de Rothschild.

The two men first met in the 1980s, when the baron and his wife, Beatrice, were visiting her home, the Maremma. In this aspiring southern part of Tuscany, which extends out towards the sea, these two experienced businessmen and wine experts placed their new wine estate, where they produce wine of the very best quality. In 2000, they planted their first vines; they then gathered their first harvest in 2003. During the early days, their oenological consultant was Christian le Sommer from Château Lafite Rothschild, near Bordeaux. Today, the oenologist Alessandro Cellai takes care of quality maintenance on the vineyards and in the cellar. The red-wine grape varieties Sangiovese, Cabernet Sauvignon, Merlot and Nero d'Avola, and the white-wine variety Vermentino grow on 80 hectares of the 500-hectare estate, which lies between the well-known appellations of Bolgheri and Scansano. In accordance with the practice of French châteaux, three collections of different qualities are marketed: the Poggio alla Guardia, a good basic wine; Le Sughere di Frassinello, an upscale middle range (in France often referred to as a *Second vin*); and the Rocca di Frassinello, the top quality or *Grand vin* of the estate. The wines are exported to 55 countries around the world.

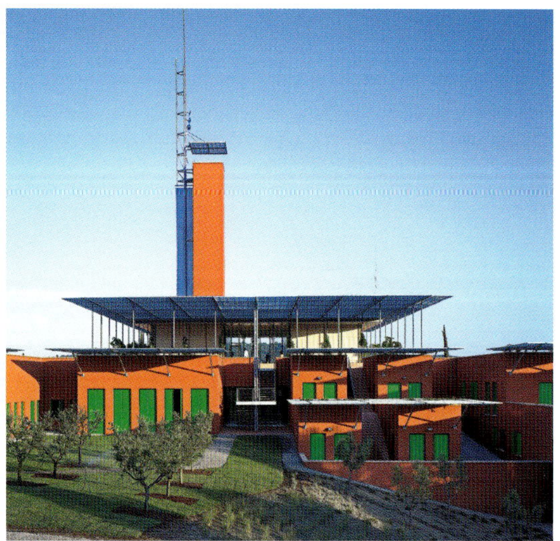

In 2001, the wine estate commissioned the architect Renzo Piano with the building of a new barrel cellar. The structure borders the northern side of an area open on the sides (based on the example of a *sagrato*, a space for public events) on the slope of a gently rising hill. Here one can enjoy a beautiful view of the surrounding landscape. Underneath the area lies the underground barrel cellar with a 2,500-barrel capacity. It resembles an amphitheatre, but instead of people, wooden barrels sit on the steps that descend down towards the middle of the space. The tasting area is on the lowest level, in the middle of the cellar.

Light wells located all around the cellar provide a soft, subdued light as well as a visual link to the surrounding wine production areas. The only direct light source is a 1.5-by-1.5-metre opening in the

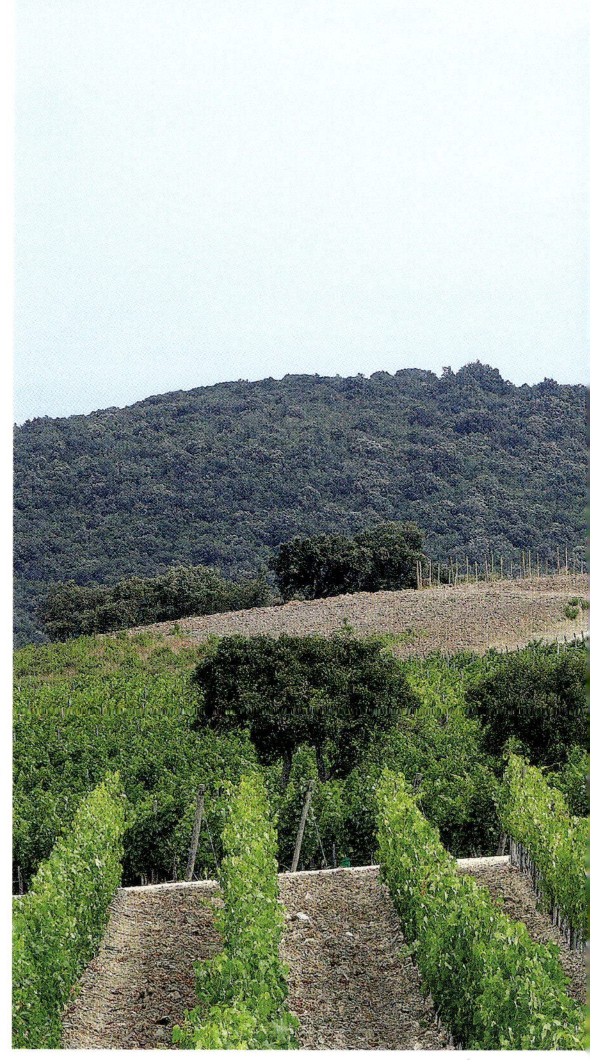

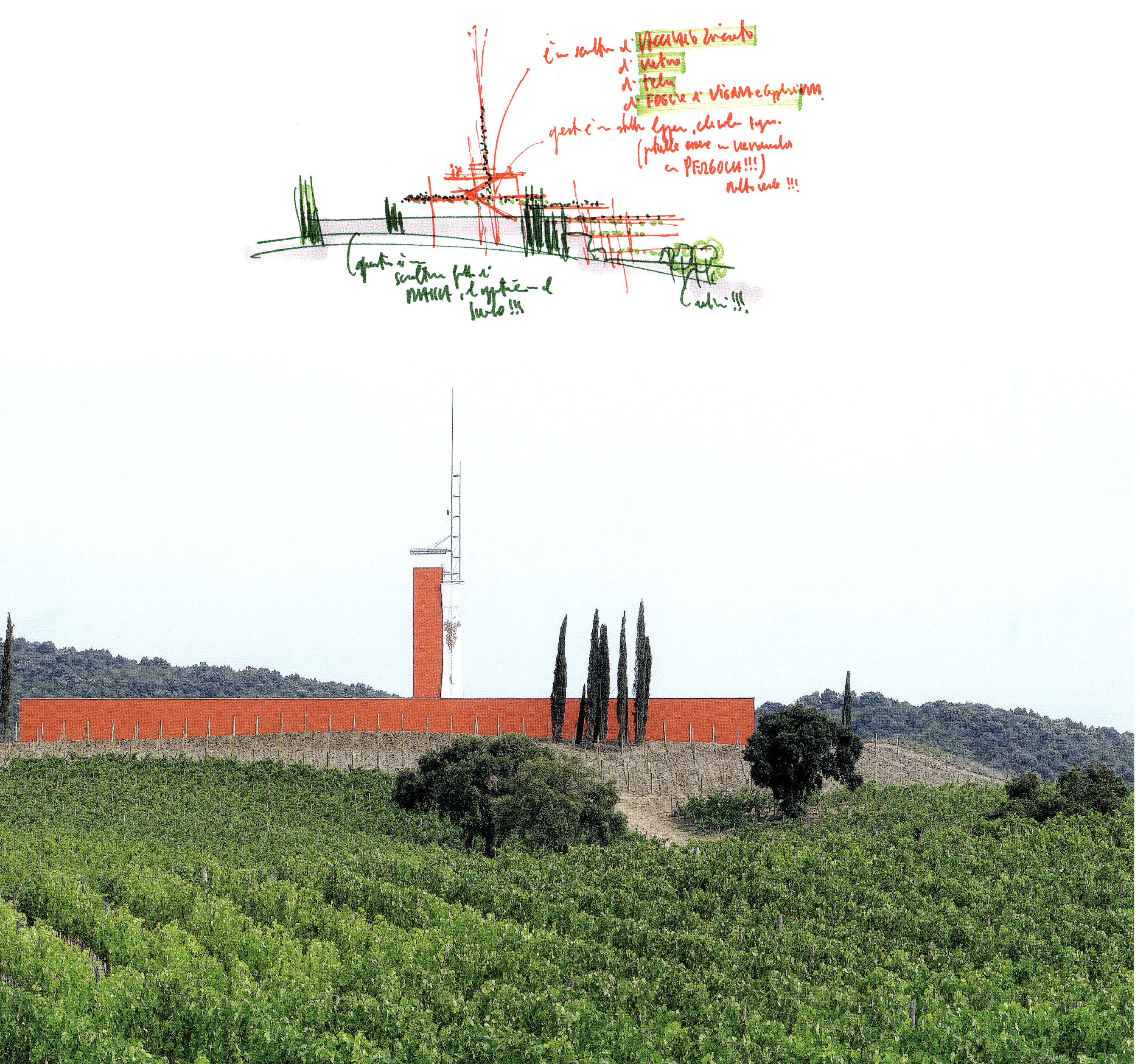

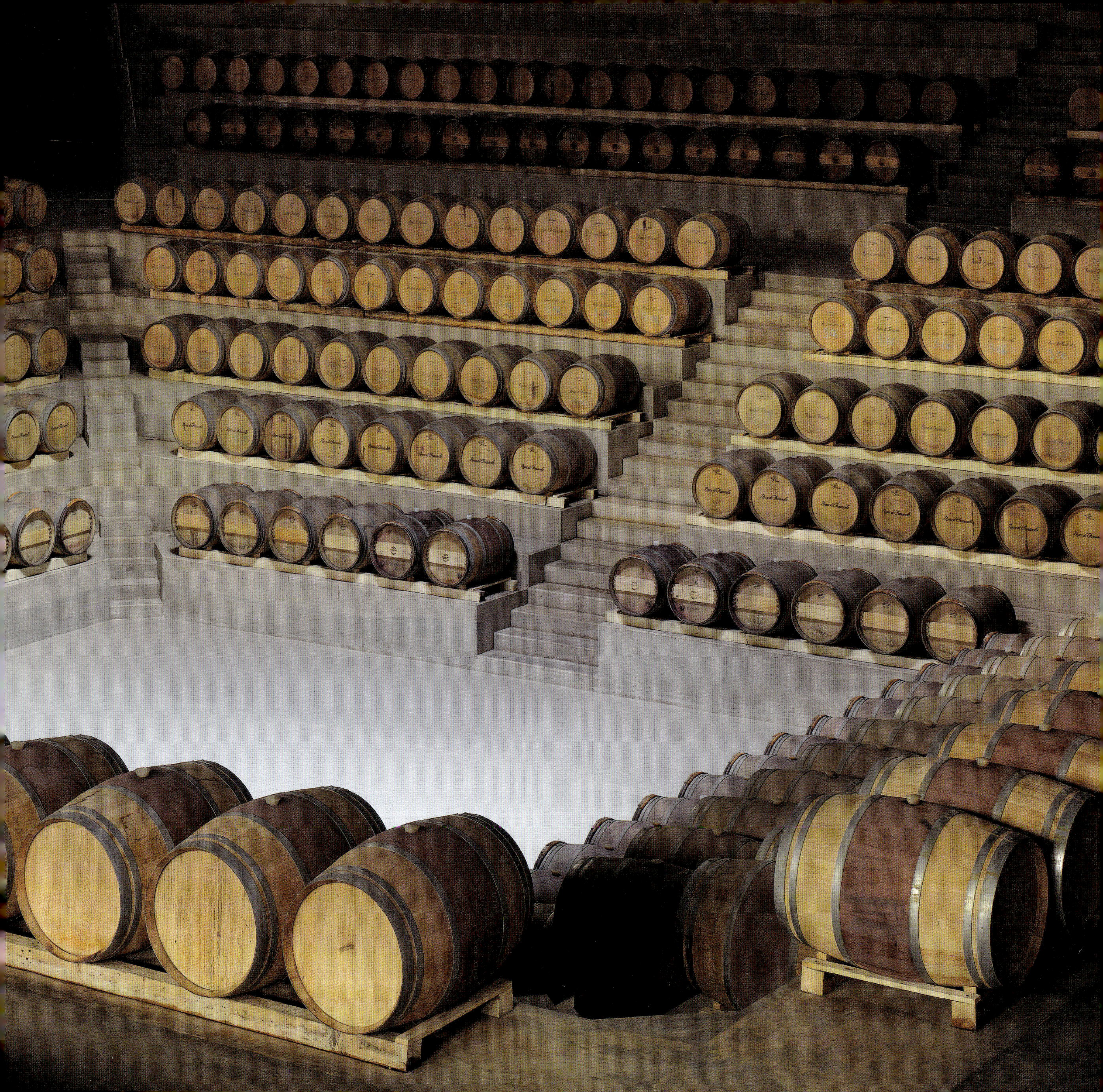

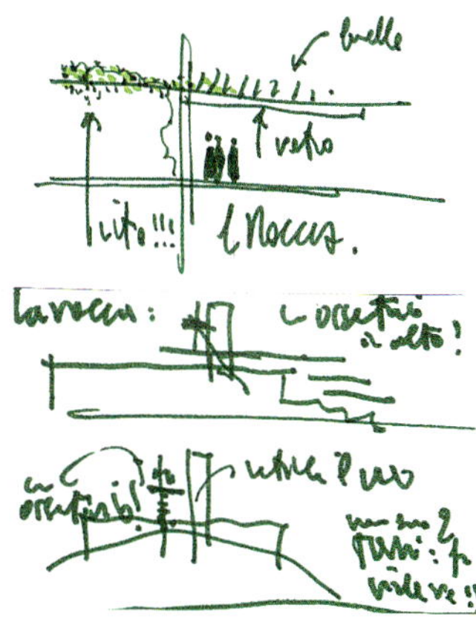

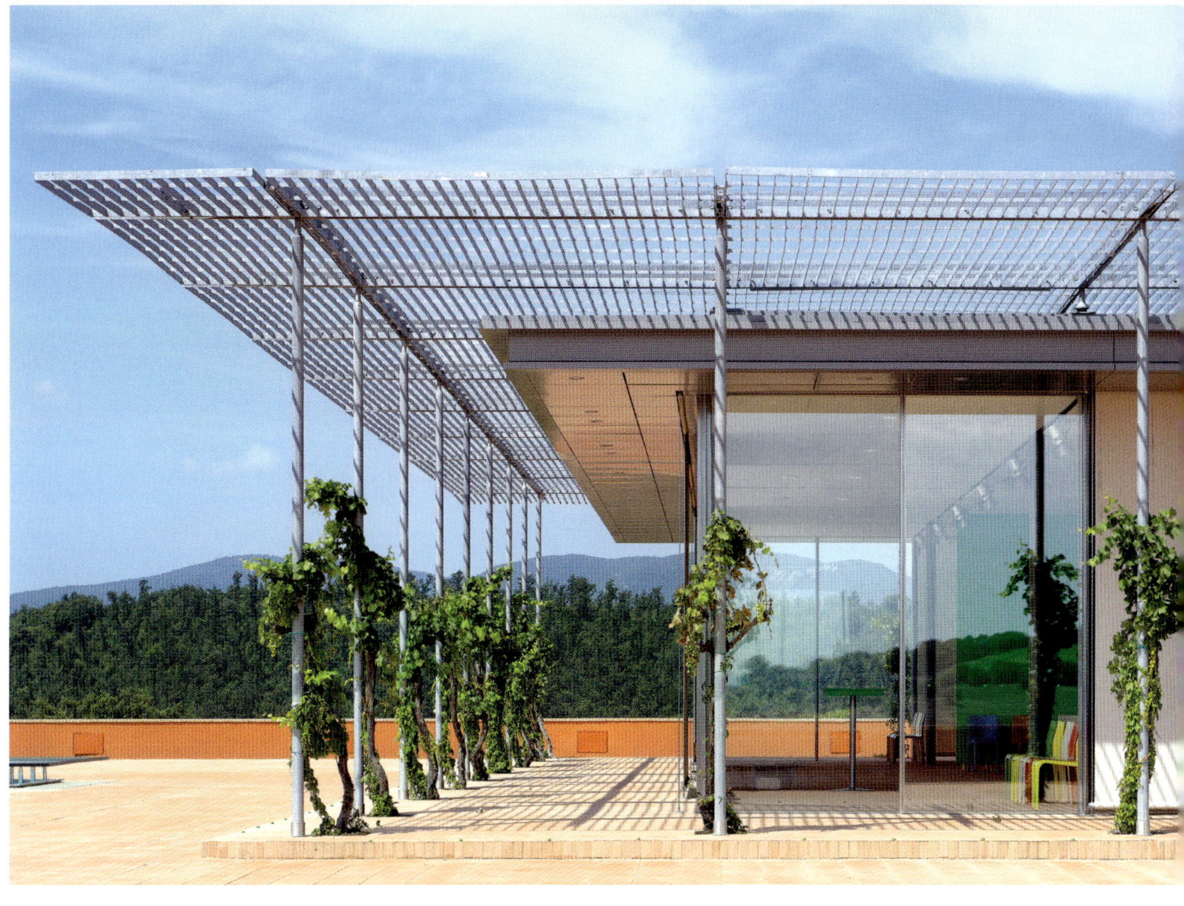

middle of the barrel cellar. This allows one to see the sky, but it also creates a dramatic atmosphere of light inside the cellar, similar to the inside of the Pantheon in Rome. The wine production areas encircle the barrel cellar. Via small openings in the ceiling, the fermentation tanks can be filled with grapes directly from the area above, which allows an optimal use of natural gravity in the production process.

The barrel cellar forms the base upon which a transparent, airy glass pavilion stands. The light-weight cube, measuring 20 by 20 metres, welcomes visitors and functions as a sales area. Its roof seems to hover overhead, like a flying carpet made of woven grape vines. The laboratories and offices are located in the eastern and western portions of the building.

Despite its size, the building does not dominate the landscape. Instead, it crouches into the slope and seems to be carrying on a dialogue with it. A creative tension exists between the rather archaic-seeming cellar and the glass construction, facilitating a dialogue between traditional winemaking and industrial production.

The wine estate's trademark – a tall, slim tower – can be seen from far away. Painted red, it recalls the towers of Tuscan city palaces, such as the square medieval towers of San Gimignano.

The external appearance of the wine estate is an expression of its philosophy. As a Franco-Italian joint venture, it aims to produce international wines. "To make great wines, you have to interpret the terroir as successfully as possible, and it varies from location to location" – this is the basic principle behind Rocca di Frassinello.

Standardized tastes are barred. In a world in which everything is becoming more homogeneous, the wine estate is fighting back in a sort of cultural crusade. Much more than just a beverage, after all, wine is still a product made painstakingly by hand.

Panerai and Piano have known each other for many years. The former was once among the first journalists to write about the architect's work, and they have been good friends since then. But that is not the only reason Piano was chosen for the project; there is also the fact that he is one of the most important contemporary architects in Italy. Interestingly, he had never before built a wine estate, although he loves wine and his father owned a small wine estate in Piedmont.

The basic tenets of the project were worked out by Piano and Panerai in a long planning process from 2001 to 2007. Piano's philosophy is not to eradicate nature through architecture, but to integrate architecture into the landscape. The resulting building is a fitting reflection of his credo.

Weingut Erich Sattler in Tadten, Austria

Architects: Architects Collective, Hohlweggasse 2/25, 1030 Vienna, www.architectscollective.net

Team: Andreas Frauscher, Patrick Herold, Richard Klinger, Kurt Sattler

Site area: 300 m²

Gross floor area: 450 m²

Start of design phase: 2009

Completion: 2010

Region: Burgenland

Contact: Obere Hauptstr. 10, 7162 Tadten www.erichsattler.at

Oenologist: Erich Sattler

Price range: €4–€30

●○○

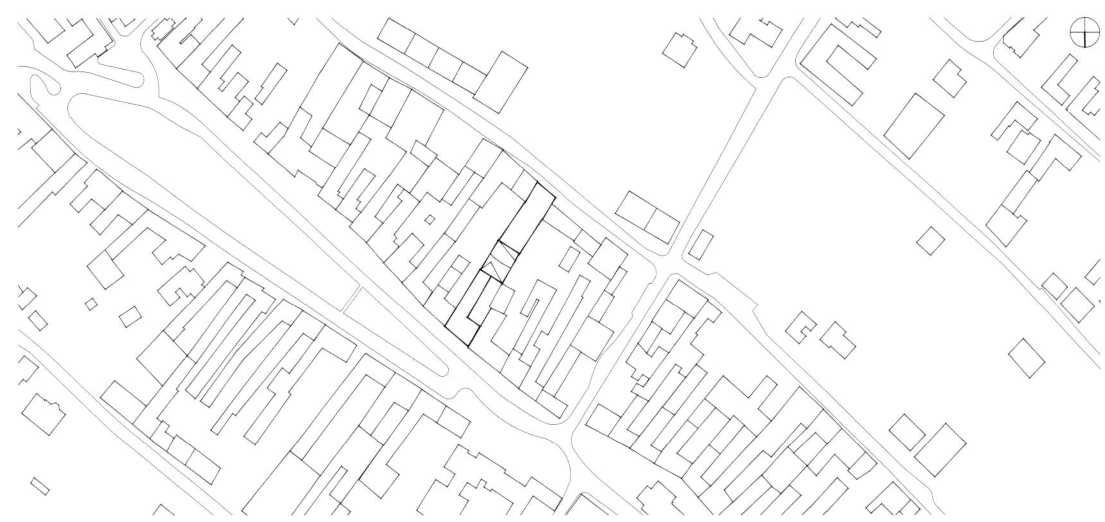

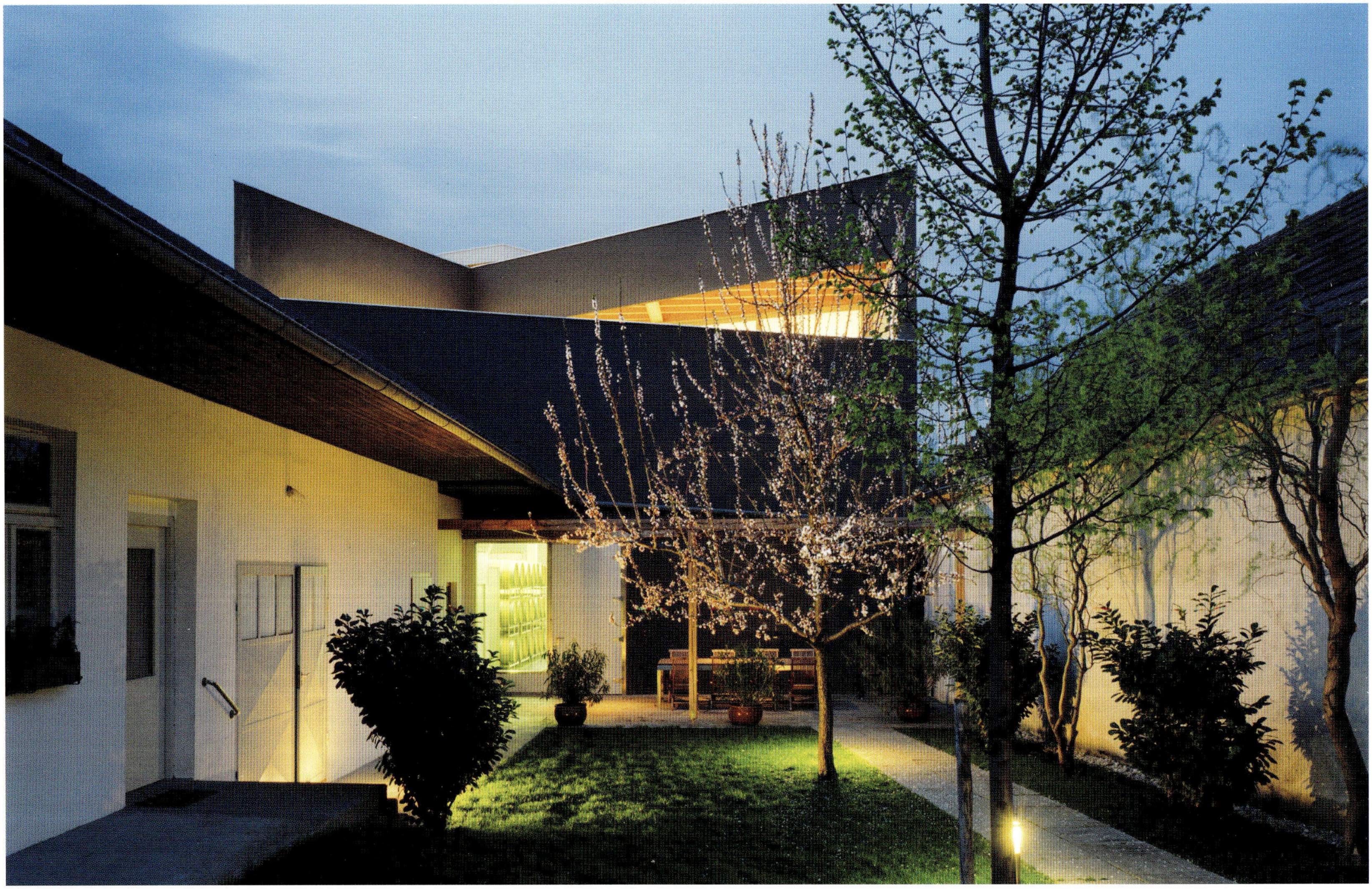

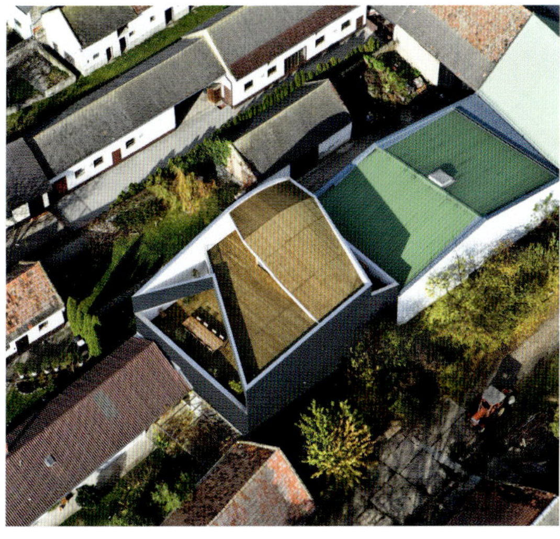

Site plan
Scale 1:2000
Floor plans
Scale 1:500

1 Barrel room
2 Tank room
3 Terrace
4 Office
5 Vestibule
6 Tasting area
7 Bedroom

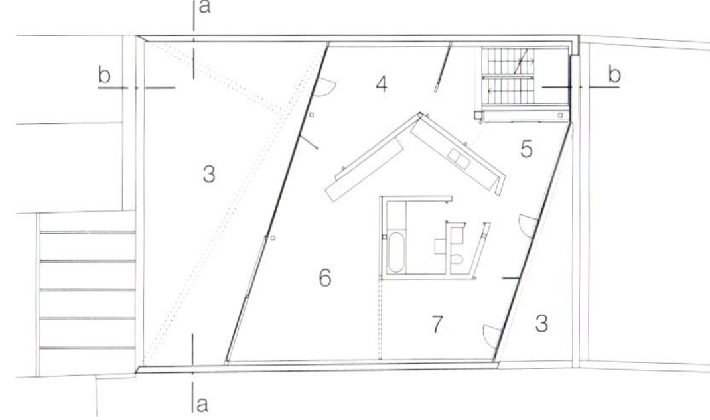

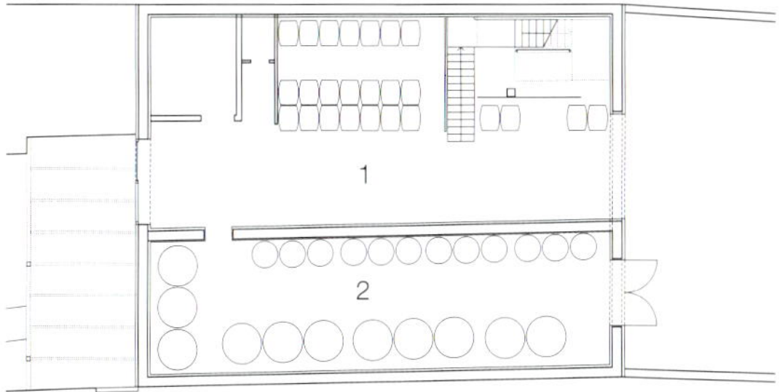

Even as a young boy, Erich Sattler played where he now passionately works: in the vineyards of his home community of Tadten, in the middle of Austria's Burgenland. After finishing his studies at the school of oenology and viticulture in Krems and at the University of Natural Resources and Life Sciences in Vienna, Sattler returned to the village of Tadten, population 1,300, and took over the family wine estate in 2000.

"I am passionate about wines, just as I love them and like to drink them," says Sattler, and one is immediately inclined to believe him. His main focus is on the red grape varieties Zweigelt and St. Laurent, which together comprise more than four fifths of his wine production. For the white wines, it's Pinot Blanc and the regional variety Welschriesling, a late-ripening grape with fruity acidity that, despite its name, has nothing to do with Riesling. They all grow on the sparse, gravelly soil that the Danube deposited here more than two million years ago on its way to the Black Sea. It's an ideal soil for producing wine, as it absorbs heat during the day and radiates it back to the vines during the night. The sparseness of the soil supports the making of red wines with velvety tannins and a playful fruitiness. The local climate, characterized by its hot, dry summers and usually sunny autumns, allows the grapes to ripen perfectly.

On his 12-hectare estate near Lake Neusiedl, Sattler produces wines with great typicity, richness and exceptional ageing potential. "From the vineyard to the bottle, everything should go through my hands," he says. "I don't want to get any bigger." But when his wine estate threatened to burst at the seams three years ago, he saw that he needed to take action. Since his brother Kurt has his own architectural practice in Vienna, the search for an architect was not hard.

Erich Sattler had particular ideas about the planned renovation. He wanted a space that could serve as a meeting place for business partners and customers alike. At the same time, he wished to have an area for cooking and eating. Since accommodation in Tadten is quite limited, it also seemed a good idea to include guest rooms for visitors at the wine estate.

The architectural challenge lay in integrating a new building into the existing space in the centre of the village. There were two older buildings and a new one on the site, which measures 12 by 120 metres. The L-shaped residential building stands near the village green; its courtyard gives access to the wine estate. On the other side of the plot, towards the vineyards, there is a production and storage building with vehicle access. This grouping of buildings led to the idea of placing the extension in the middle of the plot. Kurt Sattler and his team at Architects Collective worked out three designs for Erich Sattler to choose from. The one he selected offered a two-storey solution: the

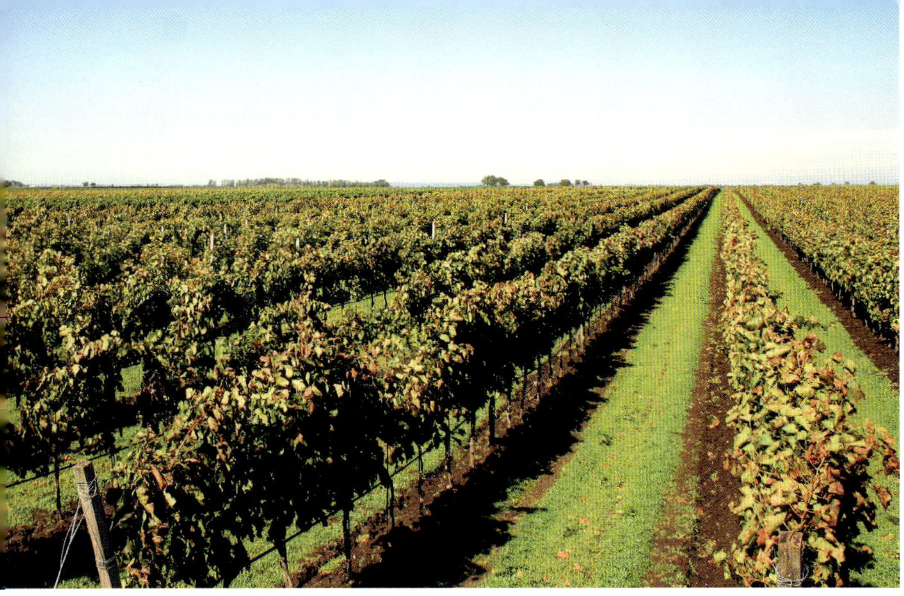

ground floor houses the barrel room, with the tasting area, kitchen, office and guest rooms on the upper floor.
The planning phase lasted for six months; the implementation, about a year. While the upper floor was still being built, the ground level was already in use for the 2009 harvest.
The different shapes of the two floors are of particular interest. The ground floor is rectangular, and the upper floor is set upon it in the shape of a parallelogram. The latter's interior rooms open out into different directions. The two basic shapes are linked via a series of diagonals, which create a flowing overall configuration. On the upper level, this gives rise to a variety of spaces with myriad geometries and angles of view. The areas left on either side of the parallelogram form two terraces, one east- and one west-facing, which can be used for events and wine presentations. The slanted and slightly arched roof is decked in wooden planks and walkable. From afar, it looks like part of an enormous wooden barrel. The roof offers an impressive, 360-degree panoramic view towards Lake Neusiedl, Slovakia and neighbouring Hungary as well as to the Alpine foothills in the distance.
Sweeping glass facades mediate the transition from interior to exterior and bring light into the rooms. Kurt Sattler and his team were inspired by the work of US artist Dan Graham, who created a stir with, among other things, his accessible pavilion in the heating power plant in Berlin-Mitte, and the "Two-Way Mirror Hedge" at the Ständehauspark in Düsseldorf. The interior itself can be used in its entirety or divided by folding walls and four large doors. In the middle of this area is a free-standing, pentagonal structure covered with wood, which contains sanitary rooms and a kitchen.
The entire construction is of concrete and masonry. The dark grey facade contrasts with the white interior. The only dashes of colour are provided by the red chairs in the tasting area.
On both ground and upper levels, the emphasis lay on easy maintenance as well as on functionality. The architects created large surfaces with as few joints as possible to make them easy to clean. To cover the bare concrete on the interior walls, they chose 10-centimetre-thick sandwich panelling for insulation. This was treated with an acid-resistant coating to make it more robust and hygienic.
It was decided not to install a cooling system on the ground floor. Although outside temperatures can exceed 30 °C during the summer, the temperature inside the barrel room does not go above 15 °C. The concrete floor was set directly into the earth without any insulation. Underfloor heating was installed on the upper level. Outside, the extensive terraces are covered with wooden decking, and an enormous awning provides shade during wine tastings. The uppermost roof terrace is reserved for private use, so only a lucky few are treated to the magnificent view from up there.
Erich Sattler is a rather reserved person, and his wine estate is designed the same way: not brash and concerned with appearances, but subdued and discreet. Only after visitors come through the entrance gate and into the courtyard does the winery open up to them – just like its wines, which take a little time to unfold after opening but then release their velvety, delicate, elegant aromas. It is this reserved elegance that unites the wines, the estate and the vintner.

Sections
Scale 1:500

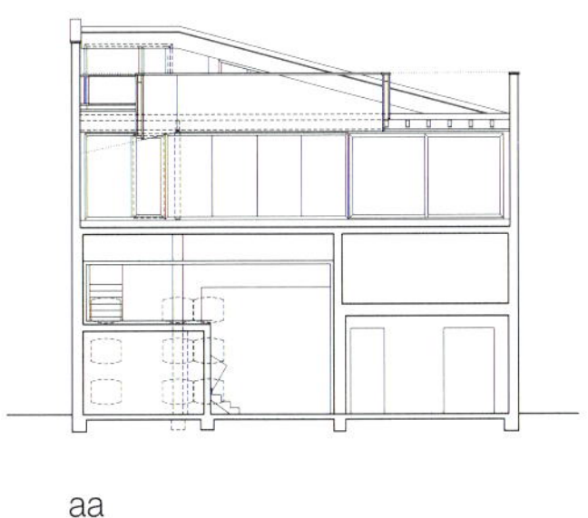

aa

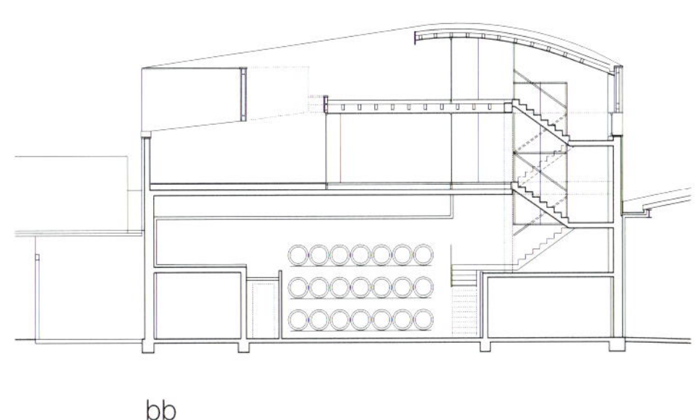

bb

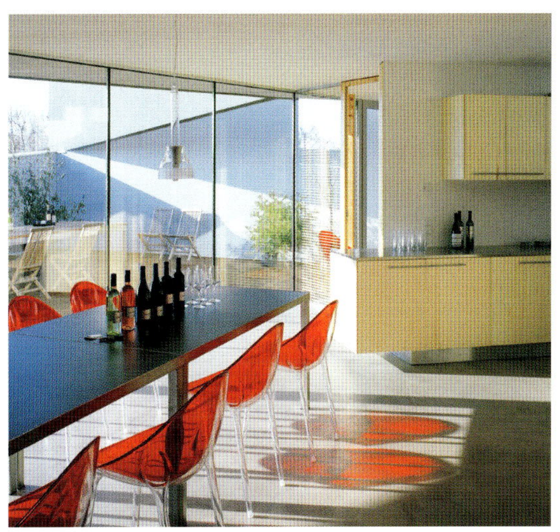

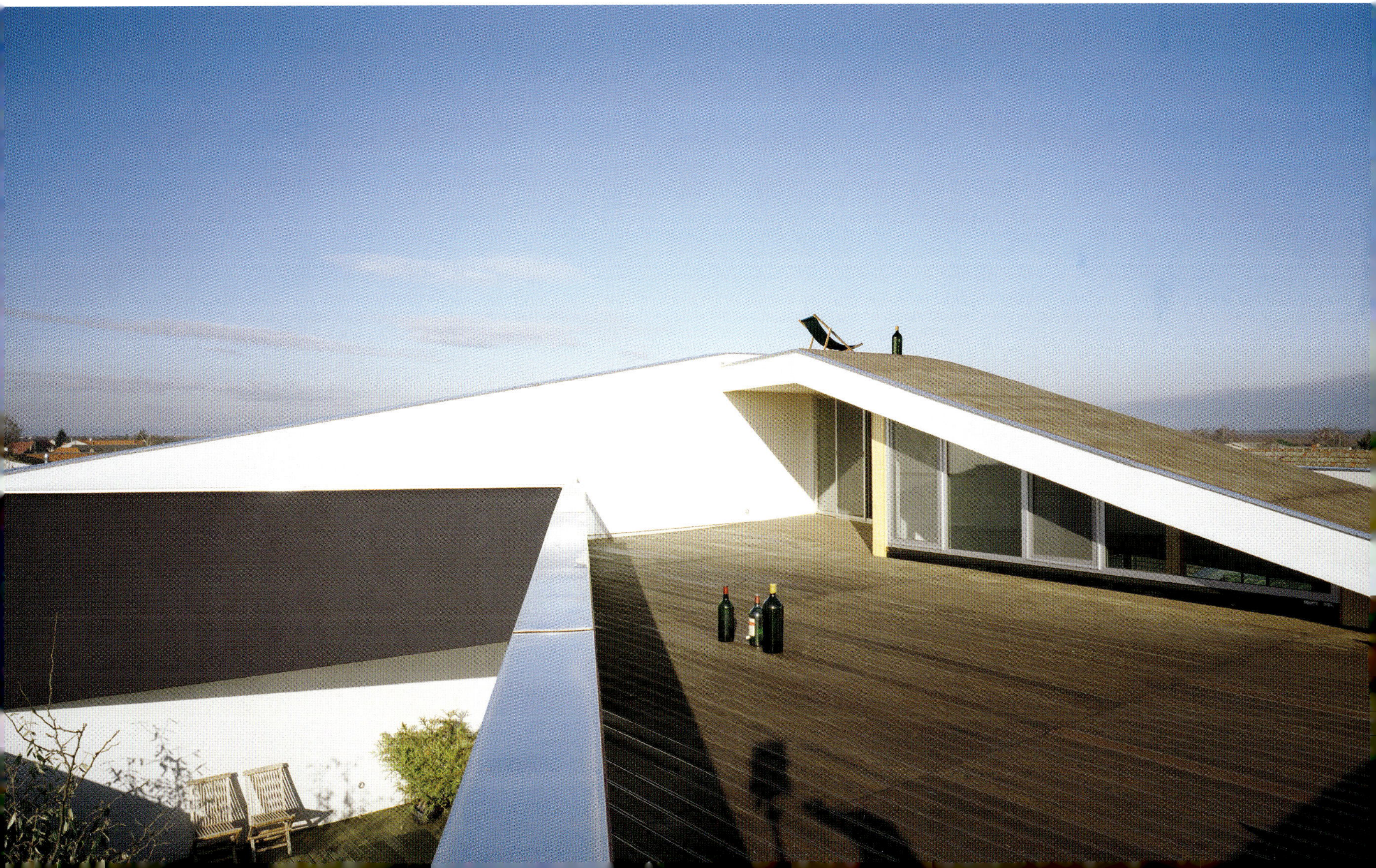

Cantina San Michele-Appiano in Appiano, Italy

Architect: Walter Angonese, Marktplatz 6, 39052 Caldaro
www.angonesewalter.it

Artistic intervention: Manfred Alois Mayr, Merano

Team: Silvia Potente

Site area: 350 m² (sales), 820 m² (barrique cellar)

Gross floor area: 422 m² (sales), 936 m² (barrique cellar)

Start of design phase: 2008

Completion: 2011

Region: Alto Adige

Contact: Via Circonvallazione 17/19, 39057 Appiano
www.stmichael.it

Oenologist: Hans Terzer

Price range: €7–€22

●●●

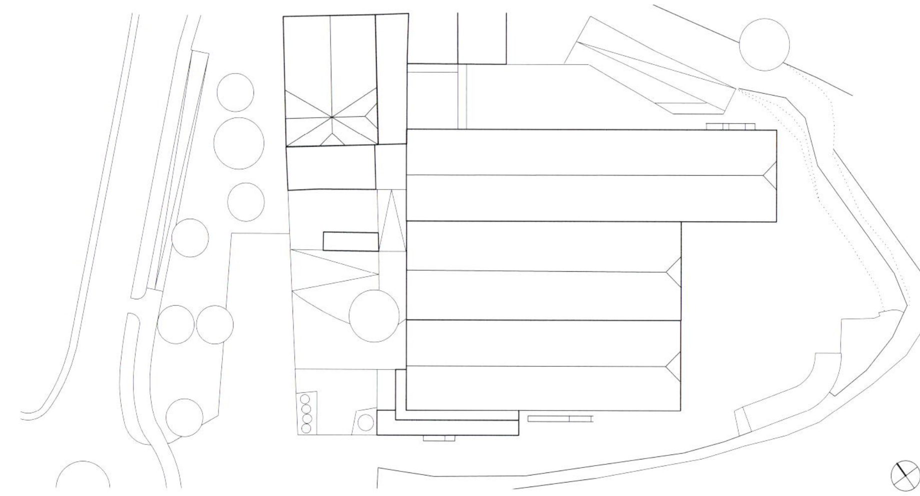

Site plan
Scale 1:1500

The San Michele-Appiano winery, founded in 1907, is located in the heart of the South Tyrolian Wine Road town of Appiano, or Eppan, where it can be seen from afar. Its 350 members deliver their grapes, tenderly cultivated on 380 hectares, to San Michele, which distributes their wines to more than 30 countries and to the top tier of Italian restaurants.

Hans Terzer, the cellarmaster, has been in charge of wine production since 1977. Anton Zublasing, himself a winegrower and one of Italy's leading oenologists, is the president of the cooperative and of the Alto Adige wine consortium, and as such constitutes the link between its members and the management. Günther Neumeir is in charge of the administration of the winery.

San Michele-Appiano's main building, built in 1909 in the Art Nouveau style, once served as the wine cellar's stately headquarters, embodying the pride of the winegrowers and the region's deep sense of tradition. Complementing this reference to the past, the newly designed barrel cellar and a wine bar/shop completed in 2011 allow a glimpse into a future that is to be marked by innovation, creativity and openness.

Terzer has been friends with architect Walter Angonese for more than 10 years. Over the course of the entire planning and building phase of the new barrique cellar and showroom, they stayed in close contact with each other and with Merano artist Manfred Alois Mayr, jointly working out the design approach.

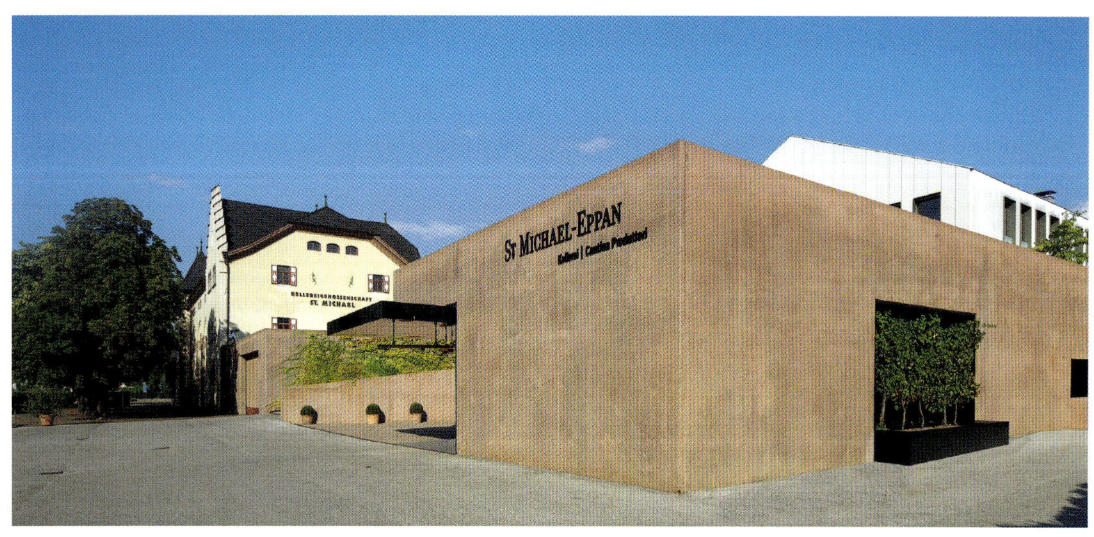

The look of the new sales space is dominated by light oak, which is found in the counters, shelves and the long table to the rear of the room. As in other wine estates, this material provides a visual link with winemaking. In spite of the heavy, solid oak and the black, three-centimetre-thick bitumen terrazzo flooring, the space appears light and open. Natural light comes in only through the glass wall in the entrance area and the patios.

Upon entering the space, one's attention is immediately caught by the lamps, which were designed by Mayr. Halogen lamps fixed to overhead cable raceways covered in gold leaf bathe the space in a warm, atmospheric light. The contrast of "lowly" material and luxurious surface comes to full effect here, with the gold playfully reflecting the light from the lamps. The interrupted cable raceways appear to be suspended in mid-air.

The undisputed stars in this space are the cellar's wines. The planners did not want to create a boutique in which architecture and furnishings would predominate and leave little room for the wine. Instead, their aim was to give the cellar's bottles pride of place.

These are on display in the oak shelves along the walls. Between the shelves, there is a strip of wood containing backlit black-and-white photographs depicting vineyards and everyday winemaking scenes. Symbolism and emotionalism suffuse the entire space, even if it is sometimes mere details, such as the barrel stoppers let into the handrail of the massive oak counter, that stimulate the senses by inviting touch.

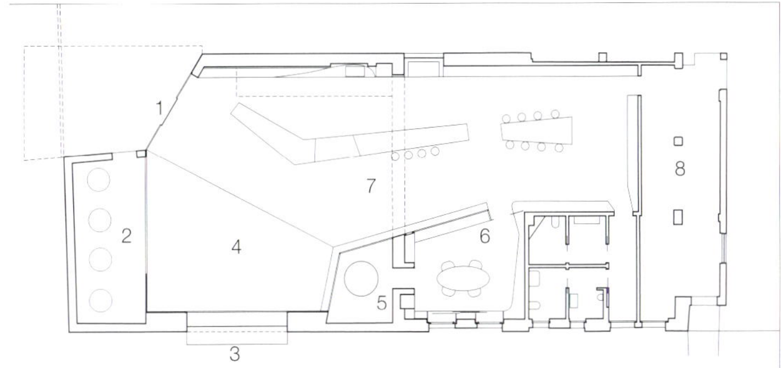

Floor plan tasting space
Scale 1:400

1 Entrance
2 Yew tree patio
3 Grapevine patio
4 Lagenbühne
5 Olivenbaum-Patio
6 Verkostungsraum
7 Verkostungs- und Verkaufsraum
8 Lager

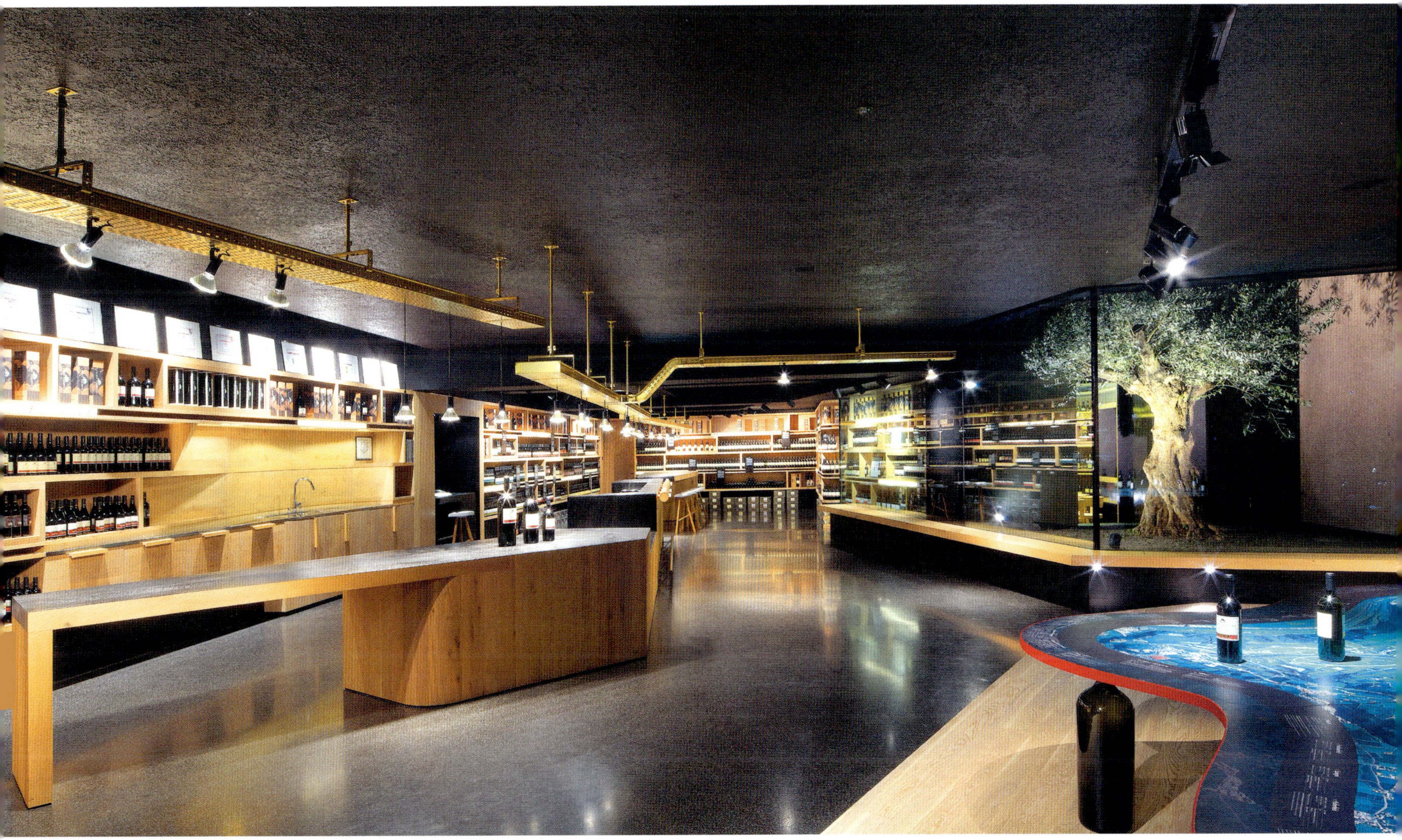

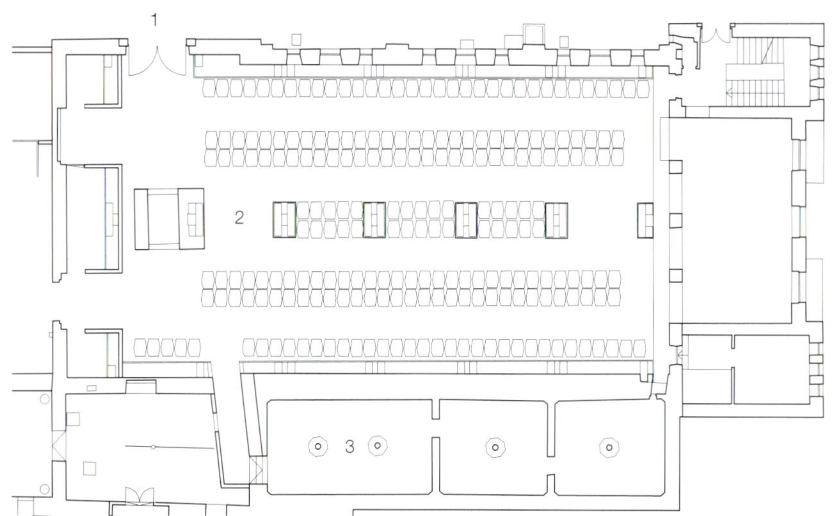

Floor plan, wine cellar
Scale 1:400

1 Entrance
2 Barrique cellar
3 Cut-open concrete tanks

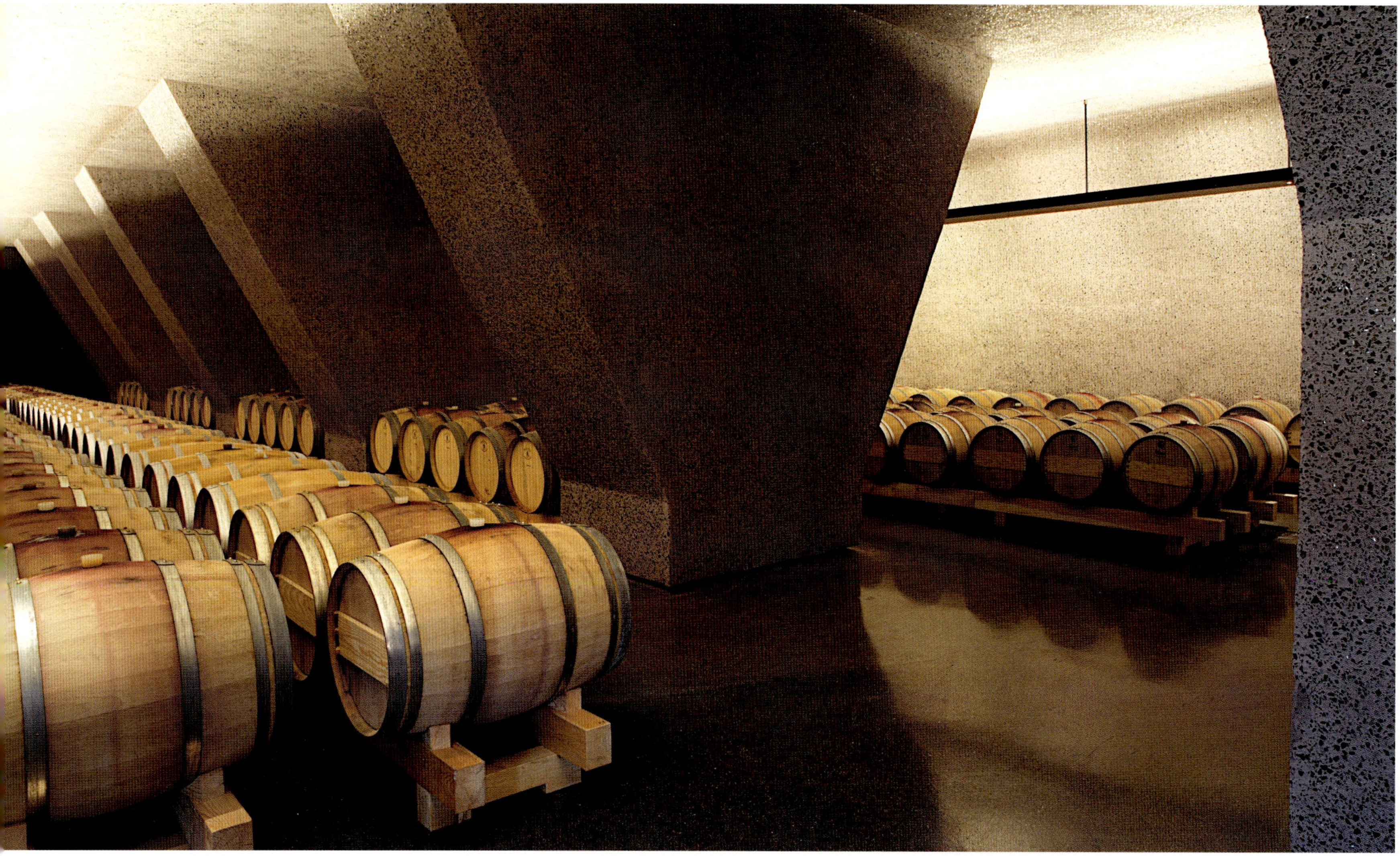

In the separate tasting room, too, oak predominates. The tables and chairs are custom-built of solid wood. A huge table stands on a slightly raised platform in the sales space. The surface of the table, which from a distance is perceived solely as a dark slab of organic form, upon closer inspection reveals itself to be a photographic overview of the cellar's vineyards. On the individual sites stand bottles of wine produced from the grapes grown there, an approach that creates an immediate and palpable link to the origin of the wines on display. The view out of the space leads across the three patios. Grapevines grow in one, an olive tree in the second, and yew trees in the third. These three typical plants from Alto Adige symbolize the flora of the surrounding landscape, while at the same time sheltering the space from the sun.

Against the light, the ceiling of the sales space initially appears black; a closer look, however, reveals large, intersecting circles of dark, muted colours. Petrol green, grey-brown and dark red are used over the table on the dais. The colours correspond to those found on the vineyard map. Above the counters and the shelves, gold, ochre and grey-blue are used, colours that harmonize with the light wood and the golden lamps. Thanks to the high-quality material used, the furnishings, though simple, appear elegant.

White wine is the mainstay of San Michele's business, accounting for 68 per cent of its production. Of this, 18 per cent are made up of Weissburgunder (Pinot Blanc). With a 17 per cent share of total production, Schiava, which is indigenous to the Alto Adige region, accounts for more than half of the red wines produced.

The Classic Line includes all the characteristic Alto Adige whites, reds and rosés in DOC quality. The Selection Line comprises an individually assembled collection of extraordinary wines from select vineyard sites. The Sanct Valentin line represents the top of the range, with wines created from individual sites with strict yield limits. This line includes the wine-loving architect's favourite wines, the Sanct Valentin Sauvignon Blanc and the Sanct Valentin Pinot Noir. Purity of tone, subtle acidity and balance characterize the San Michele wines. The uncompromising focus on quality was honoured in 2000 with the "Cellar of the Year" award.

From the 1950s to the 1970s, the Alto Adige region, like many other wine-growing regions in the world, pursued a policy of mass production. The huge subterranean concrete tanks bear witness to this time. As these had not been used for years, the San Michele-Appiano winery, too, put the tanks to good use by cutting them open and turning them into barrique cellars. The walls are clad in glass tiles, which have over the years taken on the colour of the wine and today shimmer in hues of violet and dark blue; the deposits of tartar found in the joints glitter. This is an atmospheric room that ties together the winery's past and present.

Through a passageway painted a bilious green, one arrives in the adjoining barrel cellar, which has also been updated by Angonese. The walls here feature the typical black yeast deposits. From the far end of the cellar, the opening in the middle of the opposite wall looks like a pane of green glass lit from behind. It is an incredibly effective optical illusion.

A flight of stairs of rough concrete leads up to the Art Nouveau building. The original wrought-iron banister is still in its original state, save for a new coat of dark-green paint. This, too, is evidence of the deliberate play of contrasts. From there, one arrives in the upper barrique cellar, whose original form, including supports, was "formed over", thus getting a pragmatic architectural reinterpretation. As in the sales space, the floor is of bitumen terrazzo. The walls are covered with a render studded with tiny shards of glass, which makes the entire space glitter. From afar, it looks as if minute gemstones have been set into the render.

All work was done under the close supervision of the architect and the artist, working together. Both were frequently present during the construction phase. There were numerous changes in the course of the project, which cost the client "lots of nerves", as Angonese sheepishly admits. But self-criticism and self-doubt have their uses, and the flexible response to new possibilities and situations permitted some decisions to be corrected.

It was not necessarily the aim of the project to call more attention to the winery, as San Michele-Appiano already had an established status. Rather, in their remodelling of the wine cellar, the architect and artist built on the existing facilities, combined the old and the new, and played masterfully with contrasts.

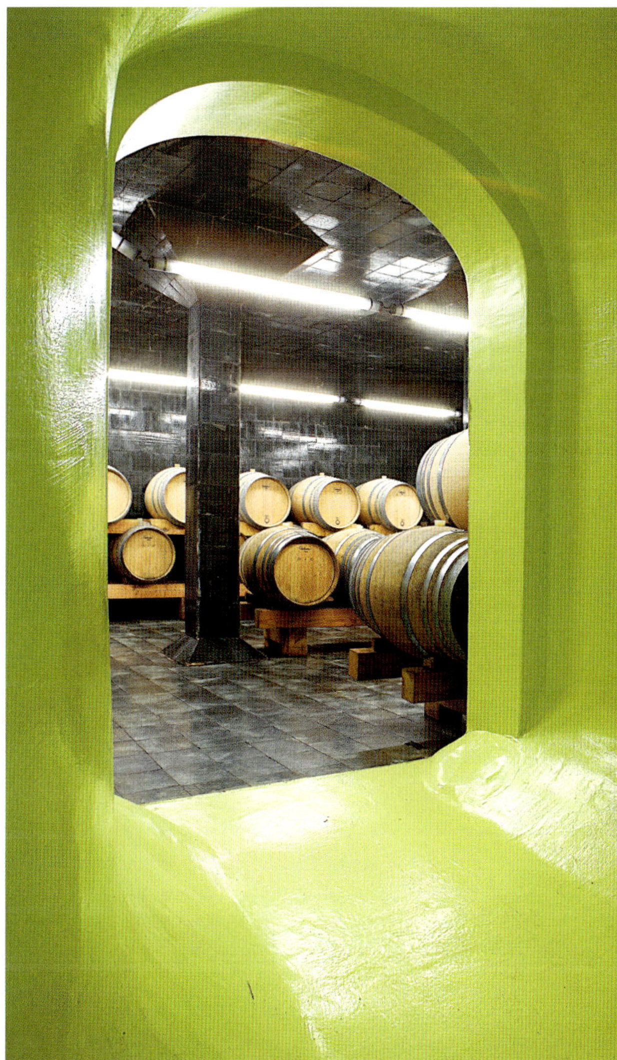

Weingut Gantenbein in Fläsch, Switzerland

Architects: Bearth & Deplazes Architekten, Chur/Zurich
Valentin Bearth – Andrea Deplazes – Daniel Ladner
Wiesentalstr. 7, 7000 Chur, www.bearth-deplazes.ch

Gross floor area: 980 m²

Start of design phase: 2006

Completion: 2008

Region: Graubündner Rheintal

Contact: Ausserdorf 38, 7306 Fläsch
www.gantenbeinwein.com

Winemaker: Daniel Gantenbein

Price range: ca. €60

●○○

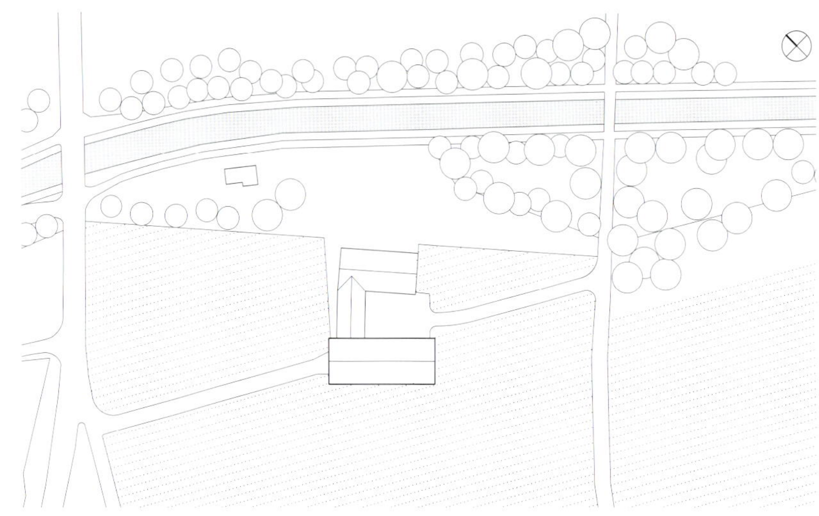

Site plan
Scale 1:2000
Section
Scale 1:500

Before the backdrop of the massive Grison Alps in the Rhine Valley of eastern Switzerland, the building nestled in the vineyard seems lightweight and almost transparent. The relief structure gives the walls the appearance of moving, and with the play of light on the sandstone bricks of the facade, every change of perspective brings a different look to the new production facility of the Gantenbein Winery in Fläsch. Completed in 2008, the structure is connected via a subterranean passage to the wine cellar built in 1996 and is the result of a unique interplay of winemaking, architecture and technological innovation.

It all started in 1982, when Martha and Daniel Gantenbein decided to take over the four-hectare vineyard belonging to Martha's parents, Leonhard and Anna Kunz, and thenceforth to focus only on their passion, wine. The businesswoman and the machine mechanic had both been fascinated by winemaking from an early age and took courses at the Wädenswil wine school on Lake Zurich to gain an in-depth knowledge of the cultivation and ageing of wine.

The vineyards, now comprising six hectares, are planted exclusively with Pinot Noir, Chardonnay and Riesling grapes, with the Pinot Noir having the lion's

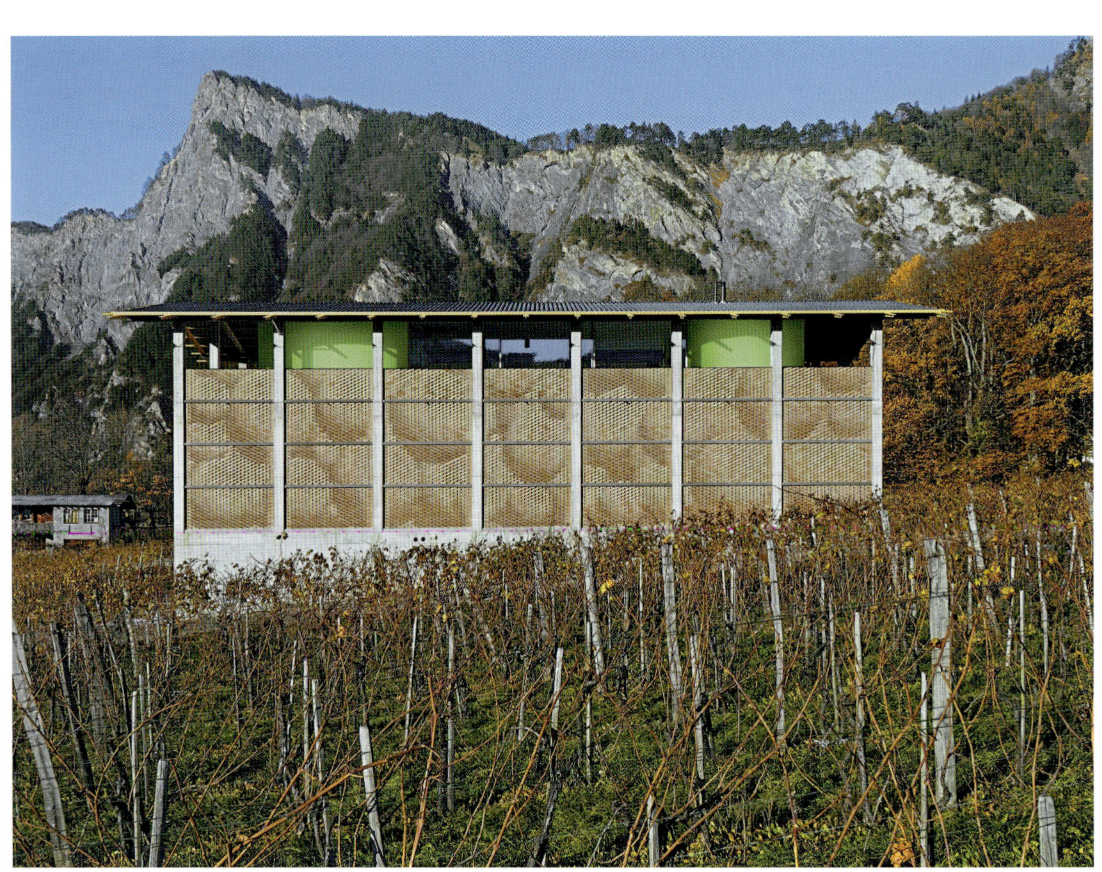

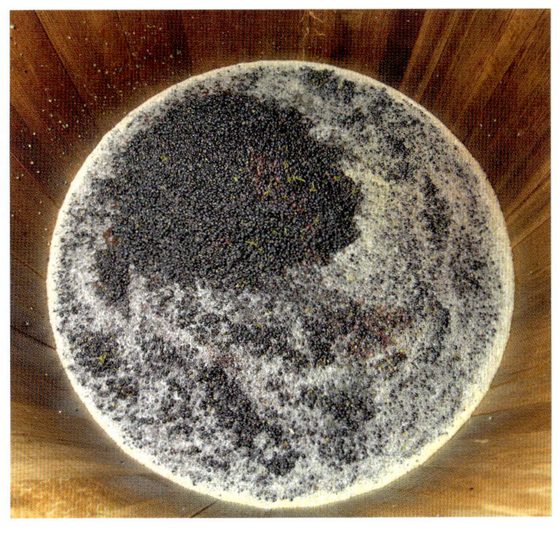

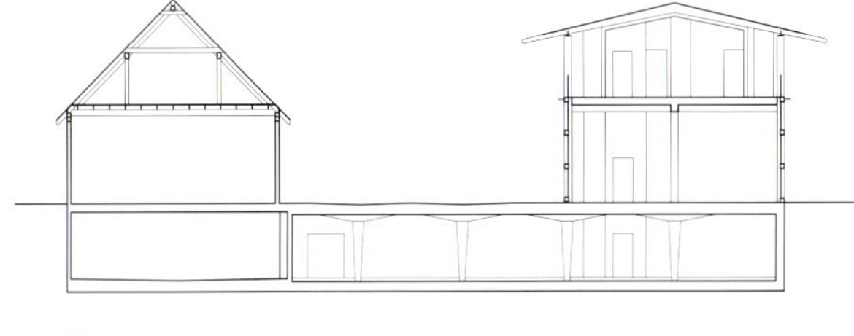

aa

share at five hectares. It is the best-known Gantenbein wine and one of the best red wines in all of Switzerland. The Gantenbeins never went in for a wide range of different wine styles and qualities; instead, their goal has been to produce one perfect wine from each variety every year. This focus, as well as an extreme yield limitation and a selection in the vineyard, has paid off. Since the early 1990s, Gantenbein wines have been celebrated by wine lovers all over the world. The great Burgundy wines, which the vintners encountered in the course of their wide-ranging travels in the perennial quest for oenological perfection, served as the inspiration for all this. Over time, the classic blue Pinot Noir vines were gradually replaced by Burgundy clones.
The Gantenbeins continue to take these trips, which are designed to keep them in a constant dialogue with their vintner friends and colleagues. Interestingly, when Daniel Gantenbein rhapsodizes about something, it is never about his own wines, but instead about the exchange of precious bottles with winemakers he is friends with, particularly from the Mosel region. The Gantenbein Riesling bears evidence of this acquaintance. In his personal trove in the subterranean wine cellar, Daniel Gantenbein keeps numerous French and German treasures.

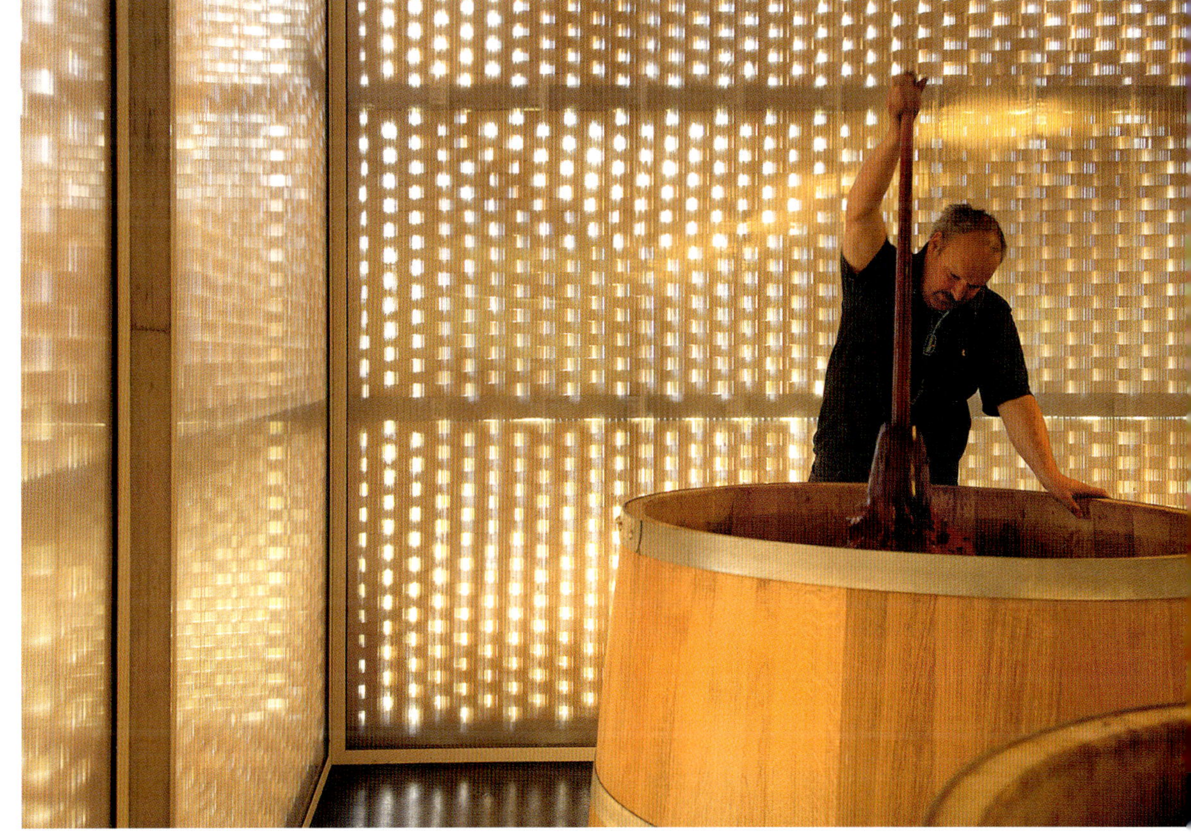

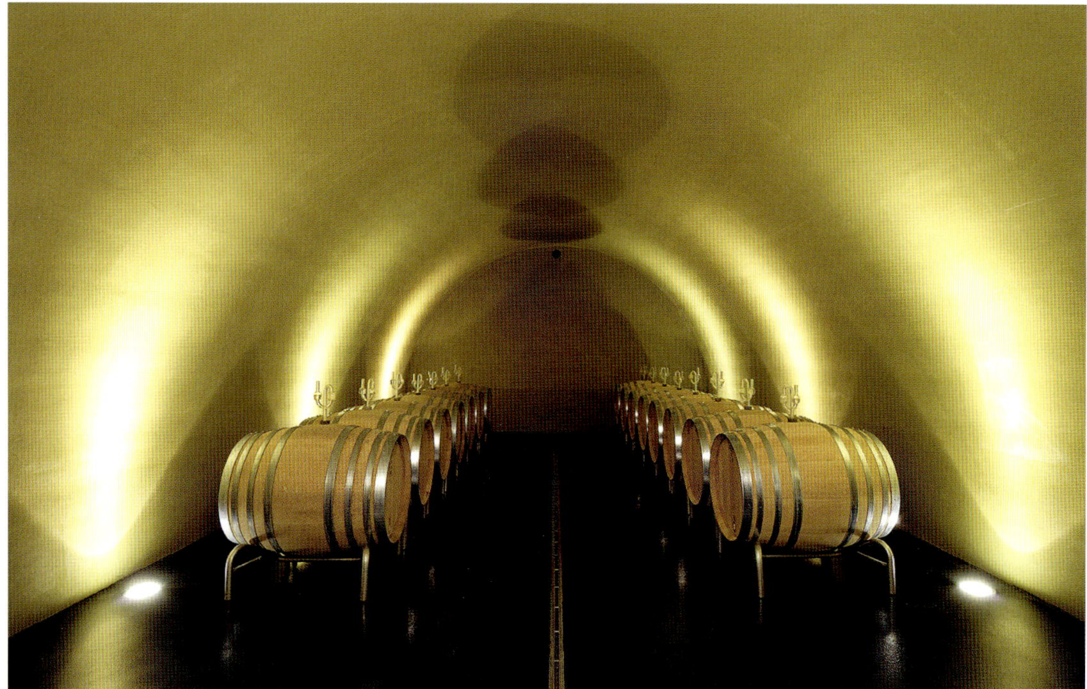

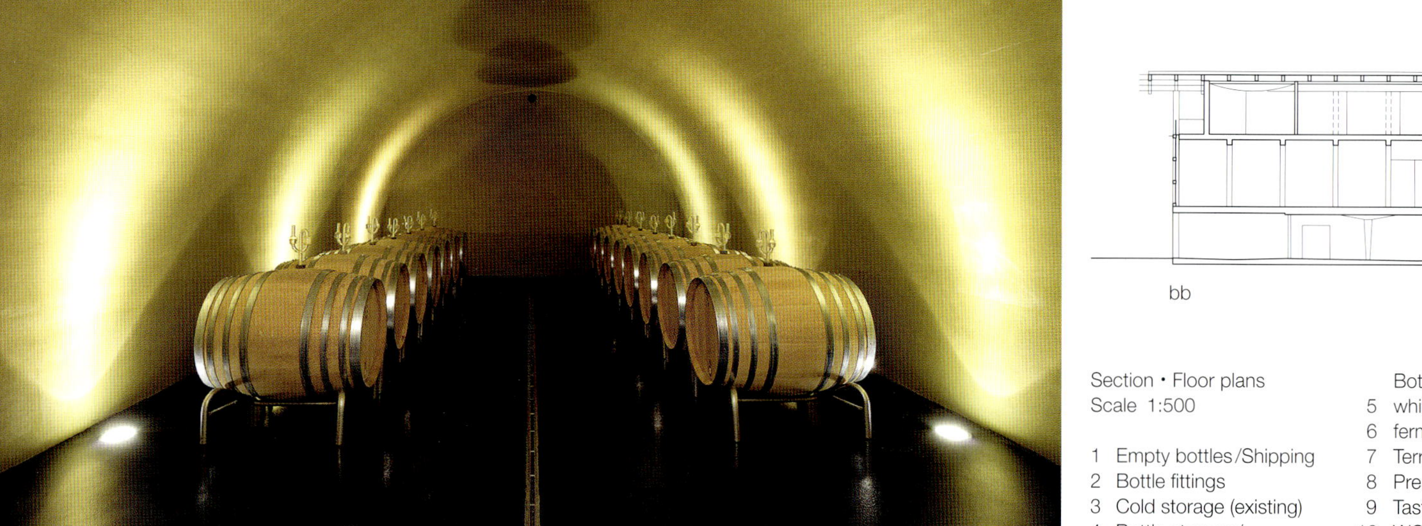

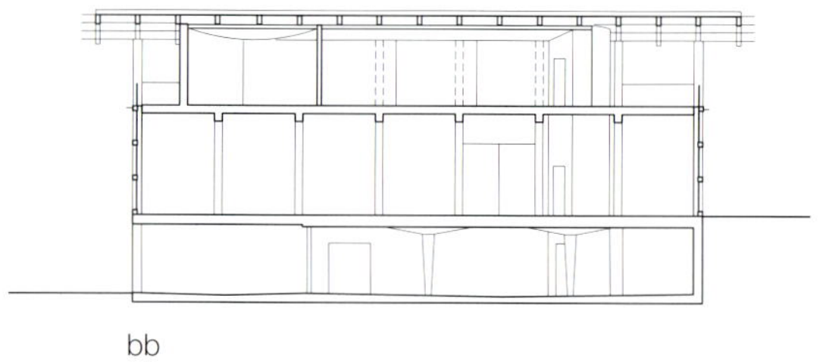

Section • Floor plans
Scale 1:500

1 Empty bottles/Shipping
2 Bottle fittings
3 Cold storage (existing)
4 Bottle storage/ Bottling (existing)
5 white wine cellar
6 fermenting cellar
7 Terrace
8 Presentation space
9 Tasting
10 WC/Coatroom

The Gantenbein wines invite comparison with the great Burgundies and the top German Rieslings, though they are in no way copies of these. Marked by their structure, depth, complexity, subtly fruity aromas and perfectly integrated wood notes, the wines come into their own after a few years in the bottle. “Great quality can only be attained if you can work in just the way you want to,” says the vintner. “We want to interfere as little as possible in the development of the wine.” After being received, the grapes are carefully crushed and then drop down into the fermentation vessel. After fermentation, the wines are clarified through the process of soutirage only. The quality is determined in the vineyard, and none of it is allowed to get lost in the cellar.

“We have decided to remain vintners,” Gantenbein explains. The wine, as the “inside” or heart of the business, was always the primary focus. Only then came the “outside” – things such as equipment, labels and new buildings. The first money that came in was invested back into high-quality wine processing equipment. In 1996, production was moved from the village to the vineyards. As the impractical, cramped cellar was bursting at the seams, the Gantenbeins first built a wine cellar and then a hall of their own design. The decision to expand followed in 2005. Alongside the two existing single-storey buildings came a new building with a logistics warehouse on the lower floor, a cuverie or press room on the ground floor and a hospitality space on the upper floor. The structure features a concrete shell covered with a simple pitched roof of corrugated sheets. The new building is connected with the existing buildings via underground passages. The flow of wine, the laws of gravity, the need for temperature regulation, and the sequence of work processes determine the layout of the space.

“Good architecture must serve its purpose 100 per cent. First comes work, then the showroom!” explains Gantenbein. It was never his intention to create a place of architectural pilgrimage or a vehicle to boost sales, but a structure in which practicality is given aesthetic expression.

Gantenbein had known some of the architects for years; but it was also on the recommendation of his brother, Köbi Gantenbein, who publishes a Swiss architectural journal, that the architectural practice Bearth & Deplazes was chosen. Basic principles of the design were worked out jointly.

The outer skin of the service building, a translucent masonry wall of offset bricks, was designed by Andrea Deplazes, professor of architecture and construction at ETH Zurich. Within the scope of a research project, Fabio Gramazio and Matthias Kohler, chair of architecture and digital fabrication at the same university, designed a robot to lay the bricks according to a predetermined pattern. Thanks to the various angles in which the individual bricks are laid in a bond pattern with open joints, the facade resembles a basket filled with grapes. The gaps in the wall let in light, but keep direct sunlight out, which makes for a pleasant working atmosphere in moderate daylight. The materials are simple: a concrete skeleton, bricks, and an interior cladding of three-layer polycarbonate panels. The temperatures in the hall do not drop below 0 °C in winter or climb above 20 °C in summer. The large, round lamps of black perforated plate on the ground floor were designed by Daniel Gantenbein’s father, who assists during the grape harvest and is in charge of the distilling of the marc. Fans mounted atop the fermentation barrels located inside provide the right circulation of air according to the weather conditions. The interior of the hall recalls the inside of a Moroccan house, where gaps between the bricks let in thin shafts of light.

A few times a year, for special occasions, the building turns into a festive hall. The parties are catered by Doris and Roland Kalberer, operator and chef, respectively, of “à table”, the hospitality space with

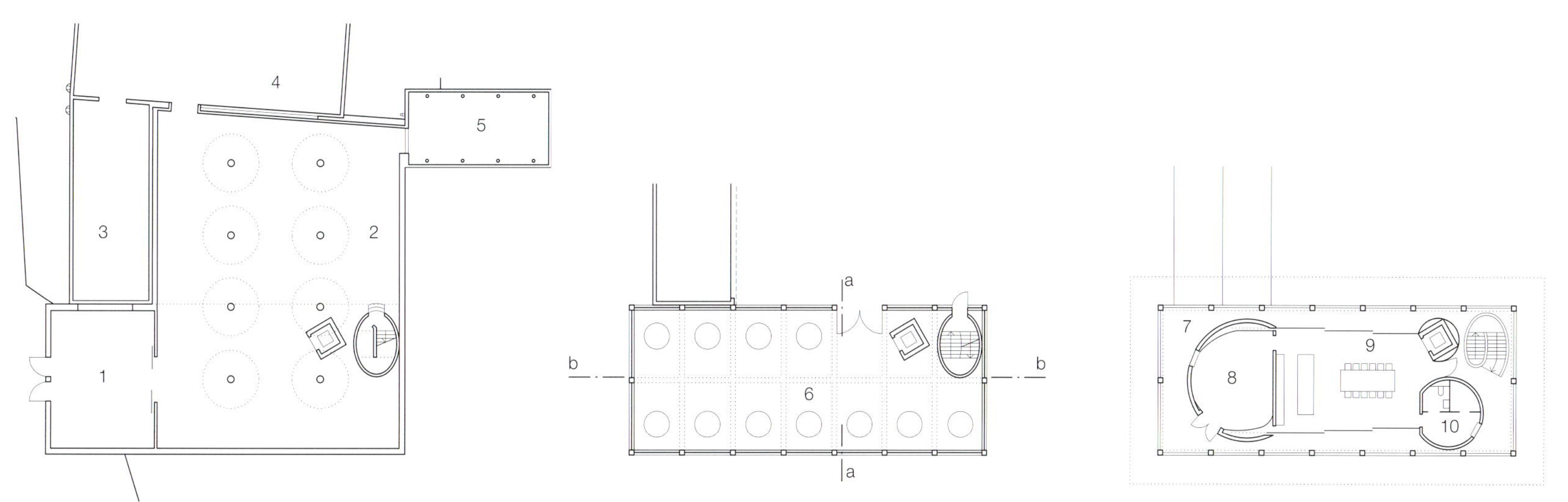
4
5
3
2
1
a
b
6
a
7
9
8
10

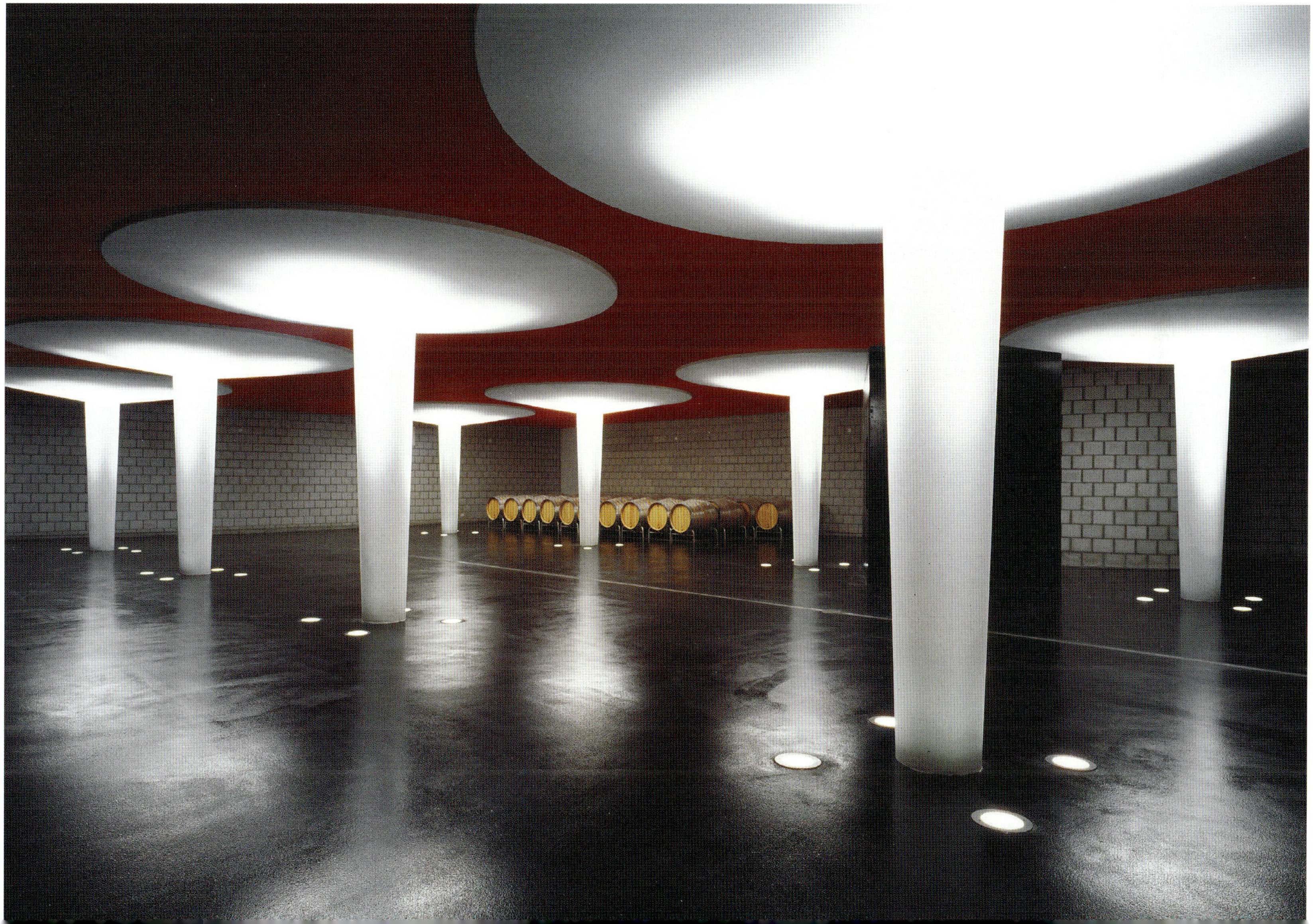

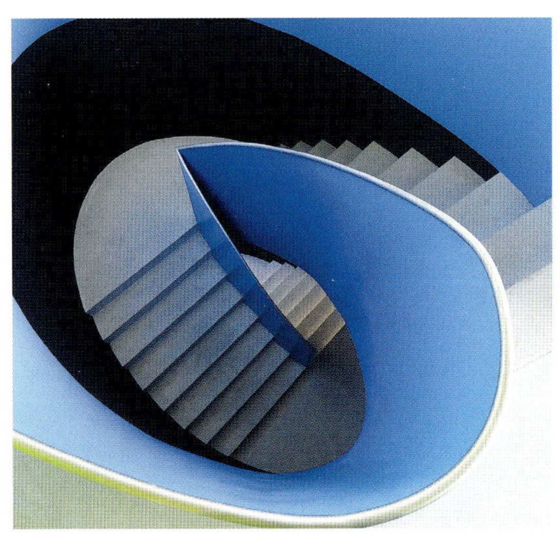

a professional kitchen located on the upper floor. Working by advance booking only, the top Swiss chef treats his guests to culinary delights of the highest order. The spaces can be booked for conferences as well. On the upper floor, too, ingenious simplicity and great artisanship go hand in hand. The floor and the sideboard are made of polished concrete; huge sliding glass doors, which allow guests to step out on to the terrace, offer a panoramic view of the Alps. A woven canopy on the ceiling sports a pattern that recalls the tendrils of a grapevine. At the very point where the windows begin, the pattern of the canopy continues in the curtains. Surrounding the two three-metre-long tables of Piedmontese walnut are 24 simple wooden chairs. This is where the guests sat who were invited to the party celebrating the completion of the project. "Good food and good wine are just as much a part of the good things in life as successful architecture," the Gantenbeins say.

Daniel Gantenbein is full of praise for the accomplishments of the builders, who worked to the highest level of their craft. When the concrete ceiling of the first storey was completed, they celebrated with a bottle of 1983 Goldkapsel by J.J. Prüm. Behind the kitchen is the lounge with its round windows and Le Corbusier armchairs. The design of the wallpaper is simple and ingenious: beech leaves were laid on paper and scanned in. The star lanterns designed by architects Bearth & Deplazes bathe the space in a diffuse light.

The cellar is accessed either via a repurposed former hospital lift or via a spiral staircase that sports the same vibrant light blue as found on the Pinot Noir labels. Both lead to the columned cellar, which is connected to the 1996 building. The white mushroom columns, lit from below, have a vaguely alien look about them. They serve both as ceiling supports and as water conduits. Somewhat hidden behind the lifts is one of the Gantenbein's personal treasure troves housing valuable bottles from the great wine regions of the world – products, to a great part, of the thriving trade that the vintners engage in with their colleagues. The columned cellar is connected to the barrique cellar for the white wines, a space painted an intense shade of ochre. Via the workroom under the older building, one arrives at the burgundy-coloured cellar where the Pinot Noir ages. The cellars in which the wines rest have clay-plastered walls, which helps to keep the humidity at the optimal level of 90 per cent.

"The existing building was the benchmark and the departure point of the extension. We as architects were fascinated by the charming, immediate practicality of this rustic architecture," explains architect Daniel Ladner, who was in the closest contact with the Gantenbeins throughout the project. He had the role of cheerleader, explainer and budget enforcer. The vintners see their philosophy as having been successfully implemented. Their friendly contact with the architects continues to this day.

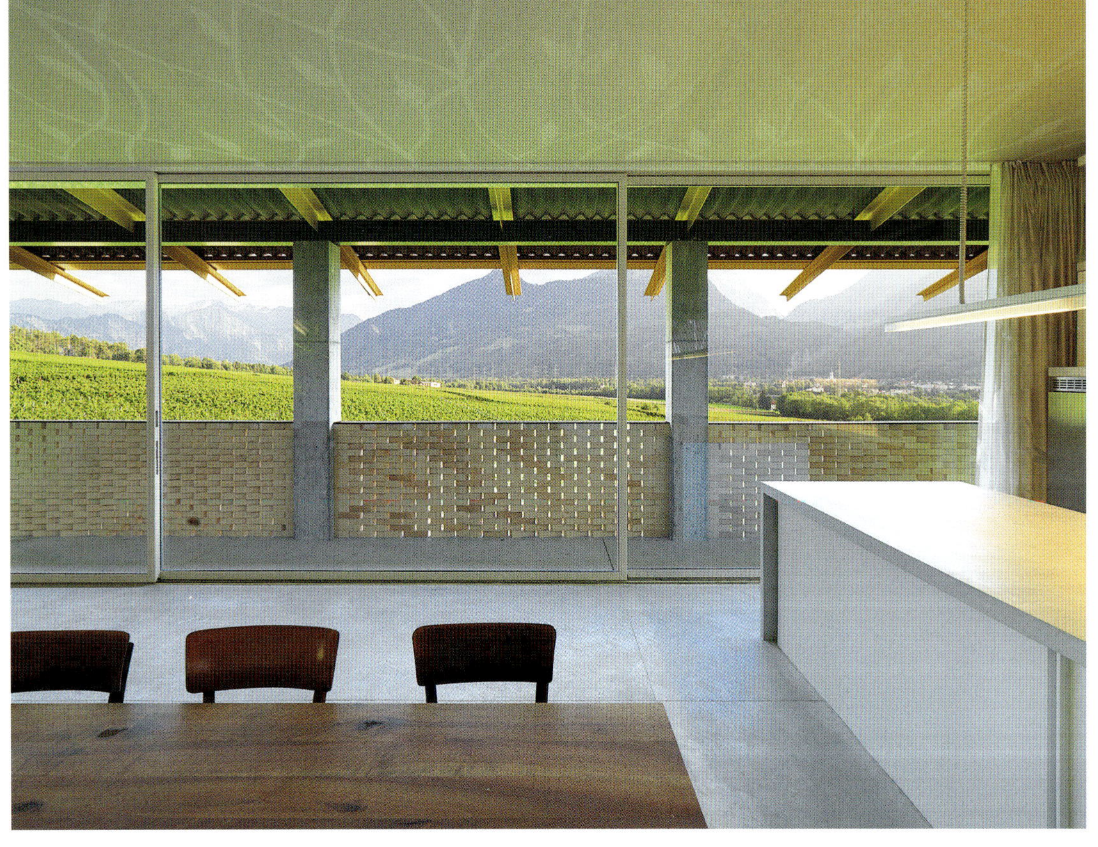

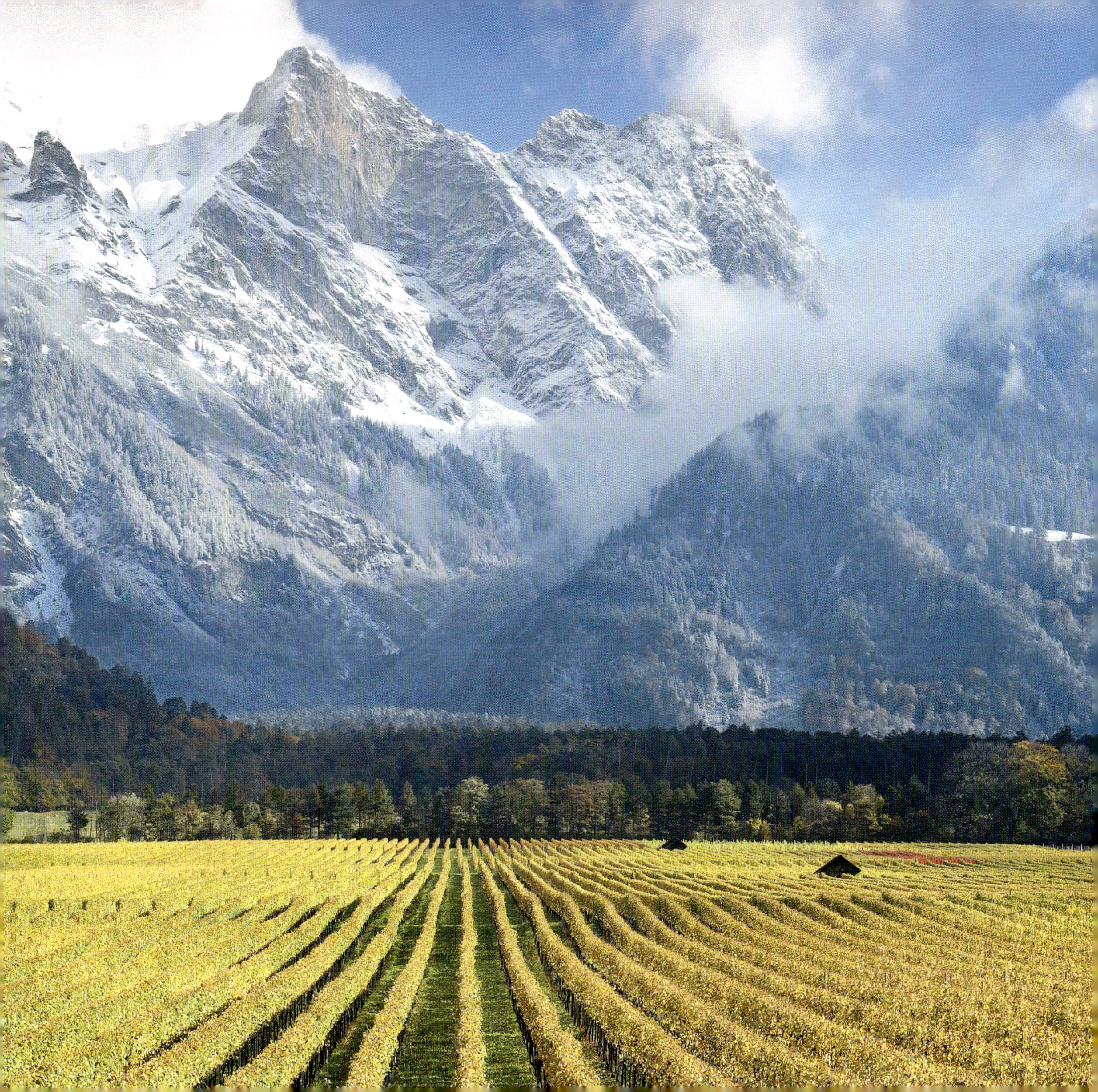

Bodegas Ysios in Laguardia, Spain

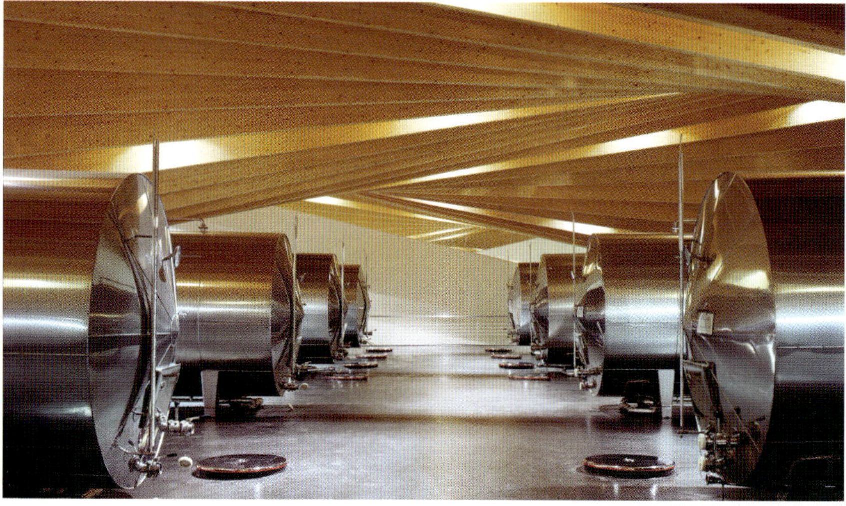

Architect: Santiago Calatrava, Parkring 11, 8002 Zurich
www.calatrava.com

Site area: 15,384 m²

Gross floor area: 8,000 m²

Start of design phase: 1998

Completion: 2001

Region: Rioja

Contact: Camino de la Hoya, 01300 Laguardia
www.ysios.com

Oenologist: Luis Zudaire

Price range: €18–€40

In this corner of Spain's Rioja Alavesa region, the mountains of the Sierra de Cantabria rise more than 1,300 metres from the ground, providing shelter from the cold and wet north-easterly winds blowing in from the Atlantic; limestone and clay soils supply the grapevines with excellent nutrients; and in spite of the comparatively rough climate, the south-facing vineyards enjoy the best possible exposure to sunlight. In the midst of this majestic scenery lies Bodegas Ysios, which, seen from afar, looks like a silvery snake undulating across the gentle green of the vineyards.

Located in Laguardia, in the Rioja Alavesa region, this impressive structure was commissioned by Domecq Bodegas, a member of the Pernod Ricard Group, and designed by the renowned Spanish architect Santiago Calatrava. Bodegas Ysios, which gets its name from the goddess Isis, the "mother of god" or "mother of the sun" of Egyptian mythology, is one of a total of seven wineries belonging to the Domecq group in the Rioja region. Every one of them stands for its own characteristic wines from different terroirs.

The vineyards of Bodegas Ysios comprise 75 hectares and are subdivided into ten sites, each of which is harvested separately by hand. Then the grapes from each plot are fermented and aged separately. Only after that does blending occur. The end results of this process are just two wines: Ysios Reserva and Ysios Edición Limitada Reserva. Both of them are reserve wines produced from 100 per cent Tempranillo grapes. Some 200,000 bottles of Ysios Reserva leave the winery every year. The reserve wine is pressed from grapes from 30-year-old vines and then aged 14 months in barriques made of 55 per cent French, 40 per cent American and five per cent Hungarian oak, which lend the Reserva its fruity aroma. These casks are usually medium toasted or medium-plus toasted, allowing them to maintain the primary aromas of the Tempranillo variety but also to impart subtle vanilla and coconut aromas to the wine. After barrel ageing, the wine is cellared in bottles for three years. Ysios Edición Limitada Reserva originates from grapevines aged over 80 years old from the Bodegas's best parcels, and it is bottled only in very good vintages. Before that, the wine ages for 18 months in barriques made of exclusively French oak. Every bottle gets its own individual number, and no more than 5,000 bottles are produced. This strict limit gives the wine the allure of the unique – a character-

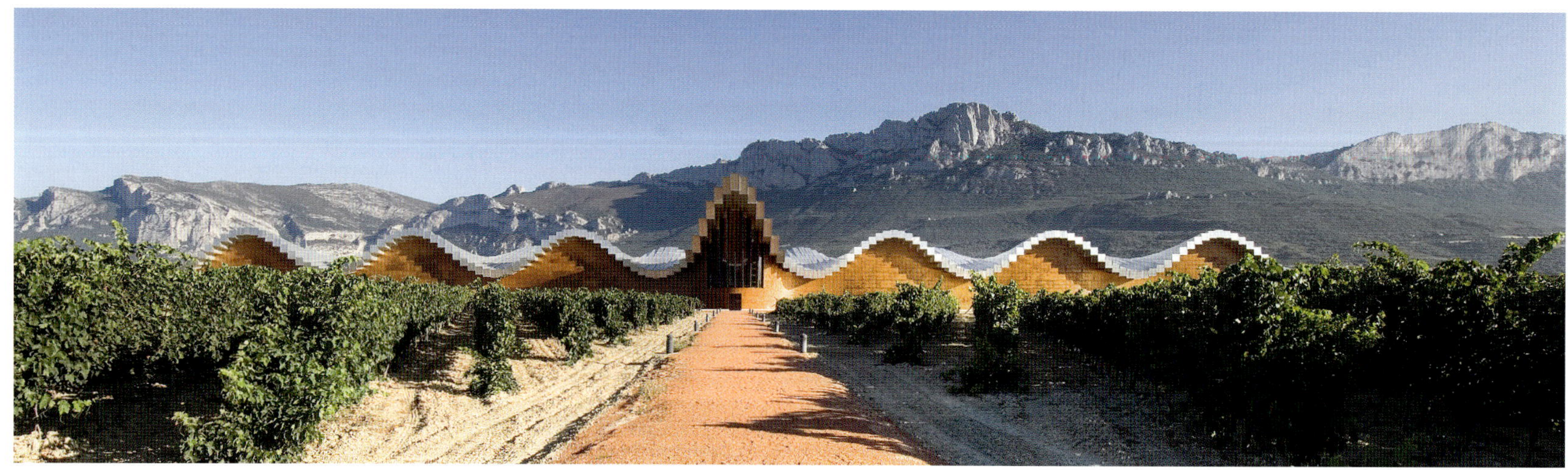

istic richly in evidence in the appearance of the winery itself.

From a bird's-eye perspective, the whole facility resembles a wine glass, with the approach and entrance forming the stem, the building itself representing its contents and the wavy form of the roof recalling large barrels lying side by side and connected by a band of silver. At the same time, in an effect intended by Calatrava, the facility follows the silhouette of the surrounding mountain range. The roof consists of rising and falling glulam timber trusses of up to 42 metres in length, clad with aluminium on the outside. It forms a stark colour contrast to the warm tone of the timber facade.

In the middle of the building, the roof pitches steeply upwards and extends far forwards. This marks the entrance to the winery, a section that contains the tasting room as well. From here, the visitor is treated to a majestic view out over the vineyards, but can also look into the barrel cellar with its overwhelming height and its 1,300 barriques. To the left of this impressive central area lies the tract with the fermentation tanks, and to the right is the bottle cellar with the bottling line. The layout of the rooms mirrors the process of wine production.

In Bodegas Ysios, Calatrava has succeeded in creating a widely celebrated architecture that shows off the particular qualities of the Ysios Reserva wines, but also speaks for itself. This is one reason why more than 20,000 visitors a year find their way to the foot of the Sierra de Cantabria.

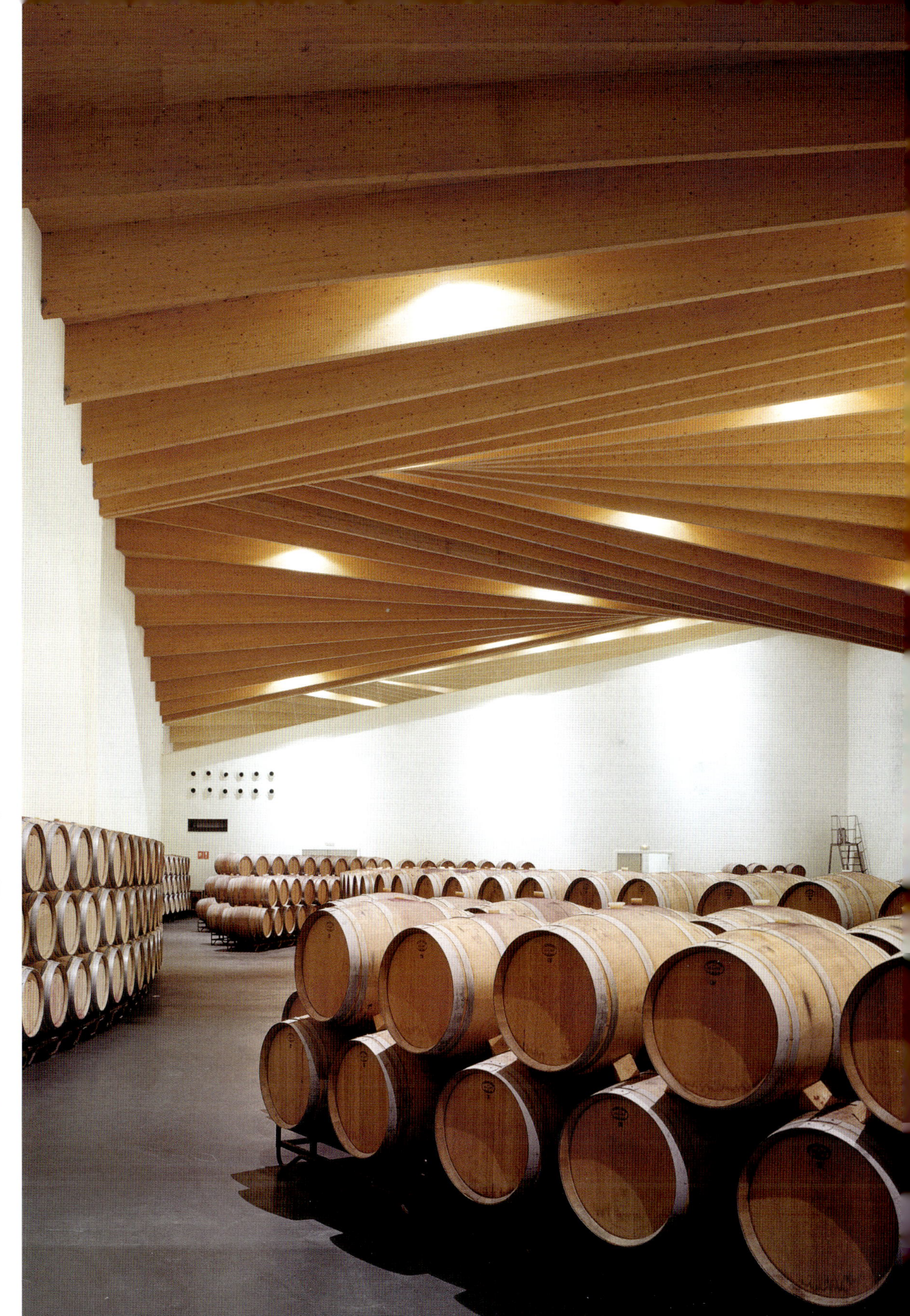

Bodega Brugarol in Palamós, Spain

Architects: RCR Arquitectes, Fontanella, 26, 17800 Olot (Girona), www.rcrarquitectes.es
Assistants: G. Puigvert, A. Lippmann
Site area: 30 hectares
Gross floor area: 981 m²
Start of design phase: 2004
Completion: 2007
Region: Catalonia
Contact: Mas Bell-Lloc, 17230 Palamós www.brugarol.com
Oenologists: Xavier Vidal, Miquel Arenas
Price range: €15–€30
●○○

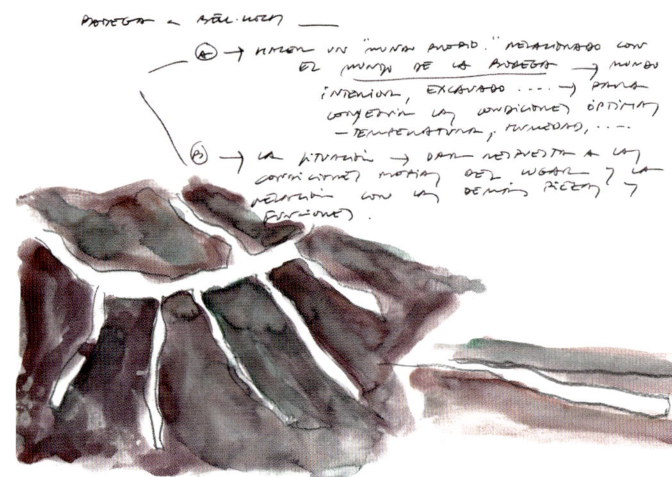

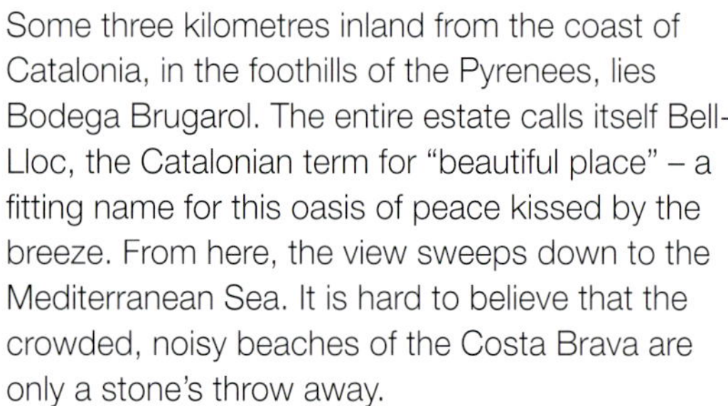

Some three kilometres inland from the coast of Catalonia, in the foothills of the Pyrenees, lies Bodega Brugarol. The entire estate calls itself Bell-Lloc, the Catalonian term for "beautiful place" – a fitting name for this oasis of peace kissed by the breeze. From here, the view sweeps down to the Mediterranean Sea. It is hard to believe that the crowded, noisy beaches of the Costa Brava are only a stone's throw away.
The old finca located in a nature preserve has been in the German Engelhorn family since 1943. Not long ago, after thinking about the matter for some time, Kurt Engelhorn decided to breathe new life into the estate. The vines were planted in 2001 and the first wine was vinified in a neighbouring winery in 2003. The goal was not to get into the winemaking business on a professional basis, but to engage in viniculture as an integral part of a holistic use of the land. What Engelhorn wanted was to set up a self-sustaining operation that included agriculture and animal husbandry. As a result, Bell-Lloc today produces not only wine, but also olive oil, olive soap, honey, jam and goat's cheese.

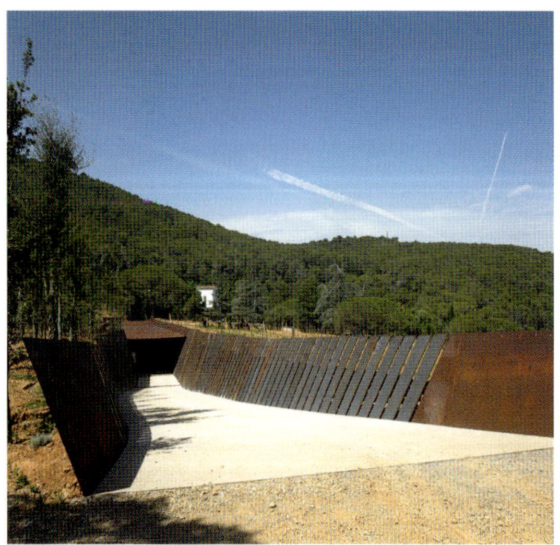

The estate includes fives hectares of vineyards that are divided into three areas. The red grape varieties of Cabernet Sauvignon and Cabernet Franc are grown directly adjacent to the bodega; the vineyards further out towards the sea feature the red varieties Garnacha and Carignan in one section and the white varieties Malvasia and Xarel-Lo in another. The vines grow in a granitic and iron-rich red soil. Two cellarmasters vinify a white wine and a red wine from the grapes, whose yield is strictly limited. The focus is on capturing the unique properties of the terroir and the grape varieties. These are fermented separately and then matured in small oak barriques. Only then are the wines blended.
In 2003, an architectural competition was tendered for the new wine cellar and won by RCR Arquitectes from Olot. The architects had had previous experience in wine architecture projects, and were already acquainted with the owners. In the course of the planning phase in 2004–2005, countless drafts were drawn up and constantly reworked until construction could finally begin in late 2005.
At first glance, the visitor does not even notice the winery and has to be told where it is. The structure is accessible only via a path through bushes and vines. Partly buried under the vineyard, the new facility blends subtly into the landscape, underscoring the concept of a strong link between building and surroundings. In this eccentric structure, architecture, sculpture and landscaping meet.
The main material used is plates of Corten steel, whose reddish-brown patina allow the building to seem to melt into the surrounding, identically coloured earth. The idea was to make and cellar the wine in the element from which it came: earth and stone. The visitor was to be given the opportunity to get to know the wine in its natural surroundings. Via gravel-covered concrete ramps on two sides, visitors enter the subterranean wine world though an honour guard of slightly outward-leaning steel plates. This is the same route that the grape harvest takes into the facility. The dumped stones that prop up the vineyard peek out through the gaps between the vertical steel plates. The ground and the spaced steel elements continue as a central theme throughout the building.
Under the roof of folded steel plates is the entrance to the tasting room and the laboratory, in which not only the wine but also the olive oil of the estate can be sampled. From here, a glass wall affords a direct view of the surrounding landscape. On the other side, a way leads past stainless-steel fermentation tanks and down into the wine cellar.
As in almost all transitions from one space to another, a sliding door of Corten steel bars the way. It takes some effort to open it, and the material squeaks with the friction produced. As the architects intended, the heaviness and solidity of the steel are palpable.

Section
Scale 1:500

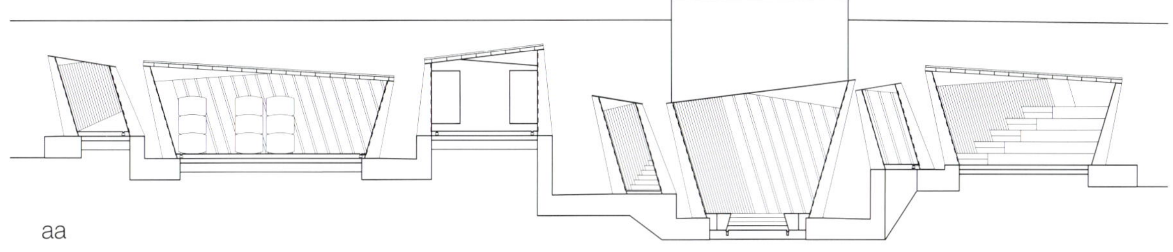

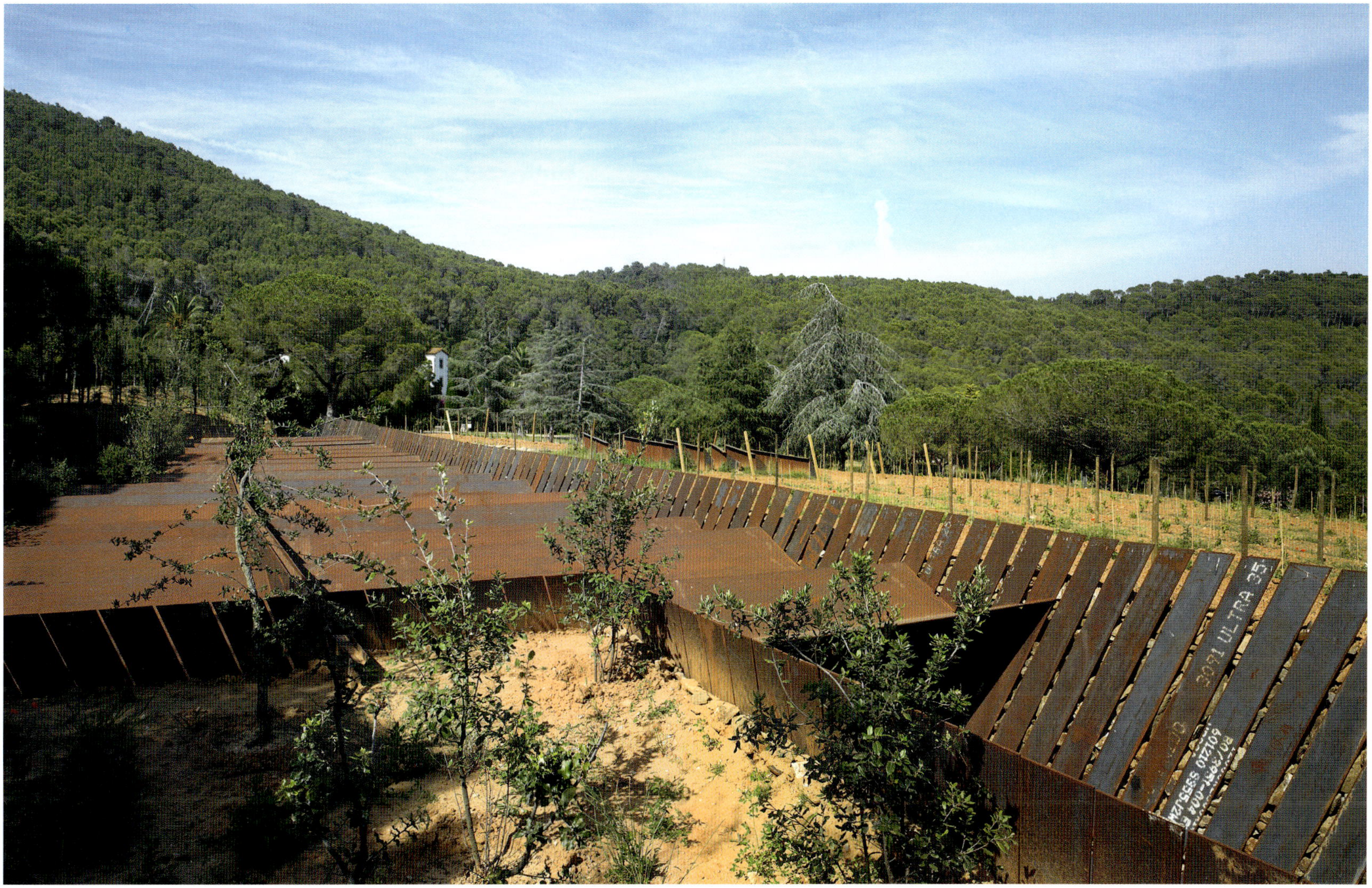

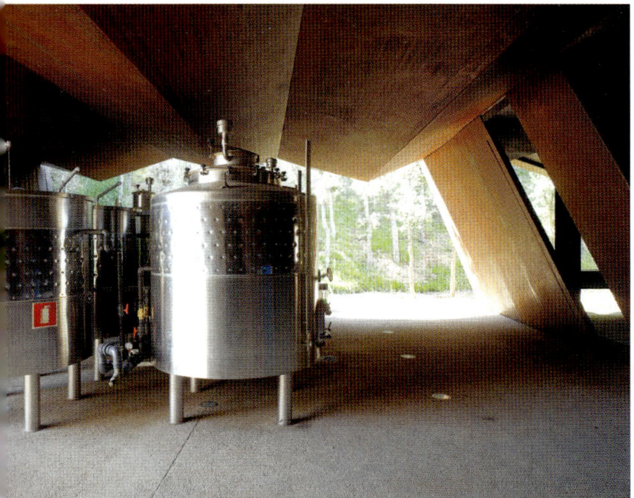

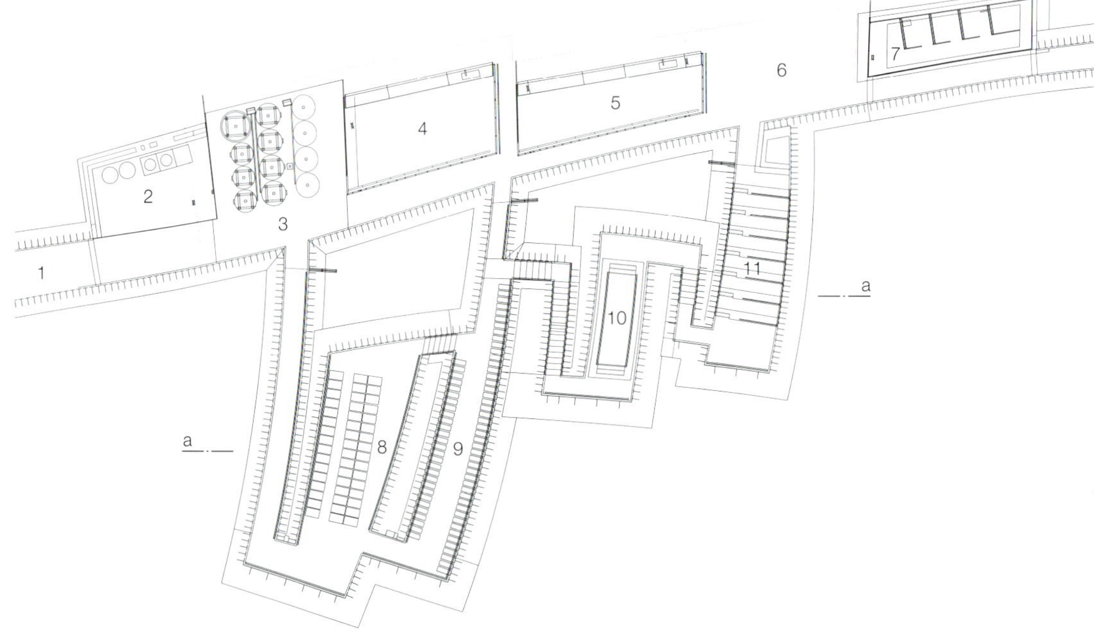

Floor plan
Scale 1:500

1 Access ramp
2 Technology
3 Fermenting cellar
4 Laboratory/Labelling room
5 Workshop
6 Multifunctional space
7 Changing rooms
8 Barrel cellar
9 Bottle cellar
10 Tasting area
11 Auditorium

A kind of obstacle course leads through the various rooms of the wine cellar. First, one enters the barrel cellar through a long corridor. The only source of light is an artificial one: a small crevice with LED lamps let into the gravel along the walls. The eyes take some time getting accustomed to the semi-darkness. Through the gaps between the steel plates that make up the walls, nature encroaches. Bits of root can be glimpsed between the stones; beetles and spiders are welcome guests. Some 50 casks standing on the natural ground are repositories for the wine, which can slumber undisturbed by bright light.

Six concrete steps lead down to the bottle ageing cellar, where up to 20,000 bottles may be stored in containers of Corten steel. The "shelves" of ceiling height are tilted to the right by 17 degrees.

From here, a sliding steel door lets one back into the entrance area. Alternatively, one can further explore the labyrinth, taking two stairs that are arranged at right angles and coming out in the tasting room, the cellar's inner sanctum. Two large concrete steps offer a place to sit; in the centre stands a simple table of rough wood. Thoughts of altars spring to mind – and indeed, the space has the air of a room for prayer or sacrifice. Overhead, shafts jut out into the open, letting sunlight – and rain – enter unimpeded. The afternoon sun flooding in makes for a fascinating, constantly changing play of light. It is pleasantly cool and very tranquil here. A six-step staircase descends to the multimedia space with a projection wall. The broad sitting steps leading down to the wall are made of concrete as well, with hemp mats the only concessions to comfort. Small, intimate concerts or lectures take place here.

The ceilings of the cellar and of the spaces above ground consist of the red-steel plates arranged in an irregular zigzag pattern resembling an outsized piece of origami. In the secluded, quiet, dark atmosphere of the wine cellar, visitors can forget the outside world and engage in subterranean meditation.

Back in daylight, in a covered open-air area between the laboratory and the workshop, Mari-Carmen Pujadas, the marketing director of Bell-Lloc, presents the bodega's two wines, which are characterized by their complexity, good length and minerality. A steel capsule sits atop the neck of the bottles, attached by a thin inner ring of rubber and a wax seal. The capsule contains all the necessary information. Otherwise, the bottles are completely bare; neither labels nor writing mar their purist look. The capsules recall the materiality of the winery. The minimalist, purist theme is evident throughout the entire concept.

The materials steel and stone as well as the subterranean arrangement of the spaces allow a natural regulation of temperature and humidity – a factor that is central to the production of wine and thus was of particular importance to the client.

The idea for the overall design concept originated with the architects, although Engelhorn took very little persuading. Everything was to be integrated perfectly into the natural landscape. From the outset, the look was to be as dark as possible, with

the sources of light reduced to a minimum. What little artificial light there is was installed by order of the building authorities.
Since June 2011, visitors wishing to spend the night at the finca are welcome to do so. The old residence and the small chapel of Santa Maria de Bell-Lloc were restored to their original states with the aim of maintaining the archaic character of the historical buildings and giving them their own face, as Engelhorn explains. The hotel, which, of course, serves its guests products made on the premises, is a refuge for those in need of a bit of tranquillity. The unspoilt landscape and the peaceful surroundings lend this place its meditative power.

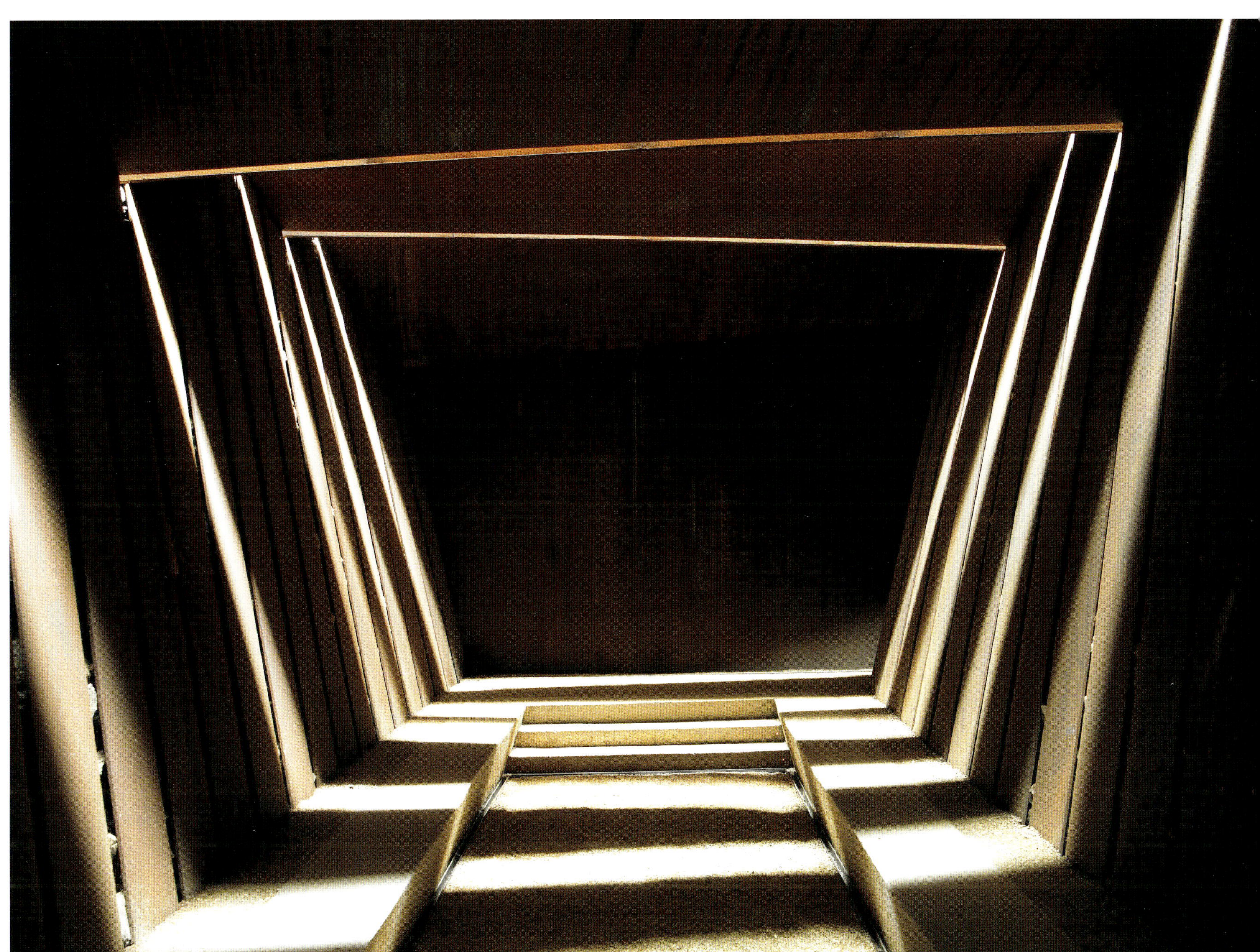

Weingut Heinrich in Gols, Austria

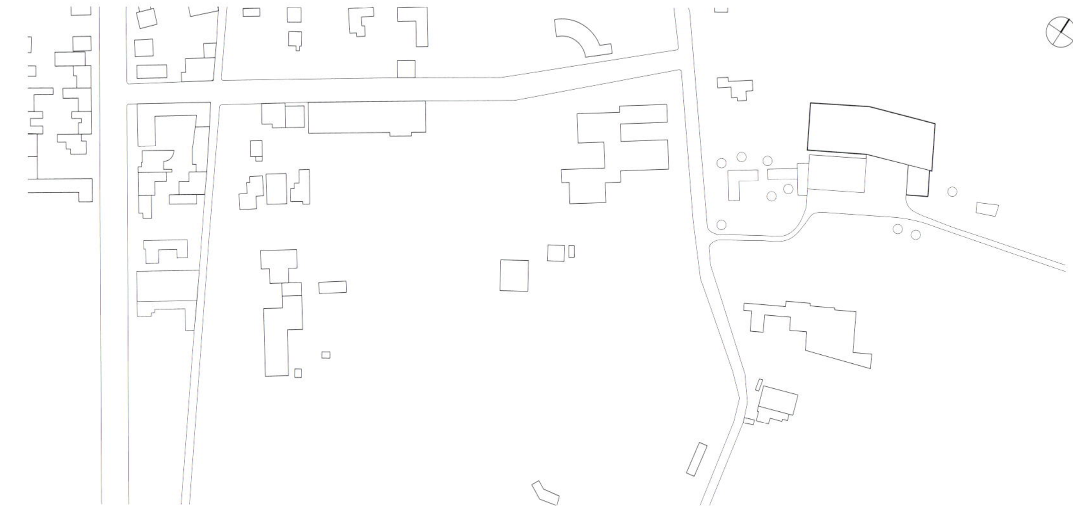

Architects: propeller z, Mariahilferstr. 101/3/55, 1060 Vienna
www.propellerz.at

Site area: 10,232 m²

Gross floor area: 4,390 m²

Start of design phase: 2007

Completion: 2008

Region: Burgenland

Contact: Baumgarten 60, 7122 Gols
www.heinrich.at

Oenologist: Gernot Heinrich

Price range: €6.50–€60

Together with his wife, Heike, Gernot Heinrich has operated the eponymous winery in eastern Austria's Burgenland with great success for more than 20 years. By now boasting 80 hectares of its own vineyards and 40 hectares' worth of additional purchases, the winery is one of the largest in all of Austria. Heinrich is also a founding member of the vintners' association Pannobile, which was launched by seven winemakers in 1994. The joint aim of the association is to produce particularly expressive wines that typify the terroir of the region and the characteristics of the various, primarily indigenous, grape varieties. The nine current members of the association collaborate mainly in the areas of quality control and marketing. Heinrich also belongs to the Premium Estates of Austria, an association formed by a few of the nation's top-tier vintners acting internationally as ambassadors of Austrian wine.

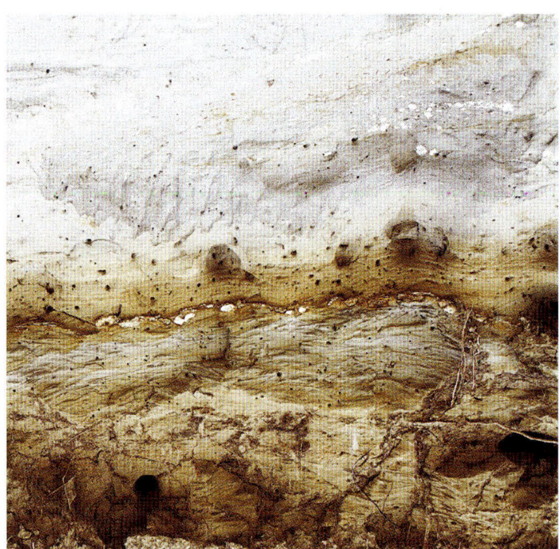

He is known for creating fascinating, age-worthy wines, primarily from the Blaufränkisch grape, which enjoys a long tradition in Burgenland. His main focus, however, is on red cuvées or blends. To create these, he vinifies the indigenous grape varieties Blaufränkisch, St. Laurent and Zweigelt, but also Pinot Noir and Merlot, using the biodynamic method and employing treatments that are, to the greatest possible extent, exclusively natural. While before the turn of the millennium the vineyards cultivated by the family business had covered less than 20 hectares, by 2007 this area had increased to 60 hectares around the northern part of Lake Neusiedl. This enormous increase in area under cultivation inevitably meant an extension of the main winery building. A lack of space had forced the owners to lease an additional hall in the neighbouring village and commission an external logistics provider with the cellaring of the bottles. What began in February of 2007 with the planning of a new hall for tractors and machinery ended in autumn 2008 – before the grape harvest – with the completion of an entirely new winery building. Three years previously, the architects, propeller z from Vienna, had already completed the winery's tasting room after a process of fruitful collaboration. Now, in the course of the initial meetings for the new project, the participants kept coming up with new ideas and considerations. Ultimately, five consecutive designs were drafted, each building on the previous one, until the decision was made to construct a whole new structure.

The architects worked out and defined the planning goals jointly with the client. These included an expansion of the barrel cellar; the creation of new storage areas for machinery, work materials and fertilizers; and an expansion of the bottle warehouse. In addition, a loading and delivery bay was to be created for vehicles, particularly for large trucks. At the same time, the new building was to be linked as closely as possible, both practically and aesthetically, to the existing winery.

In addition to these considerations, the inner layout of the building was to reflect Heinrich's philosophy of biodynamic agriculture. For an efficient utilization of the building in both agro-economic terms and in its everyday operations, the declared aim was a hangar structure with a simple, divisible and recyclable construction. And Heinrich had another request that was a bit unusual for a vintner to make: namely, that spaces should be created for the use of the workers temporarily employed on the vineyard – spaces that could be used as communal living areas, but also as dining areas and accommodation.

In the ensuing planning phase, Heinrich and his team analysed the technical requirements from a standpoint of processes and scale. These requirements were precisely set down, from the number of fermentation tanks called for to the space needed for tractors and machinery, and even down to the distances required between the tanks. During the planning and building phase, the architect commu-

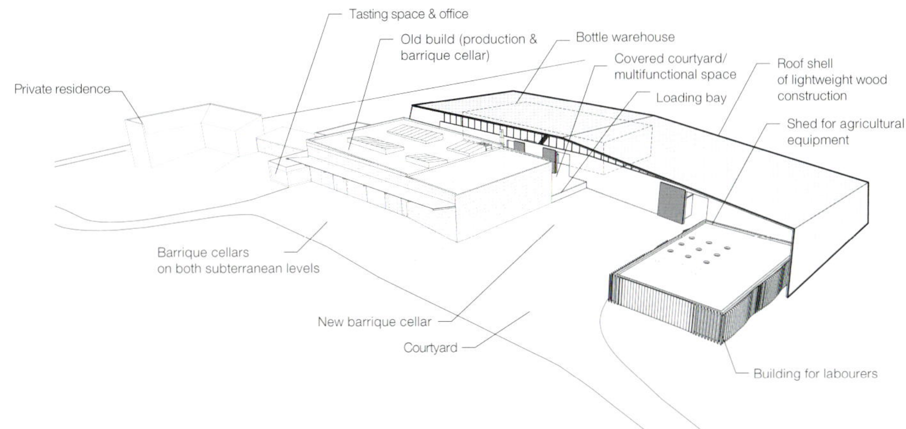

Site plan
Scale 1:5000
Perspective view of the entire facility

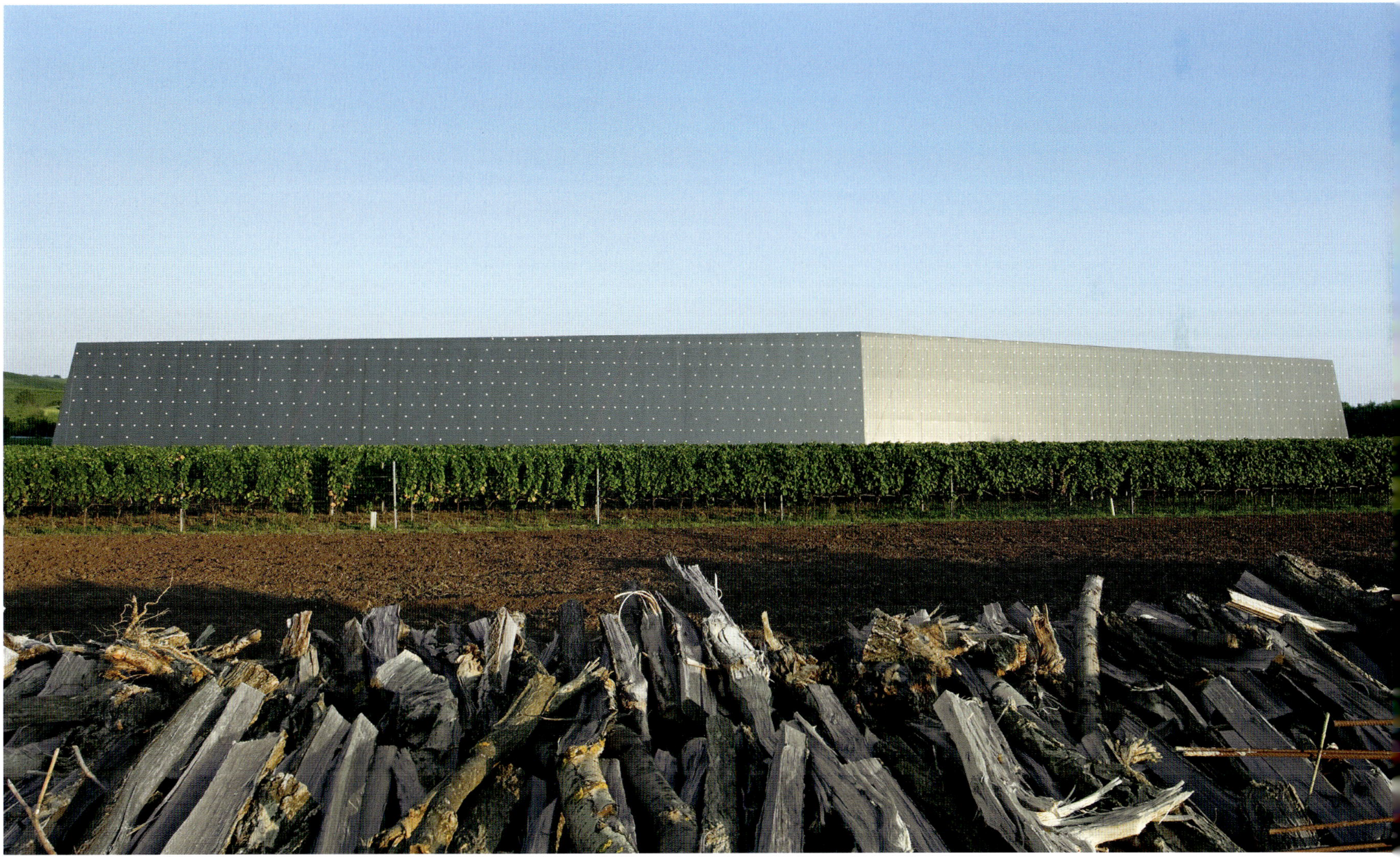

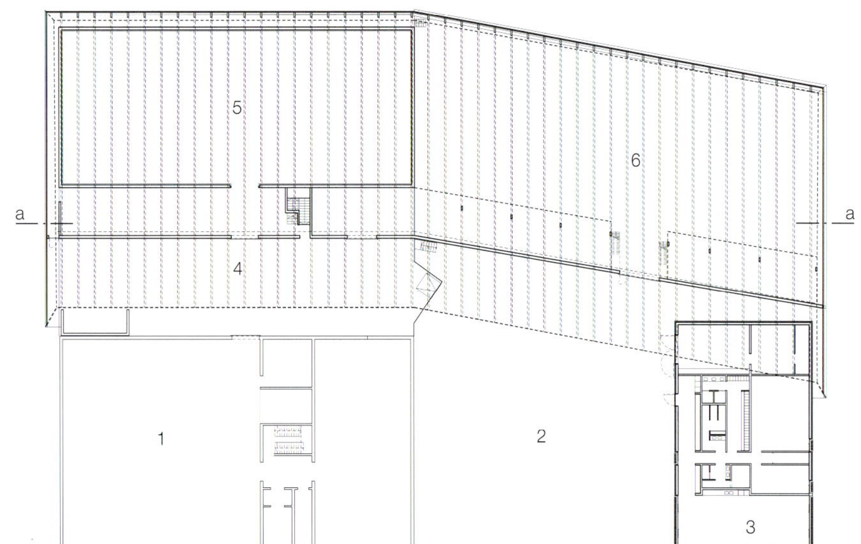

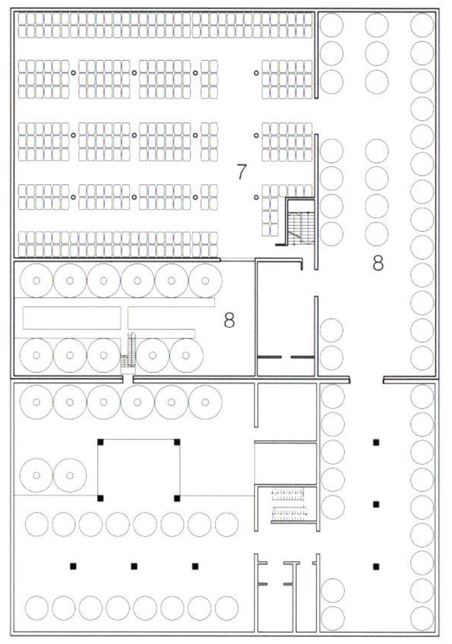

Floor plans • Section
Maßstab 1:800

1 Press room
2 Front courtyard
3 Labourers' building
4 Multifunctional area
5 Bottle cellar
6 Shed
7 Barrique cellar
8 Fermenting cellar

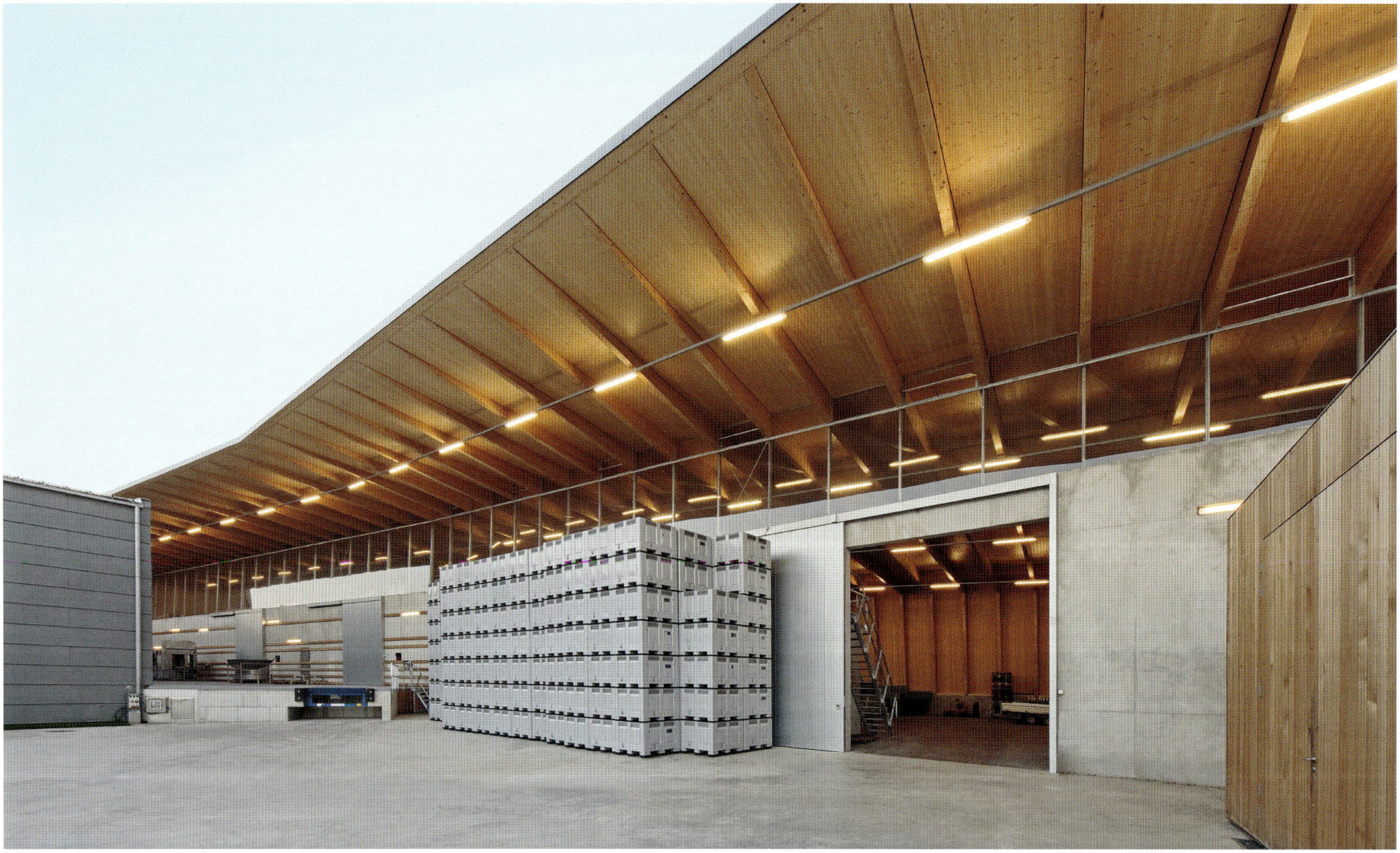

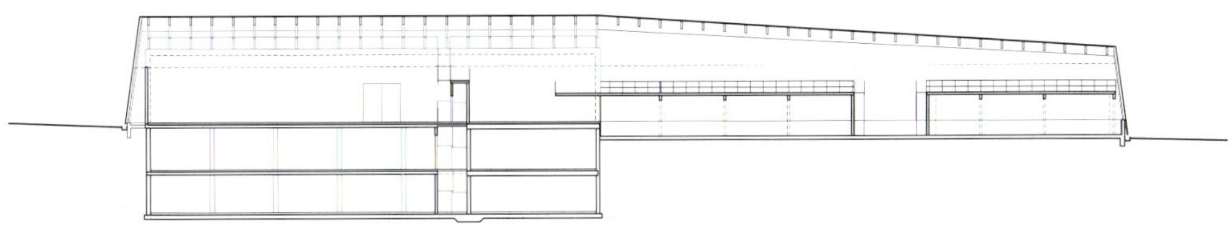

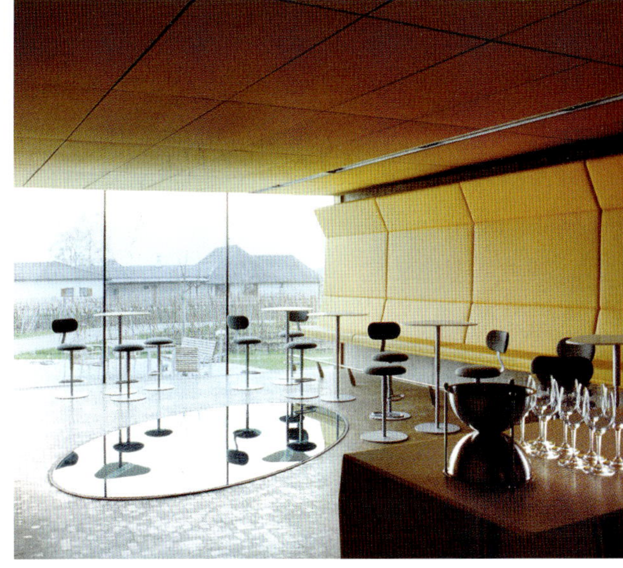

nicated with Heinrich directly, with Heinrich's cellar-master providing input on technical questions.
In a construction period of just 10 months, an impressive building went up on a 10,000-square-metre area, a building whose most striking feature is its distinctive envelope. When one approaches from the west, the highly angular structure looks hermetically sealed; still, despite its size, it fits harmoniously into the landscape. On passing, the outer skin reveals itself to be a light roof shell of about 90 by 34 metres in size that freely spans the shed and the bottle warehouse, thus positively affecting the temperature and air circulation.
Initially, Heinrich had wanted the wood of the building envelope to stay visible, as he thought that in the course of time, the colour changes that timber undergoes would allow the building to blend better into the landscape. What was ultimately implemented was a roof construction of wood sandwich panels covered with a welded black roofing membrane held in place with white vacuum fasteners. Today, the winemaker is very happy with this solution.
Under the bottle warehouse, the barrique cellar extends over two levels and is joined below ground with the existing build, the press house. Thanks to the climate-regulating effect of the surrounding earth, the temperature is naturally kept at a constant level. This is where the 500-litre oak barrels, the fermentation tanks and the large stainless steel tanks used for the blending of the wine are found.
The adjacent shed houses tractors and machinery as well as work materials and empty receptacles. If need be, an additional level can be created here for extra warehouse space. To enable operations in any weather, the roof extends out far beyond the building, creating a rain-protected, multifunctional area between the bottle warehouse and the existing build. "The large courtyard space created by the U-shaped arrangement of the buildings can be used for many purposes," explains Heinrich. For example, large coolers placed there during the harvest provide additional cooling capacity. The courtyard also serves as a manoeuvring space for trucks delivering supplies and empty bottles.
On the other side of the courtyard, the hall complex with its large freight elevator is designed to receive the grapes picked during the harvest. Via large openings in the floor, the freshly crushed grapes can drop directly into the fermentation tanks in the cellar by means of gravity rather than pumps – a factor that has a direct bearing on the quality of the wine. A further notable feature is integrated in the roof of this hall: rainwater is collected over the whole surface of the roof and utilized in the winery as non-potable water.
In order for visitors to be able to enjoy the wines in an appropriate setting, a futuristic-looking tasting room was installed. On the wall, soil profiles of the various rock and ground formations show the diversity of the surrounding terroir, which is reflected in the highly diverse Heinrich wines. They range from the well-made Red, an everyday red wine, to the top-tier Pannobile and Gabarinza wines, the latter a blend of 60 per cent Zweigelt, 30 per cent Blaufränkisch and 10 per cent Merlot. But the very pinnacle is represented by the now legendary Salzberg, which is regularly listed among the three best reds in Austria.
The vineyards on the slopes directly above the winery enjoy not just the ideal amount of sun, but a fascinatingly diverse range of soils, from silty and clayey to calcareous or sandy and gravelly, a diversity which provides the ideal ripening conditions for the very different needs of Merlot, Blaufränkisch and Zweigelt grapes, and all within a relatively small area.
After ascending the Mount Olympus of red wines, Heinrich has discovered a new playing field: the world of white wines. On the chalky and slate-based soils of the Leitha Mountains, he vinifies expressive varietal wines from Chardonnay, Neuburger and Weissburgunder (Pinot Blanc) grapes. So far, unfortunately, his production of these has barely exceeded homeopathic doses; but those who know Heinrich trust that that will change.
With this impressive building, the Heinrichs have taken an important step towards their goal of gradually expanding their wine estate.

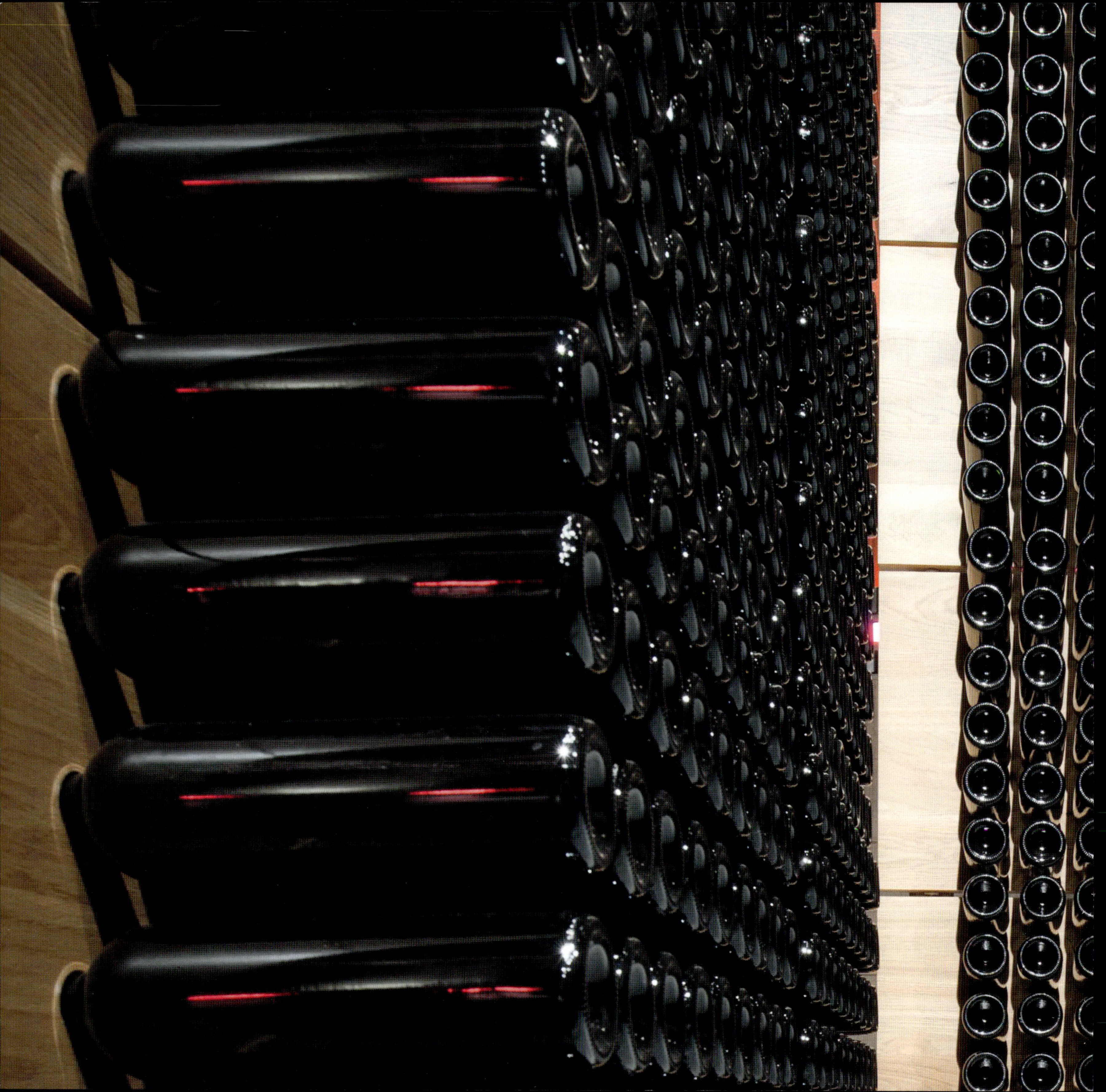

Country guide to wine and architecture in Europe

Germany

Wine production

Together, the German wine regions boast 105,000 hectares under vines. Of this area, white wine cultivation accounts for some 64 per cent and red wine and rosé 36 per cent. The leading grape varieties among the white wines are Riesling, Müller-Thurgau/Rivaner, Silvaner, Grauburgunder/Ruländer (Pinot Gris) and Weissburgunder (Pinot Blanc), with Kerner, Chardonnay, Gutedel, Traminer, Sauvignon Blanc and others playing a lesser role. The most popular red-wine varieties include Spätburgunder (Pinot Noir), Dornfelder, Portugieser, Trollinger (Schiava), Lemberger (Blaufränkisch), St. Laurent and Merlot. Depending on the vintage, *Tafelwein* (table wine) and *Landwein* (country wine) account for some 5–10 per cent of output; *Qualitätswein* (quality wine from a specific region) makes up about 60–70 per cent, and *Prädikatswein* (superior quality wine, such as Kabinett, Spätlese and Auslesen) accounts for 20–30 per cent.

Cultivation takes place primarily on steep and hilly vineyards on various types of soil. There are 13 wine regions in all, of which 11 are located in the south-west of the country. With its 65,000 hectares under cultivation, Rhineland-Palatinate is the largest wine producer of all the German states, with Baden-Württemberg coming in second with 27,000 hectares.

The number of winemaking businesses has been decreasing for decades, a trend that is affecting the smaller wineries above all. About one third of the vineyard area in Germany is cultivated by the members of the 200 winemaking cooperatives (called *Winzergenossenschaften*). Two hundred leading wineries (with a high percentage of Riesling producers) are members of VDP, an association of German superior-quality wine estates.

Rhineland-Palatinate
Six wine regions – Rheinhessen, Pfalz (Palatinate), Mosel, Nahe, Mittelrhein (UNESCO World Heritage Site) and Ahr – are located in Rhineland-Palatinate. The state accounts for 65–70 per cent of German wine production.

Baden-Württemberg
Judging by its main grape varieties, Baden is "Burgunderland": Spätburgunder (Pinot Noir), Grauburgunder (Pinot Gris) and Weissburgunder (Pinot Blanc) account for some 55 per cent of the gross vineyard area of 16,000 hectares. In Württemberg, with its 11,500 hectares of vineyards, red wine production is predominant, accounting for almost 70 per cent of total output. There is an emphasis on specialities such as Trollinger (called Vernatsch in Alto Adige), Schwarzriesling (Pinot Meunier), and Lemberger (called Blaufränkisch in Austria). Boasting an output share of more than 70 per cent, the 146 winemaking cooperatives are the main wine producers in Baden-Württemberg.

Franken / Franconia
With its 6,000 hectares under cultivation, Franconia is one of the smaller German wine regions, accounting for six per cent of output. White wines – primarily specialities such as Silvaner, Müller-Thurgau and Bacchus – predominate, making up 80 per cent of production. The majority of wines produced here are visually distinguished from others by the shape of their bottle: most Franken wines are sold in flasks – short, flattened, round-bodied bottles called *Bocksbeutel*.

Sachsen/Saxony
Europe's north-easternmost wine region is also one of the smallest German wine regions. In the Elbe valley east and west of Dresden, a broad range of predominantly white wine grapes is cultivated, mainly Müller-Thurgau, Riesling and Weissburgunder. On the producer side, the small size of Saxon winemaking businesses is notable. Some 1,800 "hobby vintners" alone, some of them with just a few rows of vines, are members of the Meissen winemaking cooperative.

Traditional wineries

Pfalz/Palatinate
- Weingut Geheimer Rat Dr. von Bassermann-Jordan, Deidesheim (extensive vaulted cellars)
- Reichsrat von Buhl, Deidesheim (mansion, historical cellar)
- Dr. Bürklin-Wolf, Wachenheim (barrel cellar, English garden)
- Fitz-Ritter, Bad Dürkheim (mansion, half-timbered inner courtyard)
- Müller-Catoir, Haardt (neo-Classical facade with column portal, interior fit-out in Gründerzeit style)

Rheingau
Alongside Schloss Vollrads, Schloss Johannisberg and Eberbach Abbey (see pp. 12ff.):
- Weingut Freiherrlich Langwerth von Simmern'sches Rentamt, Eltville (building ensemble with Renaissance residence, park)
- Weingut Robert Weil, Kiedrich (mansion in the English country style, park)

Rheinhessen
- Staatliche Weinbaudomäne Oppenheim (three-wing facility in the Art Nouveau style)
- Schloss Westerhaus, Ingelheim (neo-Baroque two-part wine estate with castle and winery buildings, impressive location)

Nahe
- Gut Hermannsberg, Niederhausen-Schlossböckelheim (formerly Preussische Weinbaudomäne, conceived as a showpiece winery, generous building complex in the Art Nouveau style)

Mosel
- Maximin Grünhaus Schlosskellerei C. von Schubert, Mertesdorf (historical building ensemble)
- Weingut Karthäuserhof, Trier-Eitelsbach (13th-century moated castle)
- Mönchhof & Joh. Jos. Christoffel Erben, Ürzig (Baroque manor, medieval vaulted cellar)
- former wine estate Julius Kayser & Co., Traben-Trarbach

Wine architecture

On the initiative of the Rhineland-Palatinate Chamber of Architects and with the support of the Rhineland-Palatinate Ministry of Viniculture and the German Winegrowers' Association, the "Architekturpreis Wein" prize for wine architecture has been awarded since 2007. Vintners and their architects in all German wine regions are eligible to win.

The following are examples of the connection between historical building culture and contemporary interior design:
- Weingut Künstler, Hochheim, Rheingau
- Weingut Forstmeister Geltz-Zilliken, Saarburg, Mosel

- Weingut Leo Fuchs, Pommern, Mosel
- Kühling-Gillot, Bodenheim, Rheinhessen
- Weingut Julius, Gundheim, Rheinhessen
- Kruger-Rumpf, Münster-Sarmsheim, Nahe

Rhineland-Palatinate
- Kreutzenberger, Kindenheim, Pfalz
- Weinmanufaktur Montana, Bensheim-Auerbach, Hessische Bergstrasse
- Weingut Schneider, Ellerstadt, Pfalz

Baden-Württemberg
In the past few decades, the winemaking cooperatives of Baden-Württemberg have invested primarily in the modernization and optimization of their production facilities, ideally leading to a "visual clean-up" of the buildings.
- Winzergenossenschaft Oberbergen
- Weingärtnergenossenschaft Eberstadt
- Weingärtner Brackenheim
- Weingärtnergenossenschaft Metzingen-Neuhausen
- Weingärtner Flein-Talheim

Franken/Franconia
Almost all projects in Franconia have focused on the areas of hospitality and customer marketing. The display and tasting spaces are part of local or regional tourism concepts:
- Cultural Centre, City of Dettelbach
- Vinothek Iphofen
- DIVINO Nordheim
- Winzergemeinschaft Franken (GWF)
- Weinhaus Hans Wirsching, Iphofen

Sachsen/Saxony
The historic legacy of Saxon wine culture, in combination with its old building culture, is lovingly maintained. Typical examples of this are the 1990–2010 renovation of the oldest wine estate of the region, Schloss Proschwitz, with its 18th-century cluster of buildings in Zadel, near Meissen, and the rebuilding of the Hoflössnitz wine estate, both of which remain popular tourist destinations.

Winzerhof Gierer in Nonnenhorn

Architects: mattes · sekiguchi partner, Wilhelmstr. 5a, 74072 Heilbronn, www.msp-architekten.com

Completion: 2007

Region: Württemberg

Contact: Sonnenbichlstrasse 31, 88149 Nonnenhorn info@winzerhof-gierer.de

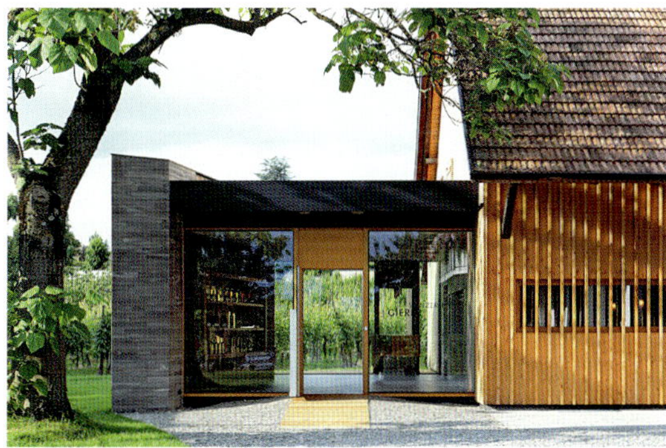

The wine-producing district of Bayerischer Bodensee, near Lake Constance, is officially an exclave of the wine region of Württemberg, a region otherwise associated with the Neckar, Rems Valley, Kocher, Jagst and Tauber areas. Not far from Lindau, Josef and Renate Gierer operate a wine farm that includes orchards, a distillery and guest rooms. When Josef Gierer took over the business from his parents, he set out not just to improve the quality of the wine, but also to increase the size of the vineyards. The resulting success dictated the next steps: a built extension of the working areas and the sales and tasting rooms. With a modern, elegant look that recalls a completely refurbished barn, the new sales and tasting extension built on to the existing building has been very popular with visitors. Moreover, it offers a view of the adjoining lakeshore, turning a tasting of the farm's impressive range of wines into a visual treat as well. A few steps away, a glass window in the floor gives the visitors a look into the oak barrel cellar. Should the popularity of their wines continue to grow, the Gierers plan to build a new bottle cellar as well as a new production building.

Staatsweingut Weinsberg in Weinsberg

Architects: Bürogemeinschaft Eisele + Mattes, heute: mattes · sekiguchi partner, Wilhelmstr. 5a, 74072 Heilbronn, www.msp-architekten.com

Completion: 1999

Region: Württemberg

Contact: Traubenplatz 5, 74189 Weinsberg www.sw-weinsberg.de

The state-owned wine estate was a product of Germany's oldest vinicultural academy (founded in 1868, now the State Teaching and Research Academy for Viticulture and Orchard Management). Its perfected cellar technique has brought forth a number of award-winning wines. The year 1999 saw the completion of a new sales space offering expert advice and tastings. Its large glass facade is conceived as an inviting shop window. The elegant presentation room harmonizes with the existing facilities, which date back to the 1970s. Four years after the sales space, the "glass production building" with an experimental winery and a sparkling-wine production facility was opened. Its equipment constitutes the state of the art in oenology.

Weingut Pauser in Flonheim

Architects: EICHLER Architekten, Hauptstr. 98, 55232 Alzey-Weinheim, www.eichler-alzey.de

Completion: 2010

Region: Rheinhessen

Contact: Im Baumfeld 40, 55237 Flonheim www.weingut-pauser.de

Over three years and three building phases, what began as a simple plan to build a new sales and tasting space for the Pauser wine estate had ballooned into a project that included a machine hall, a new barrel and bottle cellar, a new grape receiving space and finally the shop. With its angular lines, the wine production building harmonizes completely with the previously built machine hall clad in oxidized steel. The sales space offers a modern, inviting tasting room that features the materials steel, glass, wood and stone. The upper storey houses an event and reception space with a sun deck affording a panoramic view over the hilly landscape of Rheinhessen.

Jean Stodden in Rech

Architects: Architekturbüro Mertens, Hauptstr. 151a, 53474 Bad Neuenahr, www.mertens-architekt.de

Completion: 2007

Region: Ahr

Contact: Rotweinstr. 7–9, 53506 Rech/Ahr
www.stodden.de

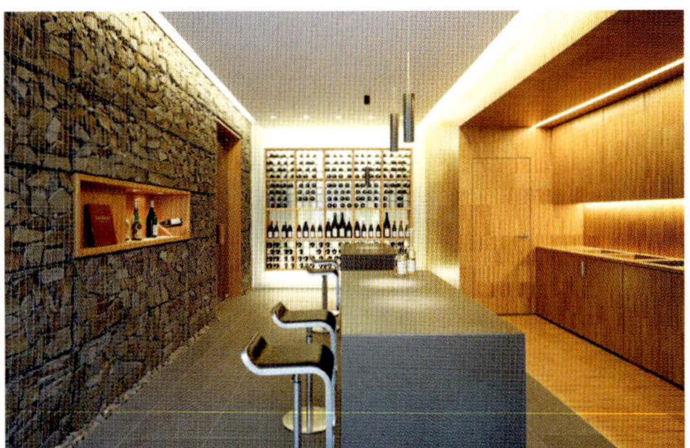

For years, Jean Stodden has been in the top league of German red-wine makers. His wines have consistently been hailed for their expressive strength, their wonderful aromas and their ageability. To achieve this, the vintner, whose family has been cultivating wine since the 16th century, lets his wines age for 16 months in special casks. Such oenological gems require a fitting setting, so a new presentation and tasting space with cellar was created. Here, materials with a strong link to wine, such as wood, natural stone and glass, were given a modern update. Wooden barrels that not only aid the "show", but also serve as red-wine storage, are integrated into the overall look, while thermally separated from the heated space by a glass wall. The logo of the winery and an open fireplace are harmoniously integrated into the interior. The result is very much in line with Stodden's wine philosophy: "Doing everything in harmony with nature to bring wine to perfection."

Weingut Bürgermeister Carl Koch Erben in Oppenheim

Architects: Gehbauer Helten Architekten, Postplatz 6, 55276 Oppenheim am Rhein, www.gehbauerhelten.de

Completion: 2002

Region: Rheinhessen

Contact: Wormser Str. 62, 55276 Oppenheim am Rhein
www.ck-wein.de

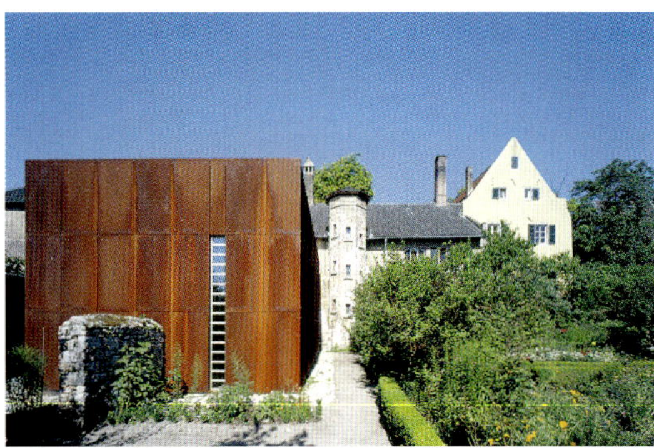

The bottling plant of Weingut Bürgermeister Carl Koch Erben in Oppenheim is evidence of how a positive and progressive attitude can facilitate the architectural rejuvenation of wineries. A building cube resembling a spatial sculpture was set beside the historical building of the estate, forming a stark contrast to the existing build. Both structures are charismatic in their own way. The many colour facets of the facade of oxidized steel and its gradual patination attractively complement the historical building of the wine estate, which was founded in the 19th century.
Looking back, architects Achim Gehbauer and Gerhardt Helten see their project as a "simple answer to complex and multifaceted considerations". They stress that the implementation of their concept would not have been possible if their client had not been open to their ideas and had confidence in their creative powers.

Vincenz Richter in Meissen

Architects: seidel + wirth, Thomas-Müntzer-Platz 9, 01307 Dresden

Completion: 2008

Region: Sachsen/Saxony

Contact: Kapitelholzsteig 1, 01662 Meissen
www.vincenz-richter.de

The Vincenz Richter wine estate in Meissen is a prime example of the sense of optimism that has brought the vintners of Saxony, in eastern Germany, to new heights, both of quality and of price. In the excellent Meissen vineyards on the slopes of the Kapitelberg, architects seidel + wirth created a building of concrete and glass to complement the historical timber-frame building from the 17th century. In order not to mar the landscape of the Spaar Mountains, the wine production area, measuring 900 square metres in total, was moved underground. The spaces for the marketing of the wines, which include a wine shop as well as tasting, teaching and exhibition spaces, encompass 250 square metres.

Schloss Wackerbarth in Radebeul

Architects: h.e.i.z.Haus Architektur.Stadtplanung, Wurzener Str. 15a, 01127 Dresden, www.heizhaus.de

Completion: 2002

Region: Sachsen/Saxony

Contact: Wackerbarthstraße 1, 01445 Radebeul
www.schloss-wackerbarth.de

The Schloss Wackerbarth wine estate, owned by the state of Saxony, exudes a fascination that is sure to affect even those visitors whose affinity to wine is not especially strong. Alongside the renovated Baroque building, the architectural highlight of the estate is the wine and sparkling-wine production facility, which in 2002 was converted to an adventure winery, in which visitors can experience the making of wine from the grape to the glass and then taste selected products afterwards. The new buildings, which are characterized by their clean lines and their tension between the old and the new, have been awarded numerous architectural prizes.

Weingut am Stein in Würzburg

Architects: hofmann keicher ring architekten, Veitshöchheimerstr. 1, 97080 Würzburg, www.hofmann-keicher-ring.de
Completion: 2005
Region: Franken / Frankonia
Contact: Mittlerer Steinbergweg 5, 97080 Würzburg www.weingut-am-stein.de

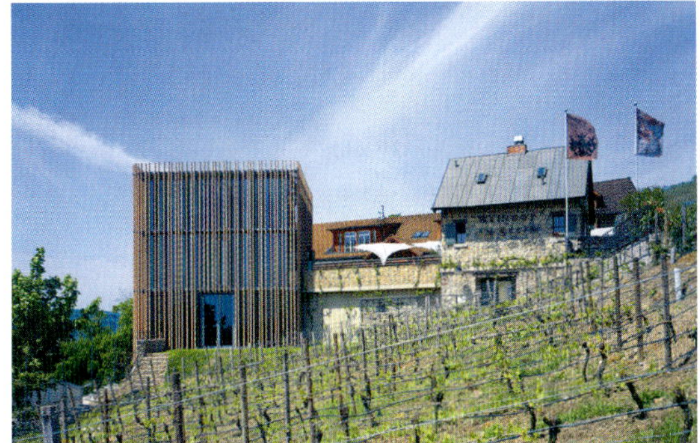

In unveiling their new wine estate on the panoramic site of the "Würzburger Stein", Ludwig and Sandra Knoll took their first and most significant step towards a rebranding of their Frankenwein. In collaboration with architects Hofmann Keicher Ring, they have created an architectural reflection of the character of the estate's wines, which are marked by their clear structures, autonomy and uncompromising quality. This ambition is manifested in two distinctive structures, the WeinWerk presentation building, measuring 10 by 10 metres, and the wine production facility, measuring 9 by 9 metres. The WeinWerk building was inspired by the vertical structure of the vineyard rows and the horizontal structure of the soil layers. The two-layered facade of green glass and vertical oak beams reflects the colours of the surrounding landscape. The wine production facility is a building of natural stone symbolizing a contemporary interpretation of typical vineyard houses. The detail-rich cubes are incorporated harmoniously into the existing ensemble, achieving a successful symbiosis of old and new that has made the wine estate an architectural attraction in the hills of the Frankenwein metropolis of Würzburg.

Staatlicher Hofkeller in Würzburg

Architects: archicult gmbh – breunig architekten, Mainleitenstr. 33, 97299 Zell am Main, www.archicult.de
Completion: 2005
Region: Franken / Frankonia
Contact: Rosenbachpalais, Residenzplatz 3, 97070 Würzburg, www.hofkeller.de

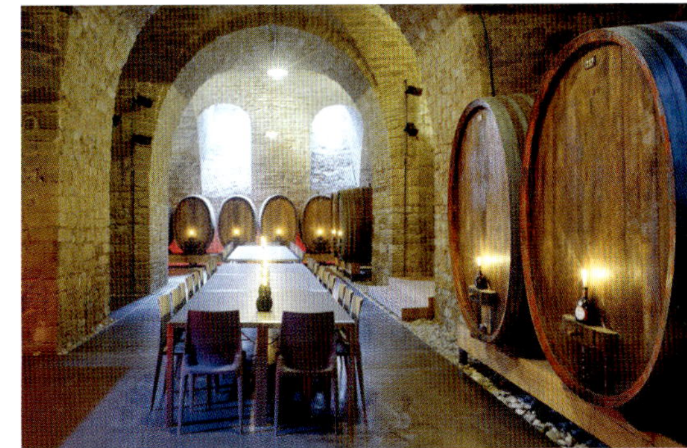

The Bavarian state-owned Hofkeller, at 120 hectares under cultivation one of the largest wine estates in Germany, is also one of the country's oldest, going back almost 300 years. The unique, historical ambience of the Hofkeller is key to the successful marketing of its wines. It is this legacy that was to be captured in a contemporary medial way for visitors to the estate. The concept of the architects is built on a multi-step solution that effectively presents historical data and facts from the Hofkeller's past, but also fulfils pragmatic functions such as tastings and sales. In this way, culture and commerce are brought together in a fitting and low-key manner. The tour starts in the sales space with its glass display areas and continues to the event pavilion with its richly ornamented facade of oxidized steel and an interior that recalls a wine bower in autumn. Finally, the visitor arrives at the historical wine cellar, whose past is shown in a timeline. The concept and planning stage of this effective, holistic presentation took several years, an investment of time that has paid off, as is evidenced by the increase in sales to private customers.

Weingut Horst Sauer in Escherndorf

Architects: Büro Reinhard May, Mergentheimer Str. 10, 97082 Würzburg, www.raymay.de
Completion: 2006
Region: Franken / Frankonia
Contact: Bocksbeutelstr. 14, 97332 Escherndorf www.weingut-horst-sauer.de

In the past few years, many winery building projects in Franconia were subject to similar constraints: there was an increased need for space but only limited area on which to create it; a new architectural language had to engage in a dialogue with the existing, varied building fabric; and in many cases, the client was not a minor vintner but a wine estate with a reputation, a rich history, and customers who often had traditional views on how "their" winery was supposed to look. Horst and Magdalena Sauer decided to accept the exciting challenge of erecting a new building with a sales space and a treasury, in which the estate's wines would be given an appropriate home. The project took more than two years to complete.

Weingut Max Müller I in Volkach

Architect: Reinhold Jäcklein, Erlachhof 5, 97332 Volkach www.jaecklein.de
Fertigstellung: 2008
Region: Franken / Frankonia
Contact: Hauptstrasse 46, 97332 Volkach www.max-mueller.de

Since 1991, the Max Müller I winery in Volkach has been housed in a Baroque building dating back to 1692, complete with an impressive vaulted cellar for its stainless-steel tanks and wooden barrels. Rainer and Monika Müller decided to transform the museum-like presentation and tasting rooms into a light-filled, inviting space with elegant furnishings and diverse materials, lighting moods and colours. Their project is a successful example how the architectural and interior-design arts of yesterday and today can coexist harmoniously side by side.

Weingut Brennfleck in Sulzfeld

Architects: Dold + Versbach, i_Park Klingholz 15, 97232 Giebelstadt, www.dold-versbach.de
Completion: 2007
Region: Franken / Frankonia
Contact: Papiusgasse 7, 97320 Sulzfeld am Main www.weingut-brennfleck.de

The question of whether – and to what degree – a project is worth all the effort, cost and commitment that go into it can, of course, be determined only in retrospect. But in the case of the Brennfleck wine estate in Sulzfeld, the Gault Millau wine guide attests that the new building measures have clearly been beneficial to the quality of the wines. The sales-boosting praise refers to Brennfleck's new wine production facility of exposed concrete and Franconian shell limestone. The new ensemble with its clean lines has optimized production processes and also gives visitors exceptional glimpses into the wine cellars, which are connected to the building by a tunnel. The contrast with the surrounding buildings of the listed estate from 1479 only adds to the appeal of the whole.

Lubentiushof in Niederfell

Architects: Hessel.Architekten, Keltenweg 27, 56626 Andernach, www.hessel-architekten.de
Completion: 2007
Region: Mosel
Contact: Kehrstraße 16, 56332 Niederfell / Mosel www.lubentiushof.de

This wine estate in Niederfell produces a "slow" wine for Riesling enthusiasts. In an almost text-book manner, a wine workshop was created for customer outreach on a tiny inner-city demolition site. With its clean form, the new build fits in effortlessly with the local building tradition. A small courtyard was created between the old and the new building. In the choice of materials and in the design of its details, the small extension is modern through and through, distinguishing itself in this way from the adjoining old build. Quarry stone was the only traditional building material used; otherwise steel, glass and wooden louvres predominate.

Austria

Wine production

Austria has 45,000 hectares under vines, of which 65.5 per cent grow white wine and 34.5 per cent red wine.
For the production of quality and premium-quality wine (Qualitätswein and Prädikatswein), 22 white wine and 13 red wine grape varieties are qualified. Grüner Veltliner is the most widely cultivated white wine grape variety (36 per cent of output), followed by Welschriesling (nine per cent), Rivaner/Müller-Thurgau and Weissburgunder (Pinot Blanc) including Chardonnay (six per cent each) and Riesling (three per cent). Among red wine varieties, Blauer Zweigelt (nine per cent) is the most dominant, followed by Blaufränkisch and Portugieser (five per cent each). As in Germany, there is a large proportion of part-time vintners with small vineyards (20,000 vintners with less than one hectare of vineyards); 6,500 wineries do their own bottling.
Grape cultivation is concentrated in four Austrian states: Lower Austria, Burgenland, Styria and Vienna. There are small vineyard areas (87 hectares) in five further federal states.
Austrian wine law distinguishes between wines without a regional appellation (country wine or Landwein, table wine or Tafelwein, and Austrian wine or österreichischer Wein) wines with a protected regional appellation (Qualitätswein and Kabinett), and Prädikatswein. Each designation comes with its own regulations concerning minimum must weight and maximum yield per hectare.

Lower Austria
Some 30,000 hectares of vineyards are spread out over eight wine districts in the Danube Plain in the north-east of the country. This is where more than 60 per cent of Austrian wine comes from, almost half of that made up of the Grüner Veltliner grape variety. The rest of the output comes from a wide selection of grapes whose resulting wines reflect the various climatic and geological factors.
Together with Burgenland, Lower Austria forms the Weinland Österreich (Wine Land Austria) wine region.

Burgenland
Some 14,600 hectares of vineyards are spread out over the four wine districts Neusiedler See (7,300 hectares), Neusiedler See/Hügelland (3,900 hectares), Mittelburgenland (2,300 hectares) and Südburgenland (500 hectares).
For a limited time, the European Union promoted Burgenland through a regional development programme. The measures permitted extensive investment in the modernization and new building of wineries and their technical equipment.

Styria
Styria accounts for some seven per cent of Austria's wine production. The total area under vines of about 3,800 hectares is spread out over the wine districts Südoststeiermark (1,350 hectares), Südsteiermark (2,350 hectares) and Weststeiermark (450 hectares). For climatic reasons, white wine cultivation predominates, accounting for 75 per cent of production. Welschriesling and Weissburgunder (Pinot Blanc) constitute the leading varieties. Of the Styrian white wines that attain an internationally recognized top quality, most are vinified from Sauvignon Blanc and Chardonnay/Morillon grapes.

Wine architecture

Notable examples of traditional wine architecture include:

- Domäne Wachau, Dürnstein (its early-18th-century Kellerschlössel, or Cellar Castle, is the Wachau region's Baroque showpiece, restored completely in 2006)
- Klosterneuburg Monastery
- Esterházy Winery, Eisenstadt (wine cultivation since the 17th century, wine museum, new production facility)

Lower Austria

In comparison with other Austrian states with wine cultivation, Lower Austria boasts a relatively modest number of modern wine architecture projects. About a dozen wine producers have taken concrete steps in that direction since 2000. The Bründlmayer wine estate in Langenlois started that as early as ten years previously, when Wilhelm Bründlmayer built a new gravity-flow winery following the principle of gentle grape processing. Other vintners followed suit in the ensuing years, constructing extensions and new builds:

- Weingut Hirsch, Kammern
- Weingut Markowitsch, Göttelsbrunn
- Weingut Ott, Feuersbrunn
- Weingut Grassl, Göttelsbrunn
- Weingut Holzapfel, Weissenkirchen
- Weingut Rudi Pichler, Wösendorf

While the winemaking cooperative Domäne Wachau (formerly Freie Weingärtner), which also runs the Kellerschlössel in the famous Kellerberg and uses it for special events, wanted just a modern sales space, the Winzer Krems cooperative (one of the largest in all of Austria, boasting 1,200 members and 1,000 hectares under cultivation) built a completely new, glass production facility under a sweeping roof construction.

Burgenland

In the course of just a few years, Burgenland has become an El Dorado of modern wine architecture. From 1999 to 2004, more than 50 winemaking businesses there undertook construction measures, ranging from modernization projects to the building of entirely new estates. The Burgenland architect Anton Mayerhofer alone handled more than 20 of these projects.
The first trailblazers included the Gesellmann and J. Heinrich wineries in Deutschkreuz and Gernot Heinrich in Gols, but primarily Franz Weninger, the Blaufränkisch specialist, who opened the way for modern architecture in winery buildings in 1998. Like many of the later projects in the region, the new production facility of the internationally renowned red-wine producer adapts to the basic form of the traditional long farm in Mittelburgenland. In collaboration with Weninger, the architects Raimund Dickinger and Kriso Leinfellner designed a clearly structured, light, south-oriented structure over a generously proportioned cellar that houses the bottling line, the tasting room and offices in addition to 500 wine casks.
With their wide variety of wine architecture, wine towns such as Gols, Horitschon, Neckenmarkt and Deutschkreuz offer the visitor a kind of permanent exhibition of contemporary wine building culture. The range of architectural expression goes from careful updates all the way to imaginative new structures the likes of which were hard to imagine here just a few short years ago. These include the ARACHON ageing cellar of the Vereinte Winzer Blaufränkischland cooperative in Horitschon, where the wine ages in 1,000 casks on 1,500 square metres and where the first storey houses not only the bottling line, but also stylish presentation and tasting rooms. Designed by architects Wilhelm Holzbauer an Dieter Irresberger and featuring a sandstone facade that blends harmoniously into the landscape, the winery is considered an aesthetic masterpiece of Burgenland wine architecture.

Styria

Parallel to the building boom in the wine industry of Burgenland, the southern part of Styria, too, witnessed a great deal of building activity in wine farms and farming estates. More than a dozen projects were realized from the late 1990s to about 2005, most of them in Leutschach, Gamlitz and Straden. The Neumeister wine estate in Straden is one of the most architecturally innovative projects, featuring a stair-like structure nestled into the hillside and a brilliant interior. More even than in other wine regions, the new buildings in southern Styria are notable for their dialogue of contrasts with the surrounding, traditional building fabric. The wine estates Regele in Ehrenhausen, Ploder-Rosenberg in St. Peter am Ottersbach and Krispel in Hof bei Straden show how dramatically the resulting solutions can differ from one another.

Loisium Visitor Centre in Langenlois

Architects: Steven Holl, 450 West 31st Street 11th Floor, 10001 New York, www.stevenholl.com
samottreinisch, Franz Sam und Irene Ott-Reinisch, Franz Josefskai 45, 1010 Vienna, www.samottreinisch.at

Region: Kamptal

Contact: Loisium Allee 1, 3550 Langenlois
www.loisium.at

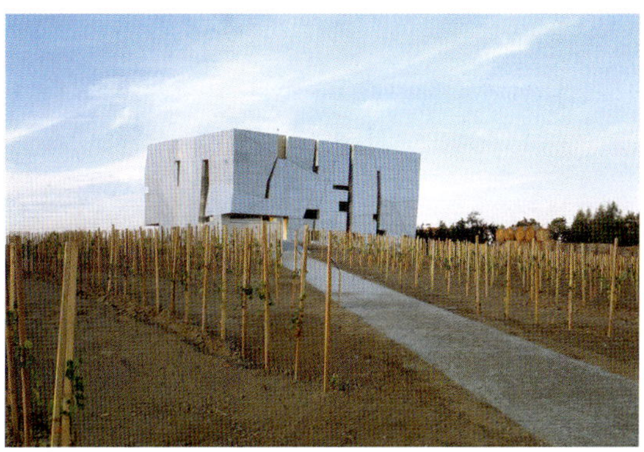

Seldom has new Austrian wine architecture been celebrated with as much media fanfare as the Loisium World of Wine. The reasons for this are as multifaceted as the entire project. In 2003, New York architect Steven Holl built something wholly new in Austria's largest wine-growing community, using an architectural language that stretched the borders of tradition and convention. The functions are spread out over three levels: underground, there is a mythical cellar world where the visitor can learn about the past and present of Austrian wine culture; at ground level, one finds the real eye-catcher, a cube-shaped structure with an unusual aluminium envelope tilted five degrees to the south. This is the tasting and sales centre for the wines from more than 100 of the region's vintners, placed in the midst of their vineyards. Those who want to learn more about the wonderful world of wine can now book a relaxing, enjoyable stay at the adjoining three-storey wine and design hotel Loisium, which "floats" on concrete pillars and was completed in 2006.

Weingut Loimer in Langenlois

Architects: Andreas Burghardt, Mariahilfer Str. 105, 1060 Vienna, www.burghardt.co.at
Completion: 2000
Region: Kamptal
Kontakt: Haindorfer Vögerlweg 23, 3550 Langenlois
www.loimer.at

Well-known vintner Fred Loimer and architect Andreas Burghardt built their Wineloft, a spectacular structure in its own way, over an 18th-century vaulted brick cellar. The building of exposed concrete and black rendering soon became a widely discussed showpiece of modern wine architecture. At first glance, the L-shaped structure seems closed and barely accessible; one lone window provides a view out on to the prime vineyards of Heiligenstein. Towards its protected courtyard, however, the structure shows its open and sun-filled face through a glass facade. In the middle of the tasting room stands a tasting table of eight metres in length, a fitting stage for the Grüner Veltliner and Riesling that have aged in the subterranean world with its geometrically arranged system of tunnels.

United Vineyards – Pfneisl in Kleinmutschen

Architect: Dietmar Gasser, Marktplatz 5, 7423 Pinkafeld
Completion: 2006
Region: Mittelburgenland
Contact: Gutshof, 7452 Kleinmutschen
www.wine-pentagon.com

To make things easier for their English-speaking clientele, the Pfneisl brothers opted for the internationally understood name United Vineyards, a decision that makes sense when one considers the increasing role that export plays for the 100-hectare wine estate. A similarly international approach is evident in the names of the wines – Pentagon, Phaeton, Platinum ¬– and in the production facility built in 2005 with architect Dietmar Gasser, which is a rectangular block of black concrete interrupted by a wide glazed entrance and some vertical slits, and sitting majestically atop a light plinth. Without a doubt, the Pfneisl winemaking family has arrived in the future of wine architecture.

Wein & Schnaps Mariell in Grosshöflein

Architects: creuz & quer, Brockmanngasse 5, 8010 Graz
Completion: 2001
Region: Neusiedler See/Hügelland
Contact: Hauptstrasse 74, 7051 Grosshöflein
www.mariell.at

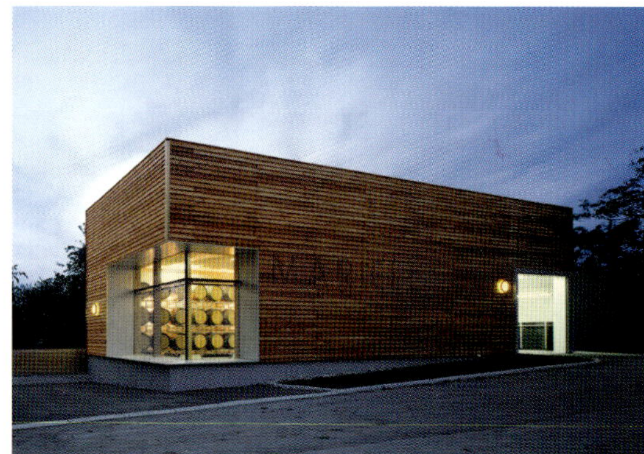

With its seven hectares of vineyards, the winery of Gabriele and Richard Mariell is one of Austria's smaller wine producers. That said, the vintners have not only made a name for themselves as makers of white and red wines, but also have became widely known for their fine spirits. Their fame, however, has spread beyond their products to encompass the production facility they erected in the middle of the old village fabric of Grosshöflein in Mittelburgenland. Reduced to clear forms and lines, the larch-clad, L-shaped block with its corners gripped by strips of sheet metal offers an engaging contrast to the surrounding traditional building fabric. Once inside, the visitor is welcomed by the quietly compelling spectacle of decoratively lined-up casks, clever lighting and a window of room height that provides a view out on to the vineyards beyond.

Weingut Pittnauer in Gols

Architects: Halbritter + Halbritter, Untere Hauptstr. 5, 7100 Neusiedl am See, www.arch-halbritter.com
AllesWirdGut Architektur, Josefstätter Str. 74/B, 1080 Vienna, www.alleswirdgut.cc
Completion: 2001
Region: Neusiedler See
Contact: Neubaugasse 90, 7122 Gols
www.pittnauer.com

What is more important, form or function? In contemporary wine architecture, planners and clients often have a clear answer to this question: both parameters should be given equal weight, so that a significant improvement in wine production efficiency is combined with an authentic, modern look. These were the criteria that guided Brigitte and Gerhard Pittnauer in the building of their new wine estate on the outskirts of Gols. Devoid of any showmanship, the structural volume of light-coloured exposed concrete with glass facades is designed within and without to ensure an optimized wine production process. Completing the Pittnauers' friendly wine world is a light-filled tasting room.

Weingut Koppitsch in Neusiedl am See

Architects: Halbritter & Hillerbrand, Untere Hauptstr. 5, 7100 Neusiedl am See, www.h2arch.at
Completion: 2010
Region: Burgenland
Contact: Oberer Satzweg 55, 7100 Neusiedl am See
www.wein-koppitsch.at

Light, friendly, unpretentious and simply likeable: this is the look of the family-run wine estate after its conversion in 2010. The building does without vibrant colour effects and modernistic structures. Only the floors and ceilings in the cellar are painted a warm red; in the other rooms, light hues predominate, even in the furnishings. The only contrasts to these are the dark lamps in the tasting room. To achieve a unified overall appearance in the wine estate, which has been subject to numerous extensions over the years, the facades of the buildings are clad with boards spaced at irregular intervals.

Weritas Wagram in Kirchberg am Wagram

Architects: gerner°gerner plus, Mariahilfer Str. 101/3/49, 1060 Vienna, www.gernergernerplus.com

Completion: 2009

Region: Wagram

Contact: Marktplatz 44, 3470 Kirchberg am Wagram www.weritas.at

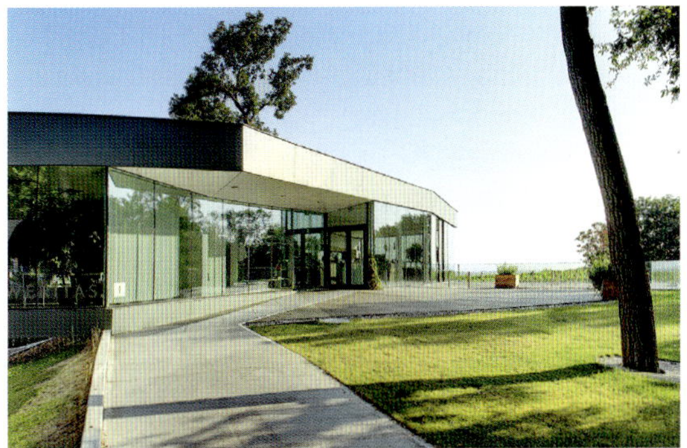

United we stand: this is the motto behind the decision of an increasing number of vintners to pool their efforts in marketing and sales in order to reach a larger number of customers than they ever could by going it alone. Such joint activities, it goes without saying, have to be accompanied with the requisite amount of fanfare. This was the insight behind the design of the new presentation and sales space built by architects Andreas and Gerda Gerner in the old market square of Kirchberg in 2009 – a commission by 54 winemakers in the Wagram wine district. The project is distinguished by its prominent location and clear design. In the building of reinforced concrete, the lower level houses the specially climate-controlled bottle cellar and the seminar rooms; the upper level, a greenish, shimmering glass cube with an extensive view over the Wagram vineyards, contains the wine shop as well as a restaurant and wine bar.

FX Pichler in Oberloiben

Architects: Architekten Tauber, Utzstr. 11, 3500 Krems www.arch-tauber.at

Completion: 2009

Region: Wachau

Contact: Oberloiben 27, 3601 Dürnstein www.fx-pichler.at

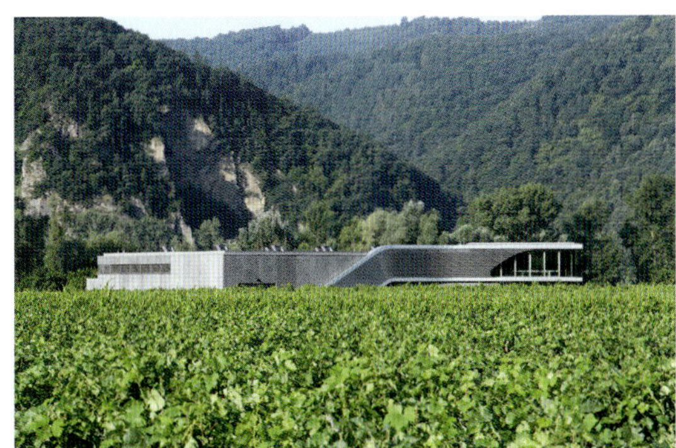

Even if the new production facility at the FX Pichler wine estate in Oberloiben, not far from Dürnstein, had not turned out as stunningly elegant as it did, it would doubtless have been the subject of critical curiosity and much discussion. But as everything that the late, legendary vintner Franz Xaver (FX) Pichler ever touched somehow turned to gold, the architecture of this project, too, far surpasses the ordinary. At the same time, the long, flat-roofed building is in no way showy; it is not even located on the main road, but tucked away behind an old vintner's house, leaving the landscape of the Wachau undisturbed. The facade design is visually sophisticated, with anthracite-coloured concrete elements and lively aluminium appliqués. A generous glass facade on the other side, as well as continuous quarried stone walls, oak board flooring and slate floors provide strong, natural accents. The furnishings in the tasting room are minimalist, featuring a huge white table and designer chairs. Planning and construction took seven years, during which time the client brought home inspirations gained on his various trips.

Weingut Sabathi in Leutschach

Architects: Wemmers Skacel Forenbacher Architects, Claudia Wemmers, Igor Skacel, Michael Forenbacher, Triesterstr. 136, 8020 Graz, www.wemmersskacel.com

Completion: 2004

Region: Südsteiermark / Styria

Contact: Pössnitz 48, 8463 Leutschach www.sabathi.com

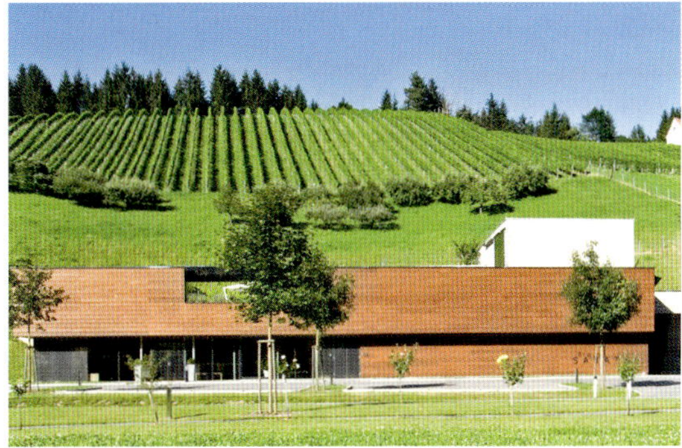

It is not only Erwin Sabathi's wines that sport a sophisticated finesse; the architecture in his wine estate in Leutschach, too, is full of surprises. The facade faced in dark, thermally treated wood announces proudly to the world that the estate uses wine barrels of toasted oak. Like some other wineries built on steep slopes in Styria, this building for wine production and tasting nestles completely into the hillside. The processing of the grapes and the downstream production steps take advantage of gravity, occurring entirely without the aid of pumps. This and the short distances are advantages that ultimately benefit the quality of the wine.

Weingut Lackner-Tinnacher in Gamlitz

Architect: Rolf Rauner, Alberstr. 8/17, 8010 Graz
www.architektur-rauner.at

Completion: 2002

Region: Südsteiermark/Styria

Contact: Steinbach 12, 8462 Gamlitz
www.tinnacher.at

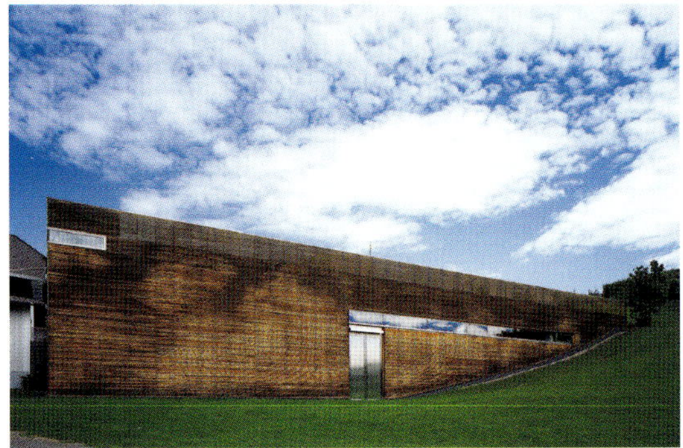

In wine estates that can look back on a rich tradition, such as Fritz and Wilma Tinnacher's winery, which goes back to the 18th century, respect for the historic legacy demands a careful approach, particularly in the implementation of new building projects. For the Tinnachers, then, it was crucial for the building housing the new tank farm and presentation rooms to be in harmonious dialogue with the old vaulted cellars. The resulting structure is faced with wooden slats that have now started to darken with age, and topped with a planted flat roof. These features, like the production facility nestled into the slope of the vineyard, are pleasantly low-key, an impression that continues inside in the modern tank farm and in the stylishly elegant tasting room under the vaulted ceiling, which was renovated in 2002. The project received an award from the Republic of Austria for its exemplary design.

Switzerland

Wine production

Vines grow in almost all Swiss cantons, but large-scale cultivation takes place in just six regions north and south of the main ridge of the Alps. Taken together, the vineyards of Switzerland cover an area of almost 15,000 hectares, making the country one of the smallest wine-growing regions of Europe. The cantons in the French-speaking part of Switzerland do the most intensive wine cultivation. Valais leads with 5,100 hectares, followed by Vaud (3,800 hectares) and Geneva (1,300 hectares). In the former two, white wine is predominant (Fendant and Perlan). In Geneva, however, red wine has now overtaken white wine cultivation. Ticino (1,000 hectares) is almost exclusively geared to red wine production, over 80 per cent of it vinified from Merlot grapes. Of the eight cantons that cultivate wine in eastern Switzerland on a total of 1,800 hectares, Graubünden or Grisons, with its Bündner Herrschaft wine district, is quantitatively not the most important, but the most significant in terms of quality.

Wine architecture

Graubünden/Grisons

While the five wine communities that make up the Bündner Herrschaft wine district are home to 60 wine-producing businesses, the number of estates that have undergone architectural changes is quite small. The few businesses that have done any conversions or new building include Weinhaus Cottinelli in Malans and Weingut Marugg in Fläsch, which built a modern, atmospheric wine cellar in which the barrels are visually accentuated with spotlights. It was designed by the Fläsch-based architect Kurt Hauenstein, whose winery projects are characterized by their clear architectural language and their orientation to the existing structures in the village, for example in their use of materials.

The architect used this very approach in his designs for Weingut Davaz in Fläsch, one of the prime producers in the Bündner Herrschaft. He began with a carriage house and a residence, both of which are marked at first sight by a refreshing inconspicuousness.

Weingut Adank in Fläsch

Architects: Kurt Hauenstein, Kirchgasse 1, 7306 Fläsch
www.atelier-f.ch

Completion: 2009

Region: Graubünden/Grisons

Contact: St. Luzi, 7306 Fläsch
www.adank-weine.ch

From 1966 to 1974, farmers and vintners in Fläsch undertook a combining of their estates and planted vines rather than crops and meadows. Since that time, the municipality has developed into a respected wine producer. It owes its reputation as the home of expressive wines primarily to its Pinot Noir, from which elegant, vigorous red wines are produced. Hansruedi Adank, who took over the winery of his parents in 1994, created quite a stir with such ruby-red Spätburgunder wines. He presents these, alongside aromatic Sauvignon Blanc and full-bodied Grauburgunder, to visitors in his new sales and tasting area, where the irregularly spaced windows cast attractive, artistically pleasing light cones on to the walls.

Scadenagut in Malans

Architects: Konrad Erhard und Daniel Schwitter, Jochstr. 1, 7000 Chur

Completion: 2004

Region: Graubünden/Grisons

Contact: Scadenaweg 1, 7208 Malans
www.malanser-weine.ch

"In the past few years, we have increasingly found that the demands of the customers go far beyond the pure quality of the wines," says Peter Wegelin, explaining his decision to build a new wine cellar and a sales and presentation space to meet the expectations of his clientele as well as fulfil his own desire for an optimization of processes. With Chur architects Konrad Erhard and Daniel Schwitter, he built a winery with a functionally designed production storey on the vineyard level, a barrique cellar underground and, on street level, a meeting space for tastings and events in a transparent glass cube.

Lavaux Vinorama in Rivaz

Architects: Fournier-Maccagnan, Atelier d'architectes, Rue du Cropt 30_cp 248, 1880 Bex, www.fourniermaccagnan.ch
Completion: 2010
Region: Vaud/Lavaux
Contact: Route du Lac 2, Case postale 118, 1071 Rivaz
www.lavaux-vinorama.ch

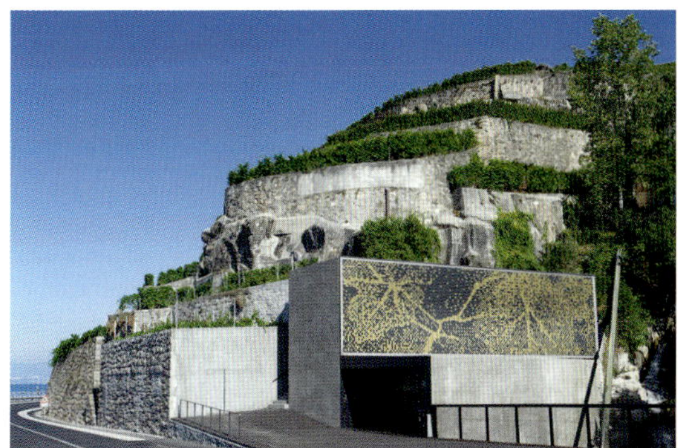

Since 2010, one of the finest vineyard landscapes of Switzerland has been enriched by an oenological and gastronomic institution with a distinctive architecture. The steep, terraced hills of the Lavaux north of Lake Geneva between Montreux and Lausanne were declared a UNESCO World Heritage Site. There, on the Lavaux wine route north of Rivaz, by the Forestay waterfalls, Lavaux Vinorama was built as a "teaching and social centre". The mighty, monolithic cube is nestled, fortress-like, into the steep slopes, its facade, decoratively designed by artist Daniel Schlaepfer, taking on the hues of the surrounding rocks and vineyard walls. The functional spaces – a wine bar serving 200 wines, a cinema and event rooms – are located on various, effectively lit levels of the low-energy building.

Cantina Ghidossi in Cadenazzo

Architect: Aurelio Galfetti, Via San Gottardo 92, 6900 Lugano-Massagno, www.aureliogalfetti.ch
Completion: 1994
Region: Ticino
Contact: Via Mirasole 8, 6500 Bellinzona/Cadenazzo
www.cantina-ghidossi.ch

The evolution of Davide Ghidossi's cantina in Cadenazzo goes back to the beginnings of modern wine architecture, when the architect Aurelio Galfetti designed the two-storey building on the steep slope for him. In his work, Galfetti favours simplicity and a focus on what is essential and natural, an approach that is reflected in his choice of forms and materials. The building project, completed in time for the 1994 wine presentation, has to this day lost none of its simple yet fascinating aura. The plants growing on it give the concrete building even more character. In this place, good wine and good architecture have been coming together joyously for decades.

Weingut Schmidheiny in Heerbrugg

Architects: Bänzigers Architektur, Kirchgasse 1, 9442 Berneck, www.baenzigersarchitektur.ch
Completion: 1999
Region: Ostschweiz
Contact: Schlossstrasse 210, 9435 Heerbrugg
www.schmidheiny.ch

The involvement of the well-known Schmidheiny business dynasty in wine cultivation goes back more than 100 years, to when the family co-founded a vintners' cooperative. In Heerbrugg, in the lovely panoramic setting of the St. Gallen Rhine valley. Thomas Schmidheiny runs a wine estate to which a spare but elegant tasting space of concrete and glass was added. An oenophile, Schmidheiny is networked with selected top wineries abroad, and recently extended his empire through the acquisition of the Höcklistein winery in Rapperswil-Jona on Lake Zurich – a modern and also architecturally attractive wine estate.

Italy

Wine production

Italy is tied with France as Europe's second-largest wine-producing country after Spain. Its 820,000 hectares of vineyards are distributed over 20 wine regions. The most wine is produced in Veneto (7.5 million hectolitres), followed by Emilia-Romagna, Apulia and Sicily (6.5 million hectolitres each). While the regions in the south produce primarily table wine and country wine, the share of quality wines (with a D.O.C. appellation) is highest in Piedmont and Trentino-Alto Adige (over 80 per cent each). In Friuli and Tuscany, quality wines account for more than half of production. The producer structure is highly heterogeneous, ranging from micro-vintners to major high-tech wineries that control a large share of Italian wine exports. Traditionally, the wine industry is based on an immense diversity of grape varieties, including several hundred indigenous varieties that are often confined to a small local area. "International" varieties, such as Cabernet, Merlot and Chardonnay, do play an ever greater role, but regional specialities such as Nebbiolo (Piedmont) and Sangiovese are cornerstones of the Italian wine range.

Wine architecture

Northern Italy

As multifaceted as the Italian wine world is, the number of new building projects in wine estates and cellars is comparatively limited. Contemporary wine architecture enjoys its most interesting displays in the north, particularly in Trentino-Alto Adige. Since 2010, the new central winery of TERRE DA VINO, an association of cooperatives and wine estates with 5,000 hectares of vineyards, has been attracting attention with its almost industrial look. The impressive scale of the project, designed by Giovanni Arnaudo from Cuneo on a 5,000-square-metre footprint, forms a stark contrast to the traditional look of Barolo's family-owned businesses.

One of the most unusual creations of modern wine architecture is found in the Colli Orientali Friuli region, in the village of Gramogliano near Corno di Rosazzo in Udine. Here, Augusto Romano Burelli and Gianfranco Roccatagliata built a 13-metre-high "wine tower" over the vaulted barrel cellar of Cantina Perusini, one of the oldest wine estates of the region. The three-storey tower recalls the sentry towers of Roman border defences. On the floor of the barrel cellar is a clock face above which a Foucault pendulum swings along with the rotation of the earth.

Central Italy

Almost all modern wine architecture projects are concentrated in Tuscany. One of the first was the winery for the estate of the former "Abbey of the Good Harvest", Badia a Coultibuono near Monti di Chianti. Architects Piero Sartago and Nathalie Grenon designed a modern "wine fort", its length punctuated by two cylindrical towers. The structure forms a noticeable counterpart to the much-visited medieval monastery in neighbouring Gaiole. Since about 2000, Maremma, a town to the south of Livorno near the Tuscan coast, has been a sort of Mecca for wine estate investors. This trend has spawned new projects, some of them quite spectacular, on which so-called star architects have been involved as well. The Ticino-based architect Mario Botta designed the Petra winery for entrepreneur Vittorio Moretti. The winery, a cylindrical central building flanked by two flat wings and clad with Verona sandstone, glows in tones of warm pink. In the interior, too, the winery is both elegant and extravagant, with ramrod-straight rows of barrels and the cellars bathed in changing colour lighting.

Angelo Gaja, a wine icon from Piedmont, commissioned Giovanni Bò to build his Cà Marcanda winery in Castegneto Carducci, and Renzo Piano planned the two-storey, amphitheatre-style underground cellar for 2,500 casks for the Rocca di Frassinello wine estate in Gavorrano (see pp. 86ff.).

The most notable creations of wine architecture in the Marche region include the barrel cellar and tasting room of Azienda Umani Ronchi, designed by Marco Vignoni.

Southern Italy

In the southern Italian region of Basilicata, which for many years did not exactly rate as the home of great wines, several ambitious wineries opened between 1998 and 2002 and opted for contemporary wine architecture. For its cellar in Serra del Granato, Cantine del Notaio went for a Mediterranean presentation. With its winery in Rionero, completed in 2002, Terra dei Re has given itself a look of measured elegance, its generous glass facades punctuated with concrete columns. In 2001, the Japanese designer Hikaru Mori and architect Domenico Santomauro built an exceptionally attractive wine estate for entrepreneur Mario Bisceglia in the midst of newly planted vineyards near Lavello, a project that sets new aesthetic standards for wineries in the south of Italy.

Italy is notable for its passion for combining wine cellars and modern art, examples of which can be found in almost all regions. One of the oldest and most renowned wine estates in Calabria, Mastroberadino in Atribalda, decided to go another way. When, following an earthquake, the vaulted cellars had to be rebuilt completely in 1980, the decision was made to complement the Classical residence by painting the vaulted ceilings of the barrel and ageing cellars with large frescoes in the Renaissance style.

Manincor in Caldaro

Architects: Walter Angonese, Marktplatz 6, 39052 Caldaro
www.angonesewalter.it
Rainer Köberl, Maria Theresien Str. 10/3, 6020 Innsbruck
www.rainerkoeberl.at
Silvia Boday, Richardsweg 1, 6020 Innsbruck
www.silviaboday.com

Completion: 2004

Region: Alto Adige

Contact: San Giuseppe al Lago 4, 39052 Caldaro
www.manincor.com

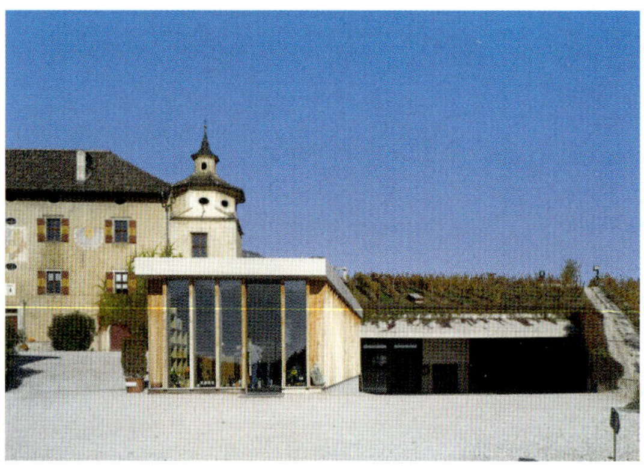

The grape harvest of the 2004 vintage marked the inauguration of the new production facility of the Manincor wine estate in Caldaro (Kaltern). The opening was preceded by three years in which Alto Adige architect Walter Angonese, his colleagues Rainer Köberl and Silvia Boday, and the client, Michael Graf Goëss-Enzenberg, were tied up almost exclusively in the ambitious project of planning a "showpiece cellar" with some 4,800 square metres of usable floor area.

Rather than being a simple appendage of the historical estate, the three-storey new build was to integrate itself as an autonomous structure into the precious earth of the surrounding hillside vineyards. The notable benefits of the building include an optimal cellar climate and a significantly improved grape-handling process as well as the communicative environment provided by the above-ground tasting and sales space. Now it has become evident also that the gradual ageing process of the exposed concrete and the cladding and staircases of oxidized steel make the structure complement the old estate building even more effectively.

"Bistrot" Elena Walch in Termeno

Architect: David Stuflesser, Petlinstrasse 18, 39046 St. Ulrich, www.dstuflesser.com
Completion: 2010
Region: Alto Adige
Contact: Via Andreas Hofer 1, 39040 Termeno
www.elenawalch.com

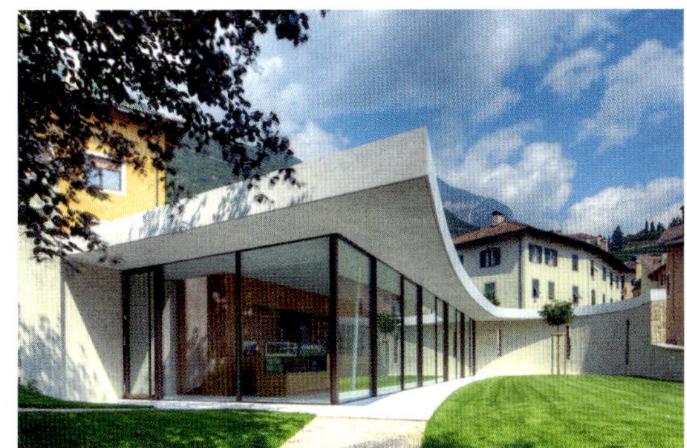

Elena Walch is one of Alto Adige's best-known ambassadors of wine. Ever since the trained architect began to run the tradition-rich Walch winery with her husband, her wines have achieved top ranks for quality, renown and popularity on the international wine scene. In the vineyards of Castel Ringberg – where top Walch wines grow – all the gastronomic stops were pulled out in the panoramic setting over Lake Caldaro. For the local marketing of the wines, an elegant wine "bistrot" was opened in the centre of Termeno (Tramin), not far from the imposing barrel cellar, in 2010. Designed by David Stuflesser and appropriately named "Le Verre capricieux", the bistro, which is located close to the main village road, opens up to the garden and is surrounded by old trees. Visitors are drawn to its inviting, friendly ambience.

Alois Lageder in Margrè

Architects: Abram & Schnabl Architekten, Via cassa di risparmio 15, 39100 Bolzano, www.abram-schnabl.com
Completion: 1995
Region: Alto Adige
Contact: Vicolo dei Conti 9, 39040 Magrè sulla Strada del Vino
www.aloislageder.eu

If the wines of Alto Adige are in increasing demand today, this is thanks in large part to local vintner visionaries such as Alois Lageder. Although he produces a million bottles these days, his wine philosophy has lost none of its autonomy and individuality. In 1997, he had a new building constructed according to ecological und building-biology criteria near the historical Löwengang estate in Magrè (Margreid). The choice of the materials wood and stone ensures a positive exchange of energy. In the cellar, the interplay of sun, air and rock produces an optimal climate for wine storage. The heart of the facility is the 15-metre-high vinification tower, which replaces mechanical pump technologies with the force of gravity.

Cantina Mezzacorona in Mezzocorona

Architects: Cecchetto & Associati, Cannaregio 563/E, 30121 Venice, www.studiocecchetto.com
Completion: 2000
Region: Trentino
Contact: Via Tonale 110, 38016 Mezzocorona
www.mezzocorona.it

When the wine production cooperative began construction of a new production facility in the mid-1990s, words such as "futuristic" and "spectacular" became attached to the project. Indeed, the concept did seem almost sensational at the time, as buildings of that scale – its footprint measures 34,590 square metres – and with such an eye-catching aesthetic were then unknown in Italy. The plant, which is designed to handle the production of wines from 1,600 member vintners and includes a production facility for the sparkling wine Rotari, was conceived with environmental impact in mind. Seventy per cent of the building's area is located underground, which significantly reduces the need for cooling.

Feudi di San Gregorio in Sorbo Serpico

Architects: ZITOMORI, Via Lamarmora 36, 20122 Mailand
www.zitomori.com
Vignelli Associates, 130 East 67th Street, New York, NY 10021, www.vignelli.com
Completion: 2003
Region: Campania
Contact: Località Cerza Grossa, 83050 Sorbo Serpico
www.feudi.it

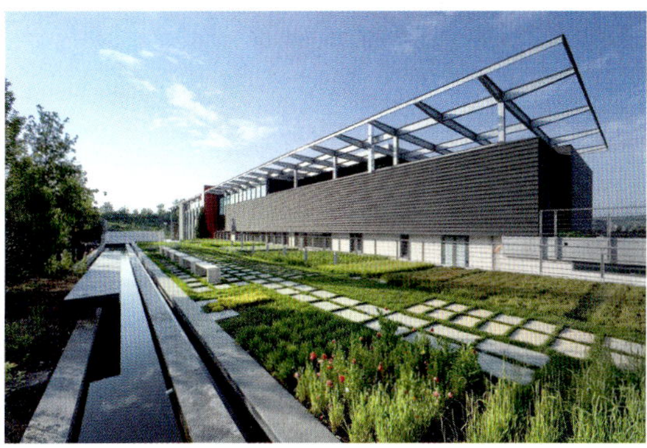

In 1986, the Ercolino and Capoldo families founded Feudi di San Gregorio with the aim of giving Campania – indeed, the whole south of Italy – a wine production facility the likes of which had not been seen before. To implement the ambitious project, 300 hectares of vines were planted near Sorbo Serpico, and Enzo Ercolino hired the Milan-based designer Hikaru Mori, the architect Maurizio Zito and the New Yorker designer couple Massimo and Lella Vignelli, all known for their creative, unusual concepts. What resulted is more than just a modern, functioning wine production facility. With a minimalist architecture that seems almost light-hearted, thanks to the surrounding gardens filled with roses, herbs, old vines and water rivulets, the complex includes a 650-metre-long ageing cellar for 6,000 barriques and an aural accompaniment of music from the Middle Ages; a central, glass tasting room; a gourmet restaurant; rooms for wine tastings and cookery courses; a wine shop; a hotel; and an amphitheatre. Under the aegis of the Vignellis, the entire interior was given a consistent design, down to the clothing of the staff and the look of the wine bottles. Since the opening in 2004, there has been a steady increase in the number of visitors and in the quality of the wine.

Wine production

If other European wine-producing countries have made great strides in the production of world-class wines in recent decades, this is thanks in large part to significant groundwork laid by France, which, among other things, has established quantitative norms that now have role-model character for virtually all wine-producing countries in the world. To name just some important milestones, France was the starting point of the global advance of the grape varieties Cabernet, Merlot and Chardonnay; pioneered the use of the small oak barrel, the barrique, in winemaking; and established the Appellation Contrôlée (AC) system of wine classification.
Vineyard area and wine output in France are decreasing, but the country still retains its first place in the international ranking with some 830,000 hectares under vines. In volume, French wine production accounts for some 20 per cent of the total worldwide figure, but its share of global quality wine production is much higher. Depending on the vintage, the country's 110,000 winery operations produce between 40 and 50 million hectolitres – six to seven billion bottles – of wine. About 73 per cent of this output is made up of red and rosé wine and 23 per cent of white wine. Of total production volume, a little less than two thirds is drunk domestically (though per capita consumption is falling markedly) and a third exported. Primarily in export, premium wines with the AC classification play an important role. On average, about half of French wines belong to this category, which can cover an entire region (such as Champagne) or the majority of it. French wine country is divided into 14 wine regions of varying size. With its 120,000 hectares, Bordeaux is the largest cultivation area for premium wines. Most red wine cultivation is of the grape varieties Grenache (94,000 hectares), Syrah (68,000 hectares), Cabernet Sauvignon (56,000 hectares) and Carignan (53,000 hectares). Among white grape varieties, the leaders are Ugni Blanc, which is cultivated for the production of cognac (83,000 hectares), followed by Chardonnay (45,000 hectares) und Sauvignon Blanc (26,000 hectares).

Wine architecture

Among the French wine regions, Bordeaux is playing a leading and multifaceted role in the evolution of wine architecture in the 21st century. As early as the 1980s, châteaux in Bordeaux underwent extensive restructuring measures, which in turn led to new building projects in the decades that followed.

As most château owners place a strong emphasis on image and on the historical legacy, most work on interiors and exteriors initially constituted "building cosmetics". Owner Olivier Bernard had his Domaine de Chevalier, a prime wine estate in Graves, completely remodelled in 1991, transforming the once almost gloomy-looking building into a light-filled, elegant and inviting structure. Château du Glana in St. Julien is another example of the trend towards an architecturally noble, subtly modern appearance. As in the 1920s, international experts were commissioned to help promote the wines by placing them in the most effective, theatre-ready setting. Architect Olivier Brochet oversaw the redesign of the cellar of Château Léoville-Poyferré in St. Julien, where walls of glass bricks, gleaming metal surfaces and intense colours surround the latest in vinification technology.

IIn a scope never before seen, commissions for numerous restorations, renovations, extensions and redesigns have been concentrated on two architectural practices: the Bordeaux-based Atelier des Architectes Mazières, which lists some two dozen châteaux among its references, and, since 1986, Jean de Gastines Architectes, based in Paris. A typical example of the Mazières style is the new cuverie of Château Branaire-Ducru in St. Julien. A far more expressive project is the white wine cellar of Château Lynch Bages in Pauillac, a row of tilted metal cubes. Metal and exposed concrete also characterize the facade of the Alain-Triaud-designed production facility at Domaine Henry Martin (Château Gloria) in Beychevelle, a structure whose angular lines are somewhat softened by a gently wavy roof. Commissioned by the entrepreneur and owner of multiple châteaux Jean-Jacques Lesgourgues, Sylvain Dubuisson built the new Château Haut Selve in Graves from 1996 to 1998, a building that set new architectural standards in its rejection of the conventions so popular in Bordeaux. The long, almost spare building, coloured a subtle pink and flanked by sculptures, houses hall-like chais for the production of red and white wines.

One of the most notable wine estates in the Bordeaux region is Château d'Arsac in Margaux, whose rigorously geometric, cobalt-blue stone decor recalls the grand buildings of Saint Petersburg. Owner Philipp Raoux commissioned Patrick Hernandez with the building of an adjacent cellar and visitor reception, the result being a perfect symbiosis of traditional building style and contemporary architecture in aluminium, wood and glass.

The most famous flagships of the wine scene have now joined the Bordeaux building boom. In 2002, the Swiss architects Herzog & de Meuron redesigned the refectory for Château Pétrus, producer of one of the world's most expensive wines, and the Mazières practice oversaw the new cellar building there in 2011. With Richard Perduzzi, Bernard Mazières also designed the new chai of the Rothschild-owned Château Clerc Millon in Paulliac.

Château Cos d'Estournel in Saint-Estèphe

Architects: Wilmotte & Associés, 68 rue du Faubourg, St Antoine, 75012 Paris, www.wilmotte.fr with Jacques Garcia

Completion: 2008

Region: Bordeaux

Contact: 33180 Saint-Estèphe

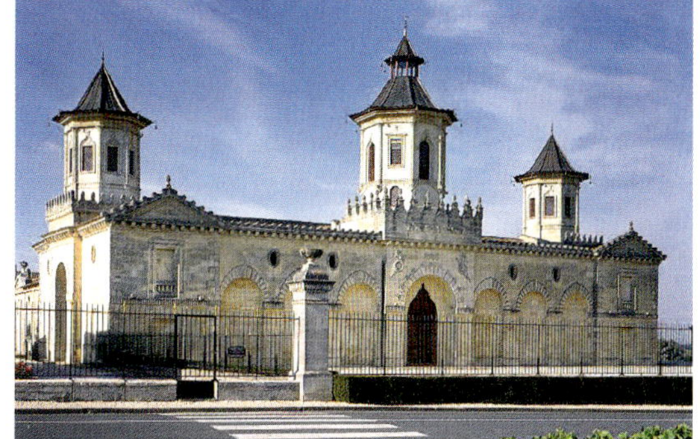

Some of the biggest challenges that architects face are projects that can hardly escape the influence of neighbouring structures. In the case of Cos d'Estournel in St-Estèphe, built by its founder in the oriental style, that is especially tricky. After the hotelier Michel Reybier, who owns further wine estates in Bordeaux and Tokaji, acquired Cos d'Estournel in 2000, he had a new winery built for €35 million behind the pagoda-decorated facade, a project that took from 2006 to 2008 to complete. Jean-Michel Wilmotte designed the production facility and the cellar; Jacques Garcia was responsible for the design of the exterior and interior. With its clear, unprepossessing external appearance, the winery completely refuses to engage in a style competition with the old build, reserving all its glamour for the inside. There, in an atmosphere of luxury and prestige, and with the help of the most up-to-date gravity-flow and cooling technology, the state of the art of premium winemaking is presented. In the fermentation cellar, 72 gleaming stainless-steel tanks are lined up in a row, a glass skywalk gives visitors a view down on a sea of barriques, and glass columns provide almost mystical light effects.

Château Faugères in Saint-Étienne-de-Lisse

Architect: Mario Botta Architetto, Via Beroldingen 26, 6850 Mendrisio, www.botta.ch

Completion: 2008

Region: Bordeaux

Contact: 33330 Saint-Étienne-de-Lisse, Saint-Émilion www.chateau-faugeres.com

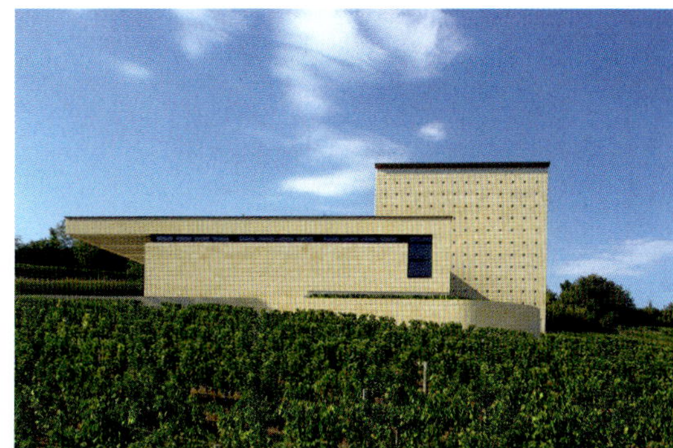

After a construction period of more than two years, two Swiss, the Basle entrepreneur Silvio Denz and the Ticino architect Mario Botta, completed a post-modern winery building on a sloping vineyard, a structure that looks more like a church building than a repository for valuable red wines. A three-storey-tall tower illuminated by LED spotlights houses offices and tasting rooms, and the subterranean cellar contains fermentation and ageing barrels (more than 1,000 barriques). The building has cost the new owner of Faugères at least 8 million. That said, no expense was spared anywhere: the facility features a computer-controlled grape selection process, chilled rooms for the grapes and 50 oak barrels for the fermentation of red wine. The entire production meets the standards of the ISO norm for environmentally friendly wine production, which is far from the case in many other Bordelais wineries.

Château Cheval Blanc in Saint-Émilion

Architect: Christian de Portzamparc, 1, rue de l'Aubade, 75014 Paris, www.chdeportzamparc.com

Completion: 2011

Region: Bordeaux

Contact: 33330 Saint-Émilion www.chateau-cheval-blanc.com

Pritzker Prize-winner Christian de Portzamparc was commissioned with building a new production facility at Château Cheval Blanc in Saint-Émilion. The project as completed aroused the most contradictory reactions: on the one hand, it was hailed as one of the most successful examples of new architecture in Bordeaux; on the other, it was criticized for not fitting in at all with the neighbouring 19th-century estate. The white, shell-like building is meant to convey the noble sensuality and elegance of the Cheval Blanc wines. The fermentation cellar features various technological flourishes, including 59 glass-clad, amphora-shaped concrete containers in which the grapes from the 44 plots of the Cheval Blanc vineyards ferment separately from one another.

Château Villemaurine in Saint-Émilion

Architektin: Marie-Laurence Vizerie, 7, Rue Abbé Lewden, 33500 Libourne

Completion: 2009

Region: Bordeaux

Contact: Lieu dit Villemaurine, 3330 Saint Émilion www.villemaurine.com

The cellars of Château Villemaurine have become one of the most popular tourist attractions in Saint-Émilion. They include a labyrinth of pathways from the Middle Ages and cave-like rooms, which are presented to visitors in a light and sound show. Justin Onclin acquired the Grand Cru Classé estate in 2007; in 2009, architect Marie-Laurence Vizerie added a new production facility equipped with the latest in vinification technology. Connected to the neighbouring château via a glass passage, the building represents the modern end point of the timeline through centuries of wine production in Saint-Émilion.

Spain

Wine production

Virtually nowhere else in Europe was the transition from archaic wine cultivation to modern wine production as rapid and far-reaching as it was in Spain. The vineyard area of the Mediterranean "wine giant" has shrunk by almost one quarter over the past two decades, which is a far greater decrease than has occurred in Italy and France in the same time period. Still, with its 1.1 million hectares under vines, Spain is still by far the world's largest wine-growing country by area. On the other hand, Spain's vineyards do not produce the same yield as those in other European countries. Its scarce rainfall and dry soils call for certain grape varieties and cultivation methods that naturally limit the harvest yield per hectare. There are, even so, large regional differences in the quantity as well as the quality produced.
Wine grapes are grown in almost all areas of the country, but the regions in the north-west, on the upper Ebro, in the Duero valley and in Catalonia are traditionally seen as the most important areas for the production of quality wines. The country's leading wine region is Rioja, with 63,500 hectares under vines and 1,000 wine producers, followed by Navarra, which has 18,400 hectares. La Mancha, found in the central plateau in the middle of Spain, is the country's largest wine cultivation area, but, like large areas of the Levante, is regarded as the home of simple table wines. Mainly, this is where the Airén and Garnacha grape varieties are cultivated for the production of cheap consumer wines. As for more sophisticated wines, these are vinified primarily in the north from the Garnacha and Tempranillo varieties. Internationally widespread varieties such as Cabernet, Merlot and Chardonnay are increasingly being used to produce higher-quality wines.

Wine architecture

From the mid-19th century onwards, the sales successes of the wine, Sherry and Cava producers led to the creation of large-scale wineries to be able to handle the harvests grown on the vintners' immense vineyard holdings, most of them between 500 and several thousand hectares in size. The most impressive building projects were undertaken by the Andalusian Sherry producers, who built "cathedral-bodegas", and by the producers of the Spanish sparkling-wine speciality, Cava, primarily the Catalonia-based Codorníu company. Its Celler Gran, built in 1901–1905 in the Modernismo (Spanish Art Nouveau) style, is a famous example of the influence of Modernismo on the winery architecture of the time. It is now a museum.

The Codorníu group expanded in the 20th century with the acquisition of further Cava- and wine-producing concerns, such as the Penedès winery built by José María Sala for the Bach brothers in a slight twist on the Classical style in 1918. The Masía Bach, which welcomes visitors to its opulent spaces, was expanded in 1988–2010 by architect Domingo Triay, who added modern service buildings. Triay modernized other Codorníu-owned wine and Cava holdings as well, among them Bodegas Bilbaínas, founded in 1901 in Haro, Rioja, and the largest Codorníu bodega, Raïmat, which was built in 1918 by Rubío i Bellver in Lleida and whose grounds include a 17th-century castle. The typical architectural features of the time survived the modernization measures largely intact. From the early 1950s, shipyard buildings as found in Barcelona inspired the Cava producer Rondel, which also belongs to the Codorníu group. Its pride and joy is its Salón Noble, which was designed by Lluís Bonet i Garí, a student of Antoni Gaudí.

Wineries that look more like church naves than like agro-industrial buildings emerged in the early 1920s, most of them commissioned by winemaking cooperatives and designed by Gaudí student Cèsar Martinell. Martinell is the true "father of the wine cathedrals", creating some 40 wineries with artistic brick halls, primarily in the Catalonian wine region around Tarragona. His most impressive works include the wineries he completed for the cooperatives El Pinell de Brai (1919) and Sant Cugat del Vallès (1921). L'Espluga de Francolí, an agricultural cooperative, commissioned a winery complex consisting of three halls of 12 metres in height, two of which were designed by Pere Domènech i Roura around 1913.

Through a continuous process of mergers, the wine cooperatives grew to several thousands of hectares in size, but this expansion process was not accompanied by a commensurate development in the architecture of their facilities. In contrast to the situation in other European countries, winery businesses were usually separate from the private residences of the owners, so for a long time, the Spanish wine landscape was characterized by simple, exclusively functional agricultural buildings.

Unencumbered by any historical building fabric, the Bordeaux-based architect Philippe Mazières, himself the owner of a vineyard in his home country, built Bodega Viña Real on a rise near Logroño for the tradition-rich family business CVNE. The wine estate was inaugurated in 2004 in the presence of King Juan Carlos. The symbolic form of the central winery building is borrowed from a fermentation vat; the circular arrangement of the barriques and columns recalls the famous example of Château Lafite Rothschild.
A number of other winery buildings have been erected on hillsides to enable a gravity-flow movement of grapes and must. These include Bodegas Baigorri near Samaniego, built by Ignacio Quemada Arquitectos; and the largest Rioja winery, Bodegas Juan Alcorta in Logroño, only a small part of whose immense facilities (45,000 square metres, 25 million bottles produced each year, 75,000 barriques) are visible from the outside.

Wine production of high quality is not limited to Rioja and its northern neighbour Navarra. Wineries in other northern and north-western parts of the country, too, have for the past several years been producing award-winning, first-rate wines. These advances have often been accompanied by the installation of new winery technology in combination with the architecture to go with it. A prime example of this is the Castilian wine region Ribera del Duero, where the area under vines has expanded to more than 20,000 hectares over the past few decades and which can now be called a kind of birthplace of cutting-edge wine architecture. Thanks in no small part to EU funding, the late 1990s saw the launch of numerous new winery projects with an architecture that set new standards. These include the bodegas listed below by region:

Galicia
- Dominio Do Bibei, Ribeira Sacra

Rioja
- Bodegas Antión, Elciego
- Bodegas Baigorri, Samaniego
- Bodega Contador, San Vicente de la Sonsierra
- Bodegas Darien, Logroño
- Institucional de la Grajera, Logroño
- Bodegas Regalía de Ollauri, Ollauri

Somontano
- Bodegas Laus, Barbastro

Ribera del Duero
- Bodegas y Viñedos Qumrán, Peñafiel

Penedès
- Mas Rodó Vitivinícola, Sant Pere Sacarrera

Castile-La Mancha
- Casalobos, Ciudad Real

Señorío Otazu in Echauri

Architects: Jaime Gaztelu Quijano, Takonera Kalea, 4, 31001 Pamplona,
Arenas y Asociados, P. Eduardo Dato, 21 Bajo, 28010 Madrid, www.arenasing.com

Completion: 2001

Region: Navarra

Contact: 31174 Echauri
www.otazu.com

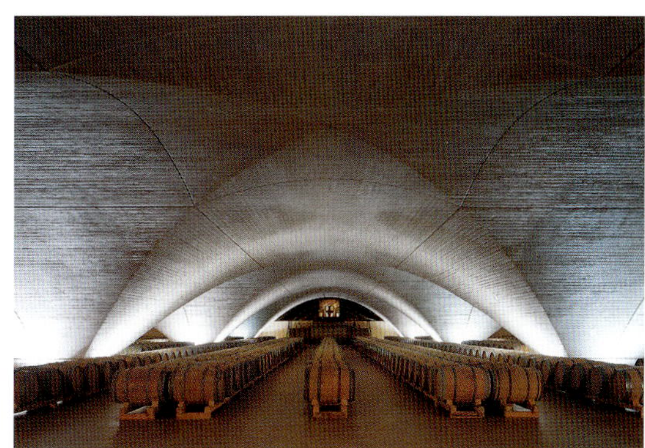

Señorio Otazu, founded in 1989 by Carlos Biurrun, is the most northerly winery in the Navarra region. It is located on the premises of an old estate that produced wines probably as early as the 14th century. Since 1860, this has been the site of a finca modelled on a French wine estate, where receptions and wine tastings are held. The U-shaped facility of historical and new buildings brings together tradition and modernity in an unusual way. In 1997, the addition of a subterranean cellar caused quite a stir. Built by architect Jaime Gaztelu Quijano and engineer Juan José Arenas, the cellar features a massive vaulted ceiling of reinforced concrete which is composed of nine square sections with spans of 18 metres each and a clear height of six metres. In contrast to traditional vaulted ceilings, the arches do not rest on supporting columns, but directly on the floor. The pine used to shutter the exposed concrete gives the surface a decorative structure that lends the ageing cellar a unique note.

Señorío de Arínzano in Aberin

Architect: Rafael Moneo, Cinca 5, 28002 Madrid

Completion: 2002

Region: Navarra

Contact: Carretera Estella-Tafalla n-132 km. 3, 31264 Aberin
www.arinzano.com

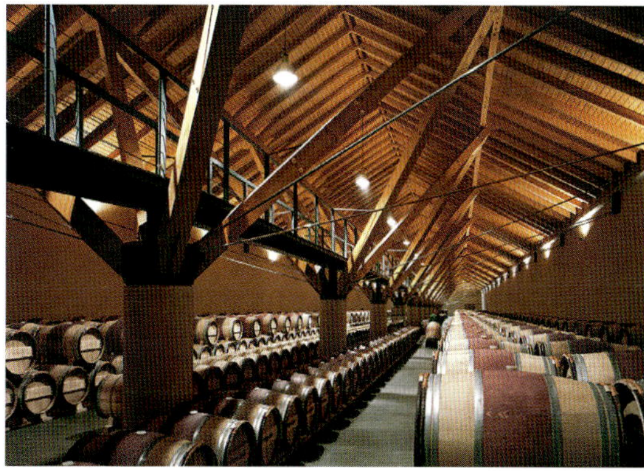

In 1988, the largest family-owned winery in Navarra, Bodegas Chivite, acquired an estate near Estella that was composed of several historical houses, including an 18th-century mansion and a fortified tower from the Middle Ages. The goal was to produce top-notch wines there. After the clearing of the former croplands and the subsequent planting of grapevines, the Chivite family commissioned Rafael Moneo with the building of the ultramodern winery Señorio de Arínzano. The facility, inaugurated in 2002, envelops the three old buildings with its two wings, adapting to them with its colour-coordinated exposed concrete and a pitched roof. The layout of the building echoes the steps in the wine-production process, with the first wing encompassing the steps from the receiving to the processing of the grapes, and the second, larger and somewhat lowered wing housing the fermentation vats, the ageing cellars and the bottling line and finally the tasting room. Not only the wine barrels, but the entire roof construction is of oak – a reference to the holm oaks that have been growing in the neighbouring woods for hundreds of years.

Bodega Tandem in Lorca

Architects: VF arquitectos, Avda Marcelo Celayeta 75, 31014 Pamplona, www.vfarquitectos.com

Completion: 2007

Region: Navarra

Contact: Ctra. Pamplona – Logroño km. 35,9, 31292 Lácar
www.tandem.es

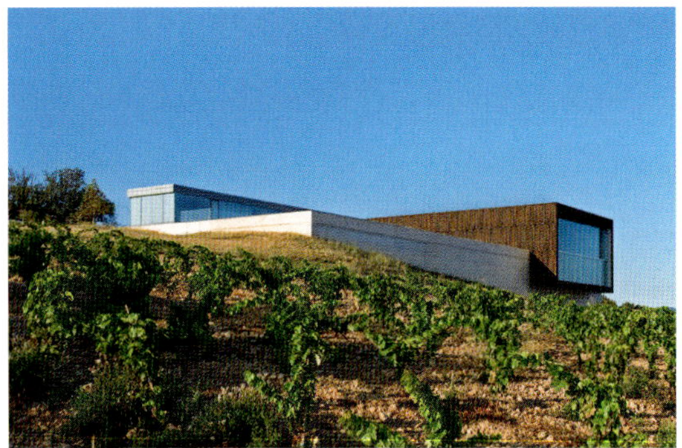

The name of this relatively young bodega, which was founded in 2003, goes back to the union of several wine professionals, including oenologist Alicia Erayalar and managing director José-Maria Fraile, and wine enthusiasts, who jointly – in tandem – took on the project of running a first-rate winery for red wine in Navarra. The plans were first forged a few years previously, before the acquisition of 22 hectares of prime vineyards in the Yerri Valley, not far from the Route of Santiago de Compostela. The design and fit-out of the winery was done by the young architects José Luis Vélaz Ballesteros and Iván Fernández Prados. The production facility building, completed in 2007, is divided into two parts, one below and one above ground, and consists entirely of concrete. Its most distinctive feature is a large window that is illuminated at night to – as tradition demands – light the way for the pilgrims en route to Santiago.

Bodega Irius in Barbastro

Architects: JMP y Asociados, C/Arrúbal, no. 2, 26006 Logroño, www.jmarinopascual.com

Completion: 2008

Region: Somontano

Contact: Ctra. Basbastro – Monzón km. 155 (N 240), 22300 Barbastro
www.bodegairius.com

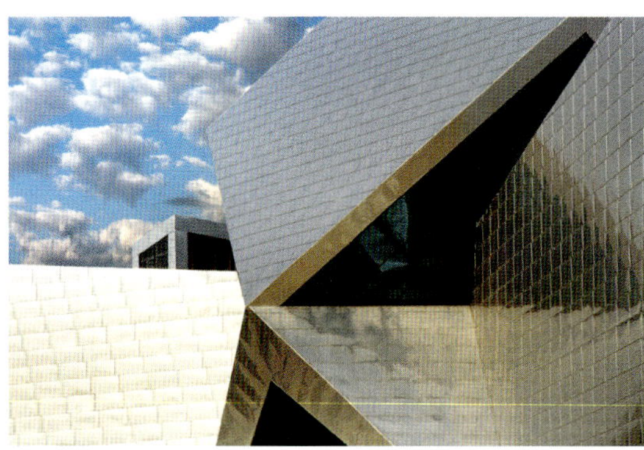

In Bodega Irius, Jésus Marino Pascual has created a project that shows a different and surprising face every time the time of day, season, or position of the viewer changes. Set in the midst of vineyards in Barbastro, in the Somontano region, the winery draws attention to itself not only because of its imaginative composition of stainless steel and glass topped with prism-like structures, but also because of the glowing lighting effects that emanate from the building. The cubes and angles of the outside find their complement in the metallic interior fit-out, part of which is vibrantly coloured. Irius, opened in 2008, is also influenced strongly by the principles of bioclimatic architecture, which is oriented towards natural energy efficiency. Twenty-seven metres of the 54-metre-high building complex are buried in the ground, allowing savings of up to 70 per cent in cooling costs.

The grapes from the 350 hectares of vineyards are harvested in the cool evening and night hours to better conserve their aromas. Special technologies for quality optimization, some of them patented, were designed for the transport and processing of the grapes.

Bodega Waltraud in Vilafranca del Penedès

Architects: BC Estudio, Plaza Equilaz 10 Ent. 3a, 08017 Barcelona, www.bcarquitectos.com

Completion: 2009

Region: Penedès

Contact: Pacs del Penedès, Vilafranca del Penedès
www.torres.es

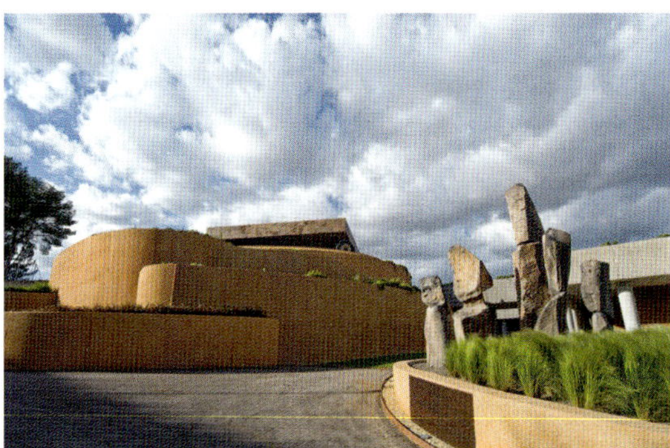

Miguel Torres has been called the uncrowned king of Spanish wine, or, at least, its most famous ambassador. Indeed, he not only turned the winery that his father founded, with its 1,700 hectares of vineyards, into one of the leading family-owned wine businesses in Spain, but he is also known for his numerous innovations and initiatives. Bodega Waltraud, named after Torres's wife, was built in 2008, joining the five estates that had made up the Torres empire until that point. Javier Barba, a proponent of "green architecture", built the winery for some €12 million in the Torres-owned Pacs del Penedès near Vilafranca del Penedès. On its green roofs, it boasts a photovoltaic plant that delivers power for the lighting of the entire complex. In the centre of the aesthetically designed facility, which is harmoniously integrated into the surrounding landscape, is an interior courtyard lined with columns. The larger part of the structure is buried up to 11 metres deep in the ground to achieve optimal natural cooling. There is where one finds the ageing cellar housing 3,000 barriques filled with the estate's top wines.

López de Heredia in Haro

Architects: Zaha Hadid Architects, 10 Bowling Green Lane, London EC1R0BQ, www. zaha-hadid.com
Completion: 2006
Region: Rioja
Contact: Avda. de Vizcaya, 3, 26200 Haro
www.lopezdeheredia.com

One of the most noticeable wineries in Rioja is López de Heredia Viña Tondonia, whose production facility is crowned by a striking outlook tower (*Txori Toki* in Basque) that offers a lovely view over the vineyards. The buildings, which are more than 100 years old and cover an area of almost 20,000 square metres (3,500 square metres of which are cellars for 15,000 barriques), were joined in 2002 by a new pavilion. Designed by Zaha Hadid, the building consists of a gleaming, golden steel structure housing the sales boutique. With a little imagination, the pavilion recalls a dented wine bottle lying on its side.

Marqués de Riscal in Elciego

Architects: Gehry Partners, 12541 Beatrice Street, Los Angeles, CA 90066, www.foga.com
Completion: 2006
Region: Rioja
Contact: C/Torrea 1, 01340 Elciego
www.marquesderiscal.com

Marqués de Riscal is not only the oldest bodega in Rioja; thanks to its futuristic-looking architecture, it has also achieved a worldwide reputation as one of the most popular examples of new building in Spain's wine regions. Adjacent to the old build of the winery, which goes back to the year 1860, American architect Frank O. Gehry designed a luxury wine hotel with a conference centre, restaurants and a wine bar. The nested building cubes – which, Gehry explains, are inspired by wine crates – were covered with wavy, variously coloured strips of titanium.

Bodega Martín Berdugo in Aranda de Duero

Architects: vi.vo architecture.landscape, Badenerstr. 125, 8004 Zurich, www.vi-vo.ch
Completion: 2004
Region: Ribera del Duero
Contact: Crta de la Colonia, 09400 Aranda de Duero
www.martinberdugo.com

The warehouse designed by architects Maria Viné and Vicky Daroca for Bodega y Viñedos Martín Berdugo in Aranda de Duero, Burgos province, in 2004, is among the examples of extraordinary architecture in the Ribera del Duero region. The extremely simple and solid-seeming building, which picks up the colours of its surroundings, is a skeleton construction with concrete facade elements of various sizes and thicknesses jutting out. These help liven up the facades, which are otherwise interrupted by just a few aluminium windows and two sliding gates, lending the complex the apperance of a "wine fort".

Bodegas Protos in Peñafiel

Architects: Rogers Stirk Harbour + Partners, Thames Wharf, Rainville Road, London W6 9HA, www.richardrogers.co.uk
Alonso Balaguer y Arquitectos Asociados, Carrer de la Riba, 36, 08950 Esplugues de Llobregat, www.alonsobalaguer.es
Completion: 2008
Region: Ribera del Duero
Contact: Bodegas Protos, 24–28, 47300 Peñafiel
www.bodegasprotos.com

Alongside major wineries such as the Codorníu-affiliated Bodega Legaris near Curiel de Duero (built in 2004 by Domingo Triay), Bodegas Protos, a former wine cooperative in Peñafiel, is among the most interesting architectural examples in the Ribera del Duero region. Designed in 2005 by Rogers Stirk Harbour + Partners and Alonso Balaguer, the project is an architecturally brilliant mixture of austerity and elegance, an impressive interpretation of contemporary building arts, and a fascinating contrast to the adjacent historical cooperative winery building from the 1920s.

Ferrer Bobet in Falset

Architects: Espinet/Ubach Arquitectes i Associats, Camp 63, 08002 Barcelona, www.espinet-ubach.com
Completion: 2002
Region: Montsant
Contact: Carretera Falset a Porrera km 6,5, 43730 Falset
www.ferrerbobet.com

Like the prow of an ocean liner, the building of the bodega rises from a vineyard-covered hill near Falset, in the mountainous Priorat. In 2002, Sergi Ferrer-Salat, CEO of a pharmaceutical company and a wine enthusiast, and Raül Bobet, former deputy head of Bodegas Miguel Torres, realized their vision of a technologically perfect and environmentally friendly winery. The building, in which only the visitor reception, bottling line and shipping department are located at ground level, blends into the surrounding landscape, thanks also its reddish colour scheme, which picks up the colour of the locally predominant stone. Ever since its first vintage, 2005, the bodega has enjoyed international renown for its excellent quality.

Pagos del Rey in Rueda

Completion: 2002
Region: Rueda
Contact: Avenida Morejona, 6, 47490 Rueda
www.pagosdelrey.com

The Ribera del Duero region owes its reputation to flagship enterprises such as Bodegas Vega Sicilia, from whose – now expanded and modernized – cellars have emerged some of Spain's most expensive wines, or the Pesquera wine estate, whose creations have caused a stir worldwide since the 1980s. The past few decades have seen the expansion of the region's vineyard acreage as well as of the capacity of is wineries. The largest among these is Pagos del Rey, which belongs to the Félix Solis wine estate and was built in 2002 for €22 million. The complex structure of concrete and glass contains, among other things, a storeroom for 8,000 barriques.

Further countries

From Asia Minor, wine culture spread via the Mediterranean into the temperate zones of Europe between the 40th and 50th parallels. Depending on the respective geographical conditions and the local population's consumption patterns, wine cultivation assumed varying degrees of importance. On average, the wine industry accounts for 6.5 per cent of total agricultural sales. Still, wine cultivation is present in all countries of central and southern Europe, a group that currently constitutes 23 states.
Put together, all the wine-growing areas in the region take up close to 44 million hectares, equivalent to a share of some 55 per cent of global vineyard area. As the average yield per hectare is higher in Europe than on other continents, Europe's wine industry accounts for almost 70 per cent of global wine production. The past few decades, however, have witnessed a clear shift here. While grubbing-up schemes and structural transformations have decreased Europe's vineyard area by almost 10 million hectares, the same period has seen a marked increase in cultivation area in the southern hemisphere and in Asia.
In the statistical mean, the wine production of Italy, France and Spain together constitutes almost 95 per cent of Europe's total wine output. Of the other wine-producing countries on the European continent, Germany, Portugal, Romania, Greece and Hungary are in leading positions, producing a long-term annual average of between 10 and 3 million hectolitres. Despite all the differences in planting, varieties and vinification techniques, the countries with less wine-growing area, too, boast a historically significant wine culture that goes back thousands of years.

Portugal
In terms of output, Portugal comes in 10th place in the international wine rankings. The fact that the popularity of its wines – other than port wine – is hardly increasing outside its borders, is not attributable to any problems with quality. Rather, the Portuguese terms on the labels denoting geographical origin, grape varieties and quality classifications are often poorly understood internationally. To insiders, however, they often signal authentic wines that are usually made from grapes grown exclusively in Portugal – grapes that thrive in the Atlantic climate and bring forth notable wines.
For many years, Portugal's wine industry was heavily traditional. The port houses in Vila Nova de Gaia, resembling huge, monotonous warehouses, or the major cooperative wineries are evidence of this. But while the prevailing conservatism, primarily among the owners of smaller quintas, is slowly giving way to a certain openness towards new ideas, this trend has not yet made itself felt in architectural projects. The winery landscape is still characterized by numerous estates built in the typical Portuguese style. In the past few years, these have been joined by only few new facilities that could be called representative of modern wine architecture. Besides the wineries introduced in the Projects section, these include Quinta do Encontro in São Lourenço do Bairo, some 30 kilometres from Coimbra in the Bairrada region. The circular winery building was designed by Pedro Mateus and completed in 2008. Two years previously, Casa da Torre, a project designed by Castanheira & Bastai Arquitectos, opened in Vila Nova de Famalição, north of Porto.

Greece
Ancient Hellas, the founder of western building and wine culture, was for a long time tied to its historic legacy and traditions. Its grape plantations total 100,000 hectares in area, which roughly equals the German acreage, but they produce more than just wine. Thus the yield is on average merely a third of a normal harvest in Germany.
Starting in the mid-1980s, when the EU provided financial assistance, and Greek oenologists who had acquired their professional know-how abroad began to establish new facilities, the production of quality wines increased. Most of the winery buildings erected in the 1980s and particularly in the 1990s are in the typical Greek style, not least because many of them are popular stops on wine tourist routes. The prime example of this is Domaine Selladia in Maegalochori, near Pygros on Santorini. The winery, which was opened in 1990 and has become a visitor magnet, boasts wholly modern equipment, but its architecture nevertheless bows to local traditions. The Boutari family, who own this estate and who call a total of six wine estates their own, built Domaine Fantaxometocho near Heraklion on Crete in the 1990s, giving the island one of its most modern wineries.
The most impressive wine estate on Crete, Domain Zacharioudaki, is located at an altitude of about 500 metres on a hill near Plouti. It was built in early 2000 by the publisher Stilianos Zacharioudakis. Behind the facades of natural stone, a 2,000-square-metre winery boasting state-of-the-art equipment is spread out over three levels. An elegant dining room on the upper storey offers a grand panoramic view.
One of the most notable projects of new Greek wine architecture is Ktima Pavlidis in northern Greece, near Kokkinogia in Drama, the architecture and grape varieties of which are strongly influenced by the countries of the western Mediterranean.
Finally, there are also several interesting new winery buildings in Attica, near Athens. These include the Strofilia winery, not far from the village of Anavyssos, which is specialized in white wine production; and Papagiannakos in Markopoulo near Mesogia, Greece's first bioclimatic winery, which was awarded an architectural prize in 2008.

Hungary
A dozen countries in central and south-eastern Europe have been cultivating wine for centuries, but only few of them are pursuing a progressive course in their vineyards and cellars to supplement their ancient traditions. These countries include Hungary and Slovenia, where new winery buildings are visual proof of the changes that have taken place since the 1990s. In Hungary, primarily in the Tokaji region, some of these have resulted from investments undertaken by western European wine companies. But initiatives by traditional Hungarian wineries, too, are culminating in notable buildings, such as the new winery built by the Millenary Benedictine Abbey of Pannonhalma not far from its Baroque cloister complex, which was recognized by UNESCO as a World Heritage Site.

Füleky Pincészet in Bodrogkeresztúr

Architects: Építesz Stúdió, Krisztina körút 71, 1016 Budapest, www.epstudio.hu
Completion: 2010
Region: Tokaj
Contact: Iskola köz 15, 3916 Bodrogkeresztúr
www.tokaj.org

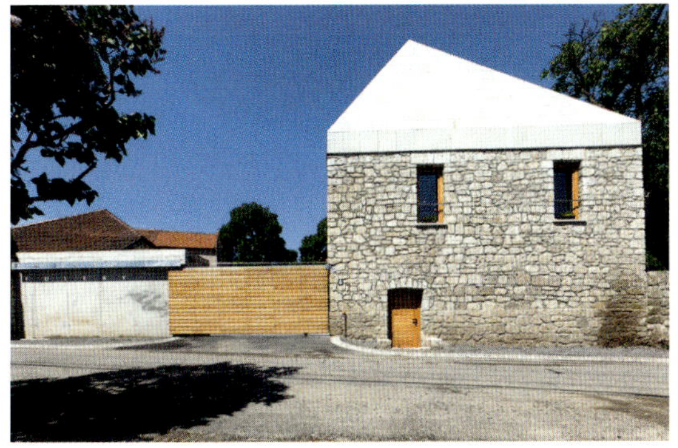

Among the new facilities in the region that brings forth the famous Tokaji wine, this project, completed in 2010, is notable for its adaptation to the surrounding old building fabric. Owner Péter Lovas commissioned the architects Épitesz Stúdió to design a new structure on the site of an older building next to the village church in the historic centre of Tokaj. But the old building was not immediately torn down; rather, its rendering was removed and parts of the wall featuring the volcanic, greyish-yellow tuff typical of the region recovered. Then the old stones were placed on the outside and inside of the reinforced-steel building. The roof is covered with stone slabs of the type found in the surrounding structures as well.

Bazaltbor Winery in Badacsony

Architects: PLANT – Atelier Péter Kis, Evetke út 2, 1121 Budapest, www.plant.co.hu
Completion: 2010
Region: Balaton
Contact: Római út 199, 8261 Badacsony
www.laposa.hu

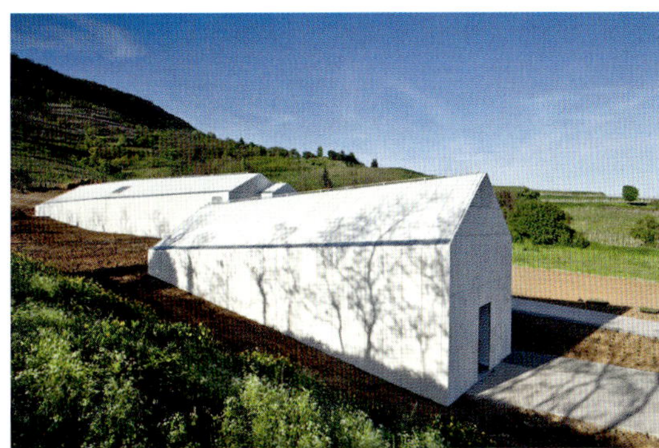

Designed by Budapest-based architect Péter Kis, the Bazaltbor ("Basalt wine") winery in Badacsony, on Lake Balaton, presents itself as a modern fairy-tale castle with a facade completely enveloped in vines. The production facility, which was inaugurated in 2010, has a footprint of almost 420 square metres and a facade of prefab concrete components into which vine-like structures have been etched – a pattern that continues over the glass and metal panels as well. The vaulted cellar is lined with traditional brickwork.

Klet Brič Winery in Dekani

Architects: Boris Podrecca, Jörgerbadgasse 8, 1170 Vienna with Marko Lavrenčič, www.podrecca.at
Completion: 2002
Region: Primorje/Istria
Contact: Dekani 3a, 6271 Dekani
www.vinabric.si

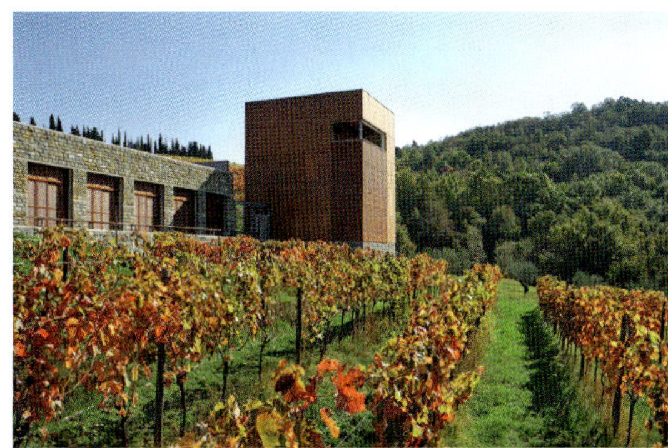

Although completed as early as 2002, Klet Brič, located near Novi Brič on the Istrian peninsula, is still Slovenia's architectural showpiece winery. It was built by the Istrian architects Boris Podrecca and Marko Lavrenčič far from the main road, on a site that was especially landscaped for the project. The location, 400 metres above sea level, offers a lovely panoramic view. The building consists of two differently designed structures for different functions. The complex includes a tower house and, set back, the private residence of the client.

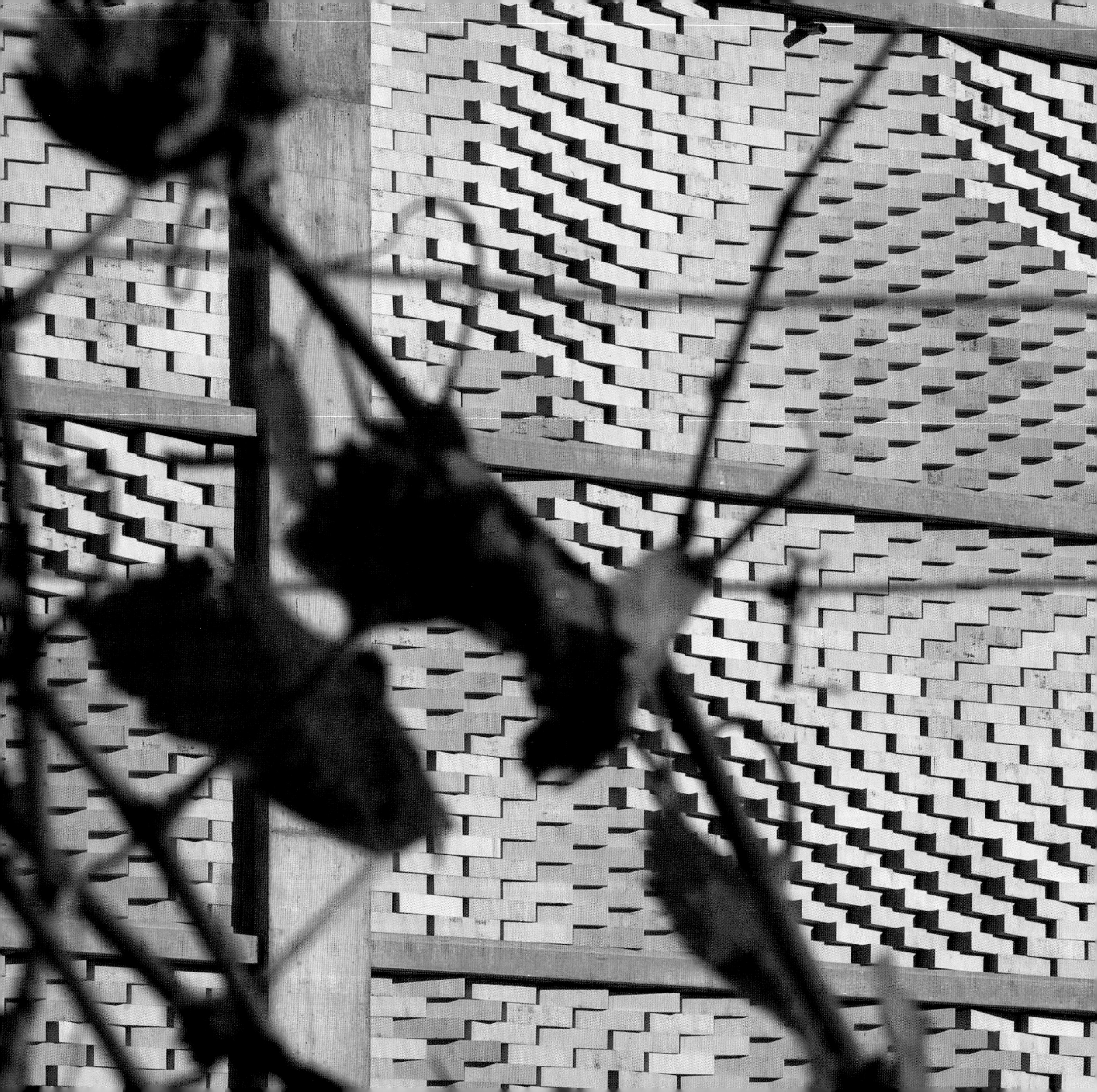

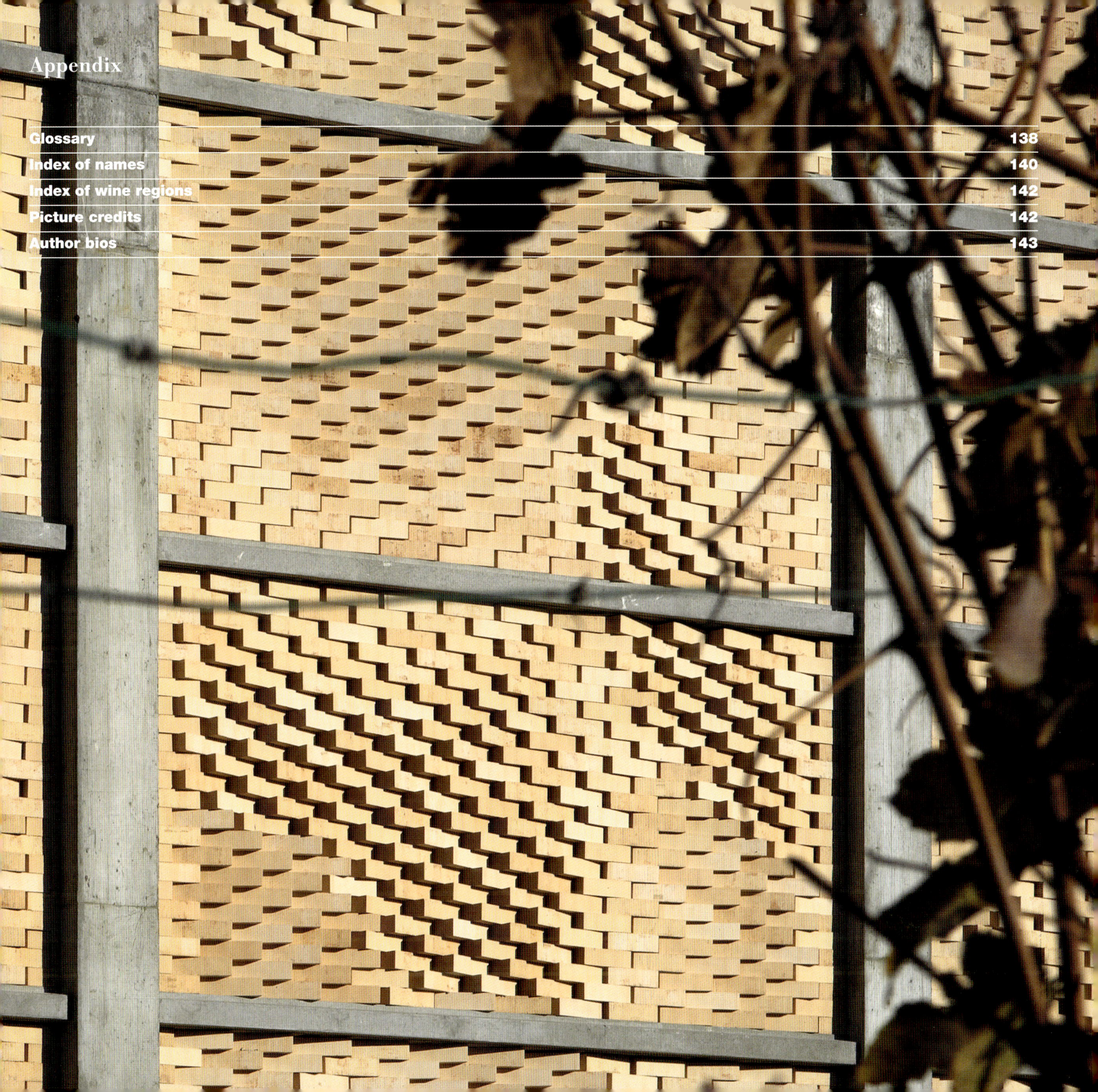

Appendix

Glossary

adega
The Portuguese term for a wine estate or wine cellar.

aerate
To bring wine in contact with air. This activates the yeast in the fermentation process.

ageing
The storing of wine for the purpose of improving its taste. During ageing, young wine undergoes internal processes that alter and mature its taste and aromas. Wine is aged in a barrel or tank first, then in a bottle.

alcohol content
The alcohol content of a wine has to be declared on its label. It can range from about 9 per cent by volume to about 15 per cent. The average alcohol content of wines has increased in the past few years, owing to warmer climates and changing consumer preferences. To manage alcohol levels, winemakers have various technical and microbiological processes at their disposal. Red wines often have a higher alcohol content than white wines. Fortified wines, such as port oder Sherry, have alcohol added to them during production, reaching an alcohol content of 16 to 22 per cent.

amphora
A ceramic vessel that was used to store liquids, such as wine, in ancient times.

appellation
An indication of the geographic origin of the wine and of various related quality criteria and restrictions. Official appellation systems, all of them based on the French Appellation d'Origine Contrôlée, have been set up in several wine-producing countries. They are a country's laws for growing and making wine in a certain region, and are attempts to impose a set of consistent quality criteria that are transparent for the consumer.

barrel
A staved vessel with flat ends and a bulge in the middle. Thanks to their shape, barrels can be stored vertically or horizontally. Small barrels can also be rolled easily.
Before being bottled, wine is often aged in barrels. The duration of the typical barrel ageing process ranges from just a few months to five years, with some exceptional wines being aged for up to ten years. Depending on the size of the barrel, the type of wood used, and the length of time the wine is kept inside, the barrel imparts some aromas and flavours to the wine. This effect is strongest when the barrel is new.
Barrels permit a slow exposure of their contents to oxygen. The wine inside must be topped up continually to replace the quantities lost to evaporation. The maintenance of barrels involves a thorough cleaning and treatment to prevent mould.
The capacity of barrels ranges from 100 to 2,600 litres, with custom-built historical barrels boasting an even larger size. Most wineries nowadays use small (ca. 225-litre) barrels called barriques, but these cannot completely replace large barrels. Depending on its size, a wooden barrel costs between €300 and €700.

barrique
The most widely used type of barrel in winemaking, with a capacity of 215 to 230 litres. Barriques are made of oak, primarily from France. After assembly, the casks can be toasted (flamed), which imparts smokey aromas to the wood. As the use of barriques is quite expensive, some vintners add oak chips or powder to their wines instead. See also **barrel**.

blend (also **cuvée**)
A wine created from a mixture of different grape varieties.

Bocksbeutel
A 0.75-litre flask, or flat ellipsoidal bottle, that is traditionally used for wines in the wine region of Franconia. Similarly shaped bottles are used for Portuguese and Hungarian wines as well.

bodega
The Spanish term for a wine estate or wine cellar.

bottle ageing
Depending on their variety, origin, vintage, and how they are made, wines undergo different ageing processes in the bottle. Wines that have been bottled shortly after vinification can still taste slightly yeasty. A balance of tastes is achieved with increasing age. Crisp wines ripen and age more quickly than do sweeter wines, and wines with low acidity age faster than more acidic ones. Red wines that have a good balance of alcohol and tannins, and that are made from varieties such as Cabernet Sauvignon, Syrah, Merlot and Pinot Noir, may even be suitable for laying down for ten years in ideal storage conditions.

bottling line
A mechanized production line that fills wine into bottles.

bung
A conical or cylindrical stopper for plugging up the opening of a barrel.

bunghole
An opening that has been bored into a barrel to enable removal or aeration of its contents.

cantina
An Italian term for a winery or wine cellar.

cap
The solid matter, consisting mainly of grape skins and seeds, that rises to the top during the fermentation process of red wine. To increase the contact of the wine with the skins, and to prevent the cap from drying out, winemakers use one of several methods of pushing the cap back down into the must.

capsule
A metal or plastic wrapper covering the cork and the top of the neck of a wine bottle. In addition to decorating the bottle, the capsule keeps the cork from becoming dirty and drying out.

Cava
A Spanish sparkling wine made according to the méthode champenoise.

cave
An underground cellar for storing wine.

cellar
In wineries, the barrel cellar is used for the ageing of wines. The conditions required for wine storage are: a constant, cool room climate, and an environment that is free of shocks, strong smells, and strong direct light. These conditions are most easily fulfilled in underground cellars, but many new winery businesses avoid the high cost of establishing one by opting instead for a large, multifunctional storage building.

cellarmaster
A person who is in charge of the cellars at a winery and whose main job it is to supervise and monitor the ageing process of the wines produced there.

chai
The French name for a building used to store barrels of wine. Different kinds of wine are usually stored in separate *chais*, as they require different storage conditions.

chaptalization
The process of adding sugar to the must before fermentation to increase the alcohol content of the resulting wine.

château
The French term for a wine estate with its own vineyards. Originally simply the word for "castle".

clarification
The removal of undesirable substances from the wine. Clarification methods include filtration, racking and fining.

cooperage
A facility for the making of barrels and casks; also, the barrels produced at such a facility.

cooperative
See **winemaking cooperative**.

cru
French term that can refer to a particular style, origin or quality of a wine; the land on which the wine grows; or a particular vineyard or estate that produced the wine. A grand cru wine is one of the region's best.

crush
To gently break the skins of the harvested grapes, releasing their juices, in preparation for the further steps in the winemaking process. The crushing process produces must.

crusher
A mechanical device through which the grapes pass after the sorting process. The crusher breaks open the skins of the grapes to release the juices while leaving the seeds intact. This prevents the tannins in the seeds from seeping into the must.

cuve
The French term for a fermentation container.

cuvée
The French term for a blend.

cuverie
The French term for the fermenting cellar.

destemming
The process of separating the grapes from the stems and leaves in preparation for crushing.

disgorgement (also **dégorgement**)
A step in the production of sparkling wine according to the méthode champenoise, in which the sediment that has settled to the neck of the upside-down bottle is removed by freezing the neck of the bottle and then pulling out the "plug" of frozen wine and lees.

domaine
Another word for château.

Domäne
In Germany, a large wine estate, usually one owned by the state or by a member of the former nobility.

extraction
The transfer of flavours, aromas and colour from the grapeskins to the wine. Excessive extraction should be avoided, as it can give the wine harsh tannins.

fermentation
A biochemical process in which yeast breaks down the sugars in grape juice into carbon dioxide and ethanol, producing wine. The process takes place in fermentation containers such as vats, often under strictly temperature-controlled conditions.

fermenting cellar
The space in which the fermentation containers are located.

filtration
The process of removing impurities or particles from the wine by passing it through a fine filter.

fining
A method of removing impurities from a wine by adding a substance – traditionally egg white, now a fine clay – to the top and letting it sink to the bottom, taking the impurities with it.

finish
The sensation left in one's mouth after one has tasted a wine.

fortified wine
Wine that has had alcohol added to it to stop the fermentation process. Fortified wines have a higher alcohol content and a longer shelf life than non-fortified wines. They include Sherry, port, madeira and marsala.

Grand vin
The French term for the top, or first-label, wine produced by a wine estate.

gravity-flow winery
A winery that uses gravity rather than pumps to move the grapes and wine gently from one step in the production process to another.

green harvesting
The removal of immature and inferior bunches of grapes in the vineyard to decrease the yield and improve the quality of the grapes remaining on the vine.

Kellerei
German term for a winery with or without its own vineyards.

label
A piece of printed paper stuck on to a wine bottle, providing information about its contents. Some of this information is required and strictly regulated by law. Labels are usually featured on the front and back of the bottle and – along with the capsule – contribute significantly to its appearance.

Landwein
German wine classification indicating a wine regulated by less stringent controls (similar to the French term *vin de pays*). A classification one step up from *Tafelwein* (French: *vin de table*).

lees
Sediment consisting of dead and residual yeast. The lees are removed before bottling, except in the making of sparkling wine according to the méthode champenoise.

maceration
The process that follows the crushing of the grapes in the making of red wine. In maceration, the must is left alone for a time to let the tannins, colour and flavour compounds of the grapeskins, seeds and stem fragments leach into the wine. This gives red wine its characteristic colour and flavour; rosé wines are allowed to macerate only briefly.

malolactic fermentation (also **secondary fermentation**)
A secondary fermentation of red wine, in which bacteria convert the malic acid in the wine into the milder lactic acid.

marc
see **pomace**

méthode champenoise
A special method of making sparkling wine that was pioneered in the Champagne region of France.

must
The mixture of juice, pulp, grapeskins, seeds and stem fragments that is produced by crushing the grapes.

nose
A wine-tasting term that describes a wine's aroma or bouquet.

oenologist
An expert in wine and winemaking.

oenology
The science of wine and winemaking.

palate
A wine-tasting term that describes the feel and taste of a wine in one's mouth.

pomace (also **marc**)
The solid remains of the grapes after pressing for juice. It is sometimes used to produce pomace brandy, such as grappa.

press
The equipment for, or act of, releasing the grape juice from the solid matter of the fruit after crushing and maceration.

racking (also **soutirage**)
The process of siphoning wine off the lees into another container. Racking is repeated, sometimes several times, to help to clarify the wine during the ageing process and to prevent the development of bitter tastes. The process is particularly significant when dealing with wine ageing in barriques.

remontage (also **pumping over**)
The process of pumping the juice or must back over the cap (solid matter that has floated to the top during maceration) to increase the wine's exposure to the grapeskins.

riddling rack (also **pupitre**)
A special rack that suspends bottles of sparkling wine at an upside-down angle for the special bottle fermentation they require. Riddling racks enable the daily shaking and shifting of the bottles called for by the méthode champenoise.

Second vin
The French term for a wine estate's second-label wine, i.e. one that does not meet the same exacting standards as its *Grand vin* but is produced and sold in much larger quantities.

soutirage
See **racking**.

structure
The composition of a wine; how its components such as acidity, tannins and alcohol content combine with each other.

süssreserve
Unfermented grape must used to sweeten wine.

tank
A large vessel often used for the ageing of wines. Compared to barrels, tanks are more hygienic and easier to clean, more long-lived, permit less loss of wine due to evaporation, facilitate a better utilization of space, and are able to store a range of different wines in sequence. Drawbacks include a slower wine maturation process and a lack of portability. In contrast to barrels, tanks impart no additional flavours to the wine.

tannins
Bitter, astringent chemical compounds found naturally in fruit. They are a component of the structure of wine.

terroir
The specific soil and climate conditions of a region, including its altitude and the amount of sunshine it receives. Certain terroirs are particularly suited to certain varieties of grape and wine.

toasting
The process of flaming the inside of barriques. Toasting imparts special aromas to the wood, and later to the wine it holds.

varietal
A wine made from a single grape variety.

variety
A type of grape.

vineyard
A farm or plot of land where grapes are cultivated.

viniculture
The science that deals with grapes, wine and winemaking.

vinification
The making of wine.

vinify
To make wine from grapes.

vinothèque
French term for a shop selling wine and wine-related items. Thanks to the growing popularity of wine, and the growth of wine tourism, such shops are playing an ever greater role in the self-promotion of wineries.

vintage
The year in which the grapes for a particular wine were harvested; also, the wine harvest itself.

vintner
A winemaker.

viticulture
The science of the cultivation of grapes for winemaking.

Weingut
German word for wine estate.

wine cellar
A synonym for winery; also, a storage area for wines.

wine diamonds
An informal term for the white, crystalline deposits of tartaric acid, or potassium bitartrate, made by wine.

wine estate
A winery business with its own vineyards.

winemaking cooperative
An association of vintners who have pooled their resources. The members (and joint owners) of a winemaking cooperative usually own and harvest their own, often relatively small-scale, vineyards and deliver the grapes to the cooperative for vinification and marketing.

winery
Any company, business or building that produces wine.

yeast
A microorganism used to ferment wine by converting its sugars to alcohol. Although wild yeasts are present naturally on grapes, winemakers often prefer to work with cultivated yeasts in order to control the fermentation process more closely.

yield
The quantity of wine produced by a vineyard. This is usually measured in hectolitres per hectare, though it can also be measured in tons per acre.

yield reduction
A deliberate decrease of the yield attained by taking measures to improve the quality of the grapes at the expense of quantity, with the aim of producing a higher-quality wine.

Index of names

Architects / Designers

Wine estate/Project name

Index of wine regions

Picture credits

The authors and publishers would like to express their sincere gratitude to all those who have assisted in the production of this book, be it through providing photos or artwork or granting permission to reproduce their documents or providing other information. Photographs not specifically credited are taken from the archives of architects or of the magazine "DETAIL Review of Architecture". Despite intensive endeavours, we were unable to establish copyright ownership in just a few cases; however, copyright is assured. Please notify us accordingly in such instances.

- Cover: Francisco Vieira de Campos, P–Porto

Foreword/Introduction

- p. 6 Cosima Frohnmaier, D–Munich
- pp. 8/9 Miran Kambič, SLO–Ljubljana
- p. 11 Faber & Partner, D–Düsseldorf
- pp. 12, 13 (left), 13 (centre) , 14, 15 Heinz-Gerd Woschek, D–Mainz
- p. 13 (right) Dieter Leistner/arturimages
- p. 16 Gabriele Röhle/wikipedia
- pp. 17, 19 Robert Dieth, D–St. Johann
- p. 18 Mick Rock/CEPHAS
- p. 20 Domaine les Aurelles, F–Nizas
- p. 21 Heinz-Gerd Woschek, D–Mainz
- p. 22 Roland Halbe, D–Stuttgart

Projects

- pp. 24/25 Günter Richard Wett, A–Innsbruck
- pp. 26–29 Fernando e Sérgio Guerra, P–Lisbon
- pp. 30–33 Nigel Young/Foster + Partners
- pp. 34–37 Hertha Hurnaus, A–Vienna
- pp. 38/39 Günter Richard Wett, A–Innsbruck
- pp. 40–43 Serge Demailly, F–La Cadière-d'Azur
- pp. 44, 46 (top) , 47, 49 (right) Alberto Plácido, P–Porto
- p. 46 (bottom), 48 Francisco Vieira de Campos, P–Porto
- p. 49 (left) Quinta do Vallado, P–Peso da Régua
- pp. 50/51 Serge Demailly, F–La Cadière-d'Azur
- pp. 52–55 Günter Richard Wett, A–Innsbruck
- pp. 56–59 Rupert Steiner, A–Vienna
- p. 60 Alexa Rainer, I–Bolzano
- p. 61 Markus Frohnmaier, D–Munich
- p. 62 Richard Becker, D–Steinheim
- p. 63 Gerhard Hagen/poolima
- pp. 64/65 Roland Halbe, D–Stuttgart
- pp. 66–67 Antje Quiram, D–Stuttgart
- pp. 68–71 Rita Burmester, P–Porto
- pp. 72–75 Gerhard Hagen/poolima
- p. 76 Domaine les Aurelles, F–Nizas
- pp. 77–79 Serge Demailly, F–La Cadière-d'Azur
- pp. 80–85 Fernando e Sérgio Guerra, P–Lisbon
- pp. 86–89 Michel Denancé, F–Paris
- pp. 90–93 Wolfgang Thaler, A–Vienna
- pp. 94–97 Günter Richard Wett, A–Innsbruck
- pp. 98–103 Ralph Feiner, CH–Malans
- p. 104 (top) , 105 Roland Halbe/arturimages
- p. 104 (bottom) Thomas Mayer/arturimages
- pp. 106–109 Eugeni Pons, E–Lloret
- p. 110 Weingut Heinrich, A–Gols
- pp. 111–113 Hertha Hurnaus, A–Vienna

Country guide to wine and architecture

- pp. 114/115 Nigel Young/Foster + Partners
- p. 117 Dietmar Strauß, D–Besigheim
- p. 118 (left) Palladium Photodesign, D–Cologne
- p. 118 (right) Dieter Leistner, D–Würzburg
- p. 119 (left) Gerhard Hagen/arturimages
- p. 119 (right) Thomas Nutt, D–Hamburg
- p. 121 Margherita Spiluttini, A–Vienna
- p. 122 Angelo Kaunat, A–Salzburg
- p. 123 (left) gerner°gerner plus | matthias raiger
- p. 123 (centre) Bernd Tauber, A–Krems
- p. 123 (right) Igor Skacel, A–Graz
- p. 124 Angelo Kaunat, A–Salzburg
- p. 125 Magali Koenig, CH–Lausanne
- p. 126 Gerhard Hagen/arturimages
- p. 127 (left) Günter Richard Wett, A–Innsbruck
- p. 127 (right) Luca Vignelli
- p. 129 (left) Karin Hessmann/arturimages
- p. 129 (right) Philippe Caumes, F–Paris
- p. 131 (left) Roland Halbe, D–Stuttgart
- p. 131 (right) Duccio Malagamba, E–Barcelona
- p. 132 (left) José Manuel Cutillas, E–Barañain
- p. 132 (centre) Adriana Landaluce, E–Logroño
- p. 132 (right) Faber & Partner, D–Düsseldorf
- p. 135 (left) Gyula Erhardt, H–Budapest
- p. 135 (centre) Zsolt Batár, H–Budapest
- p. 135 (right) Miran Kambič, SLO–Ljubljana
- pp. 136/137 Ralph Feiner, CH–Malans

Facility size

The symbols featured in the Projects section denote the average annual gross output of the respective facility in bottles:

●○○ up to 150,000 bottles
●●○ 150,000–500,000 bottles
●●● 500,000 bottles and above

Author bios

Heinz-Gert Woschek
born in 1937
Born in one of the best vintage years, Heinz-Gert Woschek was lucky enough to be exposed to the world of wine at a very early point in his career. Ever since, he has dedicated the larger part of his life to the enthusiastic service of wine culture.

Woschek has done public-relations work for national agricultural and wine institutions in Germany, France, Italy and Austria; held trade fairs, seminars and workshops; and organized and moderated symposia on wine and architecture in conjunction with the Rhineland-Palatinate Chamber of Architects.
In addition to producing various television and radio programmes, Woschek has written several specialist books and guides on wine, gastronomy and tourism. He has also published and edited a number of books and magazines on the topics of wine and travel.

Denis Duhme
born in 1966
Studied forestry and economics at Freiburg; worked in the engineered-wood industry in a senior capacity from 1994 to 2009; became a partner at nolte Parkettmanufaktur GmbH, a maker of parquet flooring in Bielefeld, Germany, in 2010.

Duhme's great passion – aside from the hunt – is wine. To acquire an in-depth knowledge in the field, he completed a multi-year training course at the Austrian Wine Academy in cooperation with the Wine & Spirit Education Trust (WSET) in London. After getting his Diploma in Wines and Spirits, he founded the weinintensiv wine school in Cologne. Duhme is the author of *weinkompakt*, a small wine guide aimed at wine novices as well as connoisseurs. He owns a vineyard near the Ruwer River, where he has produced Rieslings for the past three years.

Katrin Friederichs
born in 1971
Studied German and English studies, pedagogy and philosophy in Duisburg; became a regional sales manager for Zeter – Die Weinagentur GmbH & Co. KG, a wholesale distributor of wine in Neustadt/Weinstrasse, in 2011.

Ever since her student days, the Diploma Graduate in Wines and Spirits has been passionately interested in wine. In addition to her years of experience in the wine industry, primarily in distribution and sales, Friederichs has enjoyed a long and successful track record as a provider of seminars and further training.
The Ruhr native has spent the past two years in the Mosel and Palatine regions. In that time she began to write about the "most fascinating drink in the world" and the people and landscapes that bring it to life.

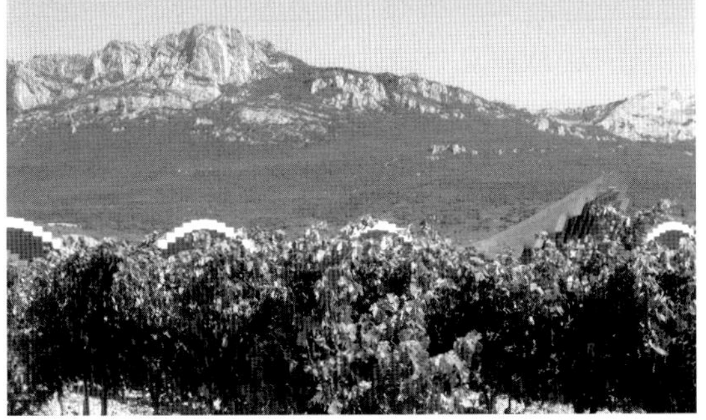

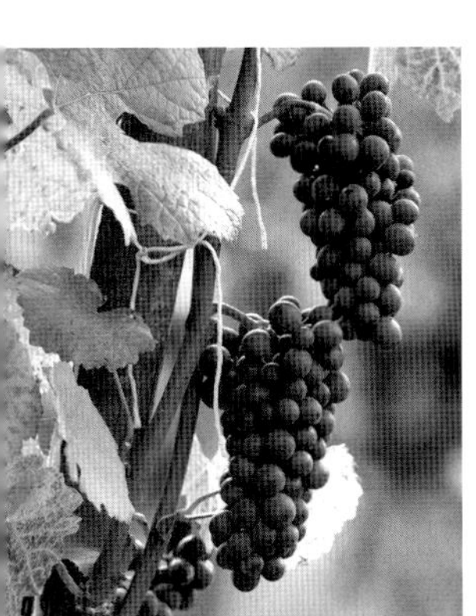

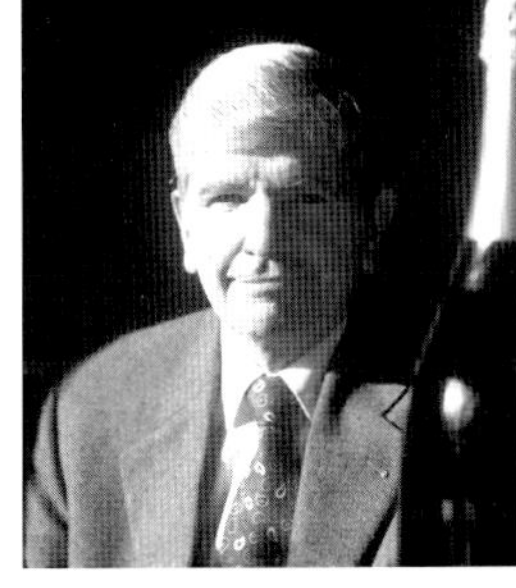

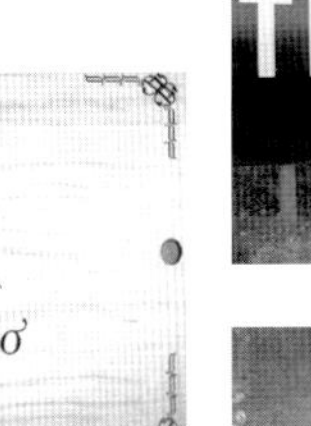

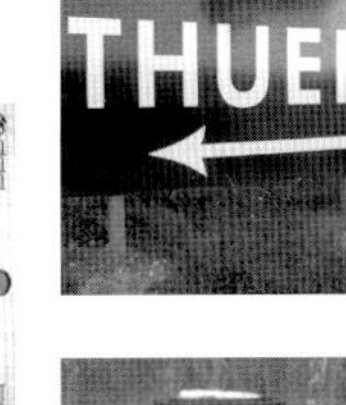

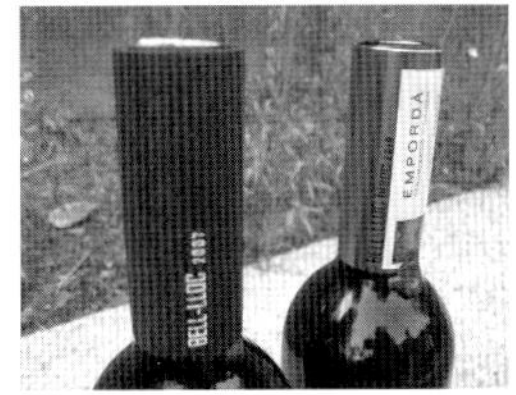

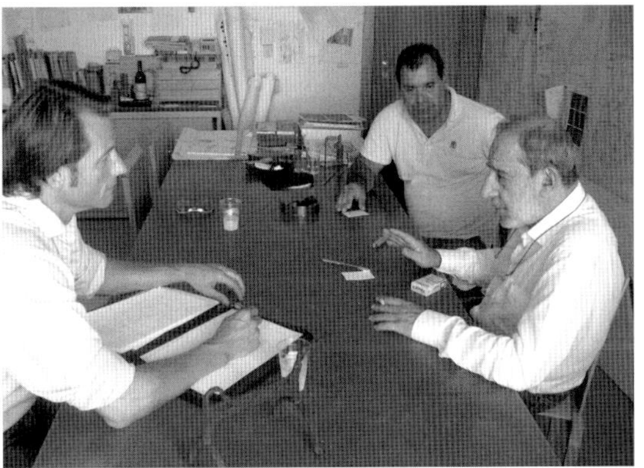

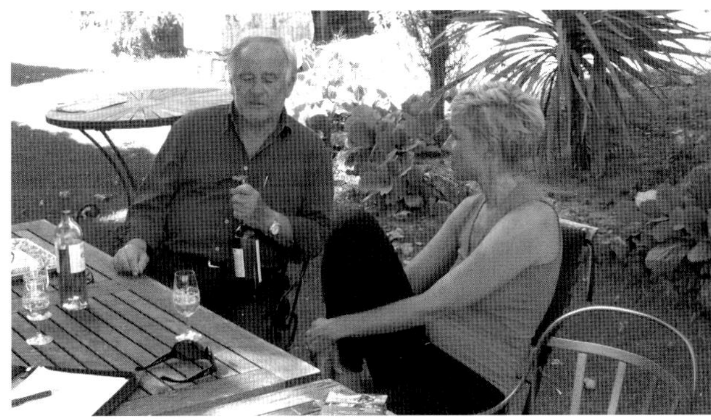

At left: Heinz-Gert Woschek; centre: Denis Duhme interviewing Álvaro Siza Vieira; above: Katrin Friederichs interviewing Jean-Louis Croquet

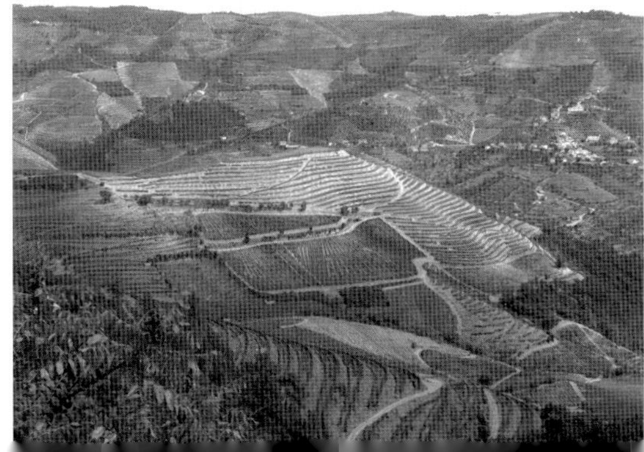